Knowledge Management and Industry Revolution 4.0

Scrivener Publishing
100 Cummings Center, Suite 541J
Beverly, MA 01915-6106

Publishers at Scrivener
Martin Scrivener (martin@scrivenerpublishing.com)
Phillip Carmical (pcarmical@scrivenerpublishing.com)

Knowledge Management and Industry Revolution 4.0

Edited by

Rajendra Kumar

Dept. of Computer Science & Engineering, Sharda University, Greater Noida, India

Vishal Jain

Dept. of Computer Science & Engineering, Sharda University, Greater Noida, India

Venus C. Ibarra

San Pablo Colleges, Laguna, Philippines

Corrienna Abdul Talib

Dept. of Educational Science, Mathematics and Creative Multimedia, Universiti Teknologi Malaysia

and

Vinay Kukreja

Centre for Research Impact & Outcome, Chitkara University Institute of Engineering and Technology, Chitkara University, Punjab, India

Scrivener Publishing

WILEY

This edition first published 2024 by John Wiley & Sons, Inc., 111 River Street, Hoboken, NJ 07030, USA and Scrivener Publishing LLC, 100 Cummings Center, Suite 541J, Beverly, MA 01915, USA

For more information about Scrivener publications please visit www.scrivenerpublishing.com.

Wiley Global Headquarters
111 River Street, Hoboken, NJ 07030, USA

For details of our global editorial offices, customer services, and more information about Wiley products visit us at www.wiley.com.

Library of Congress Cataloging-in-Publication Data

ISBN 978-1-394-24261-0

Cover image: Pixabay.Com
Cover design by Russell Richardson

Set in size of 11pt and Minion Pro by Manila Typesetting Company, Makati, Philippines

Printed in the USA

10 9 8 7 6 5 4 3 2 1

Contents

Preface

This book focuses on how the practices of Industrial Revolution 4.0 and knowledge management interact to create value. This volume mainly discusses the impact and challenges of knowledge management in the Fourth Industrial Revolution. In recent years, the value chain relationships and related activities have taken advantage of new technologies, but a new era is beginning and the existing conceptual frameworks require a roadmap for innovation strategies and effective implementation. The material collected herein includes case studies contributed from researchers and industry practitioners that showcase the impact of practices and challenges presented by technological changes, upgradation of old systems, and internal and external factors.

Knowledge Management and Industrial Revolution 4.0: Impacts and Challenges describes how knowledge management impacts the automation of the industry in secure, controlled, and optimized ways. For instance, the use of the latest technologies and sensors can lead to significant time and cost savings, and operators can utilize their machines and equipment from remote locations. The Industrial Revolution 4.0 incorporates the latest technologies for automation and, in many cases, the result is similar to working from home, even in manufacturing.

The use of deep learning should offer many quality control benefits. Furthermore, blockchain technology can help the industry with automation in secure and transparent ways. Apart from industry automation, other departments like human resources can also use effective knowledge management for better outcomes. The use of HR knowledge management allows employees to find and access the information they require without the assistance of the HR department. However, proper management is required to make all information accessible to every employee, otherwise they can become exhausted or access information not fruitful to them.

The book focuses on every aspect of the industry to help all the stakeholders of an organization. The benefits include a reduction in time required for accessing information, easier training, decreased operational expenses, improved stakeholders' satisfaction, faster problem-solving, increased pace of innovation, simpler employee review and progress reports, etc.

Chapter 1 discusses the integration of IoT (Internet of Things) into manufacturing processes. It also introduces new challenges, including cyber-security vulnerabilities and the necessity for upskilling labor forces.

Chapter 2 proposes an intelligent complex adaptive system named 4A, which insists on Agent, Algorithm, Architecture, and Adaptation. The proposed model aims to offer a more adaptable and flexible approach to KM in the context of I4.0.

Chapter 3 discusses the synergizing of knowledge management in the era of Industry 4.0.

Chapter 4 gives an overview of how knowledge production (knowledge creation, capture, sharing, and application) helps manufacturing organizations acquire new information, discuss best practices, successfully use knowledge, and incorporate new knowledge to promote innovation.

Chapter 5 sheds light on the significance of cyber security measures in safeguarding sensitive data and maintaining the integrity of interconnected systems. This comprehensive review highlights the transformative potential of Industry 4.0 and the pivotal part of knowledge management in its successful implementation.

Chapter 6 discusses the use of artificial intelligence in knowledge management and the Industrial Revolution 4.0.

Chapter 7 presents a transformative opportunity for organizations seeking enhanced efficiency and sustainable growth through the convergence of Industry 4.0 and knowledge management.

Chapter 8 provides various insights on the requirements for advanced development and dynamic change in the industrial sector.

Chapter 9 serves as a comprehensive guide for organizations seeking to harness the potential of Industry 4.0 while adeptly managing their knowledge assets.

Chapter 10 discusses the use of IoT and data analytics to enhance knowledge management in Industry 4.0.

Chapter 11 presents a study of the software-defined analysis framework for Industry 4.0, and specifically for Industrialized Control and Automation Systems (ICAS).

Chapter 12 includes the results of a survey aimed at understanding the structural relationship between interest in programming and creative attitudes among Japanese high school students as part of the knowledge management process in preparation for the Industrial Revolution 4.0.

Chapter 13 examines the concepts and roles of Blended-Mode Instruction (BMI) as an emerging knowledge management platform during the Industrial Revolution 4.0. It aims to promote Science, Technology, Reading, Engineering, Arts, and Mathematics (STREAM) education in three Southeast-Asian countries and China.

Chapter 14 gives an insightful review of advanced digital manufacturing technology solutions for Industry 4.0.

Chapter 15 presents a study for enhancing students' learning achievement, 21st-century skills, and self-regulation skills with a knowledge management and Industry 4.0 perspective.

Editors
Rajendra Kumar
Vishal Jain
Venus C. Ibarra
Corrienna Abdul Talib
Vinay Kukreja

Acknowledgement

This book is a collective effort not only by the contributors but also the publisher and its staff, reviewers, and critics. The editors are grateful to Mr. Martin Scrivener for accepting the book proposal and publishing the book within the stipulated time. Many thanks to the editorial and production team of Scrivener publishing.

Editors are thankful to the contributors of the book and all the editors who reviewed the contents with full enthusiasm.

Editors are very much thankful to Sharda University (India), San Pablo Colleges (Philippines), Universiti Teknologi Malaysia (Malaysia), and Chikara University (India) for providing necessary support and resources.

Last, but not the least, the editors are thankful to their colleagues and families for their kind cooperation and direct/indirect support.

Editors
Rajendra Kumar
Vishal Jain
Venus C. Ibarra
Corrienna Abdul Talib
Vinay Kukreja

1

The 5G Technology IR4 and Knowledge Management

Vyshali Rao K. P.[1*], Shanthi M. B.[2] and Sudhakar K. N.[3]

[1]Department of ISE, CMR Institute of Technology, Bangalore, India
[2]Department of CSE, CMR Institute of Technology, Bangalore, India
[3]SoCSE, RV University, Bangalore, India

Abstract

Often termed as Industry IR-4.0, the fourth revolution industry encompasses the merging of high-end technologies, with a distinct emphasis on the Internet of Things (IoT), within the manufacturing domain, leading to the transformation of the industrial landscape into a heightened state of intelligence. The IoT concept encompasses the interlinking of hardware devices, vehicles, and various objects embedded with sensors and connectivity software, facilitating processes like data collection, organization, and exchange. The swift growth of IoT in the present years has led to an upsurge in Internet-connected devices spurring the need for faster and more dependable networks to accommodate this expansion. The emergence of 5G networks offers a potential solution delivering enhanced speeds, reduced delay, and increased capacity compared to previous generations. These 5G networks are well positioned to support a wide variety of IoT devices, including sensors, wearable, smart cities, autonomous vehicles, and industrial factories. Thanks to its increased bandwidth and decreased latency, 5G facilitates real-time communication between devices enabling more efficient data transfers. This capability finds particular relevance in applications, such as industrial automation, where seamless real-time communication between machines enhances production processes. Notably, 5G networks for IoT offer support for extensive machine-type communications (mMTC), and they feature slicing of network, allowing network operators to develop virtual networks optimized for specific industrial IoT applications. However, while the integration of IoT into manufacturing processes brings about advantages, it also introduces new challenges, including cybersecurity vulnerabilities and the necessity for up-skilling labor forces.

**Corresponding author*: vyshali.r@cmrit.ac.in

Rajendra Kumar, Vishal Jain, Venus C. Ibarra, Corrienna Abdul Talib and Vinay Kukreja (eds.) Knowledge Management and Industry Revolution 4.0, (1–20) © 2024 Scrivener Publishing LLC

Keywords: Radio access networks (RANs), service-aligned architecture (SAA), long term evolution (LTE), industrial revolution (IR)

1.1 Introduction

The Fourth Industrial Revolution (4IR) is the upcoming level in computerizing the mass production industry. It is fueled by ingenious developments like growth of size of data and their connectivity, analytics, machine–human interaction, and elevation in robotics. The industrial revolution 4.0, commonly known as Industry 4.0, is exemplified by the integration of advanced technologies to create smart, connected, and highly automated systems [1]. One of the key enablers of Industry 4.0 is the deployment of 5G technology, which represents the 5G mobile networks. 5G is poised to revolutionize various industries by providing unprecedented levels of speed, reliability, and connectivity. In this introduction, we will explore the necessary aspects of 5G technology and its role in powering Industry 4.0.

The 5G technology is the latest improvisation in cellular communication networks succeeding the previous generation, 4G/LTE [2]. It is designed to deliver significantly faster data speeds, lower delays (the time taken by data to travel among devices), and enhanced network capacity. 5G operates on greater frequency bands and millimeter waves, enabling it to handle more significant data volumes with minimal delays. While 5G holds immense promise for Industry 4.0, its widespread implementation faces some challenges. These include the need for significant infrastructure upgrades, ensuring network security and privacy, and addressing potential grievance regarding health effects of larger frequency radio waves [3]. The 5G technology is a critical enabler of Industry 4.0 revolutionizing various sectors by providing faster and more reliable connectivity. Its implementation has the future to transform industries, boost innovation, and expose new business models that leverage the power of smart, connected systems. As 5G networks continue to expand, we can foresee a proliferation of cutting-edge technologies that will reshape our way of living, work, and having an interaction with digital age.

1.2 5G Technology Architecture

Cellular networking has evolved across successive generations with the imminent fifth generation being the latest advancement. The primary objective of preceding iterations was to provide rapid and dependable mobile services to users. However, 5G significantly broadens this objective introducing an extensive array of wireless services available to users across diverse platforms and multi-layered networks. This new generation, 5G establishes a cohesive, dynamic, and adaptable framework comprised of forward-looking technologies capable of accommodating a wide range of applications. Employing a more advanced architecture, 5G's Radio Access Networks (RANs) are not objectified by the proximity of base stations or intricate infrastructure. Instead, 5G paves the way for a flexible, disaggregated, and virtual RAN augmented by interfaces that create additional data access points.

The 5G basic network infrastructure is crucial for supporting the increased throughput demand of 5G [4]. It follows a cloud-oriented, service-aligned architecture (SAA) defined by 3GPP. This architecture encompasses various 5G functionalities, including security, authentication, session management, and data traffic accumulation from the user end. The 3rd Generation Partnership Project (3GPP) encompasses telecommunication technologies such as RAN, core transport networks, and service capabilities [5]. It has defined comprehensive system requirements for the 5G network infrastructure, which is characterized as service-oriented compared to previous generations. These services are made available via a familiar framework to networking accessibility that are available for usage. Reusability, modularity, and self-circumscription of these 5G network functionalities are added design considerations for the 5G network infrastructure described by the 3GPP specifications.

The architecture of 5G networks is designed to support faster and more reliable wireless communication. It consists of three major components, the radio access network (RAN), the root network, and user equipment (UE). The RAN includes base stations and antennas that connect devices at the end to a network. The basic network manages the flow of data and provides services like authentication and security. The UE refers to the devices used by users to access the network, such as smartphones or IoT devices [6]. Overall, the architecture of 5G networks aims to provide enhanced connectivity and enables new applications and services. The Figure 1.1 depicts the core architecture of 5G networks per 3GPP specifications.

User equipment (UE), such as smartphones or mobile devices that utilize 5G technology, establishes connections through the 5G New Radio Access Network to the 5G core and subsequently to Data Networks (DN), including the Internet.

- Access and Mobility Management Function (AMF) [7]: The AMF serves as the indigenous point of entry for UE connections. It performs tasks such as non-access stratum (NAS)

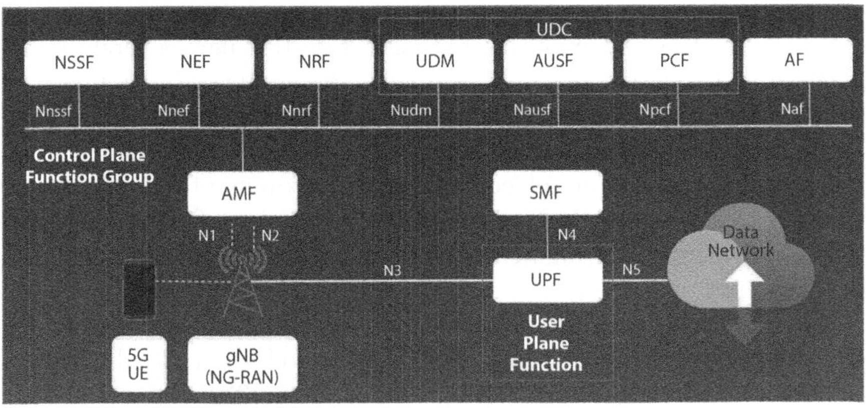

Figure 1.1 5G architecture.

signal termination, NAS encoding and protection of integrity, management of registration, connection, mobility, access authorization and authentication, and security factor management. Depending on the requested service by the UE, the AMF selects the relevant Session Management Function (SMF) to oversee the user session. Additionally, the AMF incorporates the Network Slice Selection Function (NSSF) and serves as the termination point for RAN control plane (CP) interfaces (N2).

- 5G Network Exposure Function (NEF) [8]: The NEF ensures secure and robust access to the network services and capabilities exposed by your 5G network. It provides developers and enterprises with the means to create tailored network services on-demand fostering innovation within an extended ecosystem.
- Network Repository Function (NRF) [9]: As a vital component of the 5G core, the NRF functions as an index that aids other network functions (NFs) in discovering information about other entities within the core, along with necessary service capabilities.
- Authentication Server Function (AUSF) [10]: The AUSF qualifies the AMF to authorize the UE and allow access to the 5G basic services.
- User Plane Function (UPF) [11]: The UPF supervises transporting IP datagram traffic (user plane) among the UE and other external networks.

- Additional Functions: The Session Management Function (SMF) [12], Policy Control Function (PCF), Application Function (AF), and Unified Data Management (UDM) function constitute a framework for policy control. They implement policy decisions, access subscription information, and regulate network behavior.

1.3 Technology Features of 5G

The 5G technology depicts a significant breakthrough in terms of fastness, capacity, latency, and connectivity in comparison to previous generations (such as 4G or LTE). Here are crucial features [13] and characteristics of 5G technicality.

- **Increased Speed:** The 5G presents notably elevated data transmission speeds compared to its predecessors boasting peak velocities that can attain up to 10 Gbps. This enhancement facilitates swifter downloads, uninterrupted streaming of high-definition media, and instantaneous interactions characterized by minimal latency.
- **Low Latency:** The 5G technology reduces network latency to as low as 1 millisecond (ms) providing nearly instantaneous communication between devices and minimizing delays. This is a bottle neck for applications like remote surgery, autonomous vehicles, and virtual gaming.
- **High Capacity:** 5G networks can handle a large number of interconnected devices concurrently. The technology utilizes advanced frequency bands, including higher-frequency millimeter waves, to increase network capacity and accommodate the growing number of Internet of Things (IoT) devices.
- **Enhanced Coverage:** 5G networks employ various technologies, including small cells, massive MIMO (Multiple Input Multiple Output), and beam forming, to improve coverage and signal strength. This enables reliable connectivity even in crowded areas and remote locations.
- **Network Slicing:** With the advent of 5G comes the innovative notion of network slicing, a concept enabling network operators to craft numerous virtual networks within a

solitary physical infrastructure. Each distinct network slice offers tailored communication services to cater to diverse needs encompassing aspects like ultra-low latency and ultra-high speed.

- **Enhanced Energy Efficiency:** 5G technologies aim to be more energy efficient in comparison to older generations. This is achieved through optimized network architecture, reduced power consumption of network equipment, and intelligent network management.
- **Empowering Emerging Innovations:** Anticipated to play a pivotal role, 5G is poised to facilitate the growth of nascent technologies like autonomous vehicles, augmented reality (AR), virtual reality (VR), smart cities, industrial automation, and remote telemedicine. The swift speeds, minimal latency, and extensive connectivity provided by 5G networks cater to the intricate requirements of these cutting-edge applications.
- **Security:** Enhancing the security of mobile devices and IoT systems is a perpetual priority due to the positioning of the latter at the periphery of the corporate network. The advent of 5G has brought forth heightened security measures compared to its predecessor, 4G LTE. These enhanced security measures encompass hardware security modules, proficient key management services, reliable over-the-air transmission, and fortified secure elements, among other advancements. These collective measures collectively bolster the integrity of data transmitted across the 5G network and contribute to the reinforcement of network endpoints.

1.4 Applications of 5G Technology in Industry 4.0 (4IR)

Industry 4.0, often termed as the 4th industrial revolution, envisions the digitization of production, manufacturing, and associated sectors. This epoch signifies a novel stage in the organizational structure, control mechanisms, and value generation processes within the industrial value chain. Presently, we find ourselves within the realm of the Fourth Industrial Revolution, marked by the implementation of cyber physical systems and intelligent machinery. This phase incorporates sophisticated control systems integrated with embedded software as well as elements like the Internet of Things (IoT), cloud computing, and cognitive computing. The potential of 5G technology spans across diverse industries encompassing domains from hawk to education, commute to entertainment, and intelligent homes to healthcare. It has the capacity to elevate the significance of mobile technology beyond its present status [14].

The benefits of the Fourth Industrial Revolution include the potential to enhance the accessibility and transmission of products and services for businesses, consumers, and stakeholders across the entire value chain. Initial data suggests that the effective implementation of the 4IR technology can lead to improved efficiency in supply chains and increased productivity during working hours. It also contributes to reduced factory waste and brings numerous advantages to employees, stakeholders, and consumers. The transition from traditional industrial methods to contemporary practices can be categorized into three distinct adoption pathways [15]:

- **Swift Integration:** Irrespective of a company's current technological setup, be it advanced or non-existent, certain cost-effective digital, augmented reality, and automation solutions can be swiftly incorporated without undergoing complex transition challenges.
- **Gradual Progression:** The pace of technology adoption can be influenced by a company's pre-existing technological infrastructure. Businesses with limited foundational information technology (IT), operational technology, and data infrastructure will require time to make the transition. On the other hand, technologically advanced companies are better positioned to swiftly implement new solutions.
- **Reduced or Postponed Adoption:** Even within companies boasting sophisticated technological foundations, the adoption of the latest and most cutting-edge innovations (such as comprehensive end-to-end automation) might occur at a slower pace due to the substantial capital expenditure involved and the uncertain long-term returns on investment.

5G networks have a variety of applications [16] across different industries. Some of the key applications have been discussed in the following section.

- **Next-Generation Mobile Network:** 5G is set to redefine the mobile experience by introducing an advanced wireless network that can achieve remarkable data download speeds ranging from 1 to 2 GBPS. This swiftness is akin to accessing an optic fiber connection wirelessly. Notably, 5G outperforms previous mobile transmission technologies allowing for efficient concurrent transfer of both voice and high-speed data. Particularly significant is the low latency inherent to 5G, a vital trait for applications like autonomous driving and mission-critical operations. The latency capability of 5G networks is notably under a millisecond. Employing novel radio millimeter waves for transmission, 5G utilizes a vastly broader bandwidth in comparison to lower LTE bands resulting in significantly higher data rates.

- **Entertainment and Multimedia:** Research indicates that in 2015, video downloads accounted for 55% of global mobile Internet traffic. This trend is projected to intensify driving the widespread embrace of high-definition video streaming. The 5G technology promises to introduce a high-definition virtual realm accessible on mobile devices. Rapid 4K video streaming now demands only a matter of seconds, complemented by crystal-clear audio quality. Wireless networks can effortlessly broadcast live events in high definition, while mobile devices grant access to HD TV channels without interruption. The entertainment sector is poised to reap substantial benefits from the deployment of 5G wireless networks. With the capability to offer 12 frames per second, high-resolution content, and elevated dynamic range video streaming devoid of interruptions, 5G revolutionizes the audiovisual experience. The integration of 5G's advanced technologies paves the way for augmented reality and virtual reality applications demanding HD video with minimal latency. 5G's robust capabilities aptly power these immersive experiences enhancing virtual interactions. The burgeoning popularity of high-definition virtual reality games, backed by investments from various companies, underscores the potential of 5G networks. The swift speeds of 5G networks further contribute to an enriched gaming experience through high-speed Internet connectivity.
- **Internet of Things (IoT):** Leveraging a high-powered 5G wireless network, the development potential within the Internet of Things (IoT) is extensive. IoT envisions a comprehensive network interlinking objects, appliances, sensors, devices, and applications to the Internet. The application of IoT involves the aggregation of substantial data volumes

from countless devices and sensors. The need for a capable network handling efficient data collection, processing, transmission, control, and real-time analytics is crucial. 5G emerges as a top contender for IoT applications due to its adaptability, availability of untapped spectrum, and cost-effective deployment solutions. The integration of 5G networks can furnish IoT with numerous advantages in various domains:

- **Smart Home:** The domain of intelligent home appliances and products is rapidly gaining momentum in the present market scenario. The concept of smart homes will utilize 5G networks to establish seamless connectivity among devices and enable real-time application monitoring. Smart appliances will effectively utilize the potential of the 5G wireless network facilitating remote access and configuration. Closed-circuit cameras will contribute by delivering high-quality, real-time video streams for security purposes.
- **Logistics and Shipping:** The logistics and shipment industry is poised to experience substantial advantages through the integration of intelligent 5G technology. This advancement can be effectively employed for tasks such as goods tracking, optimizing fleet management, centralized administration of databases, staff scheduling, and the real-time monitoring and reporting of deliveries.
- **Smart Cities:** Applications within smart cities, encompassing tasks like traffic management, immediate weather updates, local area broadcasting, energy management, smart power grids, street lighting control, water resource management, crowd management, and emergency responses, can seamlessly operate through a dependable 5G wireless network.
- **Industrial IoT:** The further improvisations of industries rely on intelligent wireless communications like 5G and LTE Advanced, for enhancing equipment automation, preventative maintenance, security protocols, process monitoring, intelligent packaging, efficient shipment, logistics, and resource management. The potential of smart sensor functionality is boundless offering answers for industrial IoT, ensuring smarter, safer, cost-conserving, and effective-resource-utilization industrial operations.

- **Advanced Agriculture:** In the impending era, the 5G technology is set to play a pivotal role in the agricultural sector, particularly in smart farming. By leveraging intelligent sensors with RFID mounted and GPS technology, farmers can effectively monitor the whereabouts and management of livestock. Smart sensors prove valuable in tasks such as regulating irrigation, managing access, and optimizing energy consumption.
- **Healthcare and Crucial Applications:** The realm of healthcare stands to be positively impacted by 5G technology serving as a dependable wireless network even across global distances for advanced medical procedures. This technology extends to connected classrooms enabling students to participate in seminars and important lectures. Individuals with chronic health severities will gain from smart equipment and real-time overlooking. Healthcare practitioners can engage with patients anytime, anywhere offering guidance as needed. Additionally, the realm of smart medical devices capable of remote surgeries is actively being explored by scientists. The healthcare industry necessitates the integration of all its operations through a robust network. 5G will empower this sector with smart medical devices, the Internet of Medical Things (IoMT), intelligent analytics, and cutting-edge medical radio-imaging technologies.
- **Intelligent Medical Equipment:** Including wearable [17], are designed to consistently monitor a patient's well-being and trigger alerts during uncertainties. Hospitals and medical services will promptly receive alerts in critical scenarios facilitating swift diagnosis and treatment procedures. Individuals with specific requirements could be monitored with the help of specialized stubs and exact location-tracing equipment. Accessible from anywhere, healthcare databases enable data analysis for research and treatment enhancements. Notably, medical professionals will have the capacity to swiftly share sizable files, such as MRI reports, often exceeding 1 GB in capacity, within fractions of a second via a 5G networking.
- **Autonomous Driving:** The reality of self-driving cars draws closer through the utilization of 5G wireless networks [18]. The significance of high-performing wireless connection

with minimal delay is paramount for the advancement of autonomous driving. In the forthcoming scenarios, vehicles can seamlessly communicate with intelligent traffic signs, adjacent objects, and fellow vehicles on the road. Given the split-second decisions crucial for self-driving cars to avoid collisions and ensure passenger safety, each millisecond holds great importance.

- **Drone Operations:** Drones have gained popularity for a multitude of applications spanning recreation video recording, emergency and medical assistance, efficient delivery solutions, security, and surveillance, among others. The 5G network offers robust support, facilitating swift wireless Internet connection for diverse drone operations [19] across an extensive range of uses. Especially during emergencies, such as natural disasters, drones can access areas inaccessible to humans, gathering valuable information.
- **Security and Surveillance:** The 5G wireless technology emerges as an optimal solution for preventive and supervision requirements attributing its vast bandwidth and utilization of illicit spectrum [20].

1.5 Knowledge Management in Industry 4.0

In the context of the Fourth Industrial Revolution (IR4), there are several techniques used in knowledge management [2] to effectively harness and utilize information. Some of these techniques include:

- **Data Analytics:** IR4 generates vast amounts of data. Data analysis techniques, including machine learning and artificial intelligence, can extract valuable insights from this data. By analyzing patterns and trends, organizations can make informed decisions and improve their knowledge-management processes.
- **Knowledge-Sharing Platforms:** Collaborative platforms and knowledge-sharing tools enable employees to share their expertise, experiences, and best practices. These platforms can include intranets, wikis, forums, and social networks fostering a culture of knowledge sharing and collaboration within organizations.
- **Knowledge Mapping:** Knowledge mapping involves visualizing and organizing knowledge assets within an

organization. It helps identify experts, knowledge gaps, and areas of expertise. By mapping knowledge, organizations can better understand their knowledge resources and make informed decisions about knowledge acquisition and distribution.

- **Knowledge Repositories:** Creating centralized repositories for storing and accessing knowledge is crucial in IR4. These repositories can consist of databases, document management systems, and content management systems. They provide a structured and easily accessible knowledge base for employees to retrieve information when needed.
- **Expert Systems:** Expert systems use artificial intelligence techniques to capture and replicate the knowledge and expertise of human experts. These systems can provide automated responses, recommendations, and solutions based on the captured knowledge. They help organizations leverage expert knowledge even when the experts are not physically available.
- **Continuous Learning and Training:** IR4. Emphasizes the need for continuous learning and up-skilling. Organizations can implement e-learning platforms, virtual training programs, and micro-learning techniques to ensure employees have access to relevant knowledge and skills to adapt to the rapidly changing technological landscape. These techniques in knowledge management help organizations effectively capture, organize, share, and utilize knowledge in the context of IR4 enabling them to stay competitive and innovative in the digital era.

1.5.1 Architecture of Knowledge Management

The architecture of knowledge management [21] involves the integration of advanced technologies and strategies to effectively capture, store, organize, and utilize knowledge within an organization. While there is no specific image associated with the architecture, here is a general overview of the key components [22]:

- **Data Sources**: Knowledge management in IR4. Relies on various data sources, consisting of structured and unstructured data from interior and exterior sources such as databases, documents, social media, and IoT devices.
- **Data Capture and Extraction:** Advanced technologies like artificial intelligence (AI) and machine learning (ML)

are used to capture and extract relevant knowledge from the data sources. This involves techniques such as natural language processing (NLP) for text analysis and computer vision for image and video analysis.

- **Knowledge Storage:** The extracted knowledge is stored in a centralized repository or a distributed database depending on the organization's requirements. This can include data lakes, data warehouses, or cloud-based storage solutions.
- **Knowledge Organization and Retrieval:** Knowledge is organized using taxonomies, ontologies, or metadata to enable efficient retrieval. Semantic technologies and search algorithms are employed to categorize and index the knowledge making it easily accessible to users.
- **Collaboration and Sharing:** IR4 emphasizes collaboration and sharing of knowledge. Collaborative platforms, social networks, and knowledge sharing tools are used to facilitate communication and collaboration among employees, teams, and departments.
- **Analytics and Insights:** Advanced analytics techniques, such as data mining, predictive analytics, and visualization, are applied to gain insights from the stored knowledge. This aids in identifying patterns, trends, and valuable insights that can inform decision making and foster innovation.
- **Security and Privacy:** Given the sensitive nature of knowledge, robust security measures are implemented to protect intellectual property and ensure data privacy. This includes access controls, encryption, and compliance with data protection regulations. The architecture of knowledge management in IR4 is dynamic and continuously evolving as new technologies and strategies emerge. It aims to leverage the power of data and advanced technologies to enable organizations to make informed decisions, foster innovation, and gain a competitive edge in the digital era.

1.6 The Role of 5G Technology in Knowledge Management

The 5G technology has greater ability to revolutionize knowledge management by enabling faster and more efficient data transfer. With 5G, organizations can access and share information in real time allowing for quicker decision making and collaboration. Additionally, 5G can support the usage of modern technologies like augmented reality and virtual reality, which can enhance knowledge sharing and training. Overall, the 5G technology has the ability to greatly improve knowledge-management processes and outcomes [23]. In order to optimize knowledge management for 5G, there are a few modifications that can be considered. First, it is significant to make sure that the knowledge-management systems and platforms are compatible with the elated speed and efficiency of 5G networks. This may involve upgrading hardware and software to handle the higher data transfer rates. Additionally, with the advancement of 5G, there will be a significant increase in the volume of data generated, growing exponentially. Therefore, it is crucial to enhance data storage and processing capabilities to effectively manage and analyze this vast amount of information. This could involve implementing advanced data-management techniques such as cloud-based solutions for distributed computing. Furthermore, the 5G technology enables real-time communication and collaboration, which can greatly enhance knowledge sharing and collaboration within organizations. To leverage this capability, it would be beneficial to integrate collaborative tools and platforms into the knowledge-management systems. This could include features like instant messaging, video conferencing, and virtual collaboration spaces. Last, as 5G networks enable connectivity across various devices and locations, it is important to ensure that knowledge-management systems are accessible and user-friendly on different devices such as smartphones, tablets, and laptops. This may involve developing responsive and mobile-friendly interfaces for seamless access to knowledge resources.

Overall, adapting knowledge-management systems to the advancements brought by 5G technology can greatly enhance the efficiency and effectiveness of knowledge sharing [24] and collaboration within organizations.

1.7 Challenges of Implementing 5G Technology for Knowledge Management

While 5G has the strength to greatly enhance knowledge-management tasks, there are several problems or challenges that need to be addressed in order to successfully implement it. Some of these challenges [25] include:

- **Infrastructure requirements:** 5G networks require significant core set up upgrades, including the deploying of new base stations and optical fiber cables. This can be an expensive and time-consuming task especially in regions with restricted existing infrastructure.
- **Security concerns:** As with any new technology, there are concerns around the security of 5G networks. With more devices connected to the network, there is a greater risk of cyberattacks and data breaches.
- **Interoperability issues:** There are currently multiple standards for 5G technology, which can create interoperability issues between different networks and devices. This can make it difficult to ensure seamless connectivity and data transfer.
- **Regulatory challenges:** The rollout of 5G networks is subject to regulatory approval, which can vary by country and region. This can create challenges for organizations operating in multiple jurisdictions.
- There can be some other challenges faced when implementing it in industries. One of the main difficulties is the initial cost of upgrading existing infrastructure to support 5G. This includes installing new equipment, upgrading network components, and ensuring compatibility with 5G standards. The financial investment required for this transition can be a significant hurdle for some industries.

Another challenge is the need for extensive coverage and infrastructure deployment. 5G networks rely on a dense network of small cells to provide high-speed connectivity. This means that industries may need to invest in deploying a large number of small cells to ensure reliable coverage throughout their facilities. This can be particularly challenging in remote or rural areas where infrastructure deployment may be more difficult.

Additionally, the increased complexity of 5G networks can pose challenges in terms of network management and security. With more devices connected and higher data-transfer rates, industries need to ensure robust network management systems to handle the increased traffic and maintain network performance. Moreover, the increased connectivity also raises concerns about cybersecurity and data privacy requiring industries to implement stringent security measures to protect sensitive information.

Last, the adoption of 5G technology may require industries to reevaluate their existing processes and workflows to fully leverage its capabilities. This could involve training employees on new technologies, updating protocols, and integrating 5G-enabled devices and applications into existing systems. Adapting to these changes and ensuring a smooth transition can be a time-consuming and complex task.

Despite these challenges, the potential benefits of 5G technology in industries, such as increased efficiency, faster data transfer, and improved connectivity [26], make it worth considering and addressing these difficulties.

1.8 Future Trends and Developments in 5G Technology and Knowledge Management

The future scope of 5G technology in knowledge management is quite promising. With its high-speed connectivity, low latency, and increased capacity, 5G has the potential to revolutionize how knowledge is managed and shared within organizations [27]. One significant aspect is the ability to access and share knowledge in real time. With 5G, employees can collaborate seamlessly regardless of their physical location. This means that knowledge can be shared instantly leading to faster decision making and problem solving. Additionally, 5G enables the use of advanced technologies like augmented reality (AR) and virtual reality (VR) [28], which can enhance knowledge management by providing immersive and interactive experiences for training, simulations, and remote collaboration.

Another area where 5G can have a significant impact is in the Internet of Things (IoT). With 5G's ability to connect a massive number of devices simultaneously, IoT devices can gather and transmit data in real time enabling organizations to collect valuable insights and knowledge [29]. This can lead to more informed decision making and the ability to proactively address issues. Furthermore, 5G's increased bandwidth and capacity can support the storage and processing of large amounts of data. This can enable organizations to implement advanced analytics and machine-learning algorithms [30] to extract valuable knowledge and insights from the data. This, in turn, can help in identifying patterns, trends, and correlations that may have been previously overlooked.

- **Increased adoption of 5G-enabled devices:** As more and more devices become 5G enabled, the potential for knowledge-management applications to leverage the speed and capabilities of 5G networks will increase.

- **Greater use of augmented reality and virtual reality:** 5G networks can support the use of advanced technologies like augmented reality and virtual reality, which can enhance knowledge sharing and training. As these technologies become more widely adopted, we can expect to see more knowledge-management applications leveraging them.
- **Improved data analytics:** 5G networks can enable faster and more efficient data transfer, which can support more advanced data analytics capabilities. This can help organizations to gain deeper insights into their data and make more informed decisions.
- **Increased use of edge computing:** 5G networks can facilitate edge computing, which involves processing data in proximity to its source rather than sending it to a centralized data center. This enables quicker processing and analysis of data, making it especially valuable for knowledge-management applications.

Overall, these trends and developments are likely to lead to more advanced and sophisticated knowledge-management applications that leverage the speed and capabilities of 5G networks. The future scope of 5G technology in knowledge management is vast. It has the potential to transform how knowledge is shared, accessed, and utilized within organizations leading to improved collaboration, faster decision making, and enhanced innovation.

References

1. Majid, M., Habib, S., Javed, A.R., Rizwan, M., Srivastava, G., Gadekallu, T.R., Lin, J.C., Applications of wireless sensor networks and internet of things frameworks in the industry revolution systematic literature review. *Sensors*, 22, 6, 2087, 2022.
2. Khuntia, M., Singh, D., Sahoo, S., Impact of internet of things (IoT) on 5g, in: *Intelligent and Cloud Computing: Proceedings of ICICC 2019*, vol. 2, pp. 125–136, Springer, Singapore, 2021.
3. Pons, M., Valenzuela, E., Rodríguez, B., Nolazco-Flores, J.A., Del-Valle-Soto, C., Utilization of 5g technologies in iot applications: Current limitations by

interference and network optimization difficulties - A review. *Sensors*, 23, 8, 3876, 2023.

4. Attarbashi, Z.S., Altaleb, A.E., Mohd Aman, A.H., Hassan Abdalla Hashim, A., Eker, S., A review of 5g technology: Architecture and challenges, in: *2022 IEEE 8th International Conference on Computing, Engineering and Design (ICCED)*, pp. 1–4, IEEE, 2022.
5. William, P., Choubey, S., Ramkumar, M., Verma, A., Vengatesan, K., Choubey, A., Implementation of 5G network architecture with interoperability in heterogeneous wireless environment using radio spectrum, in: *2022 International Conference on Electronics and Renewable Systems (ICEARS)*, pp. 786–791, IEEE, 2022.
6. Kazmi, S.H.A., Qamar, F., Hassan, R., Nisar, K., Chowdhry, B.S., Survey on Joint Paradigm of 5G and 1SDN Emerging Mobile Technologies: Architecture, Security, Challenges and Research Directions. *Wirel. Pers. Commun.*, 130, 4, 2753–2800, 2023.
7. Siddiqui, M.U.A., Qamar, F., Tayyab, M., Hindia, M.N., Nguyen, Q.N., Hassan, R., Mobility Management Issues and Solutions in 5G- and Beyond Networks: A Comprehensive Review. *Electronics*, 11, 9, 1366, 2022.
8. Marquez-Barja, J.M., Naudts, D., Maglogiannis, V., Hadiwardoyo, S.A., Moerman, I., Klepper, M., Kakes, G., Lian, X., Vandenberghe, W., Kusumakar, R. *et al.*, Designing a 5G Architecture to Overcome the Challenges of the Teleoperated Transport and Logistics, in: *2022 IEEE 19th Annual Consumer Communications & Networking Conference (CCNC)*, IEEE, pp. 264–267, 2022.
9. Husain, S., Kunz, A., Song, J., 3GPP 5G core network: An Overview and Future Directions. *J. Inf. Commun. Converg. Eng.*, 20, 1, 2022.
10. Chen, Z., Ao, J., Luo, W., Cheng, Z., Liu, Y., Sheng, K., Chen, L., A Dual-Factor Access Authentication Scheme for IoT Terminal in 5G Environments with Network Slice Selection. *J. Inf. Secur. Appl.*, 68, 103247, 2022.
11. Kundel, R., Meuser, T., Koppe, T., Hark, R., Steinmetz, R., User plane hardware acceleration in access networks: Experiences in Offloading Network Functions in Real 5G Deployments, in: *HICSS*, 2022.
12. Park, S., Kwon, S., Park, Y., Kim, D., You, I., Session Management for Security Systems in 5G Standalone Network. *IEEE Access*, 10, 73421–73436, 2022.
13. Attar, H., Issa, H., Ababneh, J., Abbasi, M., Solyman, A.A.A., Khosravi, M., Said Agieb, R. *et al.*, 5G System Overview for Ongoing Smart Applications: Structure, Requirements, and Specifications. *Comput. Intell. Neurosci.*, 2022, 2022.
14. Tsaramirsis, G., Kantaros, A., Al-Darraji, I., Piromalis, D., Apostolopoulos, C., Pavlopoulou, A., Alrammal, M., Ismail, Z., Buhari, S.M., Stojmenovic, M. *et al.*, A Modern Approach Towards an Industry 4.0 model: From Driving Technologies to Management. *J. Sens.*, 1–18, 2022.
15. Javaid, M., Haleem, A., Rab, S., Singh, R.P., Suman, R., Mohan, S., Progressive Schema of 5G for Industry 4.0: Features, Enablers, and Services. *Ind. Robot: Int. J. Robotics Res. Appl.*, 49, 3, 527–543, 2022.

16. Ghoraishi, M., 5G-Clarity Executive Summary, pp. 11–15, 2023.
17. Long, N., Lei, Y., Peng, L., Xu, P., Mao, P., A scoping review on monitoring mental health using smart wearable devices. *Math. Biosci. Eng*, ., 19, 8, 7899–7919, 2022.
18. Parekh, D., Poddar, N., Rajpurkar, A., Chahal, M., Kumar, N., Joshi, G.P., Cho, W., A Review on Autonomous Vehicles: Progress, Methods and Challenges. *Electronics*, 11, 14, 2162, 2022.
19. Balamurugan, N.M., Mohan, S., Adimoolam, M., John, A., Wang, W. *et al.*, DOA Tracking for Seamless Connectivity in Beamformed IoT based Drones. *Comput. Stand. Interfaces*, 79, 103564, 2022.
20. Gangwar, P.K., The Internet of Things Integration in Building Information Management Towards Construction 4.0. *J. Surv. Fish. Sci.*, 10, 2S, 1662–1671, 2023.
21. Logeshwaran, J., Kiruthiga, T., Lloret, J., A Novel Architecture of Intelligent Decision Model for Efficient Resource Allocation in 5G Broadband Communication Networks. *ICTACT J. Soft Comput.*, 13, 3, 2023.
22. Tiwari, S.P., Knowledge Management Strategies and Emerging Technologies - An Overview of the Underpinning -Concepts-Siddhartha Paul Tiwari. Authorea Preprints. 2022 Apr 20.
23. Zhao, J., Influence of Knowledge Sharing on Students' Learning Ability Under the Background of "5G + AI". *Int. J. Emerg. Technol. Learn. (iJET)*, 17, 1, 133–145, 2022.
24. Samtani, S., Zhao, Z., Krishnan, R., Secure Knowledge Management and Cybersecurity in the Era of Artificial Intelligence. *Inf. Syst. Front.*, 25, 2, 425–429, 2023.
25. Dong, X. and Yu, Y., Knowledge Management in the Digital Economy Era: Challenges and Trends, in: *The Routledge Companion to Knowledge Management*, pp. 115–127, 2022.
26. Pradhan, D., Tun, H.M., Dash, A.K., Iot: Security & Challenges of 5G Network in Smart Cities. *Asian J. Converg. Technol.*, 8, 2, 45–5, 2022, ISSN-235-1146.
27. Xu, X. and He, Y., Blockchain Application in Modern Logistics Information Sharing: A Review and Case Study Analysis. *Prod. Plan. Control*, 1–15, 2022.
28. Zhang, Z., Wen, F., Sun, Z., Guo, X., He, T., Lee, C., Artificial Intelligence-Enabled Sensing Technologies in the 5G/Internet of Things Era: from Virtual Reality/Augmented Reality to the Digital Twin. *Adv. Intell. Syst.*, 4, 7, 210028, 2022.
29. Huseien, G.F. and Shah, K.W., A Review on 5G Technology for Smart Energy Management and Smart Buildings in Singapore. *Energy AI*, 7, 100116, 2022.
30. Almutairi, M.S., Deep Learning-Based Solutions for 5G Network and 5G-Enabled Internet of Vehicles: Advances, Meta-Data Analysis, and Future Direction. *Math. Probl. Eng.*, 1–27, 2022.

2

Impact of Knowledge Management on Industry 4.0

Amala J.[1] and Anitha K.[2*]

[1]Department of Business Administration, DG Vaishnav College, Chennai, India
[2]Department of Management Studies, Faculty of Humanities and Science, Meenakshi Academy of Higher Education and Research, Chennai, India

Abstract
In today's competitive environment, governing information, which is readily available across the whole organization, is more crucial than acquiring information for determining the efficiency of the organization along with its environment, framework, and strategy. In an era marked by swift technological innovation and change, Knowledge Management (KM) plays a pivotal role as a catalyst for value creation. The imperative for organizations to accord priority to KM is underscored by its pivotal role in fostering the exchange of knowledge among employees. This exchange serves as a linchpin for heightened productivity and more judicious decision making. KM models emerge as indispensable tools, enabling organizations to deftly handle and leverage their wealth of information and expertise. The strategic implementation of a well-defined KM strategy and model empowers organizations to proactively position themselves ahead of the competitive curve. By implementing a KM strategy and model, organizations may stay ahead of the competition. There is a shortage of identification of suitable KM models that can be utilized in doing additional research, literature review, and organizational applications due to the nascent nature of the topic. The fourth industrial revolution, often known as Industry 4.0 (I4.0), which incorporates the connectivity of machines and their capacity to learn and share data autonomously, has had a significant impact on and molded KM processes. In the context of I4.0, KM is a strategic and operational function that involves both human and technology perspectives. It encompasses exploration and exploitation processes. This chapter examines the available KM

**Corresponding author*: anitharamesh211@gmail.com
Amala J.: ORCID: https://orcid.org/0000-0002-4864-4791
Anitha K.: ORCID: https://orcid.org/0000-0002-1940-2101

Rajendra Kumar, Vishal Jain, Venus C. Ibarra, Corrienna Abdul Talib and Vinay Kukreja (eds.) Knowledge Management and Industry Revolution 4.0, (21–38) © 2024 Scrivener Publishing LLC

concepts and models, including a wide range of perspectives from mechanistic to more socially oriented, and proposes a model equipped for I4.0. The authors try to propose an Intelligent Complex Adaptive System named 4A, which insists on Agent, Algorithm, Architecture, and Adaptation. The aim of this model is to offer a more adaptable and flexible approach to KM in the context of I4.0. This enables organizations to effectively navigate a rapidly changing business environment and utilize their knowledge assets to attain a competitive edge.

Keywords: Knowledge management, industry 4.0, KM models, KM strategy, I4.0, KM process, intelligent complex adaptive system, 4A

2.1 Introduction

Due to technological innovation, most organizations struggle with how to handle the information that is available both inside and outside the organization to enhance organizational effectiveness. KM is a notion that has gained popularity in recent years and helps organizations operate better overall because it is their most valuable resource [1]. From the perspective of knowledge management is the process of collecting, distributing, and applying knowledge, and it involves the socialization, externalization, combination, and internalization of knowledge, and its main goal is to enhance performance in the organization [2].

Since organizations no longer compete largely based on financial capital and strength, knowledge is the new key to success in business [3]. KM is very curial because it increases the complexity of organizational environments, which is associated with abundance of new knowledge challenges [4]. KM plays a vital role in the success of the organization implementing effective strategy [5]. As a result, in order to fully realize the value of information, it is imperative that both individuals and organizations manage and utilize knowledge properly.

2.1.1 Concept of KM

KM concentrates on four important key areas: (1) a process for finding new knowledge, i.e., acquiring new information, (2) techniques for machine learning and supervised semi-supervised data mining, i.e., procedure for acquiring accurate information, (3) source of information, i.e., how the information is gathered, (4) platforms for data management, i.e., how gathered information is stored. KM precisely in an organization is responsible for selection of information, execution, and assessment of information to attain the organization goals by improving overall performance of the organization [6].

2.1.2 Definitions

KM refers to the methodical process of seizing, organizing, storing, and allocating an organization's knowledge possessions to augment its inclusive performance, foster innovation, and improve decision making. It involves the identification, creation, acquisition, distribution, and utilization of knowledge within an organization to facilitate learning and improve productivity.

One commonly used definition of KM is "Knowledge Management is the process of capturing, distributing, and effectively using knowledge. It refers to a multi-disciplinary approach to achieving organization's objectives by making the best use of knowledge." This definition emphasizes the importance of capturing and distributing knowledge within an organization and leveraging it to achieve organizational goals.

"Through the development, capture, sharing, and efficient use of knowledge, KM is a multidisciplinary strategy for improving organizational performance [7]".

2.2 State of Art

2.2.1 Industry 4.0

Industry 4.0, which has been a pillar of German industrial policy since 2011 [8], is derived from the German phrase Industry 4.0. According to Reference [9], it alludes to a production system in which normal tasks are carried out by digitally equipped machines as they communicate with humans and other machines. Although it is primarily a utilization of technological innovation in manufacturing processes, its implementation necessitates man–machine exchange; therefore, operators should be involved from the beginning of the design process [10]. Because it affects work organization, I4.0 should not be seen as just a technology issue intended to boost productivity [11].

To generate high-quality and customized products and services, I4.0 implementation necessitates qualified people, adjusts routines, and influences planning and decision making [12]. I4.0 necessitates a combination of expertise in manufacturing technologies, total quality management, and supply chain management [13]. This calls for effective KM [14], as it necessitates increased data processing and the engagement of employees to seek autonomous solutions [10, 11]. Operators must acquire new knowledge and abilities to meet the difficulties of the digital transformation. For I4.0,

KM can support both formal and informal training [11, 15, 16]. Therefore, new HR management methods are needed, which will necessitate new KM techniques to enable efficient knowledge exchange and retention. For instance, according to References [12], [14], and [17], Virtual Factory simulations can help with issue resolution, continuous improvement, and decision-making practices that support the development of organizational culture.

2.2.2 Knowledge Management

In a nutshell, KM is a set of productive actions and processes that strive to make information useful and reusable through iterative, life-cycle-based, dynamic, and systematic exploitation and exploration [6]. I4.0 technology may lead to the emergence of KM techniques, enabling organizations to scan for and identify important bits of information and create increasingly complex applications for this knowledge [9]. To increase an organization's competitiveness, KM entails the skills of obtaining, developing, sharing, utilizing, and preserving organizational knowledge [18]. Some researchers [9, 19] advocate using KM techniques to enable reasoning based on the vast amount of data generated by the rising automatization. According to several researchers [9, 19], the adoption of KM techniques is encouraged in order to enable reasoning based on the enormous amount of data produced by greater automatization. According to Reference [20], organizations adopting the Fourth Industrial Revolution may build specialized KM techniques and strategies to make decisions based on more precise information at the individual, team, and organizational levels. Like this, Reference [21] stresses the need for organizations following the I4.0 path to develop, acquire, and transfer knowledge in a way that enables faster adaptation to changing market conditions than rivals.

Technology advancements and the ongoing innovation produced by businesses, together with knowledge development programs, have been the key drivers of growth in recent years [22]. A new systemic logic that implies knowledge is a vital component of both physical and intellectual production as well as a driver of modernization in the business environment is represented by the tremendous expansion of knowledge that we are currently experiencing [23]. To encourage innovations and new emerging technologies, information alone is insufficient because it must be managed to be accessible at the proper time and with the appropriate content [24].

2.3 Models of Knowledge Management

2.3.1 Von Krogh and Roos Model

This is the first framework that distinguishes between individualized information and societal data and determine the link between them and is illustrated in Figure 2.1. This model evaluates how knowledge enters the organization, how it is used by employees, and how it is vital to the organization and for employees. It also identifies the challenges the organization have in putting the model into practice. One of those KM models explicitly looks at the following aspects of its fundamentals, which affect the implementation of KM Strategies:

- Knowledge Professionals (Workers)
- Improved Communication Abilities
- Organizational Structure
- Network Management
- Personnel Management

2.3.2 Nonaka and Takeuchi Model

This model represents the constant advancement of knowledge; it is referred to as a spiral rather than a circle (Figure 2.2). There are two types of knowledge commonly available within business and KM, i.e., Explicit and Tacit Knowledge. Explicit Knowledge is available theoretically, which can be shared easily, but in the case of Tacit Knowledge or skill that can be

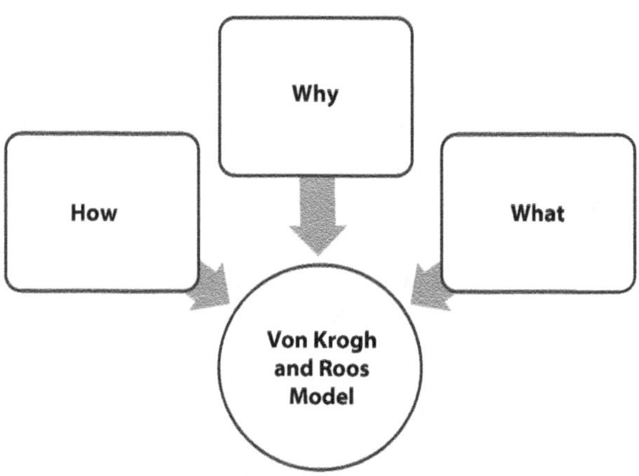

Figure 2.1 Von Krogh and Roos model.

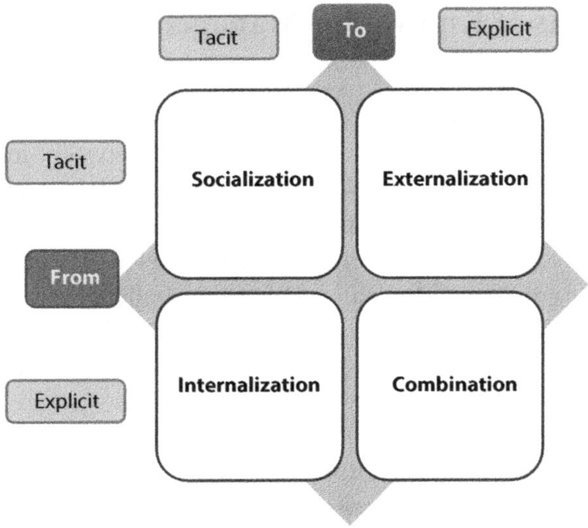

Figure 2.2 Nonaka and Takeuchi model.

acquired via experience, it cannot be shared easily and is not documented [25].

The method through which knowledge is exchanged and developed is known by Nonaka and Takeuchi as "SECI": Socialization, Externalization, Combination, and Internalization [25].

Socialization: During this process, knowledge is passed from one person to another through observation, brainstorming, and shared experience.
Externalization: In this process, Tacit knowledge will become Explicit when workers start sharing ideas, which are easily available to the entire organization.
Combination: As new information is created by combining, sorting, and categorizing practical knowledge sources, such as papers, this is the most basic type of knowledge sharing.
Internalization: Knowledge is distributed and applied across the whole enterprise; as a result, it develops by employees. As people "internalize" information and combine it with their own thoughts and experiences to produce new knowledge, it might then become tacit knowledge.

2.3.3 Choo Sense-Making KM Model

This model emphasizes on the following three principles. It is crucial for every team member to be committed to putting these interrelated ideas into

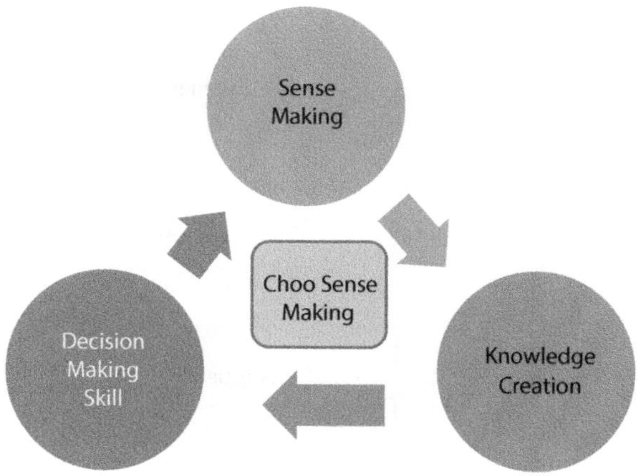

Figure 2.3 Choo sense-making KM model.

practice in order to create new knowledge and is illustrated in Figure 2.3 [26].

- Sense Making
- Knowledge Creation
- Decision-Making Skill

Sense Making: Its long-term objective is to ensure that businesses can adapt to and thrive in a changing and complicated environment through the exploration and interpretation of pertinent information that enables them to realize deviations, tendencies, and circumstances about its stakeholders, and other factors in the external environment.
Knowledge Creation: It is a procedure that enables an employer to produce or gather, establish, and develop data in order to produce innovative thoughts through corporate learning.
Decision-Making Skill: The Company must decide which choice, out of several that are feasible and provided, is the best and then follow it in accordance with the organization's plan. The limited reason concept limits the decision-making process in businesses.

2.3.4 WIIGS KM Model

The following principals are emphasized by this model [27] and is illustrated in Figure 2.4:

- Completeness

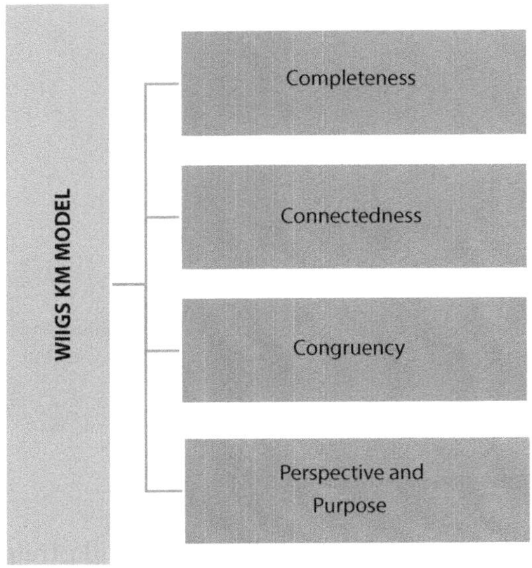

Figure 2.4 WIIGs KM model.

- Connectedness
- Congruency
- Perspective and Purpose [28]

Completeness—This explains how the information is accurately and adequately available in the Organization which is collected from different sources (Tactic and Explicit Knowledge).
Connectedness—It provides a concise description of the clear relationships between the numerous knowledge items. Most knowledge items are related to one another; hence, the more interconnected a knowledge base is, the more reliable the information is, and the more valuable it becomes.
Congruency—When all the facts, ideas, viewpoints, judgments, values, and relationships between items are consistent, they are said to have congruent knowledge. Such standards are generally not met by knowledge material.
Perspective and Purpose—It is defined as a method by which worker get knowledge, but for a particular goal and from a certain point of view. But the information available should serve both perspective and purpose.

2.3.5 Boisot I-Space

The Boisot I-Space model, developed by Ikujiro Nonaka and Georg von Krogh, is a KM framework that helps understand the dynamics of knowledge creation and transfer within organizations. It draws inspiration from the works of Michael Polanyi and forms the basis for the SECI (Socialization, Externalization, Combination, Internalization) model of knowledge conversion. The I-Space model explores the relationship between codifiability and personalization of knowledge, providing insights into how knowledge flows within different domains. The Boisot model for effective KM extricates it from a physical strength by allowing decision making based on valuable information.

Key Components of Boisot I-Space Model:
The axis represents the degree to which knowledge can be codified into explicit, formalized, and standardized forms such as documents, manuals, or databases. At one end, information is highly codified and can be easily transmitted and communicated. At the other end, information is tacit and hard to express explicitly.

Boisot's model can be envisaged as a three-dimensional block with the following extents:

- uncodified converts to codified,
- concrete converts to abstract,
- undiffused converts to diffused.

The Social Learning Cycle uses the I-Space model and depicts the dynamic flow of knowledge in six phases as shown in Figure 2.5.

Scanning: The process of screening the information that is already available.
Problem Solving: Solutions are given to the problems, which gives a clear construction and consistency to the data (knowledge becomes "codified").
Abstraction: The updated collated data are made comprehensive to an extensive assortment of circumstances (knowledge converts into "abstract").
Diffusion: These perceptions are then highlighted to the target audience in an organized and intellectual form (knowledge converts into "diffused").
Absorption: These abstract data are pragmatic to a variation of circumstances creating new erudition understandings (knowledge is absorbed and produces learned behavior and so becomes "uncodified," or "tacit").
Impacting: Intellectual data become entrenched in tangible practices, for instance in objects, rubrics, or behavior patterns (knowledge converts to "concrete").

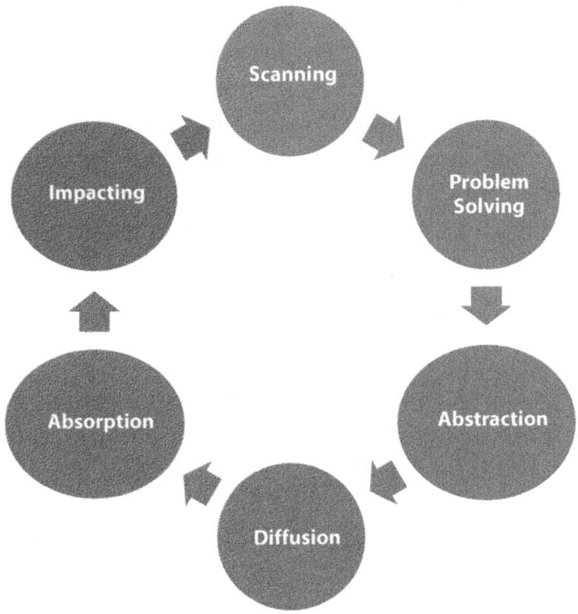

Figure 2.5 Social Learning Cycle (SLC) based on Boisot I-Space.

The Social Learning Cycle aids to relate gratified data and KM in a very operative way—the dimensions are allied to classification, knowledge creation, and information access and transfer.

The I-Space model provides a useful framework for understanding the challenges and strategies involved in managing different types of knowledge within organizations and improving knowledge creation and transfer processes.

2.3.6 ZACK Knowledge Management

Meyer and Zack introduced a model of KM that comprises the stages of a KM cycle that stresses the importance of a "refinery." The steps of the model are illustrated in Figure 2.6.

- **Acquisition:** Acquisition resolves concerns with respect to the source of raw materials such as dimensions, trustworthiness, accuracy, promptness, relevancy, expense, authority, and uniqueness. The overarching principle "garbage in, garbage out" aids as the managerial evidence. If low-quality

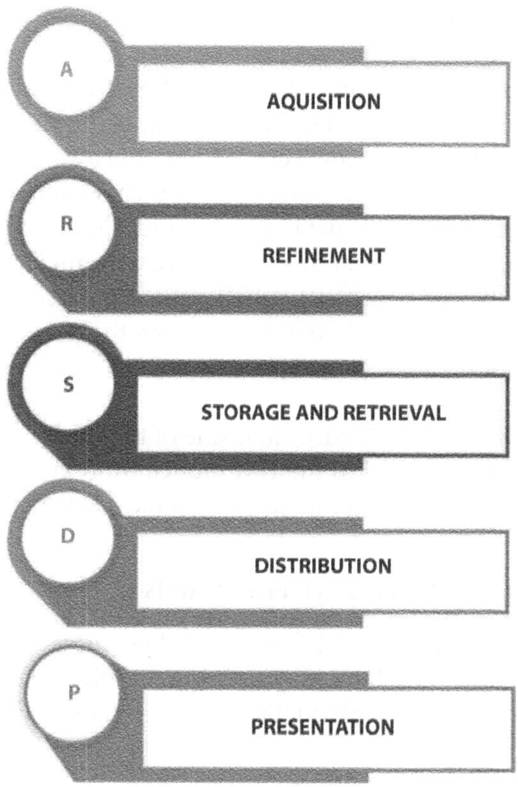

Figure 2.6 Zack model of knowledge management.

source data are used in that situation, the intellectual property produced subsequently will also be of lower quality.

- **Refinement:** Structural improvement, such as switching from one media to another, or cognitive modification, such as transformation, relabeling, searching, and combining, are termed as refinement. Refining also refers to fixing up (such as sanitizing information to guarantee total confidentiality of sources and key participants) or standardizing (such as adhering to templates of a best practice or lessons learned as used within that organization). By creating knowledge objects that are simpler to use and by better preserving the information for use in the future, this step enhances value.
- **Storage and Retrieval:** Storage or retrieval forms a bridge between the upstream addition and refinement stages that

feed the repository and downstream stages of product generation.

- **Distribution:** Distribution specifies how the product will be supplied to the customer (e.g., by fax, print, or email) and includes not only the delivery medium but also its frequency, form, language, scheduling, and other characteristics.
- **Presentation:** The data center and "refinery" operating simultaneously allows for the management of critical knowledge for a corporation. There is also the idea that they need to be upgraded constantly across the process to avert eradication.

The model presented in Figure 2.6 is one of the most complete pictures of the key elements engaged in the KM model. More precisely, the idea of refining is an important but frequently overlooked stage in the KM cycle.

2.3.7 Complex Adaptive System Models

A computational or theoretical framework known as complex adaptive system (CAS) models is helpful in examining complex systems that display emergent behavior and possess adaptive characteristics. They are made up

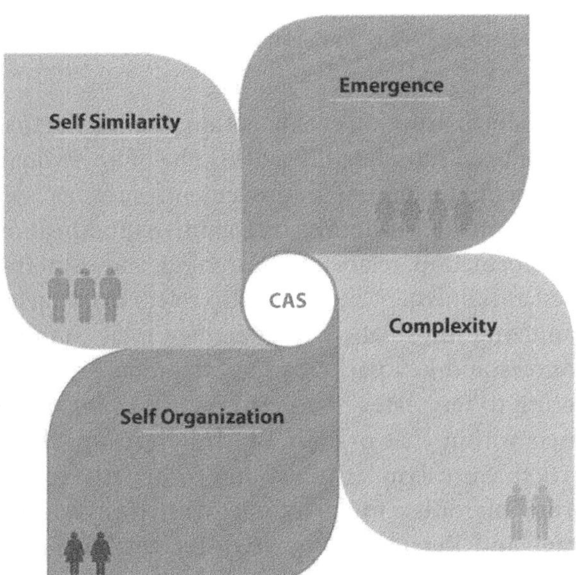

Figure 2.7 Complex adaptive system model.

of numerous interacting parts, or agents, that can modify their behavior in response to environmental changes. Because CAS models can describe the dynamics of complex systems and emergent features at higher levels, they have found diverse applications in fields ranging from computer science to biology, ecology, and sociology. Key features of complex adaptive system models are illustrated in Figure 2.7.

Usually, the idea entails hybrid behavior, where individuals serve as the deliberate elements of independent groups. Furthermore, these components are essential to the structure of the organizational hierarchy. The model demonstrates self-organizing characteristics, in which interactions and teamwork lead to the emergence of knowledge at the system level. It makes it possible for the company to better respond to developments by utilizing the collective intelligence of its employees.

2.4 Proposed Model for Industry 4.0

Understanding KM models allows organizations to determine the right course of action for managing their information and ensuring its effective utilization from a variety of knowledge sources. Organizations may improve their knowledge management processes and get better business results by selecting the right model.

Numerous studies have discussed effective combinations of I4.0 and KM. Methodologically replacing KM in the context of Industry 4.0 by digitalization, such as IoT applications, robotics, or data management, has not received much attention in study [29–31]. Intelligent methods and the ideas of complex adaptive systems are combined in a knowledge management framework called an Intelligent Complex Adaptive System (KM) model to manage knowledge effectively in a dynamic and ever-changing environment. This model aims to handle the complexities and uncertainties that modern companies face by enhancing the development, sharing, and use of information through the use of cutting-edge technology. Key attributes and features of a knowledge management (KM) model for an Intelligent Complex Adaptive System could include the following:

Agent-Based Methodology: The idea is built on an agent-based methodology, where different agents represent and manage knowledge. These agents can be people, software agents, or even AI algorithms that interact with their environment and one another to produce, distribute, and apply knowledge.

Learning and Adaptation: An agent's ability to learn and adapt is highly valued in the model. Agents are always taking in new information, learning from the past, and adapting their behavior to changing conditions. This allows the KM strategies used by the system to evolve over time.

Intelligent Algorithms: Large volumes of unstructured data are analyzed, and insights are extracted using sophisticated techniques including data mining, machine learning, and natural language processing. These algorithms aid in locating trends, patterns, and insider information about the company.

Network Structure: The model often presents the flow of knowledge within an organization as an agent network (individuals or groups) that are interconnected. The network structure facilitates the analysis of patterns of collaboration and knowledge diffusion. Through the ease of knowledge sharing between different departments and units within the organization, the strategy allows for a more complete view of its knowledge assets.

Robustness and Resilience: Similar to other complex adaptive systems, the knowledge management model demonstrates resilience and robustness. Even when there are disruptions or modifications, the system is able to bounce back and retain its KM features.

Continuous Improvement: The paradigm encourages continuous improvement through feedback loops. Reintroducing application-based information into the system enables ongoing process optimization and enhancement for knowledge management.

On the context to the above, the authors try to propose an Intelligent Complex Adaptive System named 4A, which insists on Agent, Algorithm, Architecture, and Adaptation and is illustrated in Figure 2.8.

By offering a more flexible and adaptive approach to knowledge management in Industry 4.0, this model aims to help organizations better adapt to a business environment that is changing quickly and use their knowledge assets to create a competitive edge. Through the integration of intelligent technology with complex adaptive system concepts, this approach seeks to improve internal information exchange, innovation, and decision making. The **Agent**—individuals or groups of individuals active in the organization—is the main subject of attention. **Algorithm**: a clever way to collect and integrate data; **Architecture**: a way to process the data that has been obtained; **Adapt**: a way to learn from and use the data to adapt to changing business and competitive conditions and endure soon.

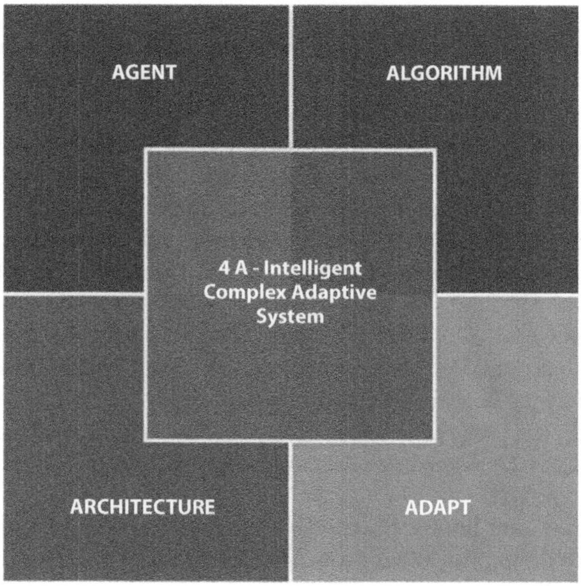

Figure 2.8 4A—Intelligent complex sdaptive system model (source: authors).

2.5 Conclusion

This study aimed to explore and evaluate the various models of knowledge management that is prevailing to improve the performance of the organizations under unpredictable contemporary business environment (I4.0). The study reinforces the conceptual understanding of KM and reviewed the existing knowledge management paradigm. After careful analysis of existing KM models, a new framework that focuses largely on the 4As (Agent, Algorithm, Architecture, and Adapt) was proposed, which will provide the organization a competitive edge. The new framework (4As) is a crucial component that an organization should realize to implement for a successful KM initiative. Therefore, the research would like to suggest using the framework as a guide for KM initiatives for a productive organization under Industry (4.0).

References

1. Palacios Marqués, D. and José Garrigós Simón, F., The effect of Knowledge Management practices on firm performance. *J. Knowl. Manag.*, 10, 3, 143–156, 2006.

2. Martínez-Martínez, A., Cegarra-Navarro, J.G., Garcia-Perez, A., Sustainability knowledge management and organisational learning in tourism: current approaches and areas for future development. *J. Sustainable Tourism*, 31, 4, 895–907, 2023.
3. Omotayo, F.O., knowledge management as an important tool in organisational management: A review of literature. *Libr. Philos. Pract.*, (e-journal). 1238, 2015. http://digitalcommons.unl.edu/libphilprac/1238
4. Durst, S. and Zieba, M., Mapping knowledge risks: Towards a better understanding of knowledge management. *Knowl. Manag. Res. Pract.*, 17, 1, 1–13, 2019.
5. Castrogiovanni, G., Ribeiro-Soriano, D., Mas-Tur, A., Roig-Tierno, N., Where to acquire knowledge: adapting knowledge management to financial institutions? *J. Bus. Res.*, 69, 5, 1812–1816, 2016.
6. Maier, R., *Knowledge management Systems, Information and Communication Technologies for Knowledge Management*, 3rd Ed., p. 57, Springer, Berlin, Germany, 2007.
7. Serenko, A. and Bontis, N., Global ranking of knowledge management and intellectual capital academic journals: 2017 update. *J. Knowl. Manag.*, 21, 3, 728–741, 2017.
8. Ghobakhloo, M., The future of manufacturing industry: a strategic roadmap toward industry 4.0. *J. Manuf. Technol. Manage.*, 29, 6, 910–936, 2018.
9. Manesh, M.F., Pellegrini, M.M., Marzi, G., Dabic, M., Knowledge management in the fourth industrial revolution: mapping the literature and scoping future avenues. *IEEE Trans. Eng. Manage.*, 68, 1, 289–300, 2021.
10. Trompisch, P., Industrie 4.0 und die Zukunft der Arbeit. *E & I Elektrotech. Inf.*, 134, 7, 370–373, 2017.
11. Kaasinen, E., Schmalfuß, F., Özturk, C., Aromaa, S., Boubekeur, M., Heilala, J., Heikkilä, P., Kuula, T., Liinasuo, M., Mach, S., Mehta, R., Petäjä, E., Walter, T., Empowering and engaging industrial workers with operator 4.0 solutions. *Comput. Ind. Eng.*, 139, 105678, 2020.
12. Kolyasnikov, M.S. and Kelchevskaya, N.R., Knowledge management strategies in companies: trends and the impact of industry 4.0. *Upravlenec*, 11, 4, 82–96, 2020.
13. Castro, J. I. D., Muniz, J., Jr., Bernardes, E., Tramarico, C.L., Logistics projects based on radio frequency identification: Multi-criteria assessment of Brazilian aircraft industry. *Pesqui. Oper.*, 41, e244928, 2021.
14. Feng, S.C., Bernstein, W.Z., Hedberg, T., Jr., Feeney, A.B., Toward knowledge management for smart manufacturing. *J. Comput. Inf. Sci. Eng.*, 17, 3, 1–40, 2017.
15. Sartori, J.T.D., Frederico, G.F., Silva, H.F.N., Organizational knowledge management in the context of supply chain 4.0: a systematic literature review and conceptual model proposal. *Knowl. Process Manage.*, 29, 2, 147–161, 2022.
16. Oztemel, E. and Gursev, S., Literature review of industry 4.0 and related technologies. *J. Intell. Manuf.*, 31, 1, 127–182, 2020.

17. Núñez-Merino, M., Maqueira-Marín, J.M., Moyano-Fuentes, J., Martínez-Jurado, P.J., Information and digital technologies of industry 4.0 and lean supply chain management: a systematic literature review. *Int. J. Prod. Res.*, 58, 16, 5034–5061, 2020.
18. Caputo, F., Garcia-Perez, A., Cillo, V., Giacosa, E., A Knowledge-based view of people and technology: directions for a value co-creation learning organization. *J. Knowl. Manag.*, 23, 7, 1314–1334, 2019.
19. Garad, A. and Gold, J., The learning-driven organization: toward an integrative model for organizational learning. *Ind. Commer. Train.*, 51, 6, 329–341, 2019.
20. Tortorella, G.L., Vergara, A.M.C., Garza-Reyes, J.A., Sawhney, R., Organizational learning paths based upon industry 4.0 adoption: An empirical study with Brazilian manufacturers. *Int. J. Prod. Econ.*, 219, 284–294, 2020.
21. Li, D., Fast-Berglund, Å., Paulin, D., Current and future Industry 4.0 capabilities for information and knowledge sharing. *Int. J. Adv. Manuf. Technol.*, 105, 9, 3951–3963, 2019.
22. da Silva Nascimento, L., Reichert, F.M., Janissek-Muniz, R., Zawislak, P.A., Dynamic interactions among knowledge management, strategic foresight, and emerging technologies. *J. Knowl. Manag.*, 25, 2, 275–297, 2020.
23. Waris, M.M., Sanin, C., Szczerbicki, E., Community of Practice for Product Innovation Towards the Establishment of Industry 4.0, in: *Intelligent Information and Database Systems. ACIIDS. Lecture Notes in Computer Science*, vol. 10752, 2018.
24. Ferreira, J., Mueller, J., Papa, A., Strategic knowledge management: theory, practice, and future challenges. *J. Knowl. Manage.*, 24, 2, 121–126, 2018.
25. Nonaka, I. and Takeuchi, H., How Japanese Companies Create the Dynamics of Innovation, in: *The Knowledge-Creating Company*, Oxford University Press, Oxford, 1995.
26. de Alvarenga Neto, R.C.D., Souza, R.R., Queiroz, J.G., Chipp, H., Knowledge management Implementation: A Process Design Proposition at Brazil's ONS (National Operator of the Interconnected Power System). *Electron. J. Knowl. Manag.*, 7, 5, 593–604, 2009.
27. Wiig, K. M., Knowledge management: an emerging discipline rooted in a long history. In C. Despres & D. Chauvel (eds.) Knowledge Horizons, The Present and thePromise of Knowledge Management. Oxford: Butterworth-Heinemann, 2000, https://doi.org/10.1016/B978-0-7506-7247-4.50004-5.
28. Dalkir, K., *Knowledge management in Theory and Practice*, The MIT Press, Cambridge, Massachusetts, 2011.
29. Azad, P., Navimipour, N.J., Rahmani, A.M., Sharifi, A., The role of structured and unstructured data managing mechanisms in the Internet of things. Cluster innovation towards the establishment of industry 4.0, in: *Asian Conference on Intelligent Information and Database Systems*, Springer, Cham, pp. 651–660, 2019.

30. Barbosa, G.F., Shiki, S.B., Da Silva, I.B., R&D roadmap for process robotization driven to the digital transformation of the industry 4.0. *Concurrent Eng.*, 28, 4, 290–304, 2020.
31. Ghanbari, Z., Navimipour, N.J., Hosseinzadeh, M., Darwesh, A., Resource allocation mechanisms and approaches on the internet of things. *Cluster Comput.*, 22, 4, 1253–1282, 2019.

3

Synergizing Knowledge Management in the Era of Industry 4.0: A Technological Revolution for Organizational Excellence

Anita Mohanty[1]*, Bright Keswani[2], Subrat Kumar Mohanty[3], Ambarish G. Mohapatra[1], Sasmita Nayak[4] and Md Mobin Akhtar[5]

[1]Electronics Engineering, Silicon Institute of Technology, Silicon University, Bhubaneswar, Odisha, India
[2]Department of Computer Engineering, Poornima University, Jaipur, India
[3]Electronics and Communication Engineering, Einstein Academy of Technology and Management, Bhubaneswar, Odisha, India
[4]Mechanical Engineering, Government College of Engineering, Kalahandi, Odisha, India
[5]Department of Basic Science, Riyadh Elm University, Riyadh, Kingdom of Saudi Arabia

Abstract
The Industrial Revolution, marked by transformative technological advancements, has evolved into the Fourth Industrial Revolution (Industry 4.0). This era is characterized by the fusion of digital technologies, artificial intelligence, and automation, ushering in a new paradigm for industries and economies worldwide. Knowledge management (KM) is pivotal in navigating this dynamic landscape. In this chapter, we explore the intricate relationship between knowledge management and the Industrial Revolution. KM empowers organizations to thrive amidst rapid change by facilitating knowledge creation, sharing, and utilization. It fosters collaboration, harnesses data-driven insights and supports agile decision making. KM also addresses challenges, such as information overload and cyber security threats, ensuring the safeguarding of valuable knowledge assets. As industries continue to transform in the Fourth Industrial Revolution, organizations prioritizing effective KM strategies are better positioned to innovate, adapt, and succeed in this era of unprecedented technological disruption.

**Corresponding author*: anitamohanty776@gmail.com

Rajendra Kumar, Vishal Jain, Venus C. Ibarra, Corrienna Abdul Talib and Vinay Kukreja (eds.) Knowledge Management and Industry Revolution 4.0, (39–86) © 2024 Scrivener Publishing LLC

***Keywords*:** Knowledge management, industrial revolution, fourth industrial revolution (Industry 4.0), digital transformation, data analytics, knowledge sharing, innovation

3.1 Introduction

The Industrial Revolution, a series of profound technological advancements that began in the late 18th century, has historically reshaped societies, economies, and industries. These monumental shifts have culminated in what we now refer to as the Fourth Industrial Revolution or Industry 4.0. This contemporary wave of innovation is characterized by the convergence of digital technologies, automation, artificial intelligence, and the Internet of Things (IoT), radically transforming the fabric of our world.

In this era of unprecedented change, the significance of knowledge management (KM) has surged to the forefront. KM, once a relatively niche discipline, has evolved into a strategic imperative for organizations seeking to thrive amidst the relentless pace of technological evolution [1]. KM, at its core, revolves around the effective creation, sharing, utilization, and protection of knowledge within an organization.

The relationship between knowledge management and the Industrial Revolution is intricate and symbiotic. In the face of information overload, organizations must develop agile strategies for capturing, analyzing, and leveraging knowledge. Collaboration, both among human teams and with intelligent machines, has become paramount. Cybersecurity challenges loom large, necessitating robust measures to safeguard intellectual property and sensitive data. Moreover, the monetization of knowledge assets and the ability to cater to customer demands through customer-centric KM practices are emerging as competitive differentiators.

3.1.1 The Foundation of Knowledge Management

In the dynamic landscape of modern industry and business, knowledge has emerged as the most valuable currency. It is the driving force behind innovation, the bedrock of informed decision making, and the key to maintaining a competitive edge. The waves of technological advancement brought about by the Industrial Revolution have heightened the significance of knowledge management (KM), making it an essential discipline for organizations seeking to thrive in the digital age [2, 3]. This chapter lays the cornerstone for our exploration of knowledge management's pivotal role in the Industrial Revolution by delving into its foundational principles, historical context, and evolutionary journey.

3.1.2 Defining Knowledge Management

At its essence, knowledge management is a systematic process that involves the creation, capture, organization, storage, retrieval, and dissemination of an organization's collective knowledge assets. This knowledge encompasses two main categories: explicit knowledge, which is codified and easily transferable, and tacit knowledge, which resides in the minds of individuals and is deeply rooted in their experiences and insights [4]. The overarching objective of knowledge management is to harness these assets effectively to enhance decision making, stimulate innovation, and improve overall organizational performance.

3.1.3 Overview of the Industrial Revolution(s)

The Industrial Revolution, a series of transformative epochs spanning from the late 18th century to the present day, has left an indelible mark on human history. It commenced with the mechanization of industry and agriculture, propelled by inventions like the steam engine. Subsequent phases witnessed the rise of electricity, the Internet, and digital technologies, revolutionizing production, communication, and commerce. These revolutions ushered in urbanization, industrial capitalism, and technological progress while also posing challenges such as labor exploitation and environmental concerns. Today, amid the Fourth Industrial Revolution (Industry 4.0), we stand at the precipice of yet another era of profound change, as digital technologies, automation, and artificial intelligence redefine the way we work, live, and interact with the world.

3.1.4 The Importance of the Relationship Between Knowledge and Industrial Progress

The connection between knowledge and industrial progress is fundamental to human advancement. Knowledge, in its myriad forms, serves as the engine propelling innovation, economic prosperity, and societal development [5]. It is the bedrock upon which industries are conceived and flourish. Throughout history, the accumulation and application of knowledge have consistently driven industrial revolutions and technological leaps. Innovation inherently linked to knowledge powers industrial evolution, enhancing efficiency, creating jobs, generating wealth, and elevating living standards. In the digital age, this synergy is more critical than ever, with the Fourth Industrial Revolution underlining knowledge's pivotal role in shaping the industries of the future. Organizations adept at harnessing and adapting their knowledge are best positioned to excel in this era of rapid change. In conclusion, the nexus between knowledge and industrial progress is a linchpin for shaping the industries of tomorrow, demanding a commitment to education, research, and innovation for sustainable growth and societal welfare.

3.2 Historical Perspective

The historical perspective of knowledge management (KM) about the Industrial Revolution provides insight into how the management of knowledge has evolved alongside the transformative changes brought about by industrialization.

3.2.1 Brief Overview of the First, Second, and Third Industrial Revolutions

To comprehend the significance of knowledge management, it is crucial to trace its roots back to the inception of industrialization. The Industrial Revolution, characterized by the mechanization of production and the increase of factories, sowed the seeds for succeeding waves of transformation. Although the early pioneers of industry did not clearly label it as such, the soul of knowledge management was already at play in their efforts to organize production processes and accumulate invaluable expertise.

As the human race transitioned into the Second and Third Industrial Revolutions, noticeable by the advent of electricity, mass production, and digitalization, the need for knowledge management became increasingly evident. With the blast of data and information, organizations recognized the significance of structuring and categorizing knowledge for efficient utilization. During this period, early knowledge management systems began to emerge, leveraging technology to stockpile and retrieve information, laying the groundwork for what would become an essential discipline in the information age.

In the present day, we discover ourselves on the cusp of the Fourth Industrial Revolution, often dubbed Industry 4.0 [6]. This age is characterized by the integration of cyber-physical systems, the proliferation of the Internet of Things (IoT), and the ubiquity of artificial intelligence (AI). Within this landscape, knowledge management has undergone a profound transformation. Knowledge is no longer confined to structured data but encompasses vast repositories of unstructured content. As such, knowledge management has evolved to become an indispensable component of the digital transformation sweeping across industries.

3.2.2 The Role of Knowledge and Innovation in Each Revolution

The role of knowledge and innovation has been instrumental in driving progress across each industrial revolution as shown in Figure 3.1 [7]. Here is a brief overview of their significance in each era:

First Industrial Revolution (Late 18th to Early 19th Century):

- Knowledge: Primarily tacit and localized, passed down through apprenticeships and craft traditions.

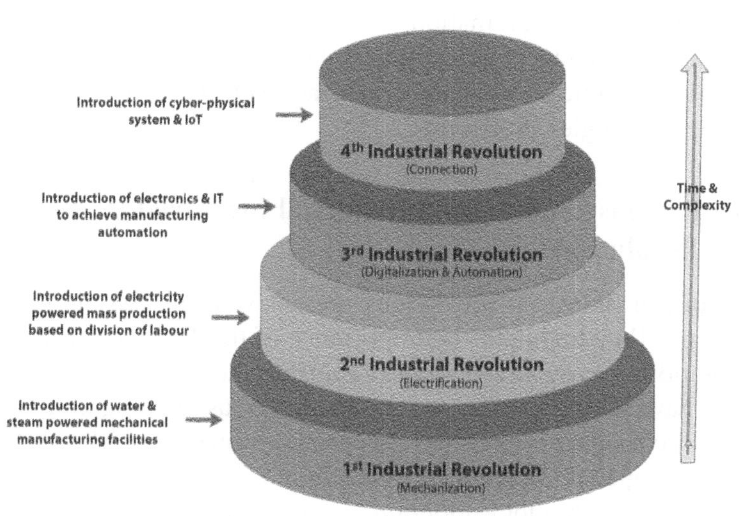

Figure 3.1 Progress of innovations during the Industrial Revolution.

- Innovation: Mechanization and steam power were groundbreaking innovations, enabling the transition from agrarian economies to industrial ones.

Second Industrial Revolution (Late 19th Century):

- Knowledge: More formalized with the emergence of scientific management principles and standardized processes.
- Innovation: Electricity, the telegraph, and assembly line techniques revolutionized industries, boosting productivity and scale.

Third Industrial Revolution (Late 20th Century):

- Knowledge: Expanded significantly with the growth of research institutions and academic knowledge.
- Innovation: Digital technologies, computing, and the Internet transformed communication, commerce, and knowledge sharing. Knowledge became more accessible and shareable.

Fourth Industrial Revolution (Present):

- Knowledge: Highly digital, with a focus on data, information, and artificial intelligence.
- Innovation: Characterized by the fusion of digital technologies, AI, and automation. This era emphasizes innovation in areas like machine learning, robotics, and IoT. Knowledge is a significant asset for organizations to tie together these technologies effectively.

3.2.3 Lessons Erudite from Historical Industrial Revolutions

The historical industrial revolutions present valuable lessons that transcend time. They highlight the importance of flexibility, innovation, and collaboration in navigating periods of transformative alteration. These revolutions have showcased the power of continuous learning and the need for ethical considerations in technological advancement. Moreover, they highlight the global interconnectedness of our world and the requirement for responsible technology adoption. As we go into the Fourth Industrial Revolution, these lessons serve as a compass, guiding us to a future where resilience, ethical awareness, and the responsible employ of technology are paramount for individual and societal success.

3.3 Knowledge Management in the Fourth Industrial Revolution (Industry 4.0)

In the Fourth Industrial Revolution, characterized by the union of digital technologies, artificial intelligence, and automation, knowledge management (KM) takes on an indispensable role. In this era of fast change, organizations must not only accumulate knowledge but also disseminate, leverage, and get used to it effectively. KM practices give the framework for achieving these objectives. They facilitate knowledge creation, capture, sharing, and analytics, empowering organizations to create data-driven decisions, foster innovation, and remain agile in the face of technological disruption. KM also addresses security concerns in defending intellectual property while enabling joint human–AI interactions. As organizations navigate the complexities of Industry 4.0, KM emerges as a linchpin for success, guiding them toward sustainable growth, competitiveness, and resilience.

3.3.1 Introduction to Industry 4.0 and Its Key Characteristics

Industry 4.0 represents a monumental leap in the evolution of industry and manufacturing. It stands as the fourth industrial revolution, building upon the foundations of mechanization, electrification, and automation [8]. This era is defined by the integration of digital technologies into every facet of industrial processes, ushering in a new era of connectivity, intelligence, and automation. Key characteristics of Industry 4.0 as shown in Figure 3.2 include:

- **Digitization:** Industry 4.0 is synonymous with the digitization of processes, products, and services. This entails the conversion of physical assets and activities into digital formats, enabling data-driven decision making and real-time insights.
- **Interconnectivity:** The Industrial Internet of Things (IIoT) is a hallmark of this revolution. Machines, devices, and sensors are interconnected, sharing data and information seamlessly. This interconnectedness enhances communication,

Figure 3.2 Characteristics of Industry 4.0.

collaboration, and the ability to monitor and control operations remotely.

- **Data Analytics and Artificial Intelligence:** Industry 4.0 leverages advanced analytics and artificial intelligence (AI) to extract meaningful insights from vast datasets. AI-driven algorithms optimize processes, predict maintenance needs, and enable autonomous decision making.
- **Human–Machine Collaboration:** While automation plays a central role, Industry 4.0 emphasizes collaboration between humans and machines. Machines handle repetitive tasks, while humans focus on creativity, problem solving, and decision making.
- **Customization and Flexibility:** Mass customization becomes feasible in Industry 4.0. Production processes can be quickly adapted to meet individual customer demands, allowing for greater flexibility and responsiveness to market changes.
- **Smart Factories:** Industry 4.0 gives rise to smart factories where production systems are self-optimizing and self-adapting. These factories are agile, efficient, and capable of producing high-quality goods with minimal waste.
- **Cyber-Physical Systems:** Physical systems are closely integrated with digital counterparts, creating cyber-physical systems. These systems monitor physical processes and make autonomous decisions, bridging the gap between the digital and physical worlds.
- **Sustainability:** Industry 4.0 offers opportunities for more sustainable practices through resource optimization, energy efficiency, and reduced waste. Smart monitoring and control systems contribute to environmental conservation.
- **Supply Chain Transparency:** Enhanced data sharing and visibility across supply chains enable better coordination,

inventory management, and responsiveness to changes in demand.
- **Security and Privacy:** As digital connectivity increases, ensuring the security and privacy of data and systems becomes paramount. Industry 4.0 necessitates robust cyber security measures.

Industry 4.0 is not merely a technological revolution; it is a transformational force reshaping industries, economies, and societies. It promises improved efficiency, innovation, and competitiveness while posing challenges related to data privacy, cyber security, and the adaptation of the workforce. Embracing and effectively navigating this era of Industry 4.0 will be pivotal for organizations seeking to thrive in an increasingly digital and interconnected world.

3.3.2 The Data-Driven Nature of Industry 4.0

Industry 4.0, the fourth industrial revolution, is characterized by its data-driven foundation [9]. At its heart lies the recognition that data are not just a valuable resource; they are the lifeblood of modern industrial and manufacturing processes. Several key aspects as shown in Figure 3.3 highlight the data-driven nature of Industry 4.0:

- **Data Collection and Sensors:** Industry 4.0 relies heavily on sensors and IoT devices to collect vast amounts of data from machines, equipment, and even products throughout the production and supply chain. These sensors continuously monitor variables, such as temperature, pressure, speed, and quality, generating a constant stream of data.
- **Big Data Analytics:** The sheer volume, velocity, and variety of data generated in Industry 4.0 necessitate advanced analytics. Big data analytics and machine learning algorithms are employed to process and analyze this wealth of information. These tools uncover patterns, trends, and anomalies that inform decision making and process optimization.
- **Predictive Maintenance:** Predictive maintenance is a most important example of how data is leveraged in Industry 4.0. By analyzing historical equipment data and real-time sensor data, organizations can forecast when machinery is likely to fail and perform maintenance proactively, minimizing downtime and reducing costs.

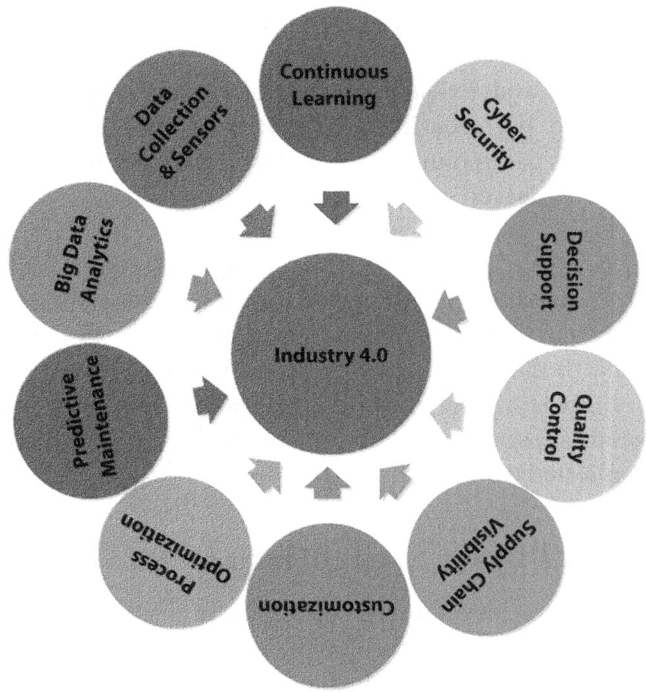

Figure 3.3 Key aspects of Industry 4.0.

- **Process Optimization:** Data-driven insights enable continuous process development. Manufacturers can recognize bottlenecks, inefficiencies, and opportunities for optimization. Real-time information feeds back into the production process, allowing for rapid adjustments and improvements.
- **Customization:** Data are utilized to tailor products and services to individual consumer preferences. By analyzing customer information and feedback, companies can create highly customized offerings, meeting the demands of a diverse and discerning market.
- **Supply Chain Visibility:** Data-driven supply chain management gives end-to-end visibility. Organizations can track inventory levels, monitor transportation routes, and respond to changes in demand on time. This enhances efficiency and decreases waste.
- **Quality Control:** Data analytics helps maintain and improve product quality. It enables real-time quality control

monitoring, reducing defects and ensuring that products meet stringent quality standards.

- **Decision Support:** In Industry 4.0, data serves as the basis for decision making at all levels. From strategic decisions on production volumes to tactical adjustments on the factory floor, data-driven insights guide choices that maximize efficiency and profitability.
- **Cyber Security:** Protecting data is paramount. Industry 4.0 necessitates robust cyber security measures to safeguard sensitive information, as interconnected systems and data sharing introduce new vulnerabilities.
- **Continuous Learning:** Data-driven organizations prioritize continuous learning. They analyze the outcomes of decisions and adapt strategies accordingly, fostering a culture of data-driven improvement.

3.3.3 The Role of Digital Technology, IoT, and AI in Industry 4.0

In Industry 4.0, the synergy of digital technology, the Internet of Things (IoT), and artificial intelligence (AI) forms the backbone of transformative change [10]. These technologies, shown in Figure 3.4, are pivotal in reshaping industries, manufacturing, and supply chains:

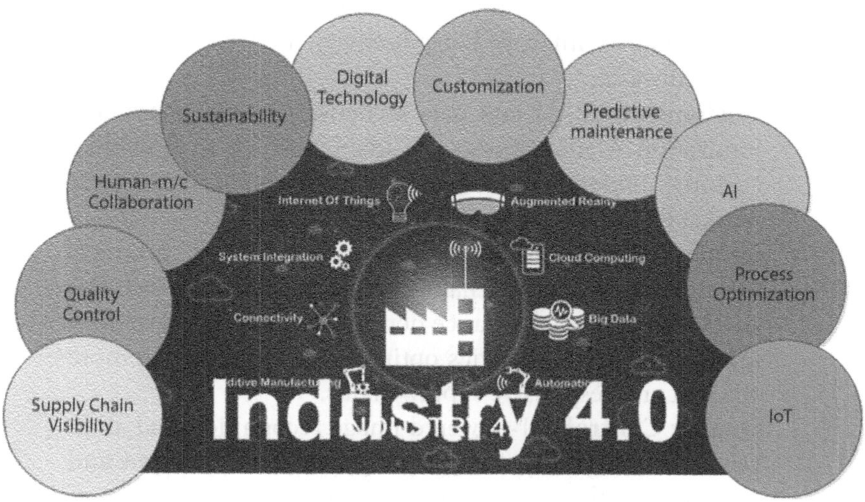

Figure 3.4 Technologies in Industry 4.0.

- **Digital Technology:** Digitalization is the foundation of Industry 4.0. It involves converting physical processes and assets into digital formats, facilitating data capture and analysis. Digital twins, virtual replicas of physical systems, enable real-time monitoring and simulation for predictive maintenance and process optimization.
- **Internet of Things (IoT):** IoT devices and sensors are ubiquitous in Industry 4.0. They collect data from machinery, products, and the environment, creating a network of interconnected assets. These data inform decision making, enhance operational efficiency, and enable proactive maintenance.
- **Artificial Intelligence (AI):** AI, including machine learning and deep learning, empowers machines and systems to learn from data, make decisions, and perform tasks autonomously. AI algorithms analyze huge datasets to expose patterns, optimize processes, and predict maintenance needs. Collaborative robots (cobots) are a key example of AI-driven automation, working alongside humans on the factory floor.
- **Predictive Maintenance:** IoT sensors and AI enable predictive maintenance, where machines self-diagnose problems based on data analysis. This proactive approach decreases downtime, increases equipment lifespan, and lowers maintenance costs.
- **Process Optimization:** Data from IoT sensors go into AI systems that optimize manufacturing processes in real-time. This leads to improved productivity, better quality, and reduced waste.
- **Customization:** AI and data analytics facilitate mass customization. Manufacturers can adapt products to individual customer preferences, meeting the requirements of a diverse market effectively.
- **Supply Chain Visibility:** IoT devices track products throughout the supply chain, providing real-time visibility. AI-driven analytics enhance demand forecasting, inventory management, and logistics optimization, resulting in more efficient and responsive supply chains.
- **Quality Control:** AI-powered image recognition and analysis improve quality control. Defects can be detected and addressed with greater accuracy, ensuring products meet stringent quality standards.

- **Human–Machine Collaboration:** AI and robotics collaborate with human workers, augmenting their capabilities. Cobots assist in repetitive or physically demanding tasks, while AI-driven analytics support decision making.
- **Sustainability:** Digital technology and AI help organizations reduce their environmental footprint. Data analysis identifies energy-saving opportunities, while IoT sensors monitor resource usage for efficient sustainability practices.

3.3.4 The Explosion of Data and Information in the Digital Age

The digital age has ushered in an era of unprecedented data proliferation, reshaping the way we live, work, and interact with the world [11, 12]. Every click, swipe, and sensor reading generates a deluge of information, contributing to the exponential growth of data. This explosion of data and information is driven by several factors:

- **Digital Transformation:** The digitization of processes, products, and services generates vast amounts of digital data. From online transactions to sensor data from IoT devices, virtually every aspect of modern life has a digital footprint.
- **Social Media and Connectivity:** Social media platforms, communication apps, and online networks facilitate constant sharing and interaction. User-generated content, including text, images, and videos, adds to the data avalanche.
- **IoT and Sensors:** The Internet of Things (IoT) connects devices and sensors, collecting real-time data from smart homes, cities, factories, and vehicles. These sensors produce continuous streams of data for analysis and decision making.
- **E-commerce and Online Services:** Online shopping, streaming, and cloud-based services produce massive datasets connected to consumer behavior, preferences, and usage patterns.
- **Machine Learning and AI:** AI systems need extensive datasets for training and learning. The more information available, the more sophisticated and precise AI algorithms become, creating a feedback loop of data generation and AI improvement.

- **Data-Driven Business Practices:** Organizations increasingly rely on data analytics to run decision making and gain a competitive edge. This demand for information has led to the collection and storage of vast datasets for business insights.
- **Research and Science:** Scientific research creates enormous volumes of data, from genomics to climate modeling. High-performance computing and big data analytics are essential for processing and extracting knowledge from these datasets.

3.4 The Intersection of Knowledge and Technology

The involvement of knowledge and technology in the Information Age has ushered in a transformative age. Education has happened to be globally reachable through online platforms and AI-driven personalization, while healthcare benefits from electronic records and data-driven diagnostics. In research and innovation, technology accelerates breakthroughs and fosters global collaboration. Businesses leverage data analytics and AI for informed decisions, while the gig economy thrives. Socially, technology redefines communication, yet raises concerns on misinformation. Cultural realms increase creative possibilities and global reach. Ethical considerations, like privacy and algorithmic bias, underscore the requirement for responsible technology use. Navigating this intersection is paramount, as it shapes our world's future, demanding stability among progress and ethical reflection.

3.4.1 How Technology Facilitates Knowledge Management

Technology has revolutionized knowledge management by giving tools and platforms that streamline the creation, storage, retrieval, and sharing of data. Knowledge management, once a cumbersome task, has become competent and effective through digital solutions. For example, knowledge repositories and content management systems permit organizations to store and organize vast amounts of data and documents, making them simply accessible to employees [13]. Collaboration tools with social platforms facilitate knowledge sharing and communication, fostering a culture of learning and innovation. Additionally, data analytics with artificial intelligence facilitate extracting valuable insights from large datasets, enabling informed decision making and continuous improvement. In essence, technology has turned into the cornerstone of modern knowledge management, enhancing productivity, innovation, and competitiveness across a variety of sectors.

3.4.2 Knowledge Management Tools and Platforms in the Digital Age

In the digital era, knowledge management techniques and platforms have become indispensable resources for organizations looking to harness the power of their collective intelligence. These methods have evolved to address the complexities of managing large amounts of information and fostering collaboration. Knowledge repositories with content management systems make easy seamless storage and recovery of documents, ensuring that vital knowledge is at employees' fingertips. Collaboration platforms, such as intranets and team communication apps, ease real-time sharing and conversation of ideas. Furthermore, advanced exploration and data analytics tools make it easier to extract insights from giant datasets, helping organizations to make knowledgeable decisions. In a world driven by data, these knowledge management techniques and platforms are the linchpins of well-organized, agile, and competitive businesses in the digital era.

3.4.3 Data Analytics and Artificial Intelligence in Knowledge Management

In the modern age, where data are generated at an unprecedented rate, harnessing its potential is critical for effective knowledge management. Data analytics and artificial intelligence (AI) have emerged as precious tools in this endeavor, revolutionizing the way organizations gather, process, and use knowledge [14].

Data analytics, the procedure of examining large datasets to extract meaningful insights, plays an essential role in knowledge management. It enables organizations to discover trends, patterns, and correlations within their data, helping them make informed decisions. In the framework of knowledge management, data analytics can help identify gaps in knowledge repositories, highlight areas where proficiency is lacking, and track the effectiveness of knowledge-sharing initiatives. By turning unprocessed data into actionable knowledge, analytics enhances the quality and relevance of information available to employees.

Artificial intelligence (AI), on the other hand, takes knowledge management to the next level. AI-powered systems can automatically classify, tag, and organize vast amounts of data, making it easily searchable and accessible. Chatbots and virtual assistants equipped with AI can give instant responses to queries, thus accelerating knowledge retrieval and improving user experiences. AI-driven recommendation engines propose related content to users, promoting continuous learning and knowledge sharing. Moreover, machine learning algorithms can predict future knowledge requirements, ensuring that organizations stay ahead of the curve.

One of the most significant advantages of data analytics and AI in knowledge management is their capability to ease personalized learning experiences. By analyzing user behavior and preferences, these technologies can adapt content recommendations, training modules, and resources to individual needs, thereby increasing employee engagement and skill development.

However, the acceptance of data analytics and AI in knowledge management also comes with challenges. Ensuring data privacy and security is dominant, as is addressing concerns about algorithmic bias. Organizations must also spend on training and upskilling their workforce to effectively leverage these technologies.

3.5 Knowledge Creation and Capture

Knowledge creation and capture are basic processes within knowledge management that drive innovation, problem solving, and organizational growth. Knowledge creation involves the growth of new insights, ideas, and expertise through a combination of individual experiences, collaborative efforts, and continuous learning. It frequently occurs organically during interactions, brainstorming sessions, and research endeavors.

Knowledge capture, otherwise, is the systematic gathering and recording of this valuable information. It deals with the preservation of the knowledge created within an organization's collective memory through documentation, databases, and digital tools [15]. Effective knowledge capture makes sure that insights and expertise are not lost when employees leave or retire, and it enables knowledge to be shared and reused across the organization.

In today's digital age, knowledge capture has been very much facilitated by technology. Document management systems, collaboration platforms, and artificial intelligence tools assist in streamlining the process, making it easier for organizations to capture, store, and retrieve knowledge efficiently. By fostering a culture of continuous learning and knowledge sharing, organizations can tie together the power of both knowledge creation and capture to stay competitive and innovative in an ever-evolving world.

3.5.1 Strategies to Foster Knowledge Creation and Capture in the Industrial Context

Creating and capturing knowledge in an industrial context is necessary for optimizing operations, enhancing innovation, and ensuring long-term competitiveness. Figure 3.5 shows strategies to effectively manage knowledge in an industrial setting:

- **Document Best Practices:** Establish standardized procedures and best practices for various industrial processes. Document these practices in manuals, checklists, or digital formats to ensure consistency and easy reference for employees.
- **Cross-Functional Teams:** Encourage cross-functional collaboration and knowledge sharing. Form teams that bring together individuals from different departments or expertise areas to solve complex problems and share insights.

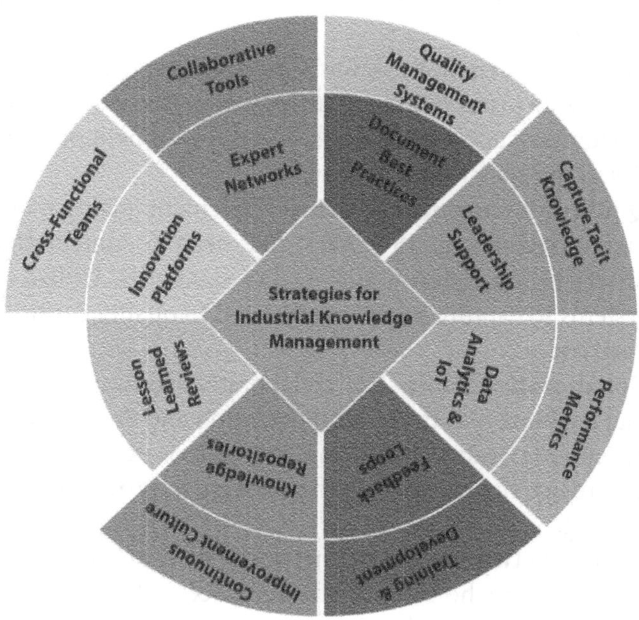

Figure 3.5 Strategies for industrial knowledge management.

- **Training and Development:** Invest in employee training and development programs to keep skills and knowledge up-to-date. Provide access to relevant courses, workshops, and certifications to foster continuous learning.
- **Knowledge Repositories:** Create digital knowledge repositories where employees can store and access information, research findings, and project documentation. Implement content management systems to organize and categorize data for easy retrieval.
- **Capture Tacit Knowledge:** Recognize the value of tacit knowledge, which resides in the minds of experienced employees. Encourage mentorship programs and facilitate knowledge transfer from retiring or departing employees to their successors.
- **Innovation Platforms:** Establish platforms or forums for employees to share innovative ideas and solutions. Encourage employees to suggest proposals for process improvements, cost-saving measures, or new product concepts.
- **Data Analytics and IoT:** Employ data analytics and Internet of Things (IoT) solutions to collect and analyze real-time data from industrial processes. Remove insights to optimize operations, predict maintenance needs, and improve efficiency.
- **Lessons Learned Reviews:** Carry out regular reviews of completed projects and initiatives to identify lessons learned. Document successes, failures, and improvement opportunities to intimate future endeavors.
- **Quality Management Systems:** Implement quality management systems (e.g., ISO 9001) that need documentation of processes, procedures, and quality standards. Utilize these systems to capture knowledge related to quality control and assurance.
- **Collaborative Tools:** Use collaborative software and tools that facilitate real-time communication and document sharing among teams. Platforms like Microsoft Teams, Slack, or project management software can improve knowledge sharing.
- **Expert Networks:** Set up networks of experts within the organization who can provide guidance and support to colleagues when needed. Encourage employees to ask for advice from subject matter experts.

- **Continuous Improvement Culture:** Foster a culture of continuous improvement where employees are encouraged to discover opportunities for enhancement and share their insights with management.
- **Performance Metrics:** Implement key performance indicators (KPIs) to evaluate the effectiveness of knowledge creation and capture initiatives. Regularly review these metrics and adjust strategies accordingly.
- **Feedback Loops:** Encourage feedback from employees at all levels. Create channels for employees to provide input on processes, suggest improvements, and report issues that can inform knowledge management efforts.
- **Leadership Support:** Ensure that leadership actively supports and promotes knowledge management initiatives. Leaders should set an example by sharing knowledge and emphasizing its importance.

3.5.2 The Vital Role of Innovation and R&D in Knowledge Generation

Innovation and Research and Development (R&D) play pivotal roles in the dynamic process of knowledge creation, propelling societies and organizations forward in an ever-evolving world [16]. They are intrinsically linked, as innovation often springs from the fruits of rigorous R&D efforts. Figure 3.6 shows how innovation and R&D contribute to the continuous expansion of human knowledge.

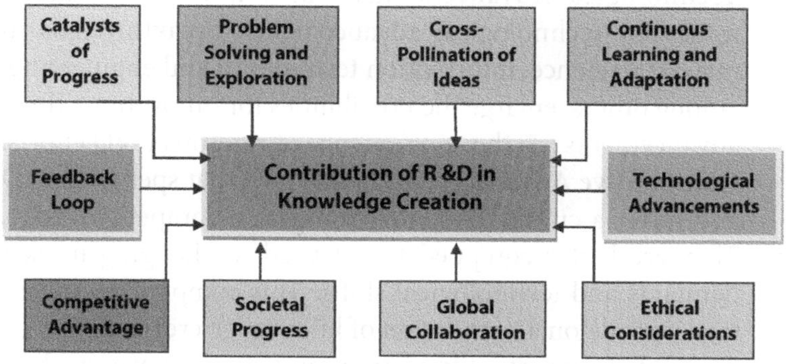

Figure 3.6 Role of R&D in knowledge creation.

- **Catalysts of Progress:** Innovation and R&D are the engines of progress. They drive the development of new technologies, products, and services by pushing the boundaries of current knowledge. Whether it is a groundbreaking scientific discovery or a new consumer gadget, knowledge creation is at the core of every innovative leap.
- **Problem Solving and Exploration:** R&D is about solving complex problems and exploring the unknown. Through systematic investigation, experimentation, and analysis, researchers expand our understanding of the world. The knowledge generated in this process forms the foundation for future innovations.
- **Cross-Pollination of Ideas:** Innovation thrives in environments where diverse ideas meet. R&D regularly involves interdisciplinary collaboration, bringing together experts from various fields. This cross-pollination of ideas leads to new perspectives and novel solutions, contributing to knowledge creation.
- **Continuous Learning and Adaptation:** Innovation and R&D need continuous learning and adaptation. Researchers and innovators must stay up-to-date with the most recent developments in their respective fields. This procedure of learning and adapting not only enhances individual expertise but also contributes to the collective knowledge pool.
- **Feedback Loop:** The process of innovation and R&D gives feedback that informs future endeavors. Whether an experiment succeeds or fails, the knowledge gained gives valuable insights. This feedback loop is necessary for refining hypotheses, strategies, and technologies.
- **Technological Advancements:** Many innovations are determined by technological advancements. Breakthroughs in materials science, information technology, and engineering, among others, enlarge the possibilities for innovation. These advancements are the consequence of rigorous R&D efforts.
- **Competitive Advantage:** Organizations that spend in R&D and foster a culture of innovation gain a competitive edge. They are better equipped to get used to changing market demands and technological shifts. This competitive advantage is made on a foundation of knowledge creation.
- **Societal Progress:** Innovation and R&D have a deep impact on societal progress. They direct to improvements in

healthcare, agriculture, energy, and countless other sectors. These advancements raise the quality of life, address global challenges, and contribute to the collective well-being of humanity.

- **Global Collaboration:** In today's interconnected world, innovation and R&D frequently involve global collaboration. Researchers and innovators from different countries work together to handle complex, global issues, fostering international knowledge exchange.
- **Ethical Considerations:** As knowledge creation accelerates, ethical considerations grow to be increasingly important. Innovators and researchers must find a way to ethical dilemmas related to privacy, security, and the responsible use of knowledge.

3.5.3 Effective Approaches for Documenting and Safeguarding Knowledge

Best practices for documenting and storing knowledge involve creating a structured and accessible repository of data that fosters competent retrieval and continuous learning. This starts with clear and standardized documentation, ensuring that knowledge is constantly recorded in a format that is easily understood. Employing a well-organized categorization system and metadata tagging facilitates competent searching and recovery. Frequently updating and maintaining the knowledge repository are crucial to keep information relevant and up-to-date. Moreover, promoting a culture of knowledge sharing and collaboration within the organization encourages employees to add their insights and expertise, enriching the repository. Last, ensuring data security, access controls, and backup procedures safeguard the valuable knowledge assets against loss or unauthorized access. These practices collectively enhance knowledge management, aiding organizations in leveraging their intellectual capital for innovation and growth.

3.6 Facilitating Knowledge Sharing and Dissemination

Knowledge sharing and distribution are significant components of effective knowledge management. When individuals and teams inside an organization openly share their expertise, insights, and lessons learned, it fosters a culture of collaboration and continuous learning. This, in turn, makes the organization capable of leveraging its collective knowledge for innovation, problem solving, and decision making [17]. To optimize knowledge sharing and distribution, organizations often use various tools and platforms, such as intranets, collaborative software, and training programs, to facilitate easy access to data and ensure that valuable knowledge reaches those who need it most. Last, a well-established knowledge sharing and distribution system empowers individuals and organizations to adapt, grow, and thrive in an ever-evolving landscape.

3.6.1 Prioritizing Intra-Organizational Knowledge Sharing

In today's fast-paced and information-driven world, the significance of sharing knowledge across an organization cannot be overstated. It serves as the lifeblood of innovation, development, and adaptability. Here are several key reasons why fostering a culture of knowledge sharing is crucial:

- **Accelerating Learning Curve:** When knowledge is shared freely, new employees can speedily learn from their more experienced colleagues. This accelerates the onboarding process and ensures with the purpose that the organization benefits from the collective wisdom of its workforce.
- **Problem Solving:** Complex challenges often need a combination of expertise from different areas. Knowledge sharing enables employees to tap into the various skill sets and experiences of their peers, leading to more effective problem solving and decision making.
- **Innovation and Creativity:** Innovation thrives in an environment where thoughts can flow freely. Sharing knowledge encourages employees to share their innovative ideas and build upon each other's concepts, fostering a culture of creativity and uninterrupted improvement.
- **Reduction of Redundancy:** Without proper knowledge sharing, employees may unknowingly duplicate work or reinvent the wheel. Sharing knowledge about ongoing projects, best practices, and past experiences helps to remove redundancy and optimize resources.
- **Improved Decision Making:** Well-versed decisions are based on comprehensive information. When knowledge

is shared transparently, leaders can construct data-driven choices that align with the organization's goals and values.

- **Employee Engagement and Satisfaction:** Employees who feel their knowledge is appreciated and actively seek opportunities to share it tend to be more engaged and satisfied in their roles. This, in turn, contributes to higher retention rates and a more optimistic work environment.
- **Risk Mitigation:** Sharing knowledge about potential risks and lessons learned from past mistakes helps the organization avoid costly errors and navigate challenges more effectively.
- **Competitive Advantage:** Organizations that excel in knowledge sharing can adapt more rapidly to changing market conditions and emerging trends. This agility provides a competitive edge in today's dynamic business landscape.
- **Organizational Memory:** Knowledge sharing creates an organizational memory that outlasts individual employees. It ensures that valuable information is not misplaced when employees leave or retire, maintaining continuity and stability.
- **Customer Satisfaction:** Knowledge sharing extends ahead of the organization to benefit customers. When employees have the right to use a wealth of information, they can better serve clients, answer questions, and address concerns, ultimately leading to higher customer satisfaction.

3.6.2 Utilizing Collaborative Tools and Platforms for Enhanced Knowledge Exchange

In the digital age, collaborative tools and platforms have revolutionized the way organizations share knowledge and foster teamwork [18]. These technologies facilitate seamless communication, information exchange, and collective learning, promoting efficiency and innovation across various sectors. Here, we explore the significance of collaborative tools and platforms for knowledge sharing.

- **Real-Time Communication:** Collaborative tools, such as instant messaging, video conferencing, and team chat platforms, enable real-time communication, breaking down geographical barriers. Teams can share insights, updates, and ideas instantly, enhancing collaboration and decision making.

- **Document Collaboration:** Cloud-based document collaboration platforms, like Google Workspace and Microsoft 365, allow multiple users to edit and comment on documents simultaneously. This streamlines the creation and refinement of shared documents, reducing version control issues.
- **Project Management:** Project management tools like Asana, Trello, and Jira enable teams to organize tasks, set deadlines, and track progress collaboratively. These platforms encourage transparency, ensuring that everyone is aligned with project goals.
- **Knowledge Repositories:** Wiki platforms, such as Confluence and MediaWiki, serve as knowledge repositories where organizations can document and share information, best practices, and policies. Users can easily access, update, and provide a collective knowledge base.
- **Virtual Workspaces:** Virtual workspaces, like Microsoft Teams and Slack, provide a centralized hub for team communication, file sharing, and integration with various apps. These platforms enhance productivity by consolidating tools into a single interface.
- **Video Conferencing and Webinars:** Video conferencing tools, like Zoom and Webex, facilitate virtual meetings, webinars, and training sessions. They enable knowledge sharing through face-to-face interactions, screen sharing, and recording capabilities.
- **Discussion Forums:** Online discussion forums and communities, such as Reddit and Stack Exchange, foster knowledge sharing among like-minded individuals. These platforms encourage open dialog, problem solving, and the exchange of expertise.
- **Social Media:** Social media platforms, like LinkedIn and Twitter, extend knowledge sharing beyond organizational boundaries. Professionals can connect, share industry insights, and participate in discussions, expanding their networks and staying updated on industry trends.
- **Collaborative Editing:** Collaborative editing tools, like Notion and Evernote, help shared note taking and knowledge organization. Teams can create, edit, and arrange notes

collaboratively, ensuring that important information is readily available.

- **Analytics and Insights:** Many collaborative platforms propose analytics and insights into user engagement and content performance. This information helps organizations track the effectiveness of their knowledge-sharing initiatives and make data-driven improvements.
- **Security and Access Control:** Collaborative tools prioritize data security, frequently providing access controls, encryption, and user authentication. This ensures that sensitive information is protected while enabling flawless knowledge sharing.
- **Mobile Accessibility:** Collaborative tools are often mobile friendly, allowing users to use knowledge and communicate on the go. This flexibility raises productivity and ensures that knowledge is accessible whenever and wherever it is needed.

3.6.3 Overcoming Challenges and Implementing Solutions in Knowledge Distribution

Knowledge distribution, the technique of disseminating valuable information and insights across an organization, is very important for fostering innovation, improving decision making, and enhancing overall productivity. On the other hand, it comes using its fair share of challenges. Here, we visualize into a few of the common challenges faced in knowledge distribution and explore potential solutions.

Challenges:

- **Information Overload:** In the era of data, employees can become devastated by the complete volume of data and knowledge available, making it difficult to discern what is relevant.
- **Silos and Fragmentation:** Knowledge is frequently distributed across departments or teams, leading to silos where valuable insights are not shared effectively.
- **Lack of Motivation:** Employees may not be willing to share knowledge due to concerns about job security, recognition, or a lack of incentives.

- **Resistance to Change:** Implementing new knowledge distribution processes or technologies may face opposition from employees accustomed to traditional methods.
- **Ineffective Tools:** Obsolete or inefficient knowledge-sharing tools can hinder the distribution process and discourage active participation.

Solutions:

- **Content Curation**: Realize content curation strategies to filter and provide relevant, high-quality information to employees. This helps combat information surplus.
- **Knowledge-Sharing Platforms:** Spend in knowledge-sharing platforms that facilitate easy access, searchability, and categorization of information, breaking down silos.
- **Recognition and Incentives:** Identify and reward employees for their knowledge-sharing efforts. Establish a tradition where sharing knowledge is seen as a valuable contribution.
- **Change Management:** Effective change management practices can facilitate employees' adapt to new knowledge distribution processes. Provide training and clear communication to address concerns and support participation.
- **Collaborative Tools:** Use modern collaborative tools and platforms that offer features, like real-time communication, document sharing, and analytics, to enhance knowledge distribution.
- **Communities of Practice:** Foster communities of practice within the organization where employees with similar interests or proficiency can collaborate and share knowledge.
- **Leadership Support:** Make sure that leaders actively participate in and support knowledge distribution efforts. Their endorsement can position the tone for the entire organization.
- **Feedback Mechanisms:** Implement feedback loops that allow employees to provide input on knowledge distribution processes and suggest improvements.
- **Content Management:** Regularly update and maintain the knowledge repository to ensure that information remains current and relevant.

- **Training and Skill Development:** Offer training programs that teach employees effective knowledge-sharing techniques and encourage continuous learning.
- **Metrics and Analytics:** Monitor and measure the effectiveness of knowledge distribution efforts using key performance indicators (KPIs) and analytics to identify areas for improvement.
- **Legal and Ethical Considerations:** Ensure that knowledge distribution complies with legal and ethical standards, particularly when handling sensitive or proprietary information.

3.7 Knowledge Transfer and Training Initiative

Knowledge transfer and training are integral components of organizational development and employee growth. Knowledge transfer involves the seamless transmission of critical expertise, insights, and best practices from experienced employees to newer team members or across departments [19, 20]. Effective training programs not only onboard new employees but also provide ongoing skill development opportunities for the entire workforce. By facilitating knowledge transfer and training, organizations ensure that valuable institutional knowledge is preserved; employees stay updated on industry trends, and the collective skill set remains competitive in a rapidly evolving business landscape.

3.7.1 Addressing the Skills Gap in the Fourth Industrial Revolution Era

The Fourth Industrial Revolution, characterized by the integration of digital technologies, artificial intelligence, automation, and data-driven decision making, has ushered in a profound transformation across industries. However, this rapid technological advancement has also given rise to a significant skill gap, where the skills demanded by the job market often outpace the skills possessed by the workforce. Effectively addressing this gap is vital for individuals, organizations, and society as a whole.

- **Continuous Learning:** Embracing a lifelong learning state of mind is essential in the Fourth Industrial Revolution. Individuals must enthusiastically seek opportunities to acquire new skills and stay updated on emerging technologies and industry trends. This can include formal education, online courses, certifications, or self-directed learning.

- **Reskilling and Upskilling:** Employers should spend on reskilling and upskilling programs to empower their workforce to adapt to changing job requirements. These programs can be tailored to the specific requirements of the organization and its employees.
- **Digital Literacy:** Digital literacy is a foundational skill in the digital era. It includes the capability to use digital tools, navigate online platforms, and understand data and analytics. Educational institutions and employers should prioritize teaching and increasing digital literacy.
- **Soft Skills:** While technical skills are vital, soft skills, such as critical thinking, problem solving, adaptability, and effective communication, stay essential. These skills facilitate individuals to navigate complex situations and collaborate effectively.
- **Industry–Academia Collaboration:** Collaboration between educational institutions and industries can facilitate bridging the skill gap. Industry input can update curriculum development, ensuring that graduates possess the skills needed for the job market.
- **Apprenticeships and Internships:** Practical experience gained through apprenticeships and internships is invaluable. These opportunities give hands-on learning and exposure to real-world challenges, preparing individuals for the workforce.
- **Diversity and Inclusion:** Embracing variety and inclusion in the workplace can help tap into a broader talent pool. Diverse teams repeatedly bring a range of perspectives and skills that can be harnessed to address the skill gap.
- **Government Support:** Governments can play a task by implementing policies that encourage investment in education and workforce development. They can also maintain initiatives that promote access to education and training for underserved communities.
- **Adaptability and Agility:** Organizations and individuals should grow adaptability and agility as core competencies. The ability to quickly learn and turn in response to changing circumstances is invaluable in a rapidly evolving job market.

- **Data-Driven Decision Making:** Organizations should leverage data analytics to discover skill gaps within their workforce and tailor training programs accordingly. Data-driven decision making ensures that resources are allocated successfully.

3.7.2 Knowledge Transfer from Seasoned Professionals to New Recruits

Knowledge transfer from experienced workers to new hires is a serious process for organizations seeking to preserve institutional wisdom and maintain a competitive edge. Experienced staff possesses valuable insights, best practices, and tacit knowledge accumulated over years of work. Effective knowledge transfer involves creating planned mentorship programs, encouraging open communication and providing opportunities for shadowing and hands-on learning. This transfer of knowledge not only accelerates the integration of new hires into the organization but also ensures the continuity of proficiency, fostering innovation and growth. It is a symbiotic progression where the wisdom of the past enriches the potential of the future, creating a thriving environment for both seasoned professionals and emerging talent.

3.7.3 Training and Development Programs Tailored for Knowledge-Intensive Industries

In knowledge-intensive industries, where intellectual assets and expertise are paramount, training and development programs play a crucial role in ensuring organizational success and competitiveness. These industries, which contain technology, finance, healthcare, and research sectors, rely on the continuous growth of their employees' skills and knowledge to remain at the front position of innovation. Here, we discover the significance of training and development programs in such knowledge-intensive environments.

- **Continuous Learning Culture:** Knowledge-intensive industries boom on innovation and adaptability. Training programs promote a culture of continuous learning, encouraging employees to stay updated with the latest technologies, industry trends, and best practices.

- **Skills Enhancement:** Fast technological advancements demand that employees acquire new skills regularly. Training and development initiatives give opportunities for employees to enhance their technical, analytical, and soft skills, ensuring they remain relevant in their roles.
- **Onboarding and Integration:** Training programs are very important for efficiently onboarding new hires. They give essential insights into the organization's culture, processes, and expectations, helping newcomers integrate seamlessly and become productive contributors.
- **Knowledge Sharing:** In industries where proficiency is highly specialized, training programs facilitate knowledge sharing from experienced professionals to newer team members. This movement of tacit knowledge is crucial for preserving institutional wisdom.
- **Compliance and Regulation:** Knowledge-intensive sectors frequently face stringent regulatory requirements. Training ensures that employees realize and adhere to these regulations, reducing compliance risks.
- **Innovation and Problem Solving:** Training programs regularly encourage creative thinking and problem-solving skills. These skills are vital in knowledge-intensive industries, where employees must tackle complex challenges and develop innovative solutions.
- **Career Development:** Employees in knowledge-intensive industries are more likely to go with organizations that offer opportunities for career growth and development. Training programs give clear paths for advancement, increasing employee retention.
- **Adaptation to Technological Changes:** As technology evolves speedily, employees need to adapt. Training programs keep employees up-to-date with the most recent tools and technologies, helping organizations leverage innovations effectively.
- **Global Competitiveness:** In a globalized world, knowledge-intensive industries struggle on a global scale. Training programs provide employees with the skills and knowledge needed to compete effectively in international markets.
- **Leadership Development:** Training programs often comprise leadership development components. Nurturing future

leaders within the organization is necessary for long-term success and innovation.

- **Data-Driven Decision Making:** In data-rich industries, employees are required to be proficient in data analysis and interpretation. Training programs educate employees on how to use data effectively in decision-making processes.
- **Customer-Centric Focus:** Several knowledge-intensive industries prioritize delivering exceptional customer experiences. Training programs encourage a customer-centric mindset, ensuring that employees understand and meet customer needs and expectations.

3.8 Strategic Knowledge Management for Fostering Innovation

Knowledge management is the foundation of innovation within organizations. By effectively capturing, organizing, and sharing knowledge, companies make an environment where employees can access a wealth of information, insights, and past experiences. This rich knowledge repository becomes the fertile ground for innovation to grow. When individuals have easy access to the collective wisdom of their colleagues, they can build upon existing knowledge, generate novel ideas, and experiment with new approaches [21]. Moreover, knowledge management promotes cross-functional collaboration, allowing diverse teams to combine their expertise and perspectives to tackle complex problems and drive innovation. In essence, knowledge management not only preserves institutional memory but also fuels the creative engine of innovation, making it a vital component of an organization's competitive strategy in today's rapidly evolving business landscape.

3.8.1 The Catalytic Role of Knowledge Management in Fueling Innovation Within the Context of Industry 4.0

In the era of Industry 4.0, characterized by the fusion of digital technologies, automation, and data-driven processes, knowledge management has emerged as a catalyst for innovation. This transformational industrial landscape demands a dynamic approach to knowledge management, one that not only preserves institutional wisdom but actively fuels the innovation engine [22]. Here, we delve into how knowledge management is the linchpin of innovation in Industry 4.0.

- **Data-Driven Decision Making:** In Industry 4.0, vast amounts of data are generated by connected devices and systems. Knowledge management systems that capture, analyze, and disseminate these data empower organizations to make informed decisions, identify opportunities for improvement, and drive innovation through data-driven insights.
- **Rapid Learning and Adaptation:** Knowledge management facilitates rapid learning and adaptation to new technologies and processes. By centralizing information on emerging technologies and best practices, organizations can equip their workforce with the knowledge needed to embrace and leverage Industry 4.0 innovations.
- **Collaborative Innovation:** Industry 4.0 thrives on collaboration among humans and machines. Knowledge management platforms foster cross-functional collaboration, allowing teams to share proficiency, iterate on ideas, and co-create innovative solutions that harness the power of automation, AI, and IoT.
- **Problem Solving and Continuous Improvement:** Knowledge management encourages traditions of problem solving and continuous improvement. Employees can utilize a repository of past solutions and lessons learned, accelerating the resolution of challenges, and sparking incremental and breakthrough innovations.
- **Agility and Adaptability:** In a rapidly evolving industrial landscape, agility is paramount. Knowledge management enables organizations to stay agile by providing up-to-date information, allowing them to get used to quickly changing market conditions and technological advancements.
- **Talent Development:** Industry 4.0 needs a workforce equipped with advanced skills. Knowledge management supports talent advancement by offering training resources, expert insights, and a platform for employees to share their knowledge, fostering a skilled workforce capable of driving innovation.
- **Innovation Ecosystems:** Knowledge management extends away from the organization's boundaries, facilitating collaboration with external partners, suppliers, and customers. These

ecosystems of knowledge exchange can direct to co-innovation and the development of new products and services.

- **Risk Mitigation:** Industry 4.0 innovations come up to the inherent risks. Effective knowledge management carries risk assessment and mitigation strategies, ensuring that organizations can innovate confidently while managing potential disruptions.

3.8.2 Illustrative Case Studies of Organizations Leveraging Knowledge to Drive

Leveraging knowledge for innovation is an important strategy for organizations looking to stay competitive and adapt to evolving market dynamics. Let us look at a few case studies of organizations that have successfully harnessed their knowledge to drive innovation:

IBM's Watson: IBM's Watson is a key example of knowledge-driven innovation. It is an AI-powered cognitive computing system that leverages huge amounts of data and knowledge to solve complex problems. Watson's capability to understand, reason, and learn from data has been applied in various sectors, from healthcare (diagnosing diseases) to finance (risk assessment) and customer service (chatbots). By leveraging its wide knowledge base, IBM has transformed how industries approach problem solving and decision making.

Netflix's Recommendation System: Netflix has become compatible with personalized contented recommendations. The company's recommendation algorithm is an essential example of knowledge-driven innovation. Netflix influences user data, viewing history, and likes to recommend content modified to individual tastes. This knowledge-driven technique not only raises user engagement but also drives content creation decisions, leading to the manufacture of successful originals like "House of Cards" and "Stranger Things."

Procter & Gamble (P&G): P&G, a consumer goods giant, has a substantial history of knowledge-driven innovation. Their "Connect and Develop" strategy deals leveraging external and internal knowledge to compel product innovation. P&G collaborates with suppliers, partners, and even competitors to pass through a broader knowledge base. This technique has led to the generation of successful products like the Swiffer, which emerged from P&G's collaborative efforts.

Tesla's Autopilot: Tesla's Autopilot system is a crucial example of knowledge-driven innovation in the automotive industry. Tesla gathers information from its fleet of vehicles furnished with Autopilot technology to continually improve and refine autonomous driving capabilities. This technique permits Tesla to leverage real-world driving data and knowledge to push the boundaries of autonomous vehicle technology.
SpaceX's Reusable Rockets: SpaceX, founded by Elon Musk, revolutionized the space industry by growing sustainable rocket technology. SpaceX's engineers take control of their deep knowledge of rocketry and aerospace engineering to design, test, and iterate on reusable rockets like the Falcon 9. This pioneering method has dramatically reduced the cost of space exploration and opened up new possibilities for the industry.

3.8.3 Cultivating an Innovative Culture Through Proficient Knowledge Management Practices

In today's fast-growing business landscape, organizations are always seeking ways to stay competitive and relevant. One of the most influential tools at their disposal is innovation [23]. To foster innovation, organizations must grow a tradition that values and encourages creative thinking, problem solving, and the continuous generation of new ideas. A crucial component in building such a culture is effective knowledge management. This article takes a glance at the role of knowledge management in creating a culture of innovation and provides insights into how organizations can leverage it to run innovation.

Understanding Knowledge Management
Knowledge management refers to the systematic activity of capturing, organizing, storing, and sharing an organization's knowledge strength. These assets can hold explicit knowledge (documented information, data, and reports) and tacit knowledge (experience, expertise, and insights held by employees). Effective knowledge management makes sure that information is readily accessible to those who require it, promoting informed decision making and problem solving.

Creating a Culture of Innovation:

- **Fostering a Learning Mindset**: The foundation of traditions of innovation is a dedication to continuous learning. Organizations should hold up employees to seek out new knowledge and skills, both within and outside their roles. This holds providing access to training and development opportunities, mentoring programs, and resources that carry lifelong learning.

- **Open Communication and Collaboration**: Innovation does well in a domain where employees feel comfortable sharing their ideas and collaborating with others. Knowledge management systems should ease open communication, enabling employees to interchange ideas, feedback, and best practices seamlessly. Cross-functional teams and collaborative spaces can also help in idea sharing.
- **Recognition and Reward Systems**: To impetus innovation, organizations should start recognition and reward systems that accept and celebrate creative contributions. This can involve the two formal recognition schemes and informal gestures like praise and opportunities for advancement.
- **Risk Tolerance**: A culture of innovation grabs calculated risk taking. Employees should feel entitled to experiment with advanced ideas and approaches without fear of severe consequences for failure. Learning from mistakes should be stimulated to drive future innovation.

Leveraging Knowledge Management for Innovation:

- **Knowledge Capture and Storage**: Knowledge management systems should expertly handle and reserve valuable insights, best practices, and lessons learned. This repository of knowledge becomes a beneficial source for employees' act of looking for inspiration and information for their innovative endeavors.
- **Search and Retrieval Tools**: Implement user-friendly investigation and retrieval tools that allow employees to quickly access the information they need. This ensures that employees can get appropriate knowledge when they require it, reducing barriers to innovation.
- **Knowledge Sharing Platforms**: Make use of knowledge-sharing platforms that ease collaboration and information interchange. These platforms can include intranets, wikis, and social media-style networks where employees can contribute, give comments, and share their knowledge.

- **Data Analytics and Insights**: Leverage data analytics to get insights from your knowledge management system. Reviewing design and trends can help to identify places where innovation is most needed and guide decision making.
- **Training and Education**: Offer training and education on how to utilize knowledge management tools effectively. Ensure that employees interpret the value of knowledge sharing and how it contributes to the organization's innovation goals.

3.8.4 Knowledge Management Challenges and Solutions

In an age of huge amounts of information and rapid technological advancements, knowledge management has become a critical component of organizational success. Effective knowledge management assists organizations to capture, store, share, and utilize their collective knowledge to drive innovation and make informed decisions [24]. However, implementing and maintaining a strong knowledge management system comes with its own set of challenges. This article searches some common knowledge management challenges and offers solutions to address them.

Challenges:

1. Lack of Clear Strategy:
Solution: Develop a Clear Knowledge Management Strategy
Organizations generally dive into knowledge management without a clear strategy, resulting in scattered efforts and limited success. To overcome this challenge, it is crucial to define a well-thought-out knowledge management strategy. This strategy should line up with the organization's goals and include objectives, key performance indicators (KPIs), and a roadmap for implementation.

2. Resistance to Change:
Solution: Change Management and Employee Engagement
Employees may abide by adopting new knowledge management practices and tools due to fear of change or concerns about added workload. Implementing successful change management strategies, such as communication plans, training programs, and involving employees in the decision-making process, can assist in overcoming resistance and foster a culture of knowledge sharing.

3. Information Overload:
Solution: Content Curation and Taxonomies
Plenty of information can be overwhelming, making it challenging to find relevant knowledge. To address this issue, organizations can implement content curation techniques, where subject matter experts curate and systematize content into meaningful categories. Additionally, the use of taxonomies and metadata can help classify and tag information for easier retrieval.

4. Lack of User-Friendly Tools:
Solution: Invest in User-Friendly Knowledge Management Systems
Complex or outdated knowledge management systems can discourage users from actively participating. Invest in user-friendly and intuitive knowledge management tools and platforms that make it easy for employees to contribute, access, and share knowledge. User training and support resources should also be readily available.

5. Inadequate Knowledge Capture:
Solution: Encourage Knowledge Sharing and Documentation
Often, valuable knowledge remains tacit and unrecorded. Encourage employees to share their expertise through documentation, mentorship programs, and knowledge-sharing sessions. Recognize and reward employees for their contributions to incentivize knowledge capture.

6. Data Security and Privacy Concerns:
Solution: Implement Robust Security Measures
Protecting sensitive information is paramount. Implement strong security measures, access controls, encryption, and regular audits to ensure that confidential data remain secure. Communicate transparently with employees about data privacy measures to build trust.

7. Knowledge Silos:
Solution: Foster Collaboration and Cross-Functional Teams
Knowledge often gets trapped within departments or teams. Foster a culture of collaboration by encouraging cross-functional teams and providing platforms for interdepartmental knowledge sharing. Incentivize knowledge sharing across silos to break down barriers.

8. Knowledge Decay:
Solution: Continuous Updating and Validation
Knowledge can become outdated quickly, especially in rapidly changing industries. Implement processes for continuous knowledge updating and validation. Regularly review and verify the accuracy and relevance of stored knowledge.

9. Knowledge Management Challenges and Solutions
In today's dynamic business environment, knowledge management (KM) is pivotal for organizations seeking to stay competitive. However, they face formidable challenges: the sheer volume of data, the need for seamless cross-functional collaboration, and the risk of knowledge loss due to employee turnover. The continuous evolution of technology and communication tools further complicates the KM landscape. To tackle these problems, organizations must implement effective KM solutions. These include various practices, technologies, and methodologies, from harnessing AI and fostering a culture of knowledge sharing to embracing collaborative tools. This analysis of knowledge management challenges and solutions will suggest insights into navigating this ever-changing field.

3.9 Common Challenges in Managing Knowledge During Industrial Revolutions

Industrial revolutions have historically directed transformative changes in how societies and economies operate. From the first industrial revolution, mechanized by steam engines and mechanization, to the ongoing fourth industrial revolution, characterized by digitalization and automation, each wave has posed unique challenges in managing knowledge [25]. This article investigates the common challenges organizations face when managing knowledge during industrial revolutions and offers insights into how to address them.

1. Rapid Technological Advancements:
During industrial revolutions, technological advancements happen at an unprecedented pace. This rapid evolution can create it challenging for organizations to keep up with the latest knowledge and tools. To address this challenge, organizations should devote in continuous learning and training programs for their workforce. This ensures that employees are

outfitted and equipped with the necessary skills and knowledge to adapt to new technologies.

2. Digital Transformation:
The shift approaching digitalization is a hallmark of the fourth industrial revolution. Managing knowledge in a digital format needs robust information systems, data security, and digital literacy. Organizations should contribute in advanced knowledge management systems, cyber security measures, and digital literacy training to navigate this challenge effectively.

3. Data Overload:
In the digital era, organizations generate vast amounts of data daily. Managing and extracting very important insights from this data can be overwhelming. Employing data analytics and artificial intelligence (AI) technologies can assist organizations in sifting through and making sense of large data sets, turning them into actionable knowledge.

4. Generational Knowledge Gap:
Industrial revolutions regularly result in generational knowledge gaps, where older employees possess valuable expertise in traditional processes while younger employees are more adept with emerging technologies. Organizations should start mentorship programs and knowledge transfer initiatives to bridge this gap, ensuring the preservation and utilization of institutional knowledge.

5. Cultural Resistance to Change:
The debut of new technologies and processes can face resistance from employees accustomed to traditional ways of working. To beat this, organizations should focus on change management strategies that involve clear communication, employee engagement, and addressing concerns. Cultivating a tradition of adaptability and innovation is crucial.

6. Data Privacy and Security:
With the increasing reliance on digital data, organizations must contend with the challenges of data privacy and security. Strict compliance with data protection regulations, implementing encryption, and conducting regular security audits are vital to safeguard sensitive knowledge and information.

7. Globalization and Diverse Workforces:
Industrial revolutions have a global effect, leading to diverse workforces with varied cultural backgrounds and perspectives. Managing knowledge

across global teams needs effective communication tools, cross-cultural training, and strategies for accommodating different time zones and work styles.

8. Evolving Business Models:
Industrial revolutions generally disrupt existing business models. Organizations must continuously adapt and reinvent themselves. Knowledge management should help in the identification of new opportunities, business model innovation, and the rapid dissemination of insights and best practices.

3.9.1 Solutions and Best Practices for Overcoming Knowledge Management Obstacles

Effective knowledge management is an important success factor for organizations in today's information-driven world. However, many obstacles can slow down the efficient capture, sharing, and utilization of knowledge. To unlock the full potential of knowledge management, organizations must start solutions and best practices to overcome these challenges [26]. This article searches common knowledge management obstacles and provides practical solutions and best practices to address them.

Obstacle 1: Lack of Clear Strategy
Solution: Develop a Comprehensive Knowledge Management Strategy
A well-defined knowledge management technique is essential. It should line up with the organization's goals and objectives, outlining how knowledge will be captured, organized, shared, and utilized. The strategy should contain clear roles and responsibilities, KPIs, and a roadmap for implementation.

Obstacle 2: Resistance to Change
Solution: Implement Change Management Practices
Resistance to change is a common obstruction in knowledge management initiatives. To address this, organizations should make use of change management practices. Communicate the benefits of knowledge management, include employees in the decision-making process, provide training and support, and recognize and reward those who actively contribute to knowledge sharing.

Obstacle 3: Inadequate Technology and Tools
Solution: Invest in User-Friendly Knowledge Management Systems
Outdated or cumbersome knowledge management tools can check users from active participation. Invest in user-friendly and intuitive knowledge management systems that facilitate easy knowledge capture and retrieval. Ensure that these tools are accessible and provide adequate training and support for users.

Obstacle 4: Lack of Incentives
Solution: Implement Recognition and Reward Systems
To encourage knowledge sharing and participation, organizations should establish recognition and reward systems. Recognize employees who contribute valuable knowledge, whether through formal programs, peer recognition, or opportunities for career advancement. Highlighting the tangible benefits of sharing knowledge can motivate employees.

Obstacle 5: Information Overload
Solution: Implement Content Curation and Taxonomies
The volume of information can be overwhelming. Implement content curation practices, where subject matter experts organize and categorize knowledge. Utilize taxonomies and metadata to classify information, making it easier to search, retrieve, and navigate.

Obstacle 6: Knowledge Silos
Solution: Foster Collaboration and Cross-Functional Teams
Knowledge often gets trapped within departments or teams. Foster a culture of collaboration by promoting cross-functional teams and providing platforms for interdepartmental knowledge sharing. Encourage knowledge sharing across silos to break down barriers.

Obstacle 7: Knowledge Decay
Solution: Continuous Updating and Validation
Knowledge can become outdated quickly, especially in rapidly changing industries. Implement processes for continuous knowledge updating and validation. Regularly review and verify the accuracy and relevance of stored knowledge.

Obstacle 8: Data Security and Privacy Concerns
Solution: Prioritize Data Security
Protecting sensitive information is paramount. Implement strong security measures, access controls, encryption, and regular audits to ensure

that confidential data remains secure. Communicate transparently with employees about data privacy measures to build trust.

Obstacle 9: Cultural and Language Diversity
Solution: Multilingual and Cross-Cultural Training
In organizations with diverse cultures and languages, provide training and resources to address language barriers and cultural differences. Promote multilingual knowledge management systems and cross-cultural training to ensure that knowledge is accessible to all employees.

Obstacle 10: Lack of Leadership Support
Solution: Gain Executive Buy-In
Leadership support is important for the success of knowledge management initiatives. Educate senior executives about the benefits of knowledge management and its effect on the organization's competitiveness and innovation. Secure their buy-in and assurance to allocate resources and support the initiative.

3.9.2 The Role of Leadership and Organizational Culture in Addressing Challenges

In the complex and expeditiously changing landscape of today's business world, leadership and organizational culture play pivotal roles in addressing challenges effectively. Challenges can be categorized from technological disruptions to market shifts and global crises. This article searches how leadership and organizational culture can be harnessed to navigate these obstacles successfully.

Leadership's Role in Addressing Challenges

1. Setting a Clear Vision and Strategy:
Effective leaders give a clear vision and strategy for their organizations. They explain the purpose, direction, and goals, which act as guiding lights during challenging times. A well-communicated vision encourages and aligns the workforce toward common objectives.

2. Leading by Example:
Leadership includes modeling the behavior and values expected from employees. Leaders who show resilience, adaptability, and a growth

mindset during challenges inspire their teams to do the same. Leading by example supports a culture of perseverance and innovation.

3. Empowering and Supporting Teams:
Great leaders enable their teams to make decisions and take ownership of challenges. They supply the necessary resources, training, and support to ensure that employees have the confidence and capability to tackle obstacles effectively.

4. Effective Communication:
Communication is vital in times of challenge and uncertainty. Leaders should continue transparent and open lines of communication, providing regular updates, addressing concerns, and actively listening to feedback from employees and stakeholders.

5. Risk Management and Decision Making:
Leaders play a vital role in risk management and decision making. They must make learned choices based on data and analysis, balancing short-term and long-term considerations. A strong leadership team can cross complex decisions with confidence.

Organizational Culture's Role in Addressing Challenges

1. Resilience and Adaptability:
A resilient and adaptable organizational culture is better outfitted to handle challenges. When employees are inspired to embrace change and view obstacles as opportunities for growth, the organization becomes more agile and responsive.

2. Innovation and Creativity:
Cultures that value innovation and creativity do well during challenges. When employees are encouraged to generate and implement new ideas, the organization can find novel solutions to complex problems.

3. Collaboration and Teamwork:
A tradition that promotes collaboration and teamwork enhances problem-solving capabilities. Cross-functional collaboration permits the pooling of diverse perspectives and expertise, which can lead to more effective solutions.

4. Learning and Development:
Organizations that prioritize regular learning and development are better prepared to tackle evolving challenges. Employees who have entrance to training and growth opportunities are more adaptable and capable of acquiring new skills.

5. Ethical and Value-Driven Culture:
An ethical and value-driven culture advises decision making during challenging times. When employees share a strong moral compass and stick to a common set of values, ethical dilemmas are resolved more effectively.

6. Inclusivity and Diversity:
Inclusive and diverse cultures grasp differences and promote a broader range of perspectives. This diversity of thought can move to more comprehensive and innovative solutions to challenges.

3.10 Conclusion

This chapter underscores the crucial role of knowledge management in navigating industrial revolutions. It gives priority to the dynamic nature of knowledge management as a key tool for innovation, competitiveness, and sustainability amid rapid technological changes. Effective knowledge management empowers organizations to change challenges into opportunities, fostering growth and competitiveness in the digital age and beyond.

3.10.1 Ongoing Importance of Knowledge Management in the Face of Industrial Revolutions

In the ever-evolving landscape of industrial revolutions, knowledge management remains as important as ever. As we cross the waves of technological disruption and societal transformation, the effective capture, organization, and utilization of knowledge continue to be the linchpin of success for organizations.

Knowledge management empowers us to contain to new technologies, harness collective wisdom, and drive innovation. It allows us to stay competitive, make informed decisions, and thrive amidst change. In the face of industrial revolutions, knowledge management is not just a means; it is the compass that guides us through uncharted waters, helping us shape a sustainable and prosperous future.

3.10.2 The Potential Impact of Future Industrial Revolutions on Knowledge Management

In the forthcoming waves of industrial revolutions, the impact on knowledge management promises to be life changing. As we enter the age of the Fourth Industrial Revolution, characterized by technologies, like AI, IoT, and blockchain, the landscape of knowledge management is set to go through profound changes.

Data will drive decision making, with knowledge management evolving to not just capture but also analyze vast datasets in real time. Automation and AI integration will shift the focus from routine tasks to strategic thinking, with knowledge management facilitating the availability of pertinent information. Learning will become dynamic and personalized, delivered through knowledge management as on-demand training and AI-driven skill development recommendations. The cross-functional collaboration will be paramount in a world where industries and disciplines blend, and knowledge management will connect experts across domains.

Ethical considerations will rise in importance, and knowledge management will incorporate ethical guidelines for responsible data use. Global connectivity will foster collaboration and cultural sensitivity, transcending geographical boundaries. Security and privacy will be critical, and knowledge management will prioritize robust data security and compliance with data protection regulations. Last, agility and adaptability will be essential traits, with knowledge management enabling organizations to pivot swiftly in response to market shifts and disruptive technologies.

In the face of these changes, organizations that proactively adapt their knowledge management practices will not only survive but thrive in the Fourth Industrial Revolution, harnessing the power of data, automation, dynamic learning, cross-functional collaboration, ethics, global connectivity, security, and adaptability to drive innovation and competitiveness.

3.10.3 Final Thoughts and Recommendations for Organizations

In conclusion, as organizations navigate the uncharted waters of the Fourth Industrial Revolution, they must embrace change, prioritize continuous learning, and foster cross-functional collaboration. Data-driven decision making, ethical considerations, and robust data security should be integral to their strategies. Global connectivity and cultural adaptability are crucial, and agility is key to staying competitive. Elevating knowledge management to a strategic imperative, guided by visionary leadership, will empower organizations to not only confront the challenges but also harness the immense potential of this transformative era. By embracing these recommendations, organizations can position themselves to thrive in an era defined by rapid technological advancements and global interconnectedness, ultimately achieving sustainable growth and competitiveness.

References

1. Bandera, C., Keshtkar, F., Bartolacci, M.R., Neerudu, S., Passerini, K., Knowledge management and the entrepreneur: Insights from Ikujiro Nonaka's Dynamic Knowledge Creation model (SECI). *Int. J. Innov. Stud.*, 1, 3, 163–174, 2017.
2. Nguyen, H.N. and Mohamed, S., Leadership behaviors, organizational culture and knowledge management practices: An empirical investigation. *J. Manage. Dev.*, 30, 2, 206–221, 2011.
3. Nonaka, I. and Peltokorpi, V., Objectivity and subjectivity in knowledge management: A review of 20 top articles. *Knowl. Process Manage.*, 13, 2, 73–82, 2006.
4. Hedlund, G., A model of knowledge management and the N-form corporation. *Strateg. Manage. J.*, 15, S2, 73–90, 1994.
5. Sarina, T., Enhancing knowledge management (KM) in the fourth industrial revolution era: The role of human resource systems, in: *The Palgrave Handbook of Knowledge Management*, pp. 411–435, Springer, New York, NY, USA, 2018.
6. Muhuri, P.K., Shukla, A.K., Abraham, A., Industry 4.0: A bibleometric analysis and detailed overview. *Eng. Appl. Artif. Intell.*, 78, 218–235, 2019.
7. Anshari, M. and Hamdan, M., Understanding knowledge management and upskilling in Fourth Industrial Revolution: transformational shift and SECI model. *VINE J. Inf. Knowl. Manage. Syst.*, 52, 3, 373–393, 2022, DOI: 10.1108/VJIKMS-09-2021-0203.
8. Oztemel, E. and Gursev, S., Literature review of Industry 4.0 and related technologies. *J. Intell. Manuf.*, 31, 127–182, 2020.
9. Di Maria, E., Bettiol, M., Capestro, M., Furlan, A., Do industry 4.0 technologies lead to more (and better) knowledge?, in: *Proc. 19th Eur.Conf. Knowl. Manage., ECKM*, vol. 1, pp. 174–181, 2018.
10. Choi, B., Poon, S.K., Davis, J.G., Effects of knowledge management strategy on organizational performance: A complementarily theory-based approach. *Omega*, 36, 2, 235–251, 2008.
11. Santoro, G., Vrontis, D., Thrassou, A., Dezi, L., The internet of things: Building a knowledge management system for open innovation and knowledge management capacity. *Technol. Forecast. Soc. Change*, 136, 347–354, 2018.

12. Erickson, S. and Rothberg, H., Big data and knowledge management: Establishing a conceptual foundation. *Electron. J. Knowl. Manage.*, 12, 2, 101–109, 2014.
13. Podsakoff, P.M., MacKenzie, S.B., Podsakoff, N.P., Bachrach, D.G., Scholarly influence in the field of management: A bibliometric analysis of the determinants of university and author impact in the management literature in the past quarter century. *J. Manag.*, 34, 4, 641–720, 2008.
14. Serenko, A., Bontis, N., Booker, L., Sadeddin, K., Hardie, T., A scientometric analysis of knowledge management and intellectual capital academic literature (1994-2008). *J. Knowl. Manag.*, 14, 1, 3–23, 2010.
15. Tranfield, D., Denyer, D., Smart, P., Towards a methodology for developing evidence-informed management knowledge by means of systematic review. *Br. J. Manag.*, 14, 3, 207–222, 2003.
16. Verba, M.A., Growth and innovation in the presence of knowledge and R&D accumulation dynamics. *Econ. Innov. New Technol.*, 31, 6, 485–510, 2022, doi: https://doi.org/10.1080/10438599.2020.1828510.
17. Zheng, T., A Literature Review on Knowledge Sharing. *Open J. Soc. Sci.*, 5, 3, 51–58, 2017, DOI: 10.4236/jss.2017.53006.
18. Zhen, L., Jiang, Z., Song, H.-T., Distributed knowledge sharing for collaborative product development. *Int. J. Prod. Res.*, 49, 10, 2959–2976, 2011, doi: https://doi.org/10.1080/00207541003705864.
19. Goh, S.C., Managing effective knowledge transfer: an integrative framework and some practice implications. *J. Knowl. Manage.*, 6, 1, 23–30, 2002, doi: https://doi.org/10.1108/13673270210417664.
20. Perez-Soltero, A. *et al.*, Knowledge Transfer in Training Processes: Towards an Integrative Evaluation Model. *J. Knowl. Manage.*, 17, 1, pp.7–40, 2019, Electronic version of the article published in IUP.
21. Mardani, A., Nikoosokhan, S., Moradi, M., Doustar, M., The Relationship between Knowledge Management and Innovation Performance. *J. High Technol. Manage. Res.*, 29, 1, pp.12–26, 2018, doi: https://doi.org/10.1016/j.hitech.2018.04.002.
22. Carneiro, A., How does knowledge management influence innovation and competitiveness? *J. Knowl. Manage.*, 4, 2, 87–98, 2000, doi: https://doi.org/10.1108/13673270010372242.
23. Idreesa, H., Xub, J., Haiderc, S.A., Tehseen, S., A systematic review of knowledge management and new product development projects: Trends, issues, and challenges. *J. Innov. Knowl.*, 8, 2, 1–10, 2023, DOI: 10.1016/j.jik.2023.100350.
24. Foster, L., Wiewiora, A., Donnet, T., Integrating Knowledge Management and Governance for Innovation Outcomes: A New Framework for Managing Innovation in a Project Environment. *J. Knowl. Econ.*, 1–28, 2023.
25. Morrar, R., Arman, H., Mousa, S., The Fourth Industrial Revolution (Industry 4.0): A Social Innovation Perspective. *Technol. Innov. Manage. Rev.*, 7, 11, 12–20, 2017.
26. Nguyen, H.T., The role of knowledge management for businesses in the context of industrial revolution 4.0. *Int. J. Res. Manage.*, 1, 2, pp.7–10, 2019.

4

Improving Manufacturing: Organizational Innovation Through Effective Knowledge Management, A McElroy Knowledge Life Cycle Approach

Arpita Nayak[1]*, Atmika Patnaik[2], Ipseeta Satpathy[3], Vishal Jain[4], B.C.M. Patnaik[3] and Majidul Islam[5]

[1]KIIT School of Management, KIIT University, Bhubaneswar, India
[2]King's College, London, United Kingdom
[3]School of Management, KIIT University, Bhubaneswar, India
[4]Department of Computer Science and Engineering, School of Engineering and Technology, Sharda University, Greater Noida, India
[5]Concordia University John Molson School of Business: Montreal, QC, Canada

Abstract

Firms must rely on innovation to achieve long-term corporate success in today's continuously changing industrial environment. Growth necessitates knowledge management and a solid basis. To compete, industrial groups must have an unquenchable urge to produce. After all, improving per-product quality and cost efficiency is just half the story. To stay in business, a corporation must always create innovative methods to accomplish things. Industrial businesses must have strategic knowledge management strategies to navigate this new road. It entails learning, sharing, and using new knowledge all at the same time. This is a critical foundation for fostering an innovative culture at these organizations. McElroy's knowledge life cycle, for example, gives a view into the interconnected phases of knowledge management and discovery. The life cycle is divided into two parts. First, we must obtain new information from within and beyond; second, we must disseminate it along with internal distribution following the occurrence. Throughout the consumption phase, expertise is employed to improve processes and goods. The highest amount of creativity is attained at the inventories stage,

**Corresponding author*: 2181158@ksom.ac.in

Rajendra Kumar, Vishal Jain, Venus C. Ibarra, Corrienna Abdul Talib and Vinay Kukreja (eds.) Knowledge Management and Industry Revolution 4.0, (87–110) © 2024 Scrivener Publishing LLC

when you develop new knowledge either by effortlessly mixing or by making something entirely new. To foster such an environment of creativity, daring, and risk taking, information must flow seamlessly from collection to usage. As a result, good knowledge management provides the foundation for the development of contemporary industrial structures. This is the gathering of new data, distributing it to such individuals, and applying it to create value. As a business culture, creating a workforce centered on teamwork, learning, and innovation is required to achieve this. A collaborative culture, a learning culture, and an inventive culture, on the other hand, promote cooperation and mutual understanding, learning and training, innovation and development, and product creation. These components work together to provide continuous success and progress, allowing businesses to remain relevant in a changing industry. The purpose of this research is to offer an overview of how knowledge production (knowledge creation, capture, sharing, and application) helps manufacturing organizations acquire new information, discuss best practices, successfully use knowledge, and incorporate new knowledge to promote innovation.

Keywords: Manufacturing organizations, knowledge acquisition, knowledge management, innovation

4.1 Introduction

Porter and Millar first proposed the notion that knowledge may be exploited to gain a competitive advantage in the middle of the 1980s. By the 1990s, experts predicted that information, not money, would be the new economy's primary driver of prosperity. Ikujiro Nonaka, a Japanese philosopher, was one of the pioneers of knowledge management theory. Explicit and tacit knowledge were concepts he presented. The first one speaks of individual talents, while the second one is about written materials. The cornerstone of knowledge management is the relationship between the two types of knowledge. Knowledge is an intangible resource that has a substantial influence on an organization's success or failure. The knowledge contained within the organization in the form of people, processes, and practices is seen as a strategic asset that provides value to individual and organizational results [1]. Manufacturing has always been on the cutting edge of technology developments and organizational changes. Manufacturers confront various obstacles in today's dynamic and competitive business climate, including increased client demands, globalization, and rapid technological improvements. Manufacturers must adopt knowledge management as a strategic instrument for organizational innovation in order to stay ahead of the competition and secure long-term growth. Because a corporation's main competitive advantage is its knowledge, "knowledge management" has become a key issue.

The methods and tactics used to successfully discover, capture, organize, and utilize an organization's knowledge assets are referred to as knowledge management. Manufacturing organizations may increase operational efficiency, improve product quality, decrease costs, and stimulate innovation by embracing knowledge management throughout the whole product life cycle [2, 3]. Explicit knowledge and tacit knowledge are the two main categories in any organization. Explicit knowledge is information that is factual, including statistics, instructions, and memoranda. It is more difficult to communicate tacit knowledge. It encompasses cultural attitudes, values, and beliefs. However, tacit knowledge is even more crucial than explicit information, according to organizational learning specialist Jerry L. Wellman, when it comes to making strides in the workplace. Managers are in charge of leading their organizations toward the achievement of objectives and set objectives. Adaptability and virtuosity are required, as well as outstanding knowledge about leadership and decision-making abilities. The term "knowledge" has been seen and interpreted from several angles. Davenport and Prusak (1998) define knowledge as a combination of contextual information, framed expertise, expert competency, and value that leads to inventiveness and perfect experience. Organizational culture, skills, goodwill, instinct, and formalized theory are examples of knowledge that impacts human behavior and cognition. Many problem-solving techniques incorporate natural, informal communication and information transmission.

The disadvantage is that teams lose unrecorded, maneuver knowledge. They squander time seeking out-of-date information or "reinventing the wheel" by continuously responding to commonly asked questions. In contrast, effective knowledge management empowers teams to quickly access all available information and comply with corporate specialists for additional clarity. Employees can ask questions anonymously or offer their expertise through modern knowledge management methods, breaking down walls and establishing a live knowledge base. As a consequence, teams across departments, including R&D, sales, and help desks, can produce more value while being more efficient [4, 5]. One of the most important organizational instruments for dealing with external unpredictability is the ability to innovate. As understood through the unit of adoption, it is a new notion, practice, or commodity. Researchers have investigated innovation aptitude as a critical factor in increasing company performance, survival, development, and competitive advantage, contributing to the debate on the importance of innovation. The knowledge and competencies required for generating new commodities and/or technologies, as well as improving existing ones, may be characterized as an organization's capacity for creativity. Toyota, for example, has effectively exploited information exchange to acquire a significant competitive advantage [6]. Ineffective knowledge management leads to knowledge gaps, which lead to wasted time, lost productivity, recurrent mistakes, and employee unhappiness.

As a company grows in size, the problems associated with poor knowledge management become more serious and difficult to fix. The average person at a company with over 10,000 workers spends more than 100 min each day seeking the required information in order to carry out their duties. This might cost more than $70 million over the course of a year as teams search for answers that are typically not recorded. Lost time and efficiency can have far-reaching consequences throughout your organization. For example, in R&D, teams may accidentally copy each other's work. When salespeople are unable to give potential customers and prospects timely and accurate information, their sales performance may suffer. Because employees get obsolete, erroneous, or irrelevant information, onboarding and other training procedures are less successful [7, 8]. Effectively managing knowledge may improve almost any process since valuable details are more easily available. Improved information sharing and collaboration can increase productivity while simultaneously providing financial and cultural advantages. The primary benefit of cross-team and cross-departmental knowledge management is that it takes less time to reassemble or preserve past data. When everyone in the organization has access to the same information, your help desk and subject matter experts will devote less time addressing the same questions, and your personnel will be able to focus their attention on more essential activities.

An effective knowledge management strategy may also assist your organization's upper management. When your top executives, for example, are not idle in seeking conveniently accessible details, executive-level decision-making improves [9]. When it pertains to data, manufacturers have a unique set of challenges. They must keep track not just of the resources they consume and the products they produce but also of the machinery, tools, and methods they employ. These data may be dispersed over several places, making tracking and administration difficult. A knowledge management system (KMS) assists industrial companies in effectively managing and using their knowledge assets. A KMS makes it simpler for workers to obtain the information they need, when they need it, by centralizing and standardizing information. Manufacturing operations, product development, and supply chain management are all improved as a result. Significant insights from industrial data are centralized and made more accessible and useable through knowledge management. Manufacturers may ensure that all team members have the benefit of the most up-to-date data-backed knowledge by centralizing insights. Furthermore, information management enables manufacturers to keep track of changes and upgrades, making it simpler to detect and resolve issues. As a consequence, knowledge management may help firms improve efficiency and quality control [10].

The manufacturing workforce is aging: nearly one-quarter of everyone who works in this industry will be over 55 by 2020. Employees who leave bring years of expertise and tacit knowledge without them. This loss of expertise has the potential to damage manufacturers, resulting in poorer output and quality. Expertise management fills this need by pooling the knowledge of business workers and subject matter experts. Manufacturers can make certain that generations after them of personnel have access to this information by centralizing it. Furthermore, knowledge management will detect knowledge and skill shortages, allowing manufacturers to engage in training and development programs to keep their employees up to date. As the workforce matures, manufacturers will find knowledge management to be an increasingly crucial tool [11, 12]. The McElroy Knowledge Life Cycle Approach is an extensive structure that assists organizations in managing their knowledge assets from development and acquisition through application and replenishment. Manufacturing organizations may build a culture of ongoing education and advancement by using this strategy, allowing them to adapt successfully to changing market conditions and technology improvements. The McElroy KML model includes crucial components such as knowledge production, knowledge capture, information sharing, knowledge implementation, and knowledge assessment [13].

According to the author Begzadic, he explained in his study that McElroy KMC analyzes existing information and then identifies knowledge gaps, enabling an iterative process in which organizational requirements are cataloged and solutions to knowledge gaps are developed. The McElroy KMC is important not just for knowledge management but also for identifying knowledge material that is valuable to the organization and its personnel.

4.2 Unleashing the Innovation Possibilities: The Effectiveness of Knowledge Creation in Manufacturing Organizations

Organizations must be aware of learning organizations in order to meet the core goals of the business. Knowledge production is focused on learning from others or acquiring knowledge information from outsiders, yet it is developed via communication and interpersonal interaction within the organization. Research-based innovation initiatives between businesses and universities boost international competitiveness while offering scientific knowledge and social benefits. Industry emphasizes that the adoption of knowledge management solutions will enable more and higher quality outputs from university-based innovation projects. Knowledge creation is the procedure of creating new information, and it is at the center of the competitive edge of an organization. The production of knowledge is a critical component of problem solving. Competitive advantage is not anything more than the manner by which a company must distinguish itself from its competitors in terms of its distinct product or service offerings [14, 15]. Knowledge generation is a critical component of decision making and a driving force behind innovation and growth in a variety of disciplines. There are several forms of knowledge generation, some of which are as follows:

A) Exploration—This process of creating knowledge comprises gathering information and data through a number of methods such as experimentation, analysis, and observation.
B) Innovation—This process of creating knowledge comprises gathering information and data through a number of methods such as experimentation, analysis, and observation.
C) Combination—Combining previously gathered information or ideas from many sources to develop new insights or understanding is what knowledge production entails.

Knowledge generation is critical because it assists individuals and organizations in understanding and solving complicated issues, as well as making better and more formal judgments over time, which drives innovation and development [16]. Knowledge production is a product that functions as an interplay between knowledge and knowledge. It was founded in 1999 by two pioneers named Cook and Brown. Information generation and knowledge sharing complement one another. It suggests that information provides an effective solution through efficient practice, connection, and, most crucially, education. Furthermore, it gives complete data and information support, accounting for substantial gains in decisions to build or develop new knowledge or items. The role of knowledge creation is a vital part of the organization. Because of its importance in generating innovation, problem solving, and learning inside organizations, knowledge production is a critical component of the McElroy Knowledge Management

Life Cycle Approach. Organizations may develop a culture of continual improvement and adaptation by actively encouraging people to produce new knowledge and insights. Organizations may remain ahead of the competition by encouraging innovation and adapting to a quickly changing business environment through knowledge development. It encourages people to explore, experiment, and think beyond the box, resulting in the creation of unique goods, services, and processes [17, 18].

Furthermore, knowledge production is important in problem solving and decision making since it draws on collective intelligence and varied viewpoints to handle complicated situations. It promotes the acquisition of information and the development of skills, hence, promoting individual and organizational learning and growth. Furthermore, knowledge production expands current knowledge by building on ideas and insights given by others, resulting in a more in-depth grasp of complicated issues. Organizations acquire a competitive advantage by successfully producing and utilizing new information, allowing them to develop creative solutions, increase operational efficiency, and provide superior client experiences [19]. Knowledge generation/creation helps to preserve and expand organizational memory by ensuring that key ideas, lessons learned, and best practices are kept inside the organization for future use. Knowledge production is an essential component of the McElroy Knowledge Management Life Cycle Approach because it supports innovation, problem solving, and learning, as well as a competitive advantage, positioning organizations for long-term success in dynamic and developing business landscapes. A shift toward smart manufacturing is now taking place in the global industrial sector. The concept of smart manufacturing is firmly linked to three knowledge-driven methods of decision making for meeting client product demands, technological disruption, and security problems, and changing labor skill sets. Smart manufacturing is made possible by cutting-edge information and production technologies, which provide businesses the ability to respond quickly and securely to digitized knowledge. These judgments are driven by internal knowledge structures about certain markets, goods, material information, and procedures. Decision makers must have access to information about each manufacturing process in order to make judgments at different phases of a product's lifespan. In all stages of the lifespan, knowledge is currently not fully recorded in a digital, searchable format [20, 21]. In the industrial sector, innovation is fueled by knowledge generation. Companies can create new concepts, technologies, and production techniques by investing in research and development (R&D). Manufacturers are able to create and produce cutting-edge goods that satisfy changing client needs thanks to this knowledge-driven strategy.

Collaboration between business stakeholders, academic institutions, and research organizations also makes it easier for information to be shared, resulting in ground-breaking developments in fields like materials science, automation, and sustainable manufacturing methods. Taking into consideration the Chinese textile manufacturing organization study showed that by presenting the data in a graphical style that is easy to grasp, knowledge visualization plays a crucial role in giving users the information they need to solve problems. By identifying new alternatives and assessing the results of decisions, the tools used for knowledge visualization effectively help decision making [22].

4.3 Leveraging Manufacturing Industries' Potential Through Efficient Knowledge Capture

According to McElroy's Knowledge Management, knowledge capture is the systematic gathering, organizing, and documenting of information inside an organization. It implies gathering from individuals or groups both explicit information—codified and readily transferable—and tacit knowledge—individual experiences, ideas, and expertise—and making both of these knowledge types available for repurposing and sharing [23]. Knowledge capture is one of the steps in McElroy's Knowledge Life Cycle method to knowledge management. Extracting information from a variety of sources, including staff members, papers, databases, and other pertinent resources, is the main goal of the knowledge capture stage. Prior to information being lost or inaccessible as a result of staff churn, retirement, or other circumstances, the objective is to collect it [24]. Utilizing the tacit information held by your partners, customers, and workers to better your organization begins with effective knowledge capture. Collecting this knowledge, however, should only be the first step. Knowledge management alludes to the broader system for gathering, retrieving, analyzing, and managing information. Organizations may fully utilize the know-how of their partners and workers through good knowledge management.

This obtained knowledge has two distinct audiences in a business setting. Internal knowledge capture can help an organization become more efficient. When top talent quits, effective knowledge management practices will help in teaching a successor. When a consultant quits, a new partner may be able to take over a project more smoothly with the support of this newly acquired knowledge. External knowledge capture, on the other hand, can make it easier for clients to receive the answers they

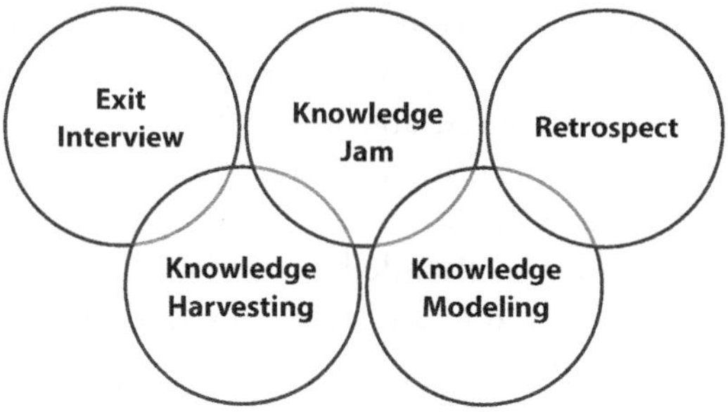

Figure 4.1 KM techniques used to capture knowledge. Source — Author's own compilation.

need, boosting their degree of happiness with your methods [25, 26]. In accordance with Gartner, knowledge capture is one of the five phases in the knowledge management procedure structure. Knowledge capture converts implicit knowledge—knowledge stored in a human being's mind—into an explicit version that the firm may access. Data on each project that an organization works on are stored in a project repository to demonstrate a capture process. This allows team members to explore the database to find knowledge from previous projects that may be applicable to current ones. There are five KM techniques that can be used to record knowledge, which are mentioned below in Figure 4.1 [27]:

Exit Interview — This is a tool used to record leaving workers' expertise. Many businesses perform departure interviews; however, they are frequently only concerned with personnel issues. Knowledge capture can be the main objective of exit interviews, which can be a component of a KM strategy.
Knowledge Harvesting — This is a tool for preserving specialist information and making it accessible to others. Expertise is transformed into knowledge assets through knowledge harvesting. The company can be shielded against costly employee departures and losses, as well as from the absence of critical skills. You may utilize a retention interview for this.
Knowledge Jam — This is a way of eliciting information through a dialog between knowers and seekers, with an integrated phase for sharing or interpreting what was learned. Knowledge Jam employs the disciplines of facilitation, discussion, and translation to bring tacit knowledge to the foreground and put it to use.
Knowledge Modeling — Known colloquially as Knowledge Capture and Modeling (KCM), is a procedure for developing a model of information or

standard specifications for a certain sort of process, facility, or product that is computer interpretable. It involves capturing and modeling information across disciplines into a reusable format with the aim of maintaining, enhancing, sharing, replacing, aggregating, and reapplying it.

Retrospect — This is an end-of-project knowledge capture meeting that is structured, facilitated, and attended by as many members of the project team as possible. It is a rapid and effective method of gathering information while the team disbands. A retrospect for one team can act as peer help for the next one if a participant from the team that will tackle a comparable business problem takes part in the conversation.

Organizations may simplify their processes and increase efficiency by using effective knowledge capture. Organizations may use the collective expertise of their workforce to optimize processes, decrease mistakes, and increase productivity by documenting best practices, SOPs, and troubleshooting strategies. As a result, expenses are reduced, quality is raised, and delivery times are shortened. Decision makers inside the organization can access a useful knowledge store that is provided via knowledge capture. Offering historical data, case studies, and insights from prior experiences, it aids in the formulation of educated decisions. Making better judgments is made possible by readily available knowledge, which lowers risks and boosts overall organizational performance [28, 29]. By maintaining the essential knowledge needed for continued operations, knowledge capture assures company continuity. Having the ability to quickly access knowledge that has been collected reduces the danger of losing important knowledge and skills in the case of personnel turnover, organizational restructuring, or unplanned interruptions. It aids in reducing the negative effects of such occurrences on organizational performance and productivity [30, 31].

Because of institutional knowledge, employees may pass on vital information and skills to new hires and everyone else in the organization for a long period. Managers and team members who benefit from having access to this knowledge are better prepared to deal with difficult situations or make difficult decisions. Using institutional knowledge, newcomers may understand the company's history, values, goods, practices, and culture. This can speed up their transition into their jobs and lessen the number of times they need to search for a particular subject matter expert to get the answers they need [32].

4.4 Knowledge Sharing as a Tool for Innovation in Manufacturing Organization

Businesses are engaged in manufacturing operations in challenging settings. Employees may benefit from one another's experiences and knowledge through promoting knowledge sharing, which speeds up learning and problem solving. Organizations may stay nimble and react to shifting market needs by exchanging best practices, lessons learned, and creative ways. Each business's data administration process runs in line with its own structure, and knowledge exchange is its common element. Today, the development and exchange of information inside businesses are essential for their success. Only 10% of the 30,000 goods that businesses in the manufacturing sector advertise annually are deemed to be successful, according to Gary Hamel's (2006) research. The study discovered that the production sector businesses' goods had a success rate of 20% or less. This implies that hundreds of billions of dollars are squandered on goods that fail on a global scale as a result of issues with organizational leadership and knowledge sharing. The efficacy of a leader ensures that an organization's goals are carried out in line with its vision and purpose, and the degree to which communication between employees and managers is positive is crucial to both the achievement of goals and the happiness of all parties, signs of low morale among the workforce in leadership [33, 34].

Employees possess a wealth of information that benefits both your firm and their coworkers. When they share knowledge, they connect more easily, perform better, and have stronger careers. One advantage of knowledge sharing for your firm is the opportunity to save money on training while still preserving information even if employees opt to work somewhere else in the future. Many employees have information that might benefit their teammates. It would be dreadful if it remained just in their minds. Knowledge sharing in organizations has the advantage of allowing knowledgeable individuals to teach others about what they know. They transform it into something that everyone can use, as well as communal knowledge that their coworkers can use in their careers. It also has the potential to create rules and strategies, as well as to streamline procedures. This ensures that employees function effectively and consistently, allowing you (and your clients) to expect the same level of productivity and quality [35]. Bloom's taxonomy of knowledge acquisition specifies six phases of knowledge acquisition: recall (the lowest form of learning), recognition, application of information, analysis, evaluation, and ultimately generation (the greatest form of learning). Employees may develop resources based on the information learned throughout the final stage of learning.

The approach to knowledge sharing is for people to constantly broaden their expertise and learn new things by creating resources that others can use and learn from. A fundamental advantage of knowledge sharing is the capacity for all team members to access information. They save an hour of waiting for a response to their inquiry or for an expert to return from vacation. They do not need to wait an hour for an answer to their issue or for a specialized knowledge worker when they get back from vacation. They may find it while they are seeking it, bring it in, and utilize it, increasing their efficiency and productivity [36, 37]. Working collaboratively across several teams or departments is common in manufacturing operations. By dismantling organizational silos and encouraging an open and transparent culture, knowledge sharing makes cooperation and teamwork easier. Employee knowledge, insight, and idea sharing encourage cross-functional teamwork, which enhances coordination, communication, and overall team performance. Working collaboratively across several teams or departments is common in manufacturing operations. By dismantling organizational silos and encouraging an open and transparent culture, knowledge sharing makes cooperation and teamwork easier. Employee knowledge, insight, and idea sharing encourage cross-functional teamwork, which enhances coordination, interactions, and overall team performance [38, 39].

The organization shows that it appreciates the knowledge and contributions of its people by actively supporting knowledge exchange. It encourages employee participation and ownership, which raises job satisfaction and drive. Employees learn from one another and acquire new skills; therefore, information sharing also presents opportunities for personal skill development and advancement. The majority of your employees will not be with your company indefinitely. They take their knowledge with them when they go. Nonetheless, if they share their implicit as well as explicit information with their coworkers, they will benefit, it will remain within your company and be used by others. This is particularly true for retirees or those nearing retirement. It would be a huge loss if those long-term employees did not add their expertise to your collective knowledge [40]. Sharing knowledge expands it rather than hoarding it. People have always passed on their gained knowledge and commercial acumen by sharing stories about their ideas, work, and experiences with younger generations. Organizations are struggling for survival in today's knowledge-based economy by becoming more agile. Using current knowledge more effectively or creating new knowledge by fusing it with existing knowledge are two possible goals of knowledge sharing. The key to effective knowledge management is information sharing. A compensation system should be in place to encourage and inspire employees who have more product knowledge to share it if they choose not to [41].

Expert David J. Skyrme defines it as "the explicit and systematic management of vital knowledge and its corresponding processes... expanding personal knowledge into organizational expertise that can be widely shared throughout an organization and appropriately applied." According to IDC, failing to share expertise costs Fortune 500 organizations at least $31.5 billion every year. It is vital to develop employee engagement by ensuring that everyone feels a part of their organization. We are aware that 80% of employees believe they should have a better understanding of how corporate decisions are made. Knowledge sharing clearly empowers employees. They are informed and understand the value placed on their ideas and experience. Employees are more interested in their work when they are involved in it and feel heard, respected, and included. Bouygues Construction employs 53,500 employees and works in 80 countries. The human resources division employs a communication and knowledge-sharing mechanism to make the entire business more socially engaged. The system provides a highly organized environment. It has developed as the go-to location for business policy and exchanges knowledge and peer recognition [42]. Knowledge sharing is the practice of disseminating information between individuals, groups, or organizations. It may promote comprehension, and a sense of purpose, and help employees improve their leadership skills.

Businesses that encourage information interchange may become more adaptable and agile, and employees may be able to develop more efficient processes and systems. An employee manual helps promote a more devoted and effective workforce [43]. Effective information exchange promotes individual and organizational learning, which accelerates and enhances product innovation. Through the research that is currently accessible, it has been demonstrated that knowledge sharing gives people, teams, and organizations the chance to improve their work [44]. The global epidemic wreaked havoc on organizations, economies, and the whole planet. Organizations will need to react to the difficulties in a variety of ways, not just by establishing remote or hybrid work environments. Businesses must place a greater focus on internal mobility and growth. Internal hiring has surged by 19% since 2019, pursuant to a LinkedIn survey. In addition, employees who have access to internal mobility are twice as likely to stay in their roles as those who do not. It is a good idea to create possibilities for information sharing with new recruits in order to get ready for internal employment prospects. Empowering your new hire to teach others and share their knowledge strengthens connections while also establishing a skilled team.

Cooley, a 1,500-lawyer global practice, needs the greatest minds available due to the intricacies of their legal job. By merging novice and experienced lawyers, they take advantage of knowledge exchange. They have thereby hastened and enhanced the efficacy of new hire onboarding. Because mentors have greater knowledge than on-the-job training or official training courses, younger attorneys may learn much faster from them. This is one of the explanations why 95% of its workers see the company as a fantastic place to work [45].

4.5 From Theories to Action: The Impact of Knowledge Application in Manufacturing Industries

Since it makes content more active and pertinent to the development of business value, using knowledge is an essential part of knowledge management. When information is employed to carry out activities and make judgments through routines and instructions, knowledge is applied. Directing is the technique of managing another person's behaviors without supplying the understanding essential for the control to take effect. Someone knowledgeable is more inclined to counsel someone else. For instance, guidance is the strategy utilized when a production worker phones an authority to ask her how to solve a certain machine problem and then resolves the problem pursuant to the expert's advice [46]. Knowledge management's primary goal, according to McElroy, is to provide organizations the ability to use information effectively to solve issues, make informed decisions, innovate, and enhance processes. Knowledge application entails actively employing knowledge to produce value and drive performance; it goes beyond merely storing and exchanging knowledge. The optimization of the production process in terms of time, cost, quality, and market adaptability is currently essential for the survival of manufacturing businesses.

Managing and processing a huge volume of data are necessary for having the appropriate information at the appropriate moment. The need for systematic management of information and knowledge grows as complexity rises. When important employees shift, it is crucial to prioritize knowledge management as a strategic component of effective company management. The notable examples of knowledge application among global manufacturing industries are Good Year (the top tire manufacturer, using eGain's virtual help and digital-first agent desktop, offers customers, retail outlets, and OEM clients contemporary digital customer care that are supported by current information), Virgin Mobile (decreased unnecessary handset swaps by 38% by using contemporary information to improve contact center service response, saving both themselves and the phone manufacturer money), etc. [47, 48]. In the industrial sector, knowledge application is of utmost importance since it fosters innovation, increased productivity, and operational excellence. First off, it gives industrial companies the ability to use collected information to optimize their operations. To simplify processes, save waste, and improve overall efficiency, this entails using best practices, lessons gained, and novel ideas.

Second, the application of knowledge is crucial for quality improvement. These benefits have been enabled by the abundance of data made available by digitalization, but there are a number of challenges that have yet to be addressed in academic literature. This is evident in both news and media, where there is an excess of knowledge on how to utilize and make the most of the wealth of data for the strategic goal of the supply chain network. Organizations may guarantee that their goods meet or surpass client expectations by using tried-and-true processes, standards, and quality control procedures. This increases customer satisfaction and loyalty [49]. In the manufacturing industry, knowledge application stimulates innovation and propels product development. Manufacturers may develop cutting-edge goods that satisfy market expectations by utilizing knowledge of new materials, technologies, and design concepts. Utilizing research and development skills may help you find new possibilities, enhance current goods, and remain ahead of the competition. The process of knowledge application benefits greatly from the created information. In reality, implicit knowledge may be pertinent to the completion of a specific task by a specific participant, such as the calculation of technical parameter values for a certain product component [50].

The application of knowledge is a potent instrument for problem solving in the industrial industry. It enables businesses to draw on the collective knowledge of their employees, making it easier to pinpoint the sources of problems, come up with workable solutions, and swiftly put corrective measures into place. For instance, a video knowledge management platform similar to YouTube called VIDIZMO Enterprise Tube makes it easy to post, share, manage, and watch videos. Users may exchange information and work together on video projects on a secure platform that allows for internal video sharing. Only authorized users are allowed to watch videos on this platform. It can import recorded meetings from Cisco Webex, MS Teams, and Zoom. It can also translate videos into more than 50 different languages and create closed captions and transcripts for films. Over 40 distinct languages are supported for user navigation on the multilingual platform. Another instance would be GE. General Electric (GE) is supporting knowledge application through its "Brilliant Factory" approach. By integrating cutting-edge technology like the IIoT and data analytics alongside employee knowledge, GE's factories are growing smart and interconnected. Real-time data analysis provides GE with knowledge-driven insights that may be used for production process optimization, downtime reduction, and overall productivity [51].

For manufacturing businesses, efficient knowledge management has been a key strategy for gaining a competitive edge in terms of product quality and the time it takes to launch new goods. It tries to properly collect and arrange information, enabling its efficient reuse for to better guide engineers, software, or even machine tools to produce sensible assessments for making decisions. This knowledge application method enables Boeing to streamline the design process, reduce errors, and enhance overall aircraft performance. The application of knowledge is a potent instrument for problem solving in the industrial industry. It enables businesses to draw on the collective knowledge of their employees, making it easier to pinpoint the sources of problems, come up with workable solutions, and swiftly put corrective measures into place. Boeing, a leading aircraft manufacturer, utilizes knowledge application in its Knowledge-Based Engineering (KBE) approach. By capturing and codifying expert knowledge into software tools, engineers can rapidly design and optimize complex aircraft systems [52]. When businesses employ pertinent information properly, they reduce the possibility of errors, eliminate duplication, boost efficiency, and continuously convert their organizational knowledge into embodied goods. The various other benefits of knowledge application in manufacturing organizations [53]:

- In the manufacturing business, knowledge application is critical to assuring product and process quality. Organizations can consistently deliver high-quality goods that fulfill client expectations by using knowledge of quality standards, inspection procedures, and quality control systems. Knowledge applications aid in the identification and resolution of quality issues, the reduction of defects, and the enhancement of customer happiness.
- To remain competitive in today's quickly changing industrial world, organizations must be inventive and adaptive. Knowledge application encourages individuals to use their

experience, think creatively, and discover unique solutions to problems. It helps businesses to respond to market changes, technology advances, and changing client needs.

- Within industrial organizations, knowledge application fosters a learning culture. Employees are encouraged to actively seek and share information, cooperate with others, and learn from their experiences. This allows information transfer across people, teams, and departments, resulting in a collective knowledge base that increases the capabilities of the organization.
- Knowledge application that is effective can lead to cost savings and increased efficiency in industrial processes. Organizations may discover areas for cost reductions, simplify processes, and reduce non-value-added tasks by using knowledge about lean concepts, process optimization, and waste reduction initiatives. As a result, cost efficiency and resource utilization increase.

4.6 Knowledge Management Practices in Global Manufacturing Organizations: Boosting Innovation and Performance

The Holy Grail makes an endlessly generous promise to whoever discovers it in these traditional romance narratives. Knowledge management holds forth the same promise of plenty to those who seek it out. For instance, it could be able to save your company $6 million annually. Unfortunately, organizations frequently fail to put effective knowledge management systems into place. Like King Arthur and his knights searching for the Holy Grail, companies looking for better knowledge management are like those groups. Knowledge management refers to giving staff members access to the appropriate knowledge at the appropriate time. Success stories of organizations that have adopted knowledge management are described below in Figure 4.2 [54]:

- Toyota — Toyota is a multinational carmaker headquartered in Aichi, Japan. The company employs over 300,000 people around the globe and is the world's 10th-largest firm in terms of profits. Toyota vigorously encourages knowledge transfer when opening a new facility. Two hundred to 300 new

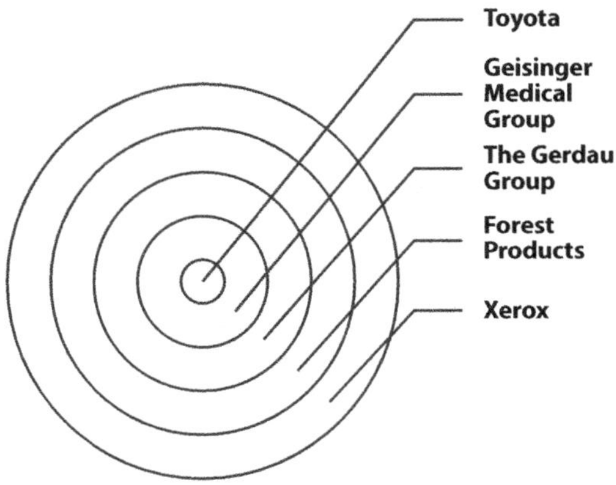

Figure 4.2 Knowledge management practices adopted by global manufacturing organizations. Source — Compiled by the Authors.

workers are sent by the corporation to a plant that already exists. They learn about the production process while working on the assembly line alongside more seasoned workers. The more recent hires are sent back to the new plant after receiving initial on-the-job training. They are supported by 200 highly skilled workers who work alongside them to guarantee that Toyota's carefully honed manufacturing system is implemented at the new location.

- Geisinger Medical — More than 2,000 medical specialists work for the Pennsylvania-based Geisinger Medical Group. The sole Level I Trauma Centre in central Pennsylvania is GMG, which offers 24/7 complicated critical care to patients who have suffered life-threatening injuries. A 40-step checklist was created by the chief of surgery at Geisinger and his colleagues to help doctors perform better bypass surgeries. The other surgeons first disapproved of the checklist, but when one or two of them started using it, everyone else started to like it. The Group saw a 99.95% compliance rate from surgeons after 200 procedures were performed using the checklist; this led to per-patient savings of $2,000, reduced bleeding, and fewer operating room intubations. The outcomes for patient health have improved as a result of this program, and outstanding doctors have been attracted and kept on. The Group has used knowledge management to significantly reduce costs, enhance patient health outcomes, and attract and keep more highly qualified medical professionals.

- The Gerdau Group — The Gerdau Group ranks as the 13th-largest steel manufacturer in the world and is the largest producer of long steel working in the Americas. The Gerdau Group reported $20 billion in sales in 2008. The business expanded swiftly, now managing 45 steel factories in 14 nations, including the US, Canada, Brazil, and Chile. Communities of practice, or teams of employees that can collaborate regardless of place and have varying levels of ability, were established by The Gerdau Group to boost operational effectiveness. An illustration of this occurred when personnel in Chile were uncertain whether to follow protocol and switch off the furnace during production shutdowns. Workers decided it was desirable to maintain the furnace blazing at a temperature of around 13,300°F after a 13-day discussion. This was due to the fact that maintaining the boiler at a lower temperature would cost less in terms of fuel use than reheating the boiler after it was switched off. Gerdau deployed the revised shutdown period at 50 sites in response to these results, which resulted in greater fuel savings and longer furnace lifespans.
- Forest Products — An experienced and senior manager was departing the company for medical reasons, leaving no one with the same expertise and abilities, and this created a problem for The Forest Products Company. To solve this, the business started a project plan to utilize the leaving manager's experience. Two "knowledge harvesters" interviewed the manager for 6 weeks to gather everything they could about the money collection system. The company eventually developed an interactive software application that could capture and transmit critical decisions made in this industry, automating many of the previously manual tasks. Over the span of 3 years, the organization earned $334,000 through this one knowledge management initiative.
- Xerox — In more than 160 countries, the 100-year-old US company Xerox Holdings Corporation sells print and digital document products and services. Due to a lack of communication among service engineers, Xerox created Eureka, its own knowledge management system. Engineers might record their solutions in Eureka, a system of information

exchange with professional accreditation. It made it possible for service engineers to sign off on articles, which improved their standing among their colleagues and inspired more workers to devote time to teaching others. As of 2016, the firm had saved over $100 million in service costs because of Eureka.

4.7 Conclusion

The McElroy KMC is a remarkable KMC that enables organizations to combine both external and internal claims on information that exists within an organization. Furthermore, the McElroy cycle fits the KM requirements. Individual and group learning captures information, knowledge claim codification organizes and stores it, and knowledge integration retrieves, distributes, and maintains it. An organization may use knowledge generation and integration to identify which knowledge is valuable and which is no longer and display it in a number of ways. The McElroy KMC is important for organizations that want to organize current information and guarantee that all knowledge incorporated is usable. Employers were questioned for the Enterprise Minnesota 2022 State of Manufacturing study, and it was discovered that 50% of them see "attracting and retaining a qualified workforce" as a major barrier to expansion. This problem is solved with a knowledge management system that raises employee satisfaction. A KMS fosters a more cooperative and encouraging work environment by facilitating employees' access to the information they require and providing them with a forum to contribute their own expertise.

References

1. Porter, M.E. and Millar, V.E., How information gives you a competitive advantage. *Harv. Bus. Rev.*, 1985.
2. Valacherry, A.K. and Pakkeerappa, P., Knowledge management in the software industry: Creating value through knowledge application. *J. Creat. Value*, *6*, 2, 249–270, 2020.
3. Ammirato, S., Linzalone, R., Felicetti, A.M., Knowledge management in pandemics. A critical literature review. *Knowl. Manag. Res. Pract.*, *19*, 4, 415–426, 2021.
4. Despres, C. and Chauvel, D., Knowledge management (s). *J. Knowl. Manag.*, 3, 2, 110–123, 1999.

5. Garstenauer, A., Blackburn, T., Olson, B., A knowledge management based approach to quality management for large manufacturing organizations. *Eng. Manage. J.*, *26*, 4, 47–58, 2014.
6. Godwin, I. and Amah, E., Knowledge management and organizational resilience in Nigerian manufacturing organizations. *Dev. Country Stud.*, *3*, 9, 104–120, 2013.
7. Davenport, T.H. and Prusak, L., *Working knowledge: How organizations manage what they know*, Harvard Business Press, Cambridge, MA, USA, 1998.
8. Singh, S.K., Gupta, S., Busso, D., Kamboj, S., Top management knowledge value, knowledge sharing practices, open innovation and organizational performance. *J. Bus. Res.*, *128*, 788–798, 2021.
9. Kruse, P. and Geißler, P., Benefiting from external knowledge in open innovation processes. *Int. J. Knowl. Syst. Sci. (IJKSS)*, *3*, 4, 16–27, 2012.
10. Ganguly, A., Talukdar, A., Chatterjee, D., Evaluating the role of social capital, tacit knowledge sharing, knowledge quality and reciprocity in determining innovation capability of an organization. *J. Knowl. Manag.*, *23*, 6, 1105–1135, 2019.
11. Games, D. and Rendi, R.P., The effects of knowledge management and risk taking on SME financial performance in creative industries in an emerging market: the mediating effect of innovation outcomes. *J. Glob. Entrep. Res.*, *9*, 1, 44, 2019.
12. Gunasekaran, A. and Ngai, E.W.T., Knowledge management in 21st century manufacturing. *Int. J. Prod. Res.*, *45*, 11, 2391–2418, 2007.
13. Feta, N.R., DEVELOPMENT OF KNOWLEDGE MANAGEMENT SYSTEM FOR JAIPONG DANCE. *Jurnal Pilar Nusa Mandiri*, *18*, 2, 107–116, 2022.
15. Koelewijn, P.A.J., Shifting towards a 2-phase approach: a qualitative study into the price determination process and knowledge management of HWPP projects, 2023.
16. Abbas, J. and Sağsan, M., Impact of knowledge management practices on green innovation and corporate sustainable development: A structural analysis. *J. Cleaner Prod.*, *229*, 611–620, 2019.
17. Ode, E. and Ayavoo, R., The mediating role of knowledge application in the relationship between knowledge management practices and firm innovation. *J. Innov. Knowl.*, *5*, 3, 210–218, 2020.
18. Hadeeba, S.O.S.B. and Yusoff, W.F.W., Proposed framework for the usage of information technology tools to enhance knowledge management process of organizations. *J. Organ. Manag. Stud.*, *2022*, 1–7, 2022.
19. Szalavetz, A., Industry 4.0 and capability development in manufacturing subsidiaries. *Technol. Forecasting Social Change*, *145*, 384–395, 2019.
20. Masenya, T.M., Integrating talent and knowledge management practices in the new normal business environment: developing future leaders in public sector organizations, in: *Navigating the new normal of business with enhanced human resource management strategies*, pp. 113–144, IGI global, Hershey, PA, USA, 2022.

21. Abraham, S.J., New Knowledge Management framework for manufacturing SMEs working in strictly regulated sectors. *Proc. Manuf.*, *54*, 290–295, 2021.
22. Feng, S.C., Bernstein, W.Z., Hedberg, T., Barnard Feeney, A., Toward knowledge management for smart manufacturing. *J. Comput. Inf. Sci. Eng.*, *17*, 3, 031016, 2017.
23. Ramis Ferrer, B., Ahmad, B., Vera, D., Lobov, A., Harrison, R., Martínez Lastra, J.L., Product, process and resource model coupling for knowledge-driven assembly automation. *at-Automatisierungstechnik*, *64*, 3, 231–243, 2016.
24. Friederich, J., Francis, D.P., Lazarova-Molnar, S., Mohamed, N., A framework for data-driven digital twins of smart manufacturing systems. *Comput. Ind.*, *136*, 103586, 2022.
25. Sonmez Cakir, F. and Adiguzel, Z., Analysis of leader effectiveness in organization and knowledge sharing behavior on employees and organization. *SAGE Open*, *10*, 1, 2158244020914634, 2020.
26. Henttonen, K., Kianto, A., Ritala, P., Knowledge sharing and individual work performance: an empirical study of a public sector organisation. *J. Knowl. Manag.*, *20*, 4, 749–768, 2016.
27. Boer, N., *Knowledge sharing within Organizations - A situated and relational Perspective.* Thesis, ISBN 90-5892-086-0, 2005.
28. Darwin, C., Building a learning organization. *Knowl. Solutions*, *57*, 54, 78–99, 2017.
29. Gagnon, M.P., Payne-Gagnon, J., Fortin, J.P., Paré, G., Côté, J., Courcy, F., A learning organization in the service of knowledge management among nurses: A case study. *Int. J. Inf. Manage.*, *35*, 5, 636–642, 2015.
30. Jin, J. and Suntrayuth, S., Knowledge Sharing Motivation, Behavior, and Creativity of Knowledge Workers in Virtual Organizations. *Discrete Dyn. Nat. Soc.*, 1–9, 2022.
31. Gyamfi, A. and Williams, I. (Eds.), *Big Data and Knowledge Sharing in Virtual Organizations*, IGI global, Hershey, PA, USA, 2019.
32. Davidavičienė, V., Al Majzoub, K., Meidute-Kavaliauskiene, I., Factors affecting knowledge sharing in virtual teams. *Sustainability*, *12*, 17, 6917, 2020.
33. Chen, I.Y., Chen, N.S., Kinshuk, Examining the factors influencing participants' knowledge sharing behavior in virtual learning communities. *J. Educ. Technol. Soc.*, *12*, 1, 134–148, 2009.
34. Perez-Araos, A., Barber, K.D., Eduardo Munive-Hernandez, J., Eldridge, S., Designing a knowledge management tool to support knowledge sharing networks. *J. Manuf. Technol. Manage.*, *18*, 2, 153–168, 2007.
35. Chinese manufacturing firms. *Bus. Strategy Environ.*, *29*, 3, 1517–1531.
36. Soto-Acosta, P., Popa, S., Palacios-Marqués, D., Social web knowledge sharing and innovation performance in knowledge-intensive manufacturing SMEs. *J. Technol. Transf.*, *42*, 425–440, 2017.

37. Szász, L., Rácz, B.G., Scherrer, M., Deflorin, P., Disseminative capabilities and manufacturing plant roles in the knowledge network of MNCs. *Int. J. Prod. Econ.*, *208*, 294–304, 2019.
38. Song, M., Yang, M.X., Zeng, K.J., Feng, W., Green knowledge sharing, stakeholder pressure, absorptive capacity, and green innovation: Evidence from Chinese manufacturing firms. *Bus. Strategy Environ.*, *29*, 3, 1517–1531, 2020.
39. Azeem, M., Ahmed, M., Haider, S., Sajjad, M., Expanding competitive advantage through organizational culture, knowledge sharing and organizational innovation. *Technol. Soc.*, *66*, 101635, 2021.
40. Yin, J., Ma, Z., Yu, H., Jia, M., Liao, G., Transformational leadership and employee knowledge sharing: Explore the mediating roles of psychological safety and team efficacy. *J. Knowl. Manag.*, *24*, 2, 150–171, 2020.
41. Al-Husseini, S., El Beltagi, I., Moizer, J., Transformational leadership and innovation: the mediating role of knowledge sharing amongst higher education faculty. *Int. J. Leadersh. Educ.*, *24*, 5, 670–693, 2021.
42. Kim, E.J. and Park, S., Transformational leadership, knowledge sharing, organizational climate and learning: an empirical study. *Leadersh. Organ. Dev. J.*, *41*, 6, 761–775, 2020.
43. Feng, C. and Ma, R., Identification of the factors that influence service innovation in manufacturing enterprises by using the fuzzy DEMATEL method. *J. Clean. Prod.*, *253*, 120002, 2020.
44. Liebowitz, J., *Building organizational intelligence: A knowledge management primer*, CRC Press, Boca Raton, FL, USA, 2019.
45. Appio, F.P., Frattini, F., Petruzzelli, A.M., Neirotti, P., Digital transformation and innovation management: A synthesis of existing research and an agenda for future studies. *J. Prod. Innovation Manage.*, *38*, 1, 4–20, 2021.
46. Rehman, U.U. and Iqbal, A., Nexus of knowledge-oriented leadership, knowledge management, innovation and organizational performance in higher education. *Bus. Process Manag. J.*, *26*, 6, 1731–1758, 2020.
47. Kozjek, D., Vrabič, R., Rihtaršič, B., Lavrač, N., Butala, P., Advancing manufacturing systems with big-data analytics: A conceptual framework. *Int. J. Comput. Integr. Manuf.*, *33*, 2, 169–188, 2020.
48. Leo Kumar, S.P., Knowledge-based expert system in manufacturing planning: state-of-the-art review. *Int. J. Prod. Res.*, *57*, 15-16, 4766–4790, 2019.
49. Lyu, M., Li, X., Chen, C.H., Achieving Knowledge-as-a-Service in IIoT-driven smart manufacturing: A crowdsourcing-based continuous enrichment method for Industrial Knowledge Graph. *Adv. Eng. Inf.*, *51*, 101494, 2022.
50. Ungermann, F., Kuhnle, A., Stricker, N., Lanza, G., Data analytics for manufacturing systems–a data-driven approach for process optimization. *Proc. CIRP*, *81*, 369–374, 2019.
51. Bai, Y., Xie, J., Wang, D., Zhang, W., Li, C., A manufacturing quality prediction model based on AdaBoost-LSTM with rough knowledge. *Comput. Ind. Eng.*, *155*, 107227, 2021.

52. Grangel-González, I., Lösch, F., ul Mehdi, A., Knowledge graphs for efficient integration and access of manufacturing data, in: *2020 25th IEEE International Conference on Emerging Technologies and Factory Automation (ETFA)*, vol. 1, pp. 93–100, IEEE, Piscataway, NJ, USA, 2020, September.
53. Kuhnle, A., May, M.C., Schäfer, L., Lanza, G., Explainable reinforcement learning in production control of job shop manufacturing system. *Int. J. Prod. Res.*, *60*, 19, 5812–5834, 2022.
54. Obradović, T., Vlačić, B., Dabić, M., Open innovation in the manufacturing industry: A review and research agenda. *Technovation*, *102*, 102221, 2021.

5

Industry 4.0 Trends and Strategies: A Modern Approach with Focus on Knowledge Management

Tarun Kumar Vashishth*, Vikas Sharma, Kewal Krishan Sharma, Bhupendra Kumar, Sachin Chaudhary and Rajneesh Panwar

School of Computer Science and Applications, IIMT University, Meerut, U.P., India

Abstract

The rapid advancement of technology has ushered in an epoch of Industry 4.0, marked by convergence of digital technologies, data-driven decision making, and interconnected systems. This review paper delves into the emerging trends and implementation strategies within Industry 4.0, with a specific emphasis on knowledge management. As organizations strive to navigate the complex landscape of Industry 4.0, effective knowledge management becomes a critical factor in harnessing the transformative potential of these technologies. The paper begins by exploring the key components and defining characteristics of Industry 4.0, highlighting its transformative impact on various sectors, from manufacturing to services. It delves into the intricate interplay between technologies, like the Internet of Things (IoT), artificial intelligence (AI), big data analytics, and cyber-physical systems, and their role in shaping the future of industries. Through this lens, the paper uncovers emerging trends that hold promise for reshaping business processes and driving innovation. One of the core focus areas of this review is knowledge management, recognized as a pivotal factor in capitalizing on Industry 4.0 advancements. The paper examines the critical role of knowledge management systems in facilitating the efficient collection, organization, and dissemination of information across organizations. It also delves into the integration of AI and machine learning in knowledge management, enabling the automation of decision-making processes and the extraction of insights from vast amounts of data. The review further explores implementation strategies for Industry 4.0 initiatives, recognizing the challenges and opportunities associated with their adoption. It emphasizes the importance of organizational readiness, leadership commitment,

**Corresponding author*: tarunvashishth@gmail.com

Rajendra Kumar, Vishal Jain, Venus C. Ibarra, Corrienna Abdul Talib and Vinay Kukreja (eds.) Knowledge Management and Industry Revolution 4.0, (111–158) © 2024 Scrivener Publishing LLC

and workforce upskilling in ensuring successful integration of Industry-4 methods. Additionally, the paper sheds light on the significance of cybersecurity measures in safeguarding sensitive data and maintaining the integrity of interconnected systems. In conclusion, this comprehensive review highlights the transformative potential of Industry 4.0 and pivotal part of knowledge management in its successful implementation. By addressing the emergence of novel technologies, trends, and challenges within Industry 4.0, organizations can gain insights into strategic approaches for leveraging these advancements effectively.

***Keywords*:** Industry 4.0 (Industry-4), emerging trends, implementation strategies, modern approaches, knowledge management

5.1 Introduction

The rapid advancement of technology has brought forth a new era in industrial development known as Industry 4.0. This transformative paradigm shift encompasses the convergence of digital technologies, cyber-physical systems, and data-driven insights to reshape industries and economies. Industry 4.0 represents a significant leap forward in manufacturing and production, where smart factories, interconnected machines, and intelligent decision making are at the forefront of operational efficiency and innovation. Journey of Industry-4 is marked by the integration of various cutting-edge technologies, including the Internet of Things (IoT), artificial intelligence (AI), big data analytics, robotics, and cloud computing (CC). These technologies are synergistically harnessed to optimize processes, enhance product quality, enable predictive maintenance, and create a more agile and responsive manufacturing ecosystem. However, the successful implementation of Industry-4 is not solely contingent on technological prowess; it necessitates strategic planning, informed decision making, and effective knowledge management. In this context, the effective management of knowledge emerges as a pivotal enabler for the realization of Industry-4 power. Knowledge, in the form of insights, expertise, data, and best practices, drives informed decision making, accelerates innovation, and facilitates adaptive responses to dynamic market demands. This chapter delves into the emerging trends and implementation strategies that underpin the Industry 4.0 revolution, with a distinct focus on the role of knowledge management in orchestrating its success.

Figure 5.1 illustrates the transformative paradigm of Industry 4.0, depicting the integration of cyber-physical systems and advanced technologies in manufacturing processes. The underlying principle of Industry 4.0 is the creation of intelligent environments where data flows seamlessly, machines communicate

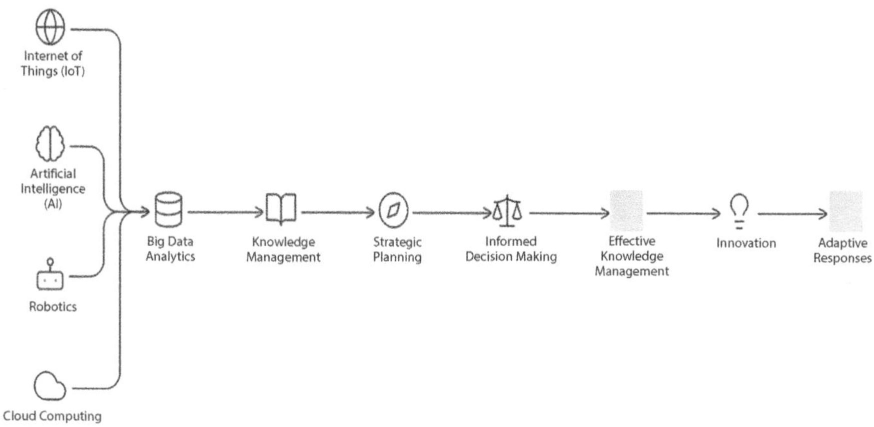

Figure 5.1 The transformative paradigm of Industry-4.

autonomously, and human–machine collaboration is optimized. As this transformative paradigm gains momentum, it is imperative to comprehend its core concepts, technological underpinnings, and the new dimensions it introduces to industrial processes. Furthermore, understanding the key trends shaping the Industry 4.0 landscape, such as digital transformation, IoT integration, big data analytics, and sustainable practices, is essential to formulate effective implementation strategies. While technological components are integral, Industry 4.0's success hinges on the strategic initiatives employed to embrace and harness these technologies. This chapter navigates the strategies that organizations can adopt to pave the way for successful Industry 4.0 integration. From building robust technological infrastructures to addressing challenges related to data security and workforce readiness, a holistic approach is required to unlock the full potential of Industry-4.

At the heart of Industry-4's evolution lies the concept of knowledge management. As organizations transition into data-driven enterprises, the ability to harness and leverage knowledge becomes a strategic differentiator. The integration of knowledge management practices empowers organizations to make informed decisions, enhance operational efficiency, and drive innovation. By capturing, sharing, and applying knowledge across the value chain, Industry 4.0 can deliver transformative outcomes that extend beyond technological advancements.

5.1.1 Background and Significance

The genesis of Industry-4 can be traced back to the fusion of digital technologies, connectivity, and automation. Figure 5.2 provides the background

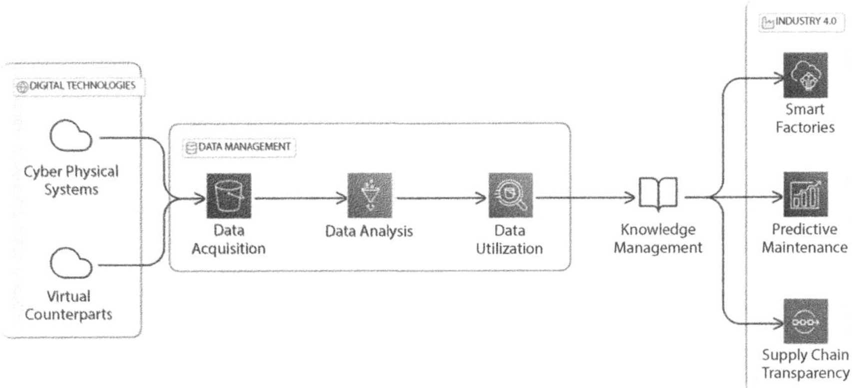

Figure 5.2 The Industry 4.0 background.

context of Industry 4.0, showcasing the evolution and integration of digital technologies in industrial processes. As a logical progression from the previous industrial revolutions, Industry 4.0 marks a paradigm shift where cyber-physical systems integrate seamlessly with virtual counterparts. This convergence facilitates a dynamic ecosystem where data becomes the lifeblood of operations, enabling informed decision making, predictive analytics, and agile responses to market dynamics. The significance of Industry 4.0 extends beyond its technological prowess. It signifies a transformative approach to manufacturing, encapsulating the principles of adaptability, efficiency, and customization. From smart factories leveraging the Internet of Things (IoT) to AI-driven predictive maintenance and blockchain-enabled chain of supply transparency, Industry-4 is a mosaic of innovations poised to redefine industries.

Within this landscape, knowledge management emerges as a pivotal catalyst. The era of Industry 4.0 generates an unprecedented volume of data, but the real value lies in harnessing these data into actionable insights. Knowledge management becomes the linchpin that connects data acquisition, analysis, and utilization, driving informed strategies that align with organizational goals.

5.1.2 Scope and Objectives

The scope of this chapter encompasses a wide spectrum of topics related to Industry-4 and its strategic implementation, underpinned by knowledge management principles. Our objectives include:

Defining Industry 4.0: We will establish a clear understanding of Industry 4.0 by delineating its core concepts and principles. Through this exploration, readers will grasp the fundamental shifts brought about by the convergence of physical and digital domains.
Exploring Modern Approaches: This chapter will delve into the contemporary strategies and approaches that organizations are adopting to leverage Industry 4.0 technologies. From IoT-driven optimization to AI-enabled predictive maintenance, we will showcase how these modern techniques redefine operational paradigms.
Knowledge Management's Role: Central to our exploration is the critical work of knowledge management in Industry 4.0. We will elucidate how efficient data collection, analysis, dissemination, and application contribute to informed decision making and sustained innovation.
Trends and Implications: We will analyze the emergent trends within the Industry 4.0 landscape, considering their implications for businesses and industries. By identifying these trends, we aim to provide readers with insights into the directions that technological advancements are steering industries.
Strategic Implementation: A significant portion of this chapter will be dedicated to discussing the strategic implementation of Industry 4.0 initiatives. It will discover how organizations can integrate knowledge management practices to maximize the benefits of Industry-4 technologies.
Real-World Examples: Drawing from real-world case studies, we will illustrate how organizations have successfully embraced Industry 4.0 with an emphasis on knowledge management. These examples will offer tangible insights into the practical applications of the theoretical concepts discussed.
Future Outlook: This chapter will conclude with a glimpse into the future trajectory of Industry 4.0 and the role of knowledge management therein. By assessing the ongoing advancements and potential challenges, we will provide readers with a forward-looking perspective.

5.2 Understanding Industry 4.0

In order to comprehend the essence of Industry 4.0, it is crucial to delve into its historical context and the transformative journey it has undertaken. This section provides a comprehensive understanding of the evolution of industrial revolutions and how they have culminated in the emergence of Industry 4.0.

5.2.1 Evolution of Industrial Revolutions

The evolution of industrial revolutions refers to the series of significant technological, economic, and societal transformations that have shaped human civilization over the past few centuries. Each industrial revolution marked a profound shift in how goods were produced, society was organized, and the economy operated. Here is an overview of the four major industrial revolutions:

Initial Industrial Revolution (Late 18–19th Century):
The First Industrial Revolution marked the shift from agrarian economies to industrialized ones. Key innovations included the steam engine, mechanized textile production, and the development of factory systems. This revolution brought about urbanization, increased productivity, and transformed traditional ways of life.

Second Industrial Revolution (Late 19–20th Century):
The Second Industrial Revolution was characterized by the expansion of industries beyond textiles and the widespread use of electricity, telegraph communication, and the internal combustion engine. This era saw the rise of mass production, assembly lines, and increased globalization of trade.

Third Industrial Revolution (Late 20th Century):
The Third Industrial Revolution was driven by advent of electronics, computing, and automation. Key developments included the rise of computers, semiconductors, telecommunications, and the internet. This revolution transformed industries, such as manufacturing, communications, and finance, and led to the digital age.

Fourth Industrial Revolution (Present and Beyond):
The Fourth Industrial Revolution, often referred to as Industry 4.0, is characterized by the convergence of digital, physical, and biological technologies. It involves technologies such as artificial intelligence, robotics, Things (IoT), biotechnology, and nanotechnology. This revolution is reshaping industries, economies, and societies, with a focus on automation, data-driven decision making, and interconnectedness.

These revolutions have not only driven economic growth but also brought about profound societal changes, altering the way people live, work, and interact. The concept of "Industry 4.0" encapsulates the ongoing Fourth Industrial Revolution, characterized by the convergence of digital, physical, and biological technologies, and the transformative impact it is

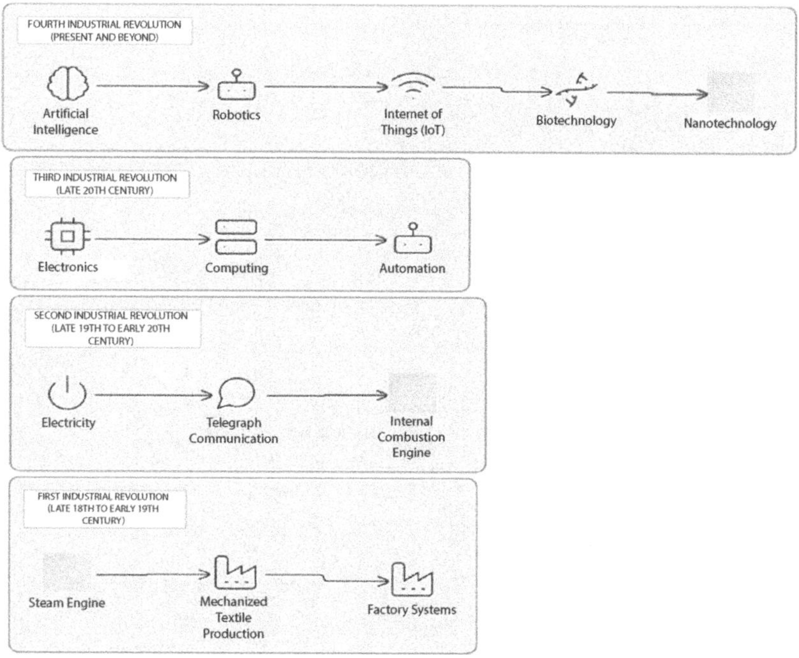

Figure 5.3 Evolution of Industry 4.

expected to have on industries and society as a whole. Figure 5.3 depicts the evolution of Industry 4.0, highlighting the progression of automation, connectivity, and data exchange in manufacturing systems over time.

5.2.2 Key Concepts of Industry 4.0

This section delves into the fundamental concepts that define Industry 4.0, shaping its principles, strategies, and implementation. These key concepts collectively drive the paradigm shift in manufacturing and pave the way for unprecedented levels of automation, connectivity, and intelligence. Figure 5.4 outlines the fundamental concepts of Industry 4.0.

Interconnectedness and Networking

Industry 4.0 thrives on the concept of interconnectedness, where machines, devices, and systems communicate seamlessly in real time. This subsection explores the significance of networked ecosystems that enable data exchange, process synchronization, and collaborative decision making.

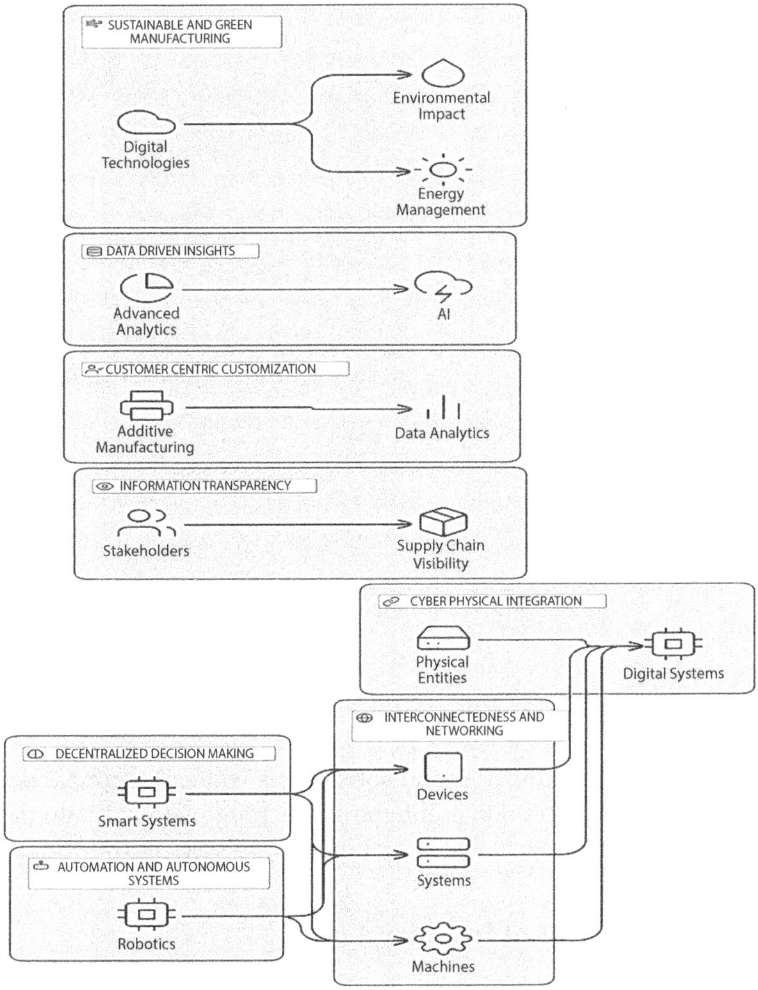

Figure 5.4 Fundamental concepts of Industry 4.0.

Cyber-Physical Integration

The combination of cyber with physical systems forms the core of Industry-4. This part explains how physical entities, equipped with sensors and actuators, are linked to digital systems, resulting in real-time data-driven control and optimization.

Information Transparency

Transparency in data sharing across value chain is pivotal in Industry-4. This subsection highlights how real-time access to accurate and relevant data empowers stakeholders to make informed decisions, optimize processes, and enhance supply chain visibility.

Decentralized Decision Making
Industry 4.0 emphasizes autonomous decision making enabled by smart systems. This part discusses how decentralized decision making based on real-time data analysis empowers machines and devices to optimize processes and adapt to changing conditions.

Customer-Centric Customization
Personalization and customization are integral to Industry 4.0. This subsection explores how technologies, like additive manufacturing and data analytics, enable the production of tailored products and services that meet individual customer needs.

Data-Driven Insights
Industry 4.0 leverages data as a valuable resource for insights and innovation. This segment emphasizes the role of advanced analytics and AI in converting data into actionable insights for optimizing operations, predicting trends, and enhancing efficiency.

Automation and Autonomous Systems
Automation is a cornerstone of Industry 4.0, enabling machines and systems to perform tasks independently. This part explains how automation, combined with AI and robotics, leads to increased efficiency, reduced human error, and improved safety.

Sustainable and Green Manufacturing
Sustainability is a driving force in Industry 4.0, promoting resource efficiency and waste reduction. This subsection explores how digital technologies contribute to eco-friendly practices, energy management, and reduced environmental impact.

5.2.3 Enabling Technologies in Industry 4.0

This section delves into the core enabling technologies that underpin Industry 4.0's transformative capabilities. It explores how these technologies converge to drive innovation, efficiency, and competitiveness in modern manufacturing and beyond. Figure 5.5 illustrates how various technologies converge to fuel innovation, enhance efficiency, and bolster competitiveness within the framework of Industry 4.0.

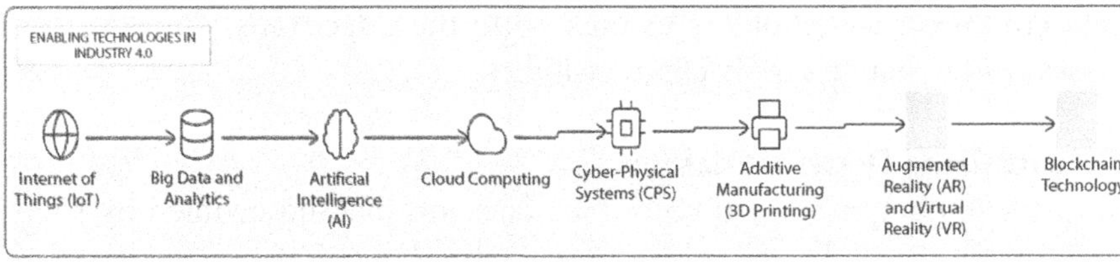

Figure 5.5 Technologies converge to drive innovation, efficiency, and competitiveness in Industry 4.0.

Internet of Things (IoT)

Discussing the IoT's pivotal role, this subsection explains how interconnected devices and sensors facilitate real-time data collection, communication, and control across various processes and systems.

Big Data and Analytics

This part emphasizes the significance of big data analytics in processing and extracting valuable insights from vast amounts of data generated by IoT devices with other sources.

Artificial Intelligence (AI)

Focusing on AI's influence, this subsection explores how machine learning, deep learning, and other AI techniques enable machines to learn from data, make informed decisions, and perform tasks that typically require human intelligence.

Cloud Computing

Detailing CC impact, this segment elaborates on its role in providing scalable and accessible resources for storing, processing, and analyzing data from connected devices.

Cyber-Physical Systems (CPS)

Discussing the fusion of physical and digital worlds, this subsection elucidates how CPS integrates computing algorithms with physical processes to optimize production and operations.

Additive Manufacturing (3D Printing)

Highlighting the potential of additive manufacturing, this part showcases how 3D printing enables rapid prototyping, customization, and sustainable production methods.

Augmented Reality (AR) and Virtual Reality (VR)
Exploring AR and VR, this subsection demonstrates how these technologies enhance training, maintenance, design, and collaboration by overlaying digital information on the real world.

Blockchain Technology
This segment introduces blockchain's role in ensuring transparency, traceability, and security in supply chains and transactions, making it a critical component of Industry 4.0.

By understanding the synergistic integration of these technologies, this section provides a comprehensive overview of how Industry 4.0 leverages their collective potential to revolutionize manufacturing and reshape business models across industries.

5.3 Literature Review

Maksim and Natalya [1] (2020) analyze the experiences of Russian and international companies in implementing scalable Industry 4.0 models. The paper establishes knowledge management principles and strategies enabling these companies to sustain their competitive positions strategically. De Bem Machado *et al.* (2022) [2] contribute to identifying a burgeoning field of research that reveals a novel and captivating connection between Knowledge Digital Transformation (DT), Management (KM), and the public sector. Manesh *et al.* (2020) [3] provide a comprehensive understanding of knowledge management (KM) processes, focusing on the precise mechanisms of knowledge creation, sharing/transfer, acquisition, storage/retrieval, and application within organizational systems. Di Maria *et al.* (2018) [4] present recent research that highlights the implications for the transformation of manufacturing processes and supply chain management. Cárdenas *et al.* (2018) [5] propose a model for managing knowledge within organizations transitioning to Industry 4.0. The model utilizes tools like Big Data to leverage competitive advantages in a context of extensive information flows, emphasizing the significance of technological solutions to analyze vast data for companies' growth in this evolving market scenario. Capestro *et al.* (2020) [6] review empirical studies concerning Industry-4 adoption, emphasizing the role of knowledge management. Anshari *et al.* (2022) [7] present findings on new skill assessment for the Fourth Industrial Revolution. The study gathers data on the role of knowledge management in creating a new set of skills or capabilities through interviews and focus group discussions. Preuveneers *et al.* (2017)

[8] conduct a survey offering insights into recent developments in intelligent manufacturing environments, highlighting research challenges and opportunities for shaping their future. Mikhalkina *et al.* (2022) [9] present a paper that underscores the significance of considering generational differences in the creation and adaptation to a new digital reality. Wagire *et al.* (2020) [10] aim to explore research dynamics and propose a taxonomy of the Industry 4.0 research landscape, outlining future research directions.

Ardito *et al.* (2018) [11] present a comprehensive overview of the evolving efforts in developing digital technologies that manage the interface between supply chain management and marketing processes. The paper highlights the role of these technologies in supporting the integration of supply chain management and marketing from an information processing perspective. Khan *et al.* (2021) [12] aim to map the expansive domain of sustainable development and explore the fundamental research domains encompassing the mentioned perspectives within the context of the Industry 4.0 framework. Souza *et al.* (2022) [13] investigate the emerging concept of TQM 4.0, elucidating its role in aligning quality management (QM) with the tenets of Industry 4.0 (I4.0). The article navigates industries toward this transformative phase, marked by adjustments across multiple domains, including QM and human resources. Whysall *et al.* (2019) [14] delve into the profound shifts in business landscapes catalyzed by the Fourth Industrial Revolution. Their analysis unveils a compelling intersection with strategic human resource management, prompting an exploration of its impact on talent management theory and practice. Barata *et al.* (2018) [15] aim to pinpoint potential avenues for forthcoming research in mobile supply chain management (mSCM) within the context of the Industry 4.0 era. Castro *et al.* (2012) [16] reveal that companies in this sector lack a synchronized knowledge management strategy and emphasize the need for intensified endeavors to enhance business competitiveness, particularly in harnessing and leveraging knowledge generated within the workplace. Furstenau *et al.* (2020) [17] direct scientific efforts toward improving economic and environmental aspects, highlighting a relative lack of attention to the social sphere. Telukdarie *et al.* (2018) [18] present a research proposal that adopts a global system approach, aligned with Industry 4.0 principles of vertical, horizontal, and total business integration, to address this challenge, encompassing ERP, manufacturing systems, and instrumentation. Kumar *et al.* (2018) [19] provide a concise introduction to the Industry 4.0 concept and outline maintenance solutions aligned with the evolving requirements of advanced manufacturing technologies and processes, in line with the vision of Industry 4.0. Tseng *et al.* (2021)

[20] analyze the current landscape of sustainable industrial and operations engineering within the context of Industry 4.0.

Liboni *et al.* (2019) [21] explore the potential impacts of Industry 4.0 on human resource management (HRM), with a specific focus on employment, job profiles, qualifications, and skill requirements within the workforce, and their implications for supply chain management (SCM). Ghobakhloo (2018) [22] conducts a comprehensive review of ongoing Industry 4.0 research, outlining its key design principles, technology trends, architectural design, and providing a strategic roadmap for manufacturers navigating the transition to Industry 4.0. Shaw *et al.* (2001) [23] propose a systematic methodology that leverages data mining and knowledge management techniques for effective marketing knowledge management and decision support. Birkel and Hartmann (2021) [24] aim to develop a comprehensive process for structured collection and processing of Industry 4.0 trend information, contributing to effective trend management. Quintas *et al.* (1997) [25] delve into the exploration of knowledge management, its significance for organizations, and its impact on individuals engaged with or within these organizations. Schniederjans *et al.* (2020) [26] aim to outline future research directions, inviting scholars to expand their horizons and utilize knowledge management to advance the research paradigm of supply chain digitization. Paschek *et al.* (2018) [27] delve into the analysis of the essential knowledge process as a foundation for performing Business Process Management (BPM) in relation to established BPM trends. Leitão *et al.* (2020) [28] aim to assess the current adoption of Industry 4.0 by examining its presence in industrial and academic research literature. Awan *et al.* (2021) [29] conduct a literature review to identify the interests and expectations of Industry 4.0 stakeholders concerning the integration of IoT in circular economy management. Fromhold-Eisebith *et al.* (2021) [30] demonstrate how the historical roots and contextual conditions of an industry influence and sometimes impede the potential of technology-driven advancements.

5.4 Emerging Trends in Industry 4.0

5.4.1 Digital Transformation and Connectivity

The evolution of Industry 4.0 has ushered in a new era of technological advancement, characterized by the integration of digital technologies into various aspects of industries and society. At the forefront of this transformation lies the paradigm of digital transformation and connectivity. This section explores the key trends within this domain that are shaping the landscape of Industry 4.0.

IoT Ecosystems

The proliferation of interconnected devices within the IoT ecosystem is a defining hallmark of Industry 4.0. As billions of devices become smart and capable of data exchange, industries are leveraging this connectivity to enhance operational efficiency, monitor equipment health, and gain real-time insights into processes. The trend here lies not just in the sheer no. of connected devices but in the orchestration of such devices to create cohesive and intelligent systems.

Edge and Fog Computing

As data generation surges due to the IoT, the conventional centralized cloud infrastructure faces challenges related to latency and bandwidth. Edge and fog computing are emerging trends that involve processing data closer to the source, enabling faster analysis and response times. This trend not only reduces the strain on networks but also supports real-time decision making and enables autonomous systems.

5G Connectivity

The advent of 5G technology is set to revolutionize Industry 4.0 by providing ultra-fast and reliable connectivity. This trend enables the seamless transfer of massive amounts of data, allowing for advanced applications like remote robotic control, augmented reality in manufacturing, and real-time analytics in logistics. The integration of 5G is poised to be a game-changer, particularly in applications that demand low latency and high bandwidth.

Digital Twins and Simulation

Digital twins, virtual replicas of physical objects or processes, are gaining traction as a powerful tool in Industry-4. These twins enable real-time monitoring, analysis, and optimization of physical assets. The trend extends to the simulation of entire systems, allowing industries to test scenarios, predict outcomes, and optimize processes without impacting the real world. This trend is significantly enhancing decision making and reducing risks.

Cybersecurity and Data Privacy

As connectivity and digitalization increase, the importance of strong cybersecurity and privacy of data measures cannot be overstated. The trend in Industry 4.0 is to embed security considerations throughout the design and implementation phases. This includes encryption, secure authentication, and continuous monitoring to safeguard sensitive data and prevent cyberattacks.

Interoperability and Standardization
The heterogeneity of technologies in Industry 4.0 ecosystems demands interoperability and standardization. The trend is toward developing common protocols and frameworks that allow seamless communication between different devices and systems. This interoperability accelerates the adoption of Industry 4.0 solutions across industries and fosters innovation through collaboration.

Digital transformation and connectivity trends within Industry-4 are pivotal in reshaping industries and economies. From IoT ecosystems to 5G connectivity, these trends are driving efficiency, innovation, and agility, while also demanding a concerted effort toward cybersecurity and interoperability. As the Industry 4.0 journey continues, embracing these trends will be paramount for organizations seeking to thrive in the era of digital transformation.

5.4.2 Integration of Cyber and Physical Systems

Industry-4 represents a paradigm shift that integrates cyber and physical systems to create intelligent and interconnected manufacturing environments. The seamless convergence of these systems is a critical implementation strategy that drives the transformative potential of Industry 4.0. This section delves into the strategies and considerations for effectively integrating cyber and physical systems. Figure 5.6 presents the architecture of cyber-physical systems (CPS), showcasing the integration of computational and physical components to enable advanced functionalities and capabilities in Industry 4.0 environments.

Cyber-Physical System (CPS) Architecture
A fundamental strategy involves designing a robust CPS architecture that enables the integration of sensors, actuators, communication networks, and data processing. CPS architecture forms the backbone for enabling real-time data exchange, decision making, and control across cyber and physical domains. It is crucial to design architectures that are scalable, adaptable, and resilient to ensure long-term success.

Sensor Integration and Data Collection
Effective integration of sensors and data collection devices in the physical environment is paramount. These sensors gather real-time data on

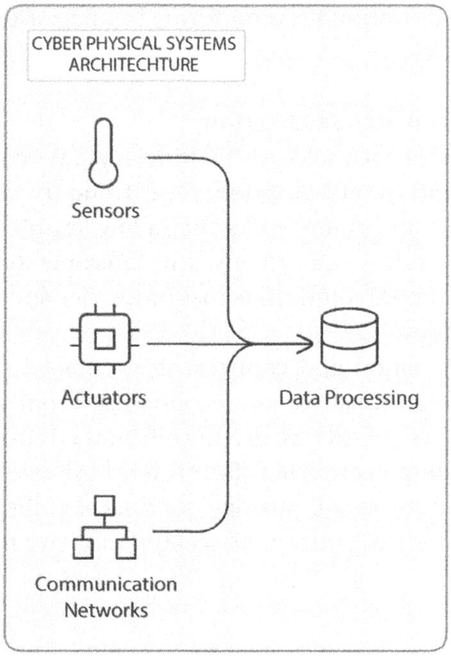

Figure 5.6 Cyber-physical systems (CPS) architecture.

processes, machine conditions, and environmental factors. The strategy here involves selecting appropriate sensors, ensuring accurate data acquisition, and establishing data pipelines that facilitate seamless transmission to the digital realm.

Connectivity and Communication Standards

A coherent communication framework is a cornerstone for cyber-physical integration. Adopting standardized communication protocols and technologies ensures interoperability between different devices and systems. Strategies involve selecting protocols, such as MQTT, OPC UA, and ensuring compatibility with existing communication infrastructure.

Edge and Cloud Computing Integration

An effective implementation strategy balances the roles of edge and cloud computing. Edge computing facilitates real-time data processing and decision making closer to data sources, reducing latency. Cloud computing enables data storage, analysis, and complex simulations. Integration strategies involve optimizing workloads, deciding which tasks are performed where, and ensuring seamless interaction between edge and cloud systems.

Digital Twin Implementation

Digital twins serve as virtual representations of physical assets or systems. Implementing digital twins involves creating accurate models, integrating real-time data, and utilizing simulation tools. This strategy enables real-time monitoring, predictive maintenance, and scenario analysis. However, digital twin implementation requires meticulous synchronization of virtual and physical entities.

Real-Time Analytics and Control

Integrating cyber and physical systems allows for real-time analytics and control. Strategies involve deploying advanced analytics tools that process real-time data, enabling insights into operational efficiencies, performance anomalies, and predictive maintenance needs. This integration leads to informed decision making and optimization of processes.

Security and Privacy Integration

Suring security of integrated systems is supreme. Implementation strategies encompass embedding security measures from the outset, employing encryption and authentication protocols, and establishing secure communication channels. Privacy-enhancing techniques should also be considered to protect sensitive data.

Continuous Monitoring and Adaptation

The landscape of Industry 4.0 is dynamic. Continuous monitoring of integrated systems, performance metrics, and feedback loops is essential. Strategies involve deploying monitoring tools, conducting regular assessments, and utilizing feedback to refine integration strategies and optimize system performance.

5.4.3 Data Governance and Security Measures

The implementation of Industry 4.0 entails harnessing vast amounts of data to drive insights and efficiency. Data governance and security measures play a crucial role in ensuring the integrity, confidentiality, and availability of these data. This section outlines key strategies for effective data governance and robust security within the context of Industry 4.0. Figure 5.7 delineates strategies aimed at empowering employees with the requisite skills to excel in the dynamic landscape of Industry 4.0, emphasizing training, upskilling, and fostering a culture of continuous learning within organizations.

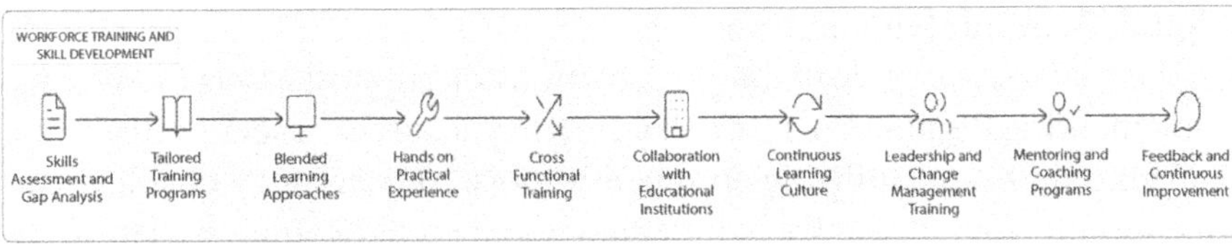

Figure 5.7 Strategies to equip employees with the skills needed to thrive in the Industry 4.0 landscape.

Data Classification and Categorization

Develop a strategy to classify and categorize data based on its sensitivity, value, and regulatory requirements. Different types of data require varying levels of protection and access control. Implement a clear data classification framework that guides how data is handled, stored, and shared across the organization.

Access Control and Authorization

Implement strong access control mechanisms to restrict data access based on roles, responsibilities, and privileges. Employ strategies, such as role-based access control (RBAC) and attribute-based access control (ABAC), to ensure that only authorized personnel can access and manipulate critical data. Regularly review and update access rights as roles evolve.

Data Encryption

Adopt robust encryption techniques to protect data both at rest and in transit. Encryption ensures that even if unauthorized access occurs, the data remains unreadable and useless to malicious actors. Implement end-to-end encryption for communication channels and employ encryption algorithms that align with industry standards.

Data Lifecycle Management

Develop a comprehensive strategy for managing data throughout its lifecycle, from creation to deletion. Define protocols for data retention, archival, and disposal. Implement data anonymization and pseudonymization techniques to protect sensitive information while allowing for meaningful analysis.

Data Auditing and Monitoring

Implement real-time data auditing and monitoring mechanisms to detect unauthorized access, data breaches, or suspicious activities. Use automated tools to track data movement, changes, and user interactions.

Establish alerts and notifications to promptly respond to potential security incidents.

Secure Data Sharing and Collaboration
In Industry 4.0 ecosystems, data sharing and collaboration are vital. Implement secure data sharing platforms and protocols that ensure data remain protected even when shared across departments, partners, or stakeholders. Consider secure data-sharing agreements and technologies like blockchain for enhanced transparency.

Incident Response and Recovery Plans
Develop robust incident response and recovery plans that outline procedures to follow in case of a security breach. Implement strategies for isolating affected systems, investigating the breach, and restoring operations. Regularly test these plans through simulated exercises to ensure readiness.

Employee Training and Awareness
Human factors remain a significant security consideration. Implement ongoing training programs to educate employees about data security best practices, the risks of social engineering, and the importance of adhering to data governance policies. Foster a culture of security awareness throughout the organization.

Regulatory Compliance
Ensure that your data governance and security strategies align with relevant industry regulations and data protection laws. Stay updated on evolving compliance requirements, and implement necessary measures to remain in compliance. This includes aspects like data breach notification and user consent.

Continuous Improvement and Adaptation
Industry 4.0 environments are dynamic and constantly evolving. Continuously assess and improve your data governance and security measures to stay ahead of emerging threats and technologies. Regularly conduct security audits and vulnerability assessments to identify potential weaknesses.

5.4.4 Workforce Training and Skill Development

As Industry 4.0 revolutionizes industries, the workforce must adapt to new technologies and methodologies. Workforce training and skill development are critical components of successful implementation. This section outlines key strategies to equip employees with the skills needed to thrive in the Industry 4.0 landscape.

Skill Assessment and Gap Analysis

Conduct a comprehensive skill assessment across your workforce to identify existing skill sets and areas requiring improvement. Perform a gap analysis to pinpoint the disparity between current skills and those demanded by Industry 4.0 technologies. This analysis forms the foundation for tailored training programs.

Tailored Training Programs

Develop customized training programs that address specific skill gaps identified in the assessment. Focus on both technical skills (such as data analytics, AI, robotics programming) and soft skills (such as adaptability, problem solving, collaboration). Design training modules that cater to various roles within the organization.

Blended Learning Approaches

Implement blended learning approaches that combine traditional classroom settings with digital platforms. Utilize e-learning modules, webinars, and virtual classrooms to provide flexible and accessible training. This approach accommodates diverse learning styles and allows employees to learn at their own pace.

Hands-on Practical Experience

Provide employees with hands-on experience through simulations, workshops, and real-world projects. Practical exposure allows individuals to apply theoretical knowledge in a controlled environment, enhancing their understanding and confidence in working with Industry 4.0 technologies.

Cross-Functional Training

Promote cross-functional training that encourages employees to learn about different aspects of Industry 4.0 technologies beyond their core responsibilities. This holistic understanding fosters collaboration, facilitates innovation, and enables employees to contribute across various domains.

Collaboration with Educational Institutions

Collaborate with educational institutions, universities, and training centers to leverage their expertise in delivering specialized Industry 4.0 training. Establish partnerships for workshops, internships, and certification programs. This collaboration ensures that your workforce stays updated with the latest advancements.

Continuous Learning Culture

Culture Cultivate is a continuous learning within group. Boost individuals to pursue further education, certifications, and skill upgrades on an ongoing basis. Implement recognition and rewards for achieving milestones in skill development.

Leadership and Change Management Training

Equip leadership teams with skills to lead and manage in the context of Industry-4. Provide training on change management, communication, and the strategic integration of new technologies. Strong leadership support is crucial for successful adoption and implementation.

Mentoring and Coaching Programs

Establish mentoring and coaching programs that pair experienced employees with those seeking skill development. Mentors can provide guidance, share insights, and offer practical advice on how to navigate the challenges posed by Industry-4 transformations.

Feedback and Continuous Improvement

Regularly gather feedback from employees regarding the effectiveness of training programs. Use this feedback to refine and enhance the training initiatives. Implement a feedback loop that ensures continuous improvement in skill development strategies.

5.4.5 Overcoming Implementation Challenges

Implementing Industry 4.0 initiatives can be complex and challenging, requiring careful planning and execution. This section outlines key strategies to overcome common implementation challenges and ensure the successful adoption of Industry 4.0 technologies.

Clear Vision and Strategy

Develop a clear vision and well-defined strategy for Industry 4.0 implementation. Align your goals with the organization's overall objectives. This strategy should outline the expected outcomes, timeline, and resource allocation, serving as a roadmap for the entire implementation process.

Change Management

Address resistance to change by emphasizing the benefits and opportunities that Industry 4.0 brings. Implement robust change management strategies that involve open communication, involving key stakeholders from various departments, and demonstrating how Industry 4.0 aligns with the organization's growth.

Pilot Projects

Initiate pilot projects to test and validate Industry 4.0 technologies on a smaller scale. Pilots provide insights into challenges and opportunities, allowing you to refine implementation strategies before scaling up. A successful pilot builds confidence and support among stakeholders.

Interdisciplinary Collaboration

Promote collaboration across different departments and teams. Cross-functional teams can provide diverse perspectives and ensure that the implementation addresses the needs of various stakeholders. Foster open communication channels to share knowledge and insights.

Technology Integration and Compatibility

Select technologies that align with your organization's existing infrastructure and processes. Focus on solutions that can integrate seamlessly with current systems. Assess the compatibility of new technologies with legacy systems and implement middleware if necessary.

Data Management and Governance

Implement robust data management practices to ensure the quality, integrity, and security of data. Establish data governance frameworks that define data ownership, access controls, and data sharing protocols. Proper data management enhances decision making and insights.

Scalability and Flexibility

Design your Industry 4.0 implementation to be scalable and adaptable. As the organization grows, the technology should be able to accommodate increased data volume and complexity. Embrace flexibility to accommodate evolving business requirements.

Skills and Training

Invest in workforce training and skill development to equip employees with the expertise to operate Industry 4.0 technologies effectively. Provide ongoing training to keep up with evolving technologies and ensure that employees are confident in using new tools.

Performance Metrics and Evaluation
Establish clear performance metrics to measure the success of Industry 4.0 implementation. Regularly assess these metrics to track progress, identify bottlenecks, and make necessary adjustments. Evaluation enables continuous improvement and optimization.

Risk Management
Anticipate and mitigate potential risks associated with Industry 4.0 implementation. Develop risk management strategies that address cybersecurity threats, system failures, and disruptions. Regularly review and update risk management plans as new challenges emerge.

Continuous Learning and Adaptation
Industry 4.0 is an ongoing journey. Foster a culture of continuous learning and adaptation. Stay updated with technological advancements and industry trends. Encourage employees and teams to proactively seek opportunities for improvement.

5.5 Knowledge Management in Industry 4.0

5.5.1 Role of Knowledge in Industry 4.0

In the context of Industry 4.0, knowledge has evolved into a strategic asset that drives innovation, efficiency, and competitiveness. The role of knowledge transcends traditional notions, becoming a cornerstone of organizational success. This section delves into the pivotal role that knowledge plays within the framework of Industry 4.0. Figure 5.8 presents the framework of Industry 4.0.

Accelerating Innovation
Information fuels innovation by serving as the bedrock upon which new ideas and technologies are built. In Industry 4.0, organizations leverage knowledge from various sources, including data analytics, research findings, and cross-disciplinary insights. This knowledge-driven innovation leads to formation of novel goods, services, and models of business.

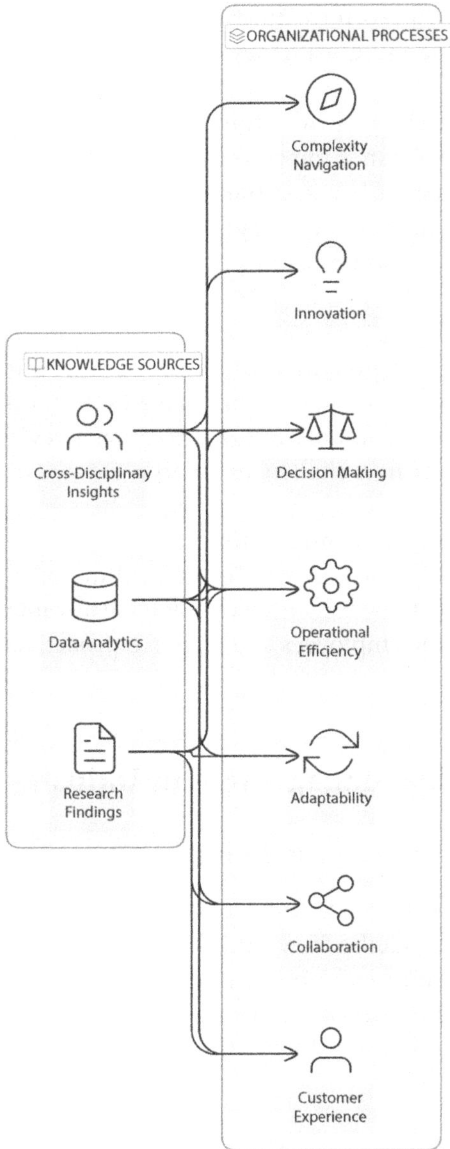

Figure 5.8 Framework of Industry-4.

Informed Decision Making

In the dynamic landscape of Industry 4.0, informed decision making is paramount. Knowledge empowers decision makers with actionable insights derived from data analysis, predictive modeling, and real-time information. The availability of accurate knowledge enhances the precision and effectiveness of strategic choices.

Enhancing Operational Efficiency
Efficiency gains in Industry 4.0 are closely tied to effective knowledge management. Organizations utilize data-driven knowledge to optimize processes, predict maintenance needs, and automate routine tasks. This integration of knowledge with operational systems streamlines workflows and reduces downtime.

Enabling Adaptability
Industry 4.0 environments are marked by rapid change and disruption. Knowledge plays a pivotal role in enabling organizations to adapt swiftly to evolving conditions. By harnessing data, trends, and insights, companies can proactively pivot strategies, modify processes, and stay ahead of market shifts.

Fostering Collaboration
Collaboration is fundamental in Industry 4.0 ecosystems, and knowledge is the currency that facilitates it. Shared knowledge fosters cross-functional collaboration, allowing diverse teams to work cohesively on projects. This collaboration amplifies problem solving, ideation, and collective intelligence.

Enhancing Customer Experience
Customer centricity is a hallmark of Industry 4.0. Knowledge enables organizations to understand customer preferences, behaviors, and needs. This knowledge-driven understanding translates into personalized experiences, customized offerings, and increased customer satisfaction.

Navigating Complexity
Industry 4.0 introduces complexity through interconnected systems and data streams. Knowledge management provides the tools to navigate this complexity. Organizations can analyze and synthesize knowledge to identify patterns, correlations, and insights that aid in unraveling intricate challenges.

5.5.2 Knowledge Acquisition and Creation

In the era of Industry 4.0, knowledge acquisition and creation take on new dimensions, driven by the influx of data and technological advancements.

This section explores the strategies and processes involved in acquiring and creating knowledge within the context of Industry 4.0.

Data-Driven Knowledge Acquisition
Industry 4.0 is characterized by the proliferation of data from various sources such as sensors, IoT devices, and production systems. Organizations must implement strategies to collect, aggregate, and analyze these data to extract valuable insights. Data-driven knowledge acquisition involves harnessing big data analytics, machine learning, and AI to derive actionable intelligence from raw data.

Sensor Networks and IoT
Utilizing sensor networks and IoT plays a pivotal role in knowledge acquisition. Sensors embedded in machines, equipment, and products capture real-time data on various parameters. These data are then used to monitor performance, identify anomalies, and optimize processes, contributing to the accumulation of knowledge.

Experimentation and Research
Innovation and knowledge creation thrive on experimentation and research. Industry 4.0 provides opportunities for organizations to conduct virtual simulations, digital prototyping, and predictive modeling. These activities enable experimentation in a controlled environment, leading to the creation of new knowledge through insights gained from these experiments.

Cross-Disciplinary Collaboration
Encouraging collaboration across diverse disciplines fosters knowledge creation. Industry 4.0's interconnected nature brings together experts from fields such as engineering, data science, and business management. By promoting cross-disciplinary collaboration, organizations create an environment where different perspectives converge to generate innovative ideas and solutions.

Innovation Hubs and Hackathons
Creating innovation hubs and organizing hackathons can facilitate the rapid generation of new knowledge. These initiatives encourage employees, stakeholders, and even external participants to collaborate on solving specific challenges. The intense and collaborative nature of these events often leads to the creation of breakthrough insights.

Knowledge Creation Culture

Cultivating a culture of continuous learning and innovation is essential for knowledge creation. Organizations should provide employees with the time, resources, and autonomy to explore new ideas and experiment with emerging technologies. Recognizing and rewarding innovative contributions reinforce this culture.

Crowd Sourcing and Open Innovation

Embracing crowd sourcing and open innovation platforms enables organizations to tap into a broader pool of expertise. External contributors—such as customers, partners, and industry experts—contribute insights, perspectives, and solutions that enrich knowledge creation processes.

Digital Twin Simulations

Digital twins—virtual replicas of physical assets or systems—are used to simulate real-world scenarios. These simulations provide insights into how systems behave under different conditions. By experimenting with digital twins, organizations acquire knowledge about potential improvements, risks, and optimizations.

5.5.3 Knowledge Sharing and Collaboration

In the dynamic landscape of Industry-4, effective knowledge sharing and collaboration are paramount for driving innovation and organizational growth. This section explores the strategies and approaches that facilitate the seamless exchange of knowledge within Industry 4.0 ecosystems.

Digital Collaboration Platforms

Implement digital collaboration platforms that enable employees to share knowledge, insights, and information in real time. These platforms offer features, such as discussion forums, chat channels, and document sharing, fostering continuous communication and collaboration among team members.

Cross-Functional Teams

As Industry 4.0 blurs the lines between departments, organizations should promote creation of cross functional teams. Such groups bring together individuals with assorted expertise to collaboratively tackle complex challenges. Cross-functional collaboration enhances knowledge sharing by leveraging insights from various domains.

Communities of Practice

Start communities of practice where employees with the same benefits or expertise can share knowledge, experiences, and best practices. These communities create spaces for informal learning, networking, and the exchange of insights that might not emerge in formal settings.

Knowledge Sharing Workshops and Seminars

Organize workshops, seminars, and knowledge-sharing sessions that provide platforms for employees to present their expertise, insights, and lessons learned. These events foster a culture of sharing and encourage employees to learn from one another's experiences.

Virtual Collaboration Tools

Leverage virtual collaboration tools AR and VR to enable remote teams to collaborate seamlessly. These tools allow for virtual meetings, collaborative design sessions, and immersive training, promoting real-time knowledge exchange regardless of geographical location.

Storytelling and Tacit Knowledge Sharing

Encourage storytelling as a means of sharing tacit knowledge—knowledge gained through experience and practice. Veteran employees can share anecdotes, case studies, and practical insights that might not be documented elsewhere. Storytelling humanizes knowledge and makes it relatable to others.

Knowledge-Sharing Metrics

Implement metrics to measure the effectiveness of knowledge-sharing initiatives. Analyze engagement levels on collaboration platforms, track participation in knowledge-sharing events, and assess the impact of shared insights on problem solving and innovation.

Leadership Role Modeling

Leader performance is a critical part in promoting a culture of knowledge sharing. When leaders actively share their expertise, insights, and experiences, it sets an example for the entire organization. This demonstrates that knowledge sharing is not only encouraged but valued at all levels.

Recognition and Rewards
Award and recognize employees who dynamically participate in knowledge sharing and collaboration efforts. Acknowledging their contributions through awards, incentives, or recognition programs reinforces the importance of sharing knowledge and encourages others to follow suit.

Knowledge-Sharing Norms
Establish norms and guidelines for knowledge sharing within the organization. Communicate expectations regarding knowledge-sharing behaviors, etiquette, and the responsible use of shared insights.

5.5.4 Knowledge Storage and Retrieval

In the era of Industry 4.0, efficient storage and retrieval of knowledge are essential for informed decision making and innovation. This section explores strategies and approaches to effectively store and retrieve knowledge within the context of Industry 4.0.

Data Lakes and Databases
Implement data lakes and databases to store a wide range of structured and unstructured data. These repositories enable organizations to consolidate knowledge from various sources, making it easily accessible for analysis and retrieval.

Semantic Indexing and Tagging
Employ semantic indexing and tagging systems to categorize and label knowledge assets. This approach enhances search ability and enables users to quickly locate relevant information based on keywords, tags, and metadata.

Knowledge Maps
Create knowledge maps that visually represent the interconnected relationships between different knowledge elements. These maps provide a holistic view of the organization's knowledge landscape, aiding in identifying gaps and opportunities.

Taxonomies and Ontologies
Develop taxonomies and ontologies that define the structure and relationships of knowledge within the organization. These frameworks help standardize terminology, ensuring consistency and facilitating accurate retrieval.

Content Management Systems
Implement content management systems (CMS) to organize and manage various types of content, including documents, presentations, videos, and images. A well-structured CMS ensures that knowledge assets are stored in an organized and accessible manner.

Search and Retrieval Algorithms
Utilize advanced search and retrieval algorithms that incorporate natural language processing (NLP) and machine learning techniques. These algorithms enhance the accuracy and relevance of search results, enabling users to find the information they need more efficiently.

Contextual Search
Implement contextual search capabilities that take into account the user's role, context, and preferences. Contextual search tailors search results to the user's specific needs, improving the accuracy of retrieved knowledge.
Knowledge Graphs
Build knowledge graphs that represent the relationships between different pieces of knowledge. These graphs visually depict how different concepts are interconnected, aiding in understanding complex relationships and facilitating knowledge discovery.

Version Control and History
Implement version control mechanisms to track changes and revisions to knowledge assets. This ensures that users have access to the latest and most accurate information while maintaining a record of historical changes.

User-Friendly Interfaces
Design user-friendly interfaces for knowledge storage and retrieval systems. Intuitive interfaces enhance user experience, encourage adoption, and minimize the learning curve for accessing knowledge.

5.6 Leveraging Knowledge Management for Successful Industry 4.0 Implementation

5.6.1 Enhancing Decision Making with Knowledge Insights

In the context of Industry-4, management of knowledge serves as a valuable tool to enhance decision-making processes. This section explores how organizations can leverage knowledge insights to inform and strategic decisions.

Data-Driven Insights
Knowledge management provides access to data-driven insights derived from various sources, including sensors, IoT devices, and analytics platforms. These insights offer a comprehensive view of operations, enabling decision makers to assess trends, identify patterns, and predict outcomes.

Real-Time Decision Support
Industry 4.0 generates real-time data that can guide immediate decision making. Knowledge management systems facilitate the aggregation and visualization of these data, empowering decision makers to respond promptly to evolving situations and make data-driven choices.

Predictive Analytics
By analyzing historical data and trends, organizations can employ predictive analytics to anticipate future scenarios. Knowledge insights enable decision makers to anticipate maintenance needs, demand fluctuations, and potential disruptions, leading to proactive decision making.

Scenario Analysis
Knowledge management supports scenario analysis, allowing organizations to simulate various situations and assess their potential impact. Decision makers can evaluate different strategies, identify potential risks, and choose the optimal course of action based on informed insights.

Cross-Functional Insights
Collaborative knowledge sharing fosters cross-functional insights. Decision makers can tap into expertise from various domains, ensuring that decisions consider multiple perspectives and potential implications across different departments.

5.6.2 Improving Process Efficiency Through Knowledge Integration

Integrating knowledge management practices with Industry 4.0 technologies enhances operational efficiency and effectiveness. This section examines how organizations can optimize processes through the integration of knowledge.

Process Optimization
Knowledge insights allow organizations to identify bottlenecks and inefficiencies within processes. By analyzing data and performance metrics, establishments can implement targeted improvements, which streamline workflows and lessen waste.

Predictive Maintenance
Incorporating knowledge about equipment conditions and historical performance data enables predictive maintenance. Organizations can schedule maintenance activities before equipment failure occurs, minimizing downtime and maximizing operational efficiency.

Workflow Automation
Knowledge-based automation enhances efficiency by automating routine tasks and processes. Organizations can use insights gained from data analysis to design automation workflows that eliminate manual interventions and reduce human error.

Continuous Monitoring and Feedback Loops
Knowledge-driven continuous monitoring allows organizations to gather real-time performance data. These data feeds into feedback loops, enabling organizations to fine-tune processes, adapt strategies, and maintain optimal efficiency levels.

5.6.3 Enabling Continuous Learning and Innovation

Knowledge management fosters a culture of continuous learning and innovation, critical for thriving in Industry 4.0. This section explores how organizations can harness knowledge to drive ongoing learning and creativity.

Knowledge-Sharing Culture
By encouraging knowledge sharing, organizations create an environment where employees contribute insights and lessons learned. This culture of open communication promotes continuous learning and ensures that valuable knowledge is circulated.

Learning from Data Insights
Real-time data insights offer opportunities for continuous learning. Organizations can analyze data to uncover emerging trends, customer preferences, and market dynamics, guiding them to adapt strategies and explore new directions.

Innovation Hubs

Establishing innovation hubs encourages employees to collaborate, brainstorm, and experiment with new ideas. These hubs foster creativity and provide a platform for knowledge sharing that fuels innovation.

Lessons Learned and Best Practices

Organizations can leverage knowledge gained from past successes and failures. Documenting lessons learned and best practices ensures that knowledge is not lost and serves as a foundation for future decision making and innovation.

5.6.4 Mitigating Risks and Enhancing Adaptability

In Industry 4.0, the ability to mitigate risks and adapt to changing conditions is crucial. Knowledge management aids organizations in addressing uncertainties and remain agile. This section explores how knowledge management contributes to risk mitigation and adaptability.

Risk Assessment and Management

Knowledge insights enable organizations to identify possible risks. By analyzing past data and trends, organizations can implement risk mitigation policies that minimize the impact of disruptions.

Crisis Management

During unexpected events, organizations can draw upon knowledge resources to implement crisis management strategies. Knowledge-sharing platforms facilitate the rapid dissemination of information and enable teams to respond effectively to crises.

Agile Decision Making

Access to real-time data and knowledge insights supports agile decision making in response to rapidly changing circumstances. Organizations can adjust strategies, supply chain operations, and production schedules based on up-to-date information.

Continuous Monitoring and Feedback

Industry 4.0 environments demand continuous monitoring and feedback. Organizations can use real-time data to track performance metrics, identify deviations from expected outcomes, and adapt strategies to ensure resilience and adaptability.

In conclusion, knowledge management is a foundational element in achieving successful Industry 4.0 implementation. By leveraging knowledge for decision making, optimizing processes, fostering innovation, and mitigating risks, organizations can navigate the complexities of Industry 4.0 with confidence and drive sustainable growth and innovation.

5.7 Case Studies: Industry 4.0 Implementation with Knowledge Management

5.7.1 Manufacturing Sector Case Study

This case study showcases the successful implementation of Industry-4 with knowledge management in manufacturing sector. The study focuses on a company, which adopted knowledge-driven strategies to enhance its manufacturing processes and overall efficiency.

Background: The manufacturing company aimed to improve its production processes, reduce downtime, and enhance product quality. They recognized that leveraging knowledge management principles could help achieve these goals in the Industry 4.0 context.

Implementation: The Company integrated data collection sensors across its production lines, capturing real-time operational data. These data were aggregated and analyzed using advanced analytics tools. Knowledge management practices were employed to categorize, store, and retrieve insights derived from these data.

Knowledge-Driven Insights: The organization's engineers and data analysts collaborated to classify patterns and variances in the data. This led to the creation of predictive maintenance models, allowing the company to anticipate machinery breakdowns and schedule maintenance proactively, minimizing production disruptions.

Cross-Functional Collaboration: Knowledge sharing was facilitated through digital platforms, enabling cross-functional collaboration among engineers, operators, and managers. Insights from different departments were integrated, leading to a holistic understanding of production processes.

Results: The knowledge-driven approach led to significant improvements in the manufacturing sector:

Reduced Downtime: Predictive maintenance reduced unplanned downtime, increasing production uptime and output.

Enhanced Quality Control: Real-time data analytics allowed quick identification of quality issues, enabling immediate corrective actions.

Streamlined Workflows: Collaborative knowledge sharing improved communication between teams, streamlining workflows and reducing inefficiencies.
Cost Savings: The reduction in downtime and improved quality control translated to cost savings and increased revenue.
Conclusion: This case study exemplifies how Industry 4.0 implementation, coupled with knowledge management, can drive substantial improvements in the manufacturing sector. By harnessing data-driven insights, facilitating cross-functional collaboration, and embracing knowledge-sharing practices, organizations can achieve enhanced efficiency, reduced costs, and increased competitiveness in the Industry 4.0 landscape.

5.7.2 Supply Chain Optimization Case Study

This case study illustrates the successful mixing of Industry-4 practices and management of knowledge principles to optimize supply chain operations.

Background: A company in the consumer goods sector aimed to enhance its supply chain efficiency by leveraging Industry 4.0 technologies while capitalizing on knowledge management strategies.
Implementation: The Company adopted a data-driven approach by implementing sensors and IoT devices across its supply chain network. These devices captured real-time data on inventory levels, demand patterns, and logistics act. The company recognized the importance of knowledge management to interpret and utilize these data effectively.
Knowledge-Driven Insights: By utilizing knowledge management platforms, the organization aggregated and analyzed the collected data. Supply chain experts collaborated with data analysts to uncover insights from the data, enabling informed decision making.
Demand Forecasting: The integration of historical data and real-time information allowed for accurate demand forecasting. This enabled the company to adjust production and inventory levels based on anticipated demand changes.
Inventory Optimization: Knowledge-driven insights facilitated better inventory management. The company could identify optimal inventory levels, reducing excess stock while ensuring availability to meet customer demands.
Logistics Efficiency: Real-time data analysis enabled proactive monitoring of transportation routes and delays. This allowed for dynamic adjustments to logistics operations, minimizing transit times and costs.

Results: The integration of Industry 4.0 and knowledge management yielded substantial improvements in supply chain optimization:
Enhanced Visibility: Real-time data insights improved visibility across the entire supply chain, from raw materials to end-user delivery.
Improved Demand Management: Accurate demand forecasting reduced the risk of stockouts and overstocking, leading to better resource allocation.
Cost Reduction: Optimized inventory levels and logistics operations translated to reduced carrying costs and transportation expenses.
Customer Satisfaction: The ability to meet customer demands promptly and accurately increased customer satisfaction and loyalty.
Conclusion: This case study showcases the transformative potential of Industry 4.0 when combined with effective knowledge management practices in supply chain optimization. By leveraging data-driven insights, facilitating collaboration, and applying knowledge management principles, organizations can achieve streamlined operations, reduced costs, and improved customer experiences within their supply chains.

5.7.3 Service Industry Transformation Case Study

This case study highlights the successful utilization of Industry 4.0 principles and knowledge management strategies to drive transformation within the service industry.

Background: A service-based company aimed to enhance its offerings and customer experiences by embracing Industry 4.0 technologies and integrating knowledge management practices.
Implementation: The Company recognized that knowledge management could play a pivotal role in utilizing data-driven insights to personalize services, optimize resource allocation, and foster innovation in the Industry 4.0 era.
Knowledge-Driven Insights: The Company implemented sensors and data collection mechanisms to gather real-time information about customer preferences, service usage patterns, and resource utilization. Knowledge management practices were applied to categorize and analyze these data effectively.
Personalized Services: By analyzing customer data and preferences, the company tailored its services to individual customer needs. This approach resulted in higher customer satisfaction and loyalty.
Resource Optimization: The organization utilized knowledge-driven insights to optimize the allocation of resources, ensuring that services were efficiently deployed based on demand patterns.

Innovation Cultivation: The Company established digital platforms for knowledge sharing and collaboration among its employees. This facilitated the exchange of insights, best practices, and creative ideas, fostering a culture of innovation.

Results: Integration of Industry-4 and management of knowledge led to notable transformations within the service industry:

Customer-Centric Approach: Personalized services improved customer satisfaction and engagement, leading to higher retention rates.

Efficient Resource Allocation: Knowledge-driven insights optimized the allocation of resources, reducing wastage and improving operational efficiency.

Enhanced Innovation: Collaborative knowledge sharing nurtured a culture of innovation, resulting in the development of new service offerings and improvements to existing processes.

Competitive Edge: The ability to offer tailored services and innovative solutions provided a competitive advantage in the service market.

Conclusion: This case study exemplifies the synergy between Industry 4.0 and knowledge management in transforming the service industry. By harnessing data-driven insights, fostering collaboration, and applying knowledge management principles, organizations can achieve customer centricity, operational efficiency, and innovation, positioning themselves as leaders in the evolving landscape of Industry 4.0.

5.8 Future Directions and Challenges

5.8.1 Evolving Trends in Industry 4.0

This section explores the evolving trends that can shape the future of Industry-4, paving the way for new opportunities and challenges.

Connected Ecosystems: Industry-4 is shifting toward more interconnected ecosystems, where smart devices, machines, and processes collaborate seamlessly. This trend emphasizes the integration of cyber and physical systems, leading to enhanced automation and decision.

Edge Computing: Edge computing is gaining prominence as data processing moves closer to the data source. This trend reduces latency, improves real-time analytics, and enables rapid response to dynamic situations, making it integral to Industry 4.0 implementations.

AI and ML: The integration of AI and machine learning continues to expand in Industry 4.0. These technologies empower systems to learn from data, make predictions, and optimize processes autonomously, leading to increased efficiency and reduced human intervention.

5G Connectivity: The advent of 5G technology facilitates faster and more reliable data transmission, enabling real-time communication between devices and systems. This trend fuels the growth of IoT applications and enhances the scalability of Industry-4 solutions.

Sustainability and Circular Economy: Industry 4.0 is evolving to align with sustainability goals and circular economy principles. Organizations are using data-driven insights to optimize resource utilization, reduce waste, and design eco-friendly products and processes.

Human–Machine Collaboration: As automation and AI advance, the focus is shifting toward human–machine collaboration. Future Industry 4.0 systems will emphasize the augmentation of human capabilities, leveraging AI to assist in complex decision making and problem solving.

Customization and Personalization: Industry 4.0 is enabling mass customization and personalized products. Ability to collect and analyze vast data allows organizations to tailor goods and facilities to individual customer needs.

Challenges: With these evolving trends come challenges:

Data Security and Privacy: Accelerating interconnectedness raises concerns about data privacy and cybersecurity. Organizations must adopt robust measures to protect sensitive information and ensure secure communication.

Skilled Workforce: As technologies advance, the demand for skilled professionals in AI, IoT, and data analytics is growing. Upskilling the workforce and bridging the skill gap will be crucial.

Integration Complexity: Integrating diverse technologies and systems can be complex. Organizations must navigate interoperability challenges to ensure seamless data flow and communication.

Ethical Considerations: The use of AI, automation, and data collection raises ethical questions about job displacement, bias in algorithms, and responsible AI use.

Regulatory Frameworks: Evolving technologies may outpace existing regulations. Developing adaptive regulatory frameworks that foster innovation while addressing concerns is a key challenge.

5.8.2 Opportunities for Further Knowledge Management Integration

This section explores the exciting opportunities that lie ahead for integrating knowledge management with evolving Industry 4.0 technologies.

AR and VR: The mixing of VR and AR with Industry 4.0 offers immersive knowledge-sharing experiences. Organizations can create virtual environments for training, troubleshooting, and collaborative problem solving, enhancing learning and decision making.

Machine Learning for Insights: As Industry 4.0 generates vast datasets, machine learning algorithms can extract valuable insights. Predictive analytics can identify patterns, anomalies, and optimization opportunities, enabling proactive decision making and process improvements.

Semantic Data Integration: Knowledge management can benefit from semantic technologies that enhance data understanding. Integrating anthologies and semantic frameworks can improve data interoperability, making it easier to extract meaningful insights from diverse sources.

Contextual Knowledge Delivery: Industry 4.0 enables context-aware systems that deliver relevant knowledge to users based on their tasks and roles. This ensures timely access to information, improving decision-making efficiency.

Collaborative Robotics: Integrating knowledge management with collaborative robots (cobots) allows workers to access real-time information and insights while working alongside robots. This enhances productivity and safety in human–robot collaboration.

Cognitive Assistants: Cognitive AI systems can act as virtual assistants, supporting users with real-time insights, recommendations, and guidance. These systems can enhance human expertise, especially in complex decision-making scenarios.

Challenges: While opportunities abound, challenges must also be addressed:

Data Quality and Relevance: Knowledge management relies on accurate and relevant data. Ensuring the quality and context of data inputs is essential for deriving meaningful insights.

Change Management: Integrating new technologies requires organizational changes. Ensuring smooth transitions and training employees to utilize these tools effectively is crucial.

User Experience: Effective integration depends on user-friendly interfaces and intuitive tools. Designing systems that cater to users' needs and preferences is essential.

Data Privacy and Ethics: As more data are shared and analyzed, ensuring data privacy and ethical use becomes paramount. Organizations must establish guidelines and practices to uphold ethical standards.

Interdisciplinary Collaboration: Integrating knowledge management with emerging technologies demands collaboration between diverse teams, including IT, data science, and domain experts.

5.8.3 Addressing Ethical and Security Concerns

As Industry 4.0 advances, addressing ethical and security concerns becomes imperative to ensure responsible and sustainable implementation. Figure 5.9 examines the societal and environmental implications within the context of Industry 4.0.

Ethical Considerations:

Job Displacement: The automation and AI-driven nature of Industry-4 can lead to concerns about job displacement. Strategies for reskilling and upskilling the workforce to match evolving job roles must be established.
Algorithmic Bias: AI models can inherit favoritisms present in data of training. Efforts should be made to develop unbiased algorithms and sure fairness in decision-making processes.
Privacy Concerns: The extensive data collection inherent to Industry 4.0 raises privacy issues. Organizations must adopt stringent data protection measures, transparent data usage policies, and anonymization techniques.
Human–Machine Interaction: Ethical dilemmas arise in human–machine interactions, such as autonomous decision making in critical scenarios. Clear guidelines for human oversight and intervention are crucial.

Security Challenges:
Cybersecurity Vulnerabilities: The interconnectedness of Industry 4.0 systems opens avenues for cyberattacks. Strengthening cybersecurity measures, employing encryption, and continuous monitoring are essential.
Data Breaches: Industry 4.0 generates vast amounts of sensitive data. Ensuring data integrity and preventing unauthorized access are crucial to avoid data breaches.

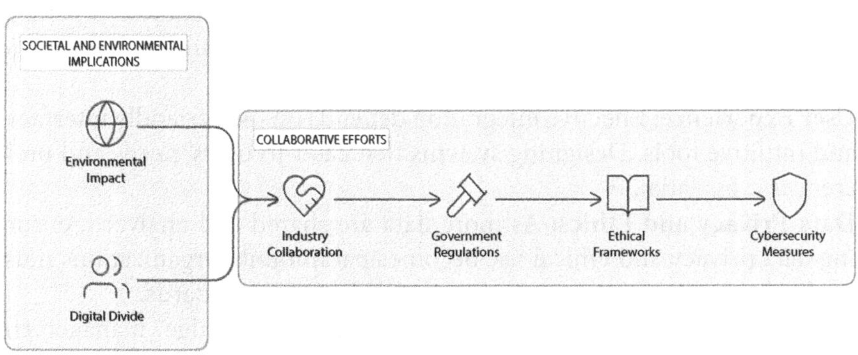

Figure 5.9 Societal and environmental implications in Industry 4.0.

Supply Chain Security: Interconnected supply chains can be targeted for attacks. Ensuring end-to-end security in the supply chain, including third-party partners, is vital.
Infrastructure Resilience: Industry 4.0 heavily relies on digital infrastructure. Preparing for infrastructure failures and establishing redundancy mechanisms is essential to minimize disruptions.

Societal and Environmental Implications:
Environmental Impact: While Industry 4.0 can enhance sustainability, increased resource consumption due to digitalization must be monitored. Adopting eco-friendly practices is important.
Digital Divide: Uneven access to Industry-4 skills can lead to a digital divide. Efforts must be made to ensure equal access and opportunities for all.

Collaborative Efforts:
Addressing these challenges requires collaborative efforts among stakeholders:
Industry Collaboration: Organizations, industries, and technology providers should collaborate to establish ethical standards, share best practices, and develop secure solutions.
Government Regulations: Governments must enact policies that balance innovation with ethical and security considerations, ensuring compliance and accountability.
Ethical Frameworks: Organizations should adopt ethical frameworks that guide decision making and AI system behavior, ensuring alignment with societal values.
Cybersecurity Measures: Continuous investment in cybersecurity measures, threat detection, and incident response capabilities is essential.

5.8.4 Regulatory and Policy Implications

As Industry 4.0 advances, regulatory and policy frameworks play a critical role in ensuring responsible and ethical adoption while fostering innovation.

Adaptive Regulatory Frameworks:

Agile Legislation: Traditional regulations may lag behind technological advancements. Governments must develop adaptive regulations that accommodate the fast-paced changes of Industry 4.0.

Interdisciplinary Collaboration: Association among policymakers, industry experts, and academia is vital to formulate active regulations that balance innovation, consumer protection, and security.

Data Governance with Ownership:

Data Ownership: The ownership of data generated by Industry 4.0 processes needs clarification. Regulations should outline data ownership rights and responsibilities, especially in cases of collaborative projects.
Cross-Border Data Flow: As data flow across borders, harmonized international protection of data regulations are necessary to preserve privacy and safety standards.

Intellectual Property and Standards:

Patent and IP Protection: Industry 4.0 innovations require robust intellectual property protection to incentivize research and development investments.
Standardization: Governments and industries should collaborate to establish interoperability standards, ensuring compatibility and seamless integration of diverse technologies.

Ethical and Social Considerations:

Ethical Guidelines: Regulatory bodies should develop ethical guidelines addressing AI, automation, and data usage, ensuring technology aligns with societal values.
Impact Assessment: Regulations should require organizations to conduct ethical and societal impact assessments before implementing Industry 4.0 technologies.

Cybersecurity and Privacy:

Cybersecurity Requirements: Regulations should mandate strong cybersecurity practices, regular audits, and incident reporting to mitigate cyber threats.
Privacy by Design: Industry 4.0 technologies should adhere to privacy by design principles, embedding privacy features into products and services.

Skills and Workforce Development:

Upskilling Initiatives: Policymakers should collaborate with educational institutions and industries to develop training programs that equip the workforce with Industry 4.0 skills.
Labor Regulations: Evolving work dynamics due to automation and AI require labor regulations that ensure fair treatment, worker protection, and job transition support.

Global Cooperation:

International Collaboration: Industry 4.0 is a global phenomenon. International collaboration is crucial to harmonize regulations and standards, facilitating seamless global operations.
Regulatory Sandboxes: Governments can create regulatory sandboxes that allow controlled experimentation with Industry 4.0 technologies, fostering innovation while assessing risks.

5.9 Conclusion

5.9.1 Recap of Key Findings

Throughout this comprehensive exploration of integration between Industry-4 and management of knowledge, several pivotal findings have emerged, underscoring the transformative potential of this synergy.

Synergistic Integration: The fusion of Industry-4 technologies, including AI, IoT, and data analytics with knowledge management principles has demonstrated the power to revolutionize industries across diverse sectors.
Data-Driven Insights: The marriage of real-time data insights and knowledge-sharing mechanisms enables informed decision making, process optimization, and innovation.
Enhanced Collaboration: Industry 4.0's interconnectedness and knowledge management's emphases on collaboration amplify each other, resulting in cross-functional teamwork that drives operational excellence.
Customer Centricity: The integration allows for personalized customer experiences, responsive supply chains, and agile product development, all of which enhance customer satisfaction and loyalty.

Continuous Learning Culture: The combination fosters a culture of continuous learning, encouraging employees to stay updated with evolving technologies and knowledge-sharing platforms.
Operational Excellence: Industry 4.0's automation capabilities, paired with knowledge management's data-driven insights, lead to streamlined processes, reduced inefficiencies, and improved productivity.
Challenges and Considerations: However, challenges, such as ethical dilemmas, cybersecurity threats, and regulatory complexities, underscore the need for careful navigation of this integration.
Future Prospects: The potential for further research lies in exploring the intersection of AI, blockchain, and IoT with knowledge management, as well as understanding the societal impacts of Industry-4.
In conclusion, integration of Industry-4 and knowledge management represents a significant leap forward for industries. As organizations embark on this journey, they must strike a balance between innovation and responsibility, leveraging this synergy to navigate challenges, drive progress, and create a sustainable and prosperous future.

5.9.2 Implications for Industries and Knowledge Management

This comprehensive exploration of combination between Industry and information management reveals profound implications for both industries and the knowledge management landscape.

Revolutionizing Industries: The fusion of Industry-4 knowledge's with knowledge management principles has the potential to revolutionize industries. Organizations that embrace this integration can achieve enhanced operational efficiency, improved decision making, and innovation across sectors.
Operational Excellence: By harnessing real-time data insights and collaborative knowledge sharing, industries can optimize processes, reduce inefficiencies, and ensure agile responses to dynamic market conditions.
Customer-Centric Transformation: The integration enables personalized customer experiences, responsive supply chains, and tailored products and services. Industries can align their offerings with individual customer preferences, fostering loyalty and differentiation.
Continuous Learning Culture: Knowledge management's emphasis on knowledge sharing aligns seamlessly with Industry 4.0's emphasis on data-driven insights. This integration fosters a culture of continuous learning, where employees adapt to technological advancements and contribute to innovation.

Innovative Practices: The fusion of technologies and knowledge management strategies opens avenues for creative problem solving and innovative practices. Cross-functional collaboration and access to real-time insights drive the development of novel solutions.
Challenges and Considerations: While the integration offers transformative benefits, organizations must navigate challenges related to ethics, security, and regulatory compliance. Striking a balance between innovation and ethical responsibility is paramount.
Reshaping Knowledge Management: The convergence of Industry-4 and knowledge expands the scope of knowledge-sharing platforms. Emerging technologies facilitate real-time knowledge delivery, collaboration, and insights extraction.
Future-Ready Organizations: Industries that embrace this integration are better positioned to thrive in an era of rapid technological advancements. They can respond swiftly to market changes, deliver exceptional customer experiences, and maintain competitive advantage.
In conclusion, integration of Industry-4 and knowledge management has reaching far away implications for industries, fostering operational excellence, customer centricity, and innovation. By aligning strategies with this integration and addressing associated challenges, organizations can position themselves as leaders in the evolving landscape of technological advancement and knowledge utilization.

5.9.3 Prospects for Future Research and Development

As we conclude this exploration of combination between Industry-4 and knowledge, several promising avenues emerge for future research and development.

Emerging Technologies: Further research can delve into the intersection of Industry 4.0 with emerging technologies such as quantum computing, edge computing, and advanced robotics. Understanding how these technologies synergize with knowledge management will unlock new dimensions of innovation.
Data Ethics and Governance: Future research should focus on establishing ethical guidelines and robust data governance frameworks. Exploring how ethical considerations evolve in a data-rich Industry 4.0 environment can guide responsible adoption.
Socioeconomic Impacts: Thoughtful broader socioeconomic implications of Industry-4's integration with knowledge management are vital.

Research can analyze its effects on employment, income distribution, and societal wellbeing.

Collaborative AI: Investigating how AI systems can collaborate with human experts in knowledge management processes will be crucial. The design of AI algorithms that complement human expertise while ensuring transparency and accountability is an avenue for exploration.

Regulatory Dynamics: The evolving regulatory landscape requires ongoing research to track changes and assess their impact on Industry 4.0 and knowledge management integration. Developing adaptable policy frameworks that foster innovation and security is essential.

Cross-Industry Applications: Exploring how the integration influences sectors beyond manufacturing, such as healthcare, finance, and education, will provide insights into its versatility and transformative potential.

Sustainability and Circular Economy: Forthcoming research must investigate how Industry-4 with knowledge management can promote sustainable practices, reduce environmental impact, and foster circular economy principles.

Ethical AI: Deepening the understanding of ethical AI development and deployment within the context of Industry 4.0 can ensure that AI systems align with human values and ethical standards.

In conclusion, the mixing of Industry-4 with management knowledge marks the beginning of a dynamic journey. Prospects for future research and development hold the promise of unraveling complexities, unlocking innovations, and shaping a responsible, ethical, and prosperous technological landscape. By embracing these opportunities, researchers, practitioners, and policymakers can collectively drive positive change and harness the full potential of this transformative integration.

References

1. Kolyasnikov, M.S. and Kelchevskaya, N.R., Knowledge management strategies in companies: Trends and the impact of Industry 4.0. *Upravlenec*, 11, 4, 82–96, 2020, doi: DOI: 10.29141/2218-5003-2020-11-4-7.
2. De Bem Machado, A., Secinaro, S., Calandra, D., Lanzalonga, F., Knowledge management and digital transformation for Industry 4.0: a structured literature review. *Knowl. Manag. Res. Pract.*, 20, 2, 320–338, 2022, doi: https://doi.org/10.1080/14778238.2021.2015261.
3. Fakhar Manesh, M.M., Pellegrini, M., Marzi, G., Dabic, M., Knowledge management in the fourth industrial revolution: Mapping the literature and

scoping future avenues. *IEEE Trans. Eng. Manage.*, 68, 1, 289–300, 2020, doi: DOI: 10.1109/TEM.2019.2963489.

4. Di Maria, E., Bettiol, M., Capestro, M., Furlan, A., Do industry 4.0 technologies lead to more (and better) knowledge?, in: *European Conference on Knowledge Management*, Academic Conferences International Limited, pp. 174–181, 2018.
5. Cárdenas, L.J.A., Ramírez, W.F.T., Rodríguez Molano, J., II, Model for the incorporation of big data in knowledge management oriented to industry 4.0, in: *Data Mining and Big Data: Third International Conference, DMBD 2018*, Shanghai, China, June 17–22, 2018, Springer International Publishing, pp. 683–693, 2018, Proceedings 3.
6. Capestro, M. and Kinkel, S., Industry 4.0 and knowledge management: A review of empirical studies, in: *Knowledge Management and Industry 4.0: New Paradigms for Value Creation*, pp. 19–52, 2020.
7. Anshari, M. and Hamdan, M., Understanding knowledge management and upskilling in Fourth Industrial Revolution: transformational shift and SECI model. *VINE J. Inf. Knowl. Manag. Syst.*, 52, 3, 373–393, 2022.
8. Preuveneers, D. and Ilie-Zudor, E., The intelligent industry of the future: A survey on emerging trends, research challenges and opportunities in Industry 4.0. *J. Ambient Intell. Smart Environ.*, 9, 3, 287–298, 2017.
9. Mikhalkina, D. and Nikitaeva, A., Trends, factors and guidelines for the development of human resources for industry 4.0, in: *Digital Transformation in Industry: Digital Twins and New Business Models*, pp. 447–459, Springer International Publishing, Cham, 2022.
10. Wagire, A.A., Rathore, A.P.S., Jain, R., Analysis and synthesis of Industry 4.0 research landscape: Using latent semantic analysis approach. *J. Manuf. Technol. Manag.*, 31, 1, 31–51, 2020.
11. Ardito, L., Petruzzelli, A.M., Panniello, U., Garavelli, A.C., Towards Industry 4.0: Mapping digital technologies for supply chain management-marketing integration. *Bus. Process Manag. J.*, 25, 2, 323–346, 2018.
12. Khan, I.S., Ahmad, M.O., Majava, J., Industry 4.0 and sustainable development: A systematic mapping of triple bottom line, Circular Economy and Sustainable Business Models perspectives. *J. Cleaner Prod.*, 297, 126655, 2021.
13. de Souza, F.F., Corsi, A., Pagani, R.N., Balbinotti, G., Kovaleski, J.L., Total quality management 4.0: Adapting quality management to Industry 4.0. *TQM J.*, 34, 4, 749–769, 2022.
14. Whysall, Z., Owtram, M., Brittain, S., The new talent management challenges of Industry 4.0. *J. Manag. Dev.*, 38, 2, 118–129, 2019.
15. Barata, J., Rupino Da Cunha, P., Stal, J., Mobile supply chain management in the Industry 4.0 era: An annotated bibliography and guide for future research. *J. Enterp. Inf. Manag.*, 31, 1, 173–192, 2018.
16. Castro Benavides, A.L., Yepes, V., Pellicer, E., Cuéllar Reyes, Á. J., Knowledge management in the construction industry: state of the art and trends in research. *Rev. Constr.*, 11, 3, 1–10, 2012.

17. Furstenau, L.B., Sott, M.K., Kipper, L.M., Machado, E.L., Lopez-Robles, J.R., Dohan, M.S., Cobo, M.J., Zahid, A., Abbasi, Q.H., Imran, M.A., Link between sustainability and industry 4.0: trends, challenges and new perspectives. *IEEE Access*, 8, 140079–140096, 2020.
18. Telukdarie, A., Buhulaiga, E., Bag, S., Gupta, S., Luo, Z., Industry 4.0 implementation for multinationals. *Process Saf. Environ. Prot.*, 118, 316–329, 2018.
19. Kumar, U. and Galar, D., Maintenance in the era of industry 4.0: issues and challenges, in: *Quality, IT and Business Operations: Modeling and Optimization*, pp. 231–250, 2018.
20. Tseng, M.-L., Tran, T.P.T., Ha, H.M., Bui, T.-D., Lim, M.K., Sustainable industrial and operation engineering trends and challenges Toward Industry 4.0: A data driven analysis. *J. Ind. Prod. Eng.*, 38, 8, 581–598, 2021.
21. Liboni, L.B., Cezarino, L.O., Jabbour, C.J.C., Oliveira, B.G., Stefanelli, N.O., Smart industry and the pathways to HRM 4.0: implications for SCM. *Supply Chain Manag.: Int. J.*, 24, 1, 124–146, 2019.
22. Ghobakhloo, M., The future of manufacturing industry: a strategic roadmap toward Industry 4.0. *J. Manuf. Technol. Manag.*, 29, 6, 910–936, 2018.
23. Shaw, M.J., Subramaniam, C., Tan, G.W., Welge, M.E., Knowledge management and data mining for marketing. *Decis. Support Syst.*, 31, 1, 127–137, 2001.
24. Birkel, H. and Hartmann, E., Development of a Trend Management Process for Supply Chain Management in the Context of Industry 4.0, in: *Digital Business Models in Industrial Ecosystems: Lessons Learned from Industry 4.0 Across Europe*, pp. 23–34, 2021.
25. Quintas, P., Lefrere, P., Jones, G., Knowledge management: a strategic agenda. *Long Range Plann.*, 30, 3, 385–391, 1997.
26. Schniederjans, D.G., Curado, C., Khalajhedayati, M., Supply chain digitisation trends: An integration of knowledge management. *Int. J. Prod. Econ.*, 220, 107439, 2020.
27. Paschek, D., Ivascu, L., Draghici, A., Knowledge management–the foundation for a successful business process management. *Proc. Social Behav. Sci.*, 238, 182–191, 2018.
28. Leitão, P., Pires, F., Karnouskos, S., Colombo, A.W., Quo vadis industry 4.0? Position, trends, and challenges. *IEEE Open J. Ind. Electron. Soc.*, 1, 298–310, 2020.
29. Awan, U., Sroufe, R., Shahbaz, M., Industry 4.0 and the circular economy: A literature review and recommendations for future research. *Bus. Strategy Environ.*, 30, 4, 2038–2060, 2021.
30. Fromhold-Eisebith, M., Marschall, P., Peters, R., Thomes, P., Torn between digitized future and context dependent past–How implementing 'Industry 4.0'production technologies could transform the German textile industry. *Technol. Forecasting Soc. Change*, 166, 120620, 2021.

6

Artificial Intelligence on Knowledge Management and Industry Revolution 4.0: Impacts and Challenges

Sridevi and Tukkappa K. Gundoor*

Department of Computer Science, Karnatak University, Dharwad, Karnataka, India

Abstract

A whole new era of business transformation is heralded by the convergence of Industry 4.0, artificial intelligence (AI), and information management. Informed decision making is made easier, and overall operational efficiency is increased when artificial intelligence (AI) is used as a catalyst for data collecting and analysis. Natural language processing (NLP) and machine learning (ML) techniques enable companies to sift through enormous databases and find crucial information for formulating corporate strategy. Knowledge workers may focus on high-value tasks that demand human creativity and intelligence since AI-powered information management solutions automate repetitive tasks like document classification and tagging. "Smart factories," defined by enhanced automation and connection via the Internet of Things (IoT), are a notion brought to Industry 4.0 by integrating AI. These factories analyze and optimize manufacturing processes in real time with the help of AI-powered technology. By anticipating and addressing possible mechanical problems early on, predictive analytics lowers downtime and enhances product quality. Production and operational efficiency rise as a result of Industry 4.0's smooth integration of AI. AI has a huge overall impact on Industry 4.0 and knowledge management. Its uses drastically change how businesses operate, giving them more agility, inventiveness, and competitive edge in the fast-paced world of modern business. By leveraging AI's capacity to gather and analyze data, businesses may make more informed and responsive decisions by gaining a

**Corresponding author*: gundoortukaram@gmail.com
Dr. Sridevi: Orcid ID: https://orcid.org/my-orcid?orcid=0000-0002-9768-1599
Tukkappa K Gundoor: Orcid ID: https://orcid.org/0000-0002-6102-0094

Rajendra Kumar, Vishal Jain, Venus C. Ibarra, Corrienna Abdul Talib and Vinay Kukreja (eds.) Knowledge Management and Industry Revolution 4.0, (159–182) © 2024 Scrivener Publishing LLC

deeper understanding of consumer behavior, market trends, and internal operational dynamics. Furthermore, integrating AI-driven technology creates new opportunities for innovation in addition to improving current procedures. The amalgamation of artificial intelligence, information management, and Industry 4.0 empowers businesses to explore novel approaches, streamline processes, and provide innovative techniques for addressing problems. AI is essentially a pillar supporting the revolution in business processes. It brings in a new era of enhanced efficiency, agility, and creativity when combined with Industry 4.0 and information management, empowering companies to adapt, expand, and take the lead in today's hectic and cutthroat business environment.

***Keywords*:** Augmented reality, artificial intelligence, blockchain, cybersecurity, industry 4.0, Internet of Things (IoT), knowledge management (KM), natural language

6.1 Introduction

AI has a big impact on Industry 4.0 and knowledge management because it makes it easier for companies to organize and use their data effectively, which improves decision making and operational effectiveness. Artificial intelligence (AI) techniques used in knowledge management, such as machine learning (ML) and natural language processing (NLP), are used to evaluate massive volumes of data and produce insights that could influence business strategy. Knowledge workers may concentrate on higher-value tasks by using AI-powered knowledge management systems to automate routine tasks like document classification and tagging. Industry 4.0 uses artificial intelligence (AI) to build highly automated, Internet of Things (IoT)-connected smart factories. AI-powered solutions that support production process optimization and real-time monitoring can anticipate and prevent machine issues. Increased productivity, decreased downtime, and improved product quality are the outcomes of this. All things considered, the use of AI in knowledge management and Industry 4.0 has the potential to transform how companies operate and increase their competitiveness, agility, and inventiveness in the present fast-paced business environment [1, 2].

Artificial intelligence (AI), a central feature of the Fourth Industrial Revolution (IR 4.0), depends critically on knowledge management (KM). Knowledge management, or KM, is the act of gathering, organizing, and applying an organization's knowledge assets to enhance creativity, problem solving, and decision making. The current era of better technology integration, or IR 4.0, is revolutionizing communities and organizations via the use of digital technologies, automation, and artificial intelligence (AI) [3–5].

6.2 Background of the Study

The background of the study provides context and rationale for investigating a particular issue or undertaking research. The context for artificial intelligence (AI) in knowledge management (KM) and the Fourth Industrial Revolution (IR 4.0) would include relevant information on the current status of AI, KM, and IR 4.0 as well as the reason for investigating their intersection.

Artificial intelligence (AI) technology has advanced significantly in recent years, particularly in the domains of machine learning, natural language processing, and cognitive computing. The Fourth Industrial Revolution (IR 4.0), which is defined by the application of digital technology, automation, and artificial intelligence (AI) across a variety of industries and enterprises, is the result of these advancements. Knowledge management (KM) has long been recognized as a crucial element of organizational success since it involves the efficient gathering, organizing, and use of knowledge assets inside an organization. Given the exponential growth of digital data and the increasing complexity of information sources, organizations find it difficult to effectively manage and use their knowledge resources [6–8].

Within IR 4.0, AI presents fresh opportunities to enhance knowledge management procedures. Artificial intelligence (AI) methods, like machine learning, natural language processing, and predictive analytics, can help businesses glean insights from vast amounts of data. They can also automate knowledge-intensive procedures, enhance the search and retrieval of relevant information, and help in decision making via cognitive computing systems. Notwithstanding the possible benefits, further study and comprehension of the uses, challenges, and implications of the intersection of AI, KM, and IR 4.0 are still required. Analyzing AI integration in knowledge management within the context of Industry 4.0 may provide useful insights into how companies might leverage these technologies to improve operational efficiency, fortify knowledge management procedures, and obtain a competitive edge. This chapter looks at the application of AI to knowledge management (KM) and what its implications are for Industry 4.0. Using case studies from real-world applications and a review of the literature, we hope to understand the current state of AI in KM, point out potential and problems, and suggest approaches for effectively integrating AI in KM practices within the framework of IR 4.0 [9–11].

6.3 Industry 4.0 Revolution

The term "Industry 4.0," or "Fourth Industrial Revolution," describes the present period of technical development and digital transformation across numerous sectors and businesses. The integration of sophisticated technology and automation has resulted in a notable transformation in the operational framework of organizations and society.

Steam and water power were used to automate manufacturing during the first industrial revolution in the 1800s. Electric power was used to mass make the second one in the early 1900s. Utilizing electronics and computer technology, the third automated production wave began in the late 1900s. The German government came up with the term "Industry 4.0" in 2011. In the "Industry 4.0" phase of the Industrial Revolution, connectivity, automation, machine learning, and real-time data are prioritized. Big data, digital technologies, machine learning, and actual production and operations are all combined in "Industry 4.0," which is the combination of IoTs and smart manufacturing. Industry 4.0 presents the requirement for real-time data connectivity and access across processes, partners, products, and people at a time when every business and organization in operation faces the same problem [12, 13].

The Fourth Industrial Revolution caused profound changes in several industries, including manufacturing, healthcare, energy, transportation, and banking. It presents opportunities for increased creativity, productivity, and economic growth. But it also brings with it concerns about the loss of jobs, moral dilemmas, and the need for workers to upgrade their skills to keep up with the rapidly changing technological environment [14, 15]. The below Figure 6.1 shows the industry revolution from industry 1.0 to industry 4.0.

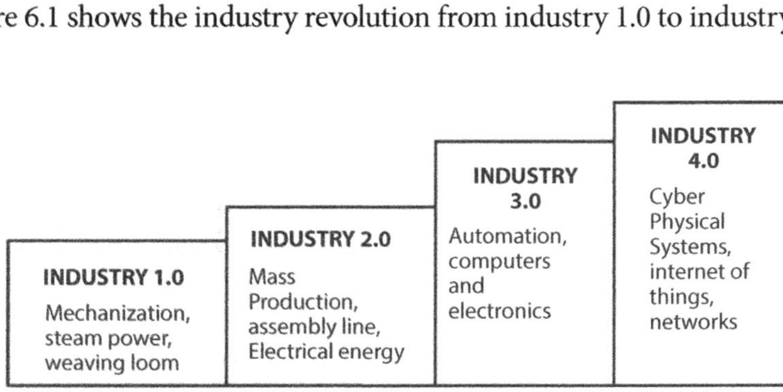

Figure 6.1 Industry revolution 4.0.

6.4 Technology is Driving Industry 4.0

Numerous new technologies that are reshaping sectors and changing business processes are driving Industry 4.0. All of these developments promote the development of intelligent, networked systems. "Industry 4.0" describes a disruptive era where advanced technologies, like artificial intelligence (AI), machine learning (ML), and the Internet of Things (IoT), are used to create networks of intelligent objects and processes that work together seamlessly. This convergence changes the way industries operate and grow by allowing firms to increase value, increase efficiency, and simplify operations across multiple sectors [16, 17]. The following is a summary of some of the key developments driving Industry 4.0:

6.4.1 The Internet of Things (IoT)

An interconnected system of machines, computers, and other items or people is known as the Internet of Things (IoT). Over a network, data can be automatically transferred. Wearable technology, linked automobiles, smart homes, smart appliances, smart cities (i.e., traffic or pollution being tracked via smart technology), and wearable smart gadgets are a few instances of IoT in operation. We are more adaptable and resource efficient thanks to IoT technology, and we can also spot development opportunities.

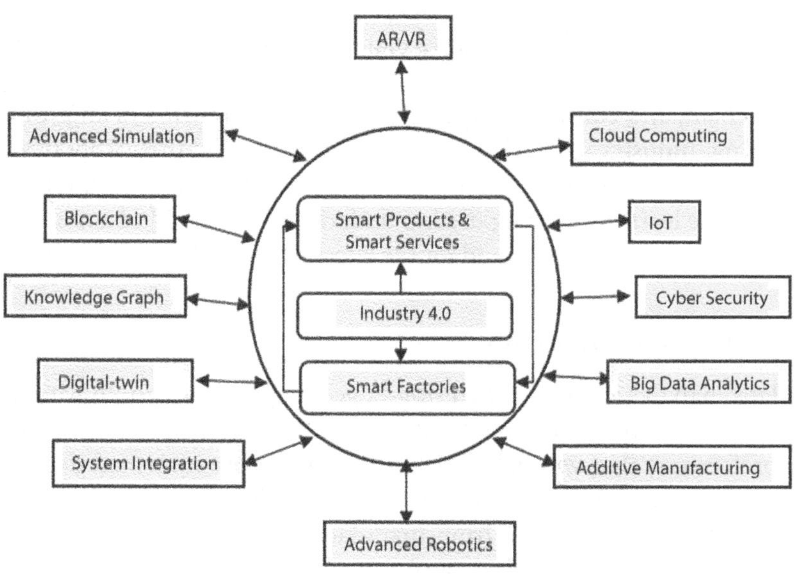

Figure 6.2 Technologies are driving Industry 4.0.

The Figure 6.2 shown below which depicts the different driving technology for Industry 4.0. (The smart thermostat should lower the temperature to save on heating expenses because no one is home during these hours.) By using sensors and other devices to collect data, optimize workflows, and spot and prevent possible issues, the Internet of Things is being utilized to build smart factories in the manufacturing sector that are more productive and efficient. IoT may be used to build smart grids that will help us use energy more efficiently and minimize our use of it. IoT has the potential to completely transform several industries besides manufacturing, including distribution, retail, and healthcare. It will also keep becoming better at anticipating human requirements and becoming more flexible in response to them.

6.4.2 AI and ML

Industry 4.0 is creating new opportunities by converting traditional production into smart manufacturing, where robots can comprehend these systems, communicate with the outside world, and intelligently adjust their behavior. Industry activity patterns have been completely transformed by artificial intelligence, which is driven by a novel method of interaction between humans and machines. Automated mechanisms are consumed by intelligent factories, which also supply digital enablers that let machinery talk to one other and the industrial systems as a whole through an IoT framework. Applications of AI and ML in Industry 4.0 have grown beyond our projections. Totally integrated, cooperative manufacturing structures that respond instantly to changing needs and situations in the intelligent factory, the supply chain, and consumer expectations are the hallmarks of smart manufacturing. Industry 4.0 is changing the automotive industry. Robotics and autonomous vehicles are still in the early stages of development and testing, but machine learning is being used to understand the world of autonomous vehicles. There is a huge demand for the latest AI and ML software products.

6.4.3 Big Data Analytics

Big data analytics is the use of cutting-edge computing technology to massive data sets in order to identify important trends, correlations, patterns, and preferences that will help businesses make more informed decisions. Big data analytics is used in a few fields of Industry 4.0, such as smart factories, where sensor data from manufacturing equipment is evaluated to forecast when maintenance and repair procedures will be required. Manufacturers who use it benefit from increased production efficiency, self-service system understanding of real-time data, predictive maintenance optimization, and automation of production management.

6.4.4 Automation and Robotics

Automation technologies connect, operate, and monitor real-time networks of gadgets, devices, machines, robots, and cloud information through the "Industrial Internet of Things" (IIoT) (via "Cloud Monitoring"). In this sense, it minimizes the need for human interaction and maximizes productivity by enabling them to learn, function, and operate automatically.

6.4.5 Cloud Computing

Industry 4.0 greatly benefits from cloud computing since it offers an adaptable and scalable platform for handling, storing, and analyzing the enormous volumes of data produced by IoT devices and other industrial systems. In Industry 4.0, cloud computing can help businesses become more competitive, efficient, and cost effective.

6.4.6 AR and VR

Future applications for virtual reality (VR) and augmented reality (AR) in gaming, marketing, e-commerce, education, and many other domains are quite promising. These technologies are renowned for their enhanced experiences, which combine augmented, three-dimensional imagery from the virtual and physical worlds. Despite the fact that it is simple to confuse the two, there are a few key distinctions.

6.4.7 Cybersecurity and Data Privacy

Robust cybersecurity measures are crucial since Industry 4.0 relies on networked systems and data sharing. Digital system integrity and dependability are preserved, and sensitive data are protected thanks to technologies including intrusion detection systems, secure communication protocols, authentication methods, and encryption.

6.4.8 Additive Manufacturing (3D Printing)

Production is now more automated, efficient, and flexible than ever in the IIoT era. These days, we can put into practice ever-more intricate technologies that bring together information systems and tangible items. Machines and devices are capable of self-adaptation through communication, data processing and exchange, context evaluation, and decision making, all of this without much assistance from human operators and independently. Due to rapid prototyping and 3D printing, additive manufacturing and smart factories have changed production.

6.4.9 Blockchain

Blockchain can efficiently, verifiably, and permanently record transactions between two parties. It is a public log of all transactions on the Bitcoin network. The reason it is named "blockchain" is that transactions are arranged into "blocks," with each block being linked to the one before it. The technology known as blockchain, which has numerous uses across numerous industries, is the foundation of cryptocurrencies, such as Bitcoin, and is utilized in Industry 4.0 to document any transaction, offers a permanent, decentralized, and safe means of storing data. The concept of transactions has been altered by blockchain technology. It is a kind of database that can be shared across several sites and has the potential to be the core technology driving the next generation of the internet.

6.5 Role of AI in KM and IR 4.0

In the context of the Fourth Industrial Revolution (IR 4.0), artificial intelligence (AI) plays a major role in knowledge management (KM). AI technology has powerful capabilities to enhance the management and utilization of corporate knowledge assets. In KM and IR 4.0, AI plays the following important functions [18]:

6.5.1 Extraction and Discovery of Knowledge

Artificial intelligence (AI) methods, like machine learning and natural language processing (NLP), can be used to extract knowledge from unstructured data sources including documents, emails, and social media. By automatically identifying and classifying relevant content, AI helps to uncover hidden patterns and crucial insights.

6.5.2 Knowledge Retrieval and Skillful Search

Artificial intelligence (AI)-powered search engines use sophisticated algorithms to interpret user searches, assess context, and provide relevant results. These systems leverage techniques to improve the accuracy and power of information retrieval, such as entity recognition, semantic search, and personalized recommendations.

6.5.3 Decision Support and Cognitive Computing

Artificial intelligence (AI) enables computer systems to mimic human intellect, reasoning, and decision making. Large data volumes can be analyzed by these systems, which can also identify patterns and provide intelligent recommendations to improve decision making in a variety of sectors, such as marketing, finance, and healthcare.

6.5.4 Virtual Assistants and Chatbots

Chatbots and virtual assistants driven by AI are becoming more common in KM and IR 4.0. These conversational agents converse with users, answer their questions, and provide guidance on a variety of topics by utilizing technologies for natural language generation and understanding. They offer a scalable and efficient way to give customers personalized information and assistance.

6.5.5 Using Machine Learning to Improve Knowledge

Machine learning algorithms can search through massive data sets for patterns and insights that humans would miss. By applying these algorithms on knowledge repositories, organizations can improve the quality of their current knowledge assets, identify gaps, and expand the processes for knowledge creation and sharing.

6.5.6 Knowledge Management and Predictive Analytics

Artificial intelligence-powered predictive analytics uses historical data and machine learning methods to forecast future trends, behaviors, and results. By making it possible to identify potential knowledge gaps and new knowledge needs, predictive analytics in knowledge management (KM) can help proactive knowledge management activities.

6.5.7 Robotic Process Automation (RPA) and Automation

Automation and AI technologies are closely associated with IR 4.0. RPA automates repetitive, rule-based tasks using artificial intelligence, freeing up human resources for higher-value tasks. By automating the knowledge management (KM) procedures of gathering, documenting, and sharing information, RPA can make sure that data are efficiently disseminated across the entire company.

All things considered, IR 4.0's integration of AI and KM offers a huge opportunity to leverage data, derive insights, improve organizational performance, and make better decisions. By leveraging AI, organizations may maximize their knowledge potential, boost productivity, and obtain a competitive advantage in the ever-evolving digital market.

6.6 The Effects of AI on IR 4.0 and KM

In the framework of the Fourth Industrial Revolution (IR 4.0), artificial intelligence (AI) has a substantial and wide-ranging impact on knowledge management (KM) [19, 20]. These are some of the main effects of AI on IR 4.0 and KM:

6.6.1 Enhanced Application and Acquisition of Knowledge

AI technologies enable organizations to mine large amounts of data for valuable patterns and insights, especially from unstructured data sources. AI methods, like machine learning and natural language processing (NLP), can help organizations uncover hidden knowledge, identify trends, and make better informed decisions based on data-driven insights.

6.6.2 Improved Search and Retrieval of Information

The effectiveness and efficiency of information retrieval are increased by AI-driven recommendation and search engines. AI systems are capable of translating user queries and comprehending context in addition to producing more accurate and relevant search results. As a result, because pertinent knowledge assets may be located more quickly and precisely, information discovery may take less time and effort.

6.6.3 Enhanced Decision Making and Cognitive Support

Cognitive computing systems powered by artificial intelligence (AI) facilitate decision making by analyzing complex data sets, identifying patterns, and providing astute guidance. Because these algorithms are faster than humans at absorbing and understanding large amounts of data, they can make more educated decisions based on data in industries like marketing, finance, and strategic planning.

6.6.4 Personalized Knowledge Delivery

AI technologies, such as chatbots and virtual assistants, enable personalized and interactive knowledge delivery. These conversational agents can understand user queries, provide instant responses, and guide users through knowledge repositories. By tailoring information to individual needs, organizations can improve user experiences, increase engagement, and ensure relevant knowledge is easily accessible.

6.6.5 Automation of Knowledge-Intensive Processes

Knowledge-intensive process engineering is still far from being mastered. When individuals or agents do a process with a substantial amount of "uncertainty," which can vary depending on a variety of criteria, including the large number of activities to be represented, their unpredictable nature, or their dependence on the situation, it is said to be knowledge intensive. In the worst scenario, tasks are primarily identified as the process progresses, and there is no pre-defined perspective of the knowledge-intensive process.

6.6.6 Improved Knowledge Creation and Innovation

AI technologies make it easier to create new knowledge and innovate by spotting patterns and insights that people might overlook. Algorithms for machine learning are capable of analyzing a variety of data sources, spotting connections, and producing fresh insights or creative solutions. This encourages innovation, continual learning, and helps businesses remain competitive in quickly changing markets.

6.6.7 Proactive Knowledge Management

Organizations can anticipate future knowledge gaps and needs with the help of AI-powered predictive analytics. Organizations can anticipate growing knowledge demands, identify prospective knowledge gaps, and take proactive steps to close those gaps by studying historical data and patterns. As a result, businesses can maintain their competitive edge, adjust to shifting market conditions, and efficiently manage their intellectual assets.

6.6.8 Enhanced Collaboration and Knowledge Sharing

Artificial intelligence (AI) technology enables intelligent tools and platforms that promote collaboration and information sharing. These technologies have the ability to suggest pertinent specialists, link people who have interests, and identify pertinent knowledge assets that may be shared. As a result, the organization's collective intelligence is increased, and cooperation and knowledge sharing are encouraged.

In general, AI has a revolutionary effect on KM and IR 4.0. Knowledge discovery, retrieval, and usage are improved, decision-making processes are strengthened, knowledge-intensive tasks are automated, innovation is encouraged, and proactive knowledge management tactics are made possible. Businesses may maximize the value of their knowledge assets, increase operational effectiveness, and acquire a competitive edge in the digital era by utilizing AI.

6.7 Key Challenges of AI in KM and IR 4.0

Despite the enormous promise that artificial intelligence (AI) presents to improve knowledge management (KM) in the framework of the Fourth Industrial Revolution (IR 4.0), businesses must confront a number of significant obstacles [21, 22]. The following are these difficulties:

6.7.1 Quality and Availability of Data

For AI systems to extract information and make judgments, readily available, high-quality data are essential. Businesses may encounter difficulties guaranteeing the accuracy, completeness, and quality of their data. Furthermore, obtaining pertinent data from several sources, particularly unstructured data, can be difficult and time consuming.

6.7.2 Ethics and Privacy Concerns

AI systems frequently handle private and sensitive data, which raises ethical and privacy problems. To preserve trust and reduce possible dangers associated with AI-enabled knowledge management, organizations need to prioritize ethical practices, ensure compliance with privacy rules, and build strong data governance frameworks.

6.7.3 Insufficient Skill and Knowledge

It takes a qualified workforce with experience in data analytics, knowledge management, and AI technologies to implement AI in KM and IR 4.0. Professionals with the required KM and AI skills are, nevertheless, hard to come by. To close this skill gap, organizations must spend in staff training and upskilling or think about forming alliances and working together.

6.7.4 Interoperability and Integration

The databases, information systems, and KM platforms that are now in use must all work seamlessly with AI systems. Securing seamless data transfer between many systems and achieving interoperability can be challenging tasks. For AI to be effectively included into KM practices, organizations need to take compatibility and integration issues into account.

6.7.5 Trust and Explainability

Frequently functioning as "black boxes," AI algorithms and models make it difficult to decipher and justify the reasons behind their judgments. It can be difficult to develop trust in AI systems in knowledge management (KM), where accountability and openness are crucial. Companies must create ways to validate and justify the outputs produced by AI in knowledge management processes, as well as explainable AI models.

6.7.6 Cultural Adoption and Change Management

Workflows, procedures, and corporate culture must all alter when AI is introduced into knowledge management. The effective adoption of AI technologies may be hampered by reluctance to change, ignorance, and concern about losing one's job. Organizations must overcome these obstacles by developing a culture that welcomes AI as a knowledge management facilitator, using effective change management techniques, and maintaining open lines of communication.

6.7.7 Fairness and Bias

Due to the biases in the data they are trained on, AI systems may exhibit biases of their own. Biases in society may be reinforced, and unfair results may result from this. For knowledge management (KM) practices to be fair and equitable, organizations need to actively address bias issues by putting in place impartial data gathering procedures, a variety of training datasets, and thorough evaluation of AI systems.

6.7.8 Cost and Scalability

Large-scale AI technology implementation can be expensive and resource intensive. Obtaining and retaining the infrastructure, processing power, and knowledge required to support AI-enabled knowledge management projects may provide difficulties for organizations. It is critical to strike a balance between the possible advantages of artificial intelligence and its cost effectiveness.

A multidimensional approach that takes organizational, social, technological, and cultural aspects into account is required to address these problems. Prioritizing data quality, privacy, and ethics is essential. Organizations also need to make workforce development investments, guarantee smooth integration, cultivate trust and openness, successfully manage change, and aggressively address biases and fairness issues. Organizations can effectively traverse the IR 4.0 terrain and optimize the advantages of AI in KM by tackling these obstacles.

6.8 Limitation of the IR 4.0 and KM

While there are many advantages to Industry 4.0 and knowledge management (KM), there are drawbacks as well that businesses must take into account. The following are some of Industry 4.0 and KM's main drawbacks:

6.8.1 Difficulties with Technological Complexity and Integration

The integration of numerous cutting-edge technologies is a key component of Industry 4.0, yet their implementation might be challenging. There are difficulties in managing interoperability, guaranteeing compatibility, and integrating various systems. To get over these obstacles, organizations must carefully plan and spend money on the infrastructure, knowledge, and integration frameworks that they will require.

6.8.2 Investment Cost and Return

The deployment of Industry 4.0 frequently necessitates large investments in trained labor, specialized technology infrastructure, and personnel. Organizations must carefully assess the return on investment (ROI) to justify these investments because the initial costs can be high. Given the anticipated benefits, the cost effectiveness of integrating Industry 4.0 technology and knowledge management methods must be taken into account.

6.8.3 Workplace Skill Gaps and Readiness

Skilled and flexible labor is needed for Industry 4.0 and knowledge management. However, within the organization, there can be opposition to change and skill gaps. The workforce must be upskilled, a learning culture must be established, and change must be managed skillfully if Industry 4.0 technologies and knowledge management techniques are to be fully utilized.

6.8.4 Privacy and Data Security Concerns

The fourth industrial revolution includes large-scale data collection, processing, and utilization. This raises concerns about privacy, protection, and data security. Organizations need to implement robust data governance frameworks, secure data management practices, and comply with privacy regulations to address these problems.

6.8.5 Bias and Ethical Considerations

Automation and artificial intelligence (AI) are two examples of Industry 4.0 technology that potentially present ethical questions and prejudices. AI programs have the potential to be biased, to reinforce injustices, or to make difficult-to-understand conclusions. To foster trust and prevent potential negative effects, organizations must address ethical issues, guarantee fairness and transparency in AI systems, and actively eliminate biases.

6.8.6 Cultural and Organizational Difficulties

Organizational culture must change to implement Industry 4.0 and KM. Cultural hurdles, ignorance, and resistance to change can all impede adoption and successful implementation. Organizations must make investments in change management techniques, cultivate a collaborative and knowledge-sharing culture, and establish an atmosphere that encourages ongoing learning and innovation.

6.8.7 Insufficient Human Engagement and Proficiency

Automation and artificial intelligence (AI) are examples of Industry 4.0 technologies that can lessen the need for human interaction in some operations. Although this increases productivity, technology may also reduce human interaction and the ability to make expert decisions and solve problems. To fully utilize the distinct advantages of both automation and human interaction, organizations must find a balance between both.

6.8.8 Error and Unpredictability

Rapid technological developments and disruptions define Industry 4.0. It might be difficult to manage uncertainty and keep up with the rate of change. To remain competitive and resilient in the face of disruption, organizations must constantly assess and adjust to new technology, market conditions, and customer preferences.

Organizations may effectively overcome the obstacles and optimize the advantages of Industry 4.0 and knowledge management deployment by recognizing and resolving these limits. To get above these obstacles and realize the full potential of these revolutionary ideas, meticulous preparation, a comprehensive strategy, and an attitude of constant learning are necessary.

6.9 Future Direction

In the context of the Fourth Industrial Revolution (IR 4.0), knowledge management (KM) is anticipated to be shaped in the future by a number of noteworthy trends and developments. The following directions could KM in IR 4.0 go in the future:

6.9.1 Better Integration of AI with KM

The integration of artificial intelligence (AI) technologies, including as machine learning, natural language processing, and cognitive computing, will continue to be crucial to knowledge management (KM). AI will enable more complex knowledge dissemination, extraction, and discovery processes, improving the effectiveness and efficiency of knowledge management practices.

6.9.2 Giving Knowledge Analytics and Insights Priority

A growing focus on knowledge analytics and the extraction of valuable insights will result from firms gathering vast amounts of data. Using sophisticated analytics techniques, like sentiment analysis, network analysis, and predictive analytics to extract valuable knowledge and patterns from a variety of data sources will enable organizations to make data-driven decisions and promote innovation.

6.9.3 Collaboration and the Management of Social Knowledge

Knowledge management's collaborative and social elements will grow in significance. Businesses will continue to encourage collaboration, education, and the sharing of implicit knowledge through the use of social collaboration platforms, enterprise social networks, and knowledge-sharing groups. Integrating AI technologies into these platforms will enhance knowledge sharing, expertise identification, and collective intelligence.

6.9.4 Integrating New Technologies with Knowledge Management

There will be a gradual growth in the integration of knowledge management (KM) with cutting-edge technologies such as blockchain, edge computing, augmented reality (AR), and virtual reality (VR). By enhancing trust, security, and knowledge asset visualization, these technologies can support more efficient training, knowledge transfer, and immersive learning experiences.

6.9.5 Prioritizing Knowledge Ethics and Bias Mitigation

An increased emphasis on bias correction and knowledge ethics will result from the growing use of AI technology in knowledge management.

Companies will endeavor to provide transparency, fairness, and accountability in AI-powered decision-making procedures. We will offer guidelines and moral precepts to lessen prejudice, safeguard privacy, and ensure moral application of AI in knowledge management.

6.9.6 Adaptive Education and Customized Information Dissemination

Knowledge transfer in knowledge management will change to become more customized and flexible. Artificial intelligence algorithms will adapt knowledge content dynamically based on user preferences, employment requirements, and learning objectives. Adaptive learning systems allow users to study at their own pace by evaluating user interactions through artificial intelligence (AI) and providing personalized learning experiences.

6.9.7 Assessing Knowledge Ecosystems and Open Knowledge

The ideas of open knowledge and knowledge ecosystems will gain traction. More and more, companies will collaborate with clients, partners, and the community at large to co-create and exchange information. The creation of knowledge ecosystems, as well as innovation, and the sharing of information across industries, will be aided by open data, open access regulations, and cooperative platforms.

6.9.8 Agile Knowledge Management and Ongoing Education

Knowledge management will adopt agile methodologies and continuous learning strategies. To help firms swiftly adapt to their changing demands, agile knowledge management will place a strong emphasis on iterative knowledge development, validation, and deployment. On-demand training, microlearning, and just-in-time knowledge support are examples of continuous learning initiatives that will allow people to acquire knowledge and skills in a flexible and personalized manner.

6.10 Research Challenges

Researchers and practitioners in the field of knowledge management (KM) in the context of the Fourth Industrial Revolution (IR 4.0) must face a number of research difficulties. Among these difficulties are:

6.10.1 The Acquisition and Extraction of Knowledge

It is still difficult to create efficient procedures for gathering and obtaining knowledge from various unstructured data sources. To improve methods for knowledge representation, knowledge extraction process automation, and knowledge discovery, research is required.

6.10.2 Knowledge Structure and Representation

The key to successful knowledge management (KM) is creating scalable, effective models for knowledge organization and representation. As data formats, ontologies, and semantic technologies advance, research is required to create novel strategies for organizing, classifying, and connecting knowledge assets.

6.10.3 Collaboration and the Sharing of Knowledge

Improving processes of collaboration and knowledge sharing both within and between ecosystems necessitates tackling issues with social dynamics, cultural obstacles, and knowledge-sharing incentives. To promote knowledge sharing and cooperation, research is required to investigate social networks, collaborative technologies, and appropriate incentives.

6.10.4 Validation of Knowledge and Quality Control

It is crucial to guarantee the authenticity and quality of knowledge assets. In the digital age, research is required to create reliable validation processes, automated quality evaluation methods, and defenses against prejudice, false information, and fake knowledge.

6.10.5 Consequences for Law and Ethics

It is important to consider the moral and legal ramifications of AI-driven KM techniques. To maintain responsible knowledge management, safeguard user privacy, and reduce biases in AI algorithms, further research is required to investigate ethical frameworks, privacy-enhancing technology, and regulatory processes.

6.10.6 Human–Machine Interaction in KM

It is essential to comprehend how AI systems and people interact in knowledge management procedures. Designing user-friendly interfaces, creating AI-supported collaborative tools that work, and investigating the role of human intuition and judgment in knowledge generation and decision making all require research.

6.10.7 Management of Change and Culture in Organizations

Overcoming corporate culture and change management obstacles is necessary for implementing KM programs and making the shift to IR 4.0. Finding tactics to develop a culture of knowledge sharing, encourage staff involvement, and handle change opposition will require research.

6.10.8 Measuring and Assessing the Impact of KM

To determine the effectiveness of KM projects, it is crucial to have strong assessment frameworks and metrics. In order to quantify knowledge-related outcomes, set up procedures for measuring them, and show the benefits and return on investment of KM activities, research is required.

6.10.9 Sustainability and Scalability

One of the challenges with KM efforts is ensuring their long-term sustainability and scalability. In the context of Industry 4.0, research is required to investigate business models that bolster the long-term sustainability of knowledge management (KM) and to address scalability challenges by developing scalable KM architectures and technologies.

6.11 Conclusion

The Fourth Industrial Revolution (IR 4.0) presents opportunities as well as problems for knowledge management (KM). The creation, sharing, and use of knowledge within businesses may change as a result of the integration of cutting-edge technology like artificial intelligence, the Internet of Things, and big data analytics. Through enhanced information discovery, tailored knowledge delivery, and data-driven decision support, AI-driven solutions give businesses a competitive edge, streamline operations, and encourage creativity. Nonetheless, several issues must be resolved for IR

4.0 and KM to be implemented successfully. These difficulties include the intricacy of fusing several technologies together, the requirement for qualified personnel, worries about data security and privacy, organizational and cultural hurdles, and the moral ramifications of AI-driven knowledge management. Careful planning, investments in people and technology, efficient change management techniques, and an emphasis on moral behavior and responsible AI are all necessary to overcome these obstacles. Trends including improved AI and KM integration, a focus on knowledge analytics and insights, collaboration and social KM, integration with emerging technologies, personalized information delivery, and continuous learning are likely to determine the future of KM in IR 4.0. These patterns draw attention to the need for investigation and creativity in fields including knowledge organization and representation, knowledge extraction and acquisition, knowledge sharing and cooperation, and the moral and legal ramifications of artificial intelligence in knowledge management.

Organizations can unleash the full potential of their knowledge assets, improve operational efficiency, encourage innovation, and adjust to the changing digital landscape by tackling these issues and embracing the promise of AI and emerging technologies. In the face of swift technology breakthroughs and market changes, KM in IR 4.0 enables firms to use knowledge as a strategic asset, make data-driven decisions, and achieve sustainable success.

References

1. Juric, B. and Fettke, P., Artificial Intelligence and Knowledge Management, in: *Encyclopedia of Knowledge Management*, Second Edition, vol. 2, pp. 160–174, 2016.
2. Armstrong, D.J., A Comparison of Human and Artificial Intelligence for Knowledge Management. *15th International Conference on Knowledge Management*, pp. 1–10, 2019.
3. Tharumarajah, A., The Integration of Knowledge Management and Artificial Intelligence. *J. Knowl. Manag.*, 22, 1, 58–80, 2018.
4. Abelha, A., Bernardes, E., Bernardino, J., Pedrosa, A., Artificial Intelligence in Knowledge Management. *Adv. Intell. Syst. Comput.*, 747, 60–69, 2019.
5. Sharma, R.R. and Al-Turjman, F., Industrial Internet of Things for Industry 4.0: Challenges and Solutions, in: *2017 International Conference on Computing, Networking and Communications (ICNC)*, IEEE, pp. 680–684, 2017.

6. Juric, B. and Fettke, P., Artificial Intelligence and Knowledge Management, in: *Encyclopaedia of Knowledge Management*, Second Edition, vol. 2, pp. 160–174, 2016.
7. Siddiqui, M.N. and Khandekar, A., Knowledge Management in Industry 4.0, in: *Industry 4.0: Challenges, Opportunities, and Solutions*, pp. 73–82, Springer, Singapore, 2018.
8. Bhowmick, S. and Nørbjerg, J., Towards Industry 4.0: A Comprehensive Review on Industrial Revolution and Future Transformation. *Proc. Comput. Sci.*, 165, 711–720, 2019.
9. Li, Z., Chen, H., Zhang, X., Knowledge Management Systems and Workforce Creativity: A Task-Technology Fit Perspective. *Inf. Manage.*, 55, 6, 681–693, 2018.
10. Bhowmick, S. and Nørbjerg, J., Towards Industry 4.0: A Comprehensive Review on Industrial Revolution and Future Transformation. *Proc. Comput. Sci.*, 165, 711–720, 2019.
11. Chiarini, A., The Role of Industry 4.0 in Worldwide Manufacturing: A Review. *J. Manuf. Technol. Manag.*, 30, 5, 934–948, 2019.
12. Lu, Y., Xu, L.D., Wang, G., Cloud manufacturing service platform for Industry 4.0. *IEEE Trans. Ind. Inf.*, 13, 4, 2140–2147, 2017.
13. Yang, H., Li, D., Wan, J., Zhou, K., Fog computing and its applications in the Industrial Internet of Things, in: *Proceedings of the International Conference on Big Data and Internet of Things*, ACM, pp. 187–191, 2017.
14. Siddiqui, M.N. and Khandekar, A., Knowledge Management in Industry 4.0, in: *Industry 4.0: Challenges, Opportunities, and Solutions*, pp. 73–82, Springer, Singapore, 2018.
15. Li, Z., Chen, H., Zhang, X., Knowledge Management Systems and Workforce Creativity: A Task-Technology Fit Perspective. *Inf. Manage.*, 55, 6, 681–693, 2018.
16. Armstrong, D.J., A Comparison of Human and Artificial Intelligence for Knowledge Management. *15th International Conference on Knowledge Management*, pp. 1–10, 2019.
17. Rieger, S., Wang, D., Stoenescu, A., Challenges and Opportunities of Artificial Intelligence for Knowledge Management: A Systematic Literature Review. *Inf. Process. Manage.*, 57, 4, 102171, 2020.
18. Papamichail, A., Chalvatzis, K., Skordoulis, M., Knowledge Management and Artificial Intelligence: The Challenges and Opportunities of Digital Transformation, in: *Proceedings of the International Conference on Management of Digital EcoSystems*, pp. 62–67, 2020.
19. Fister Jr., I. and Fister, D., Knowledge Management and Artificial Intelligence, in: *2018 International Conference on Intelligent Systems (IS)*, IEEE, pp. 377–382, 2018.
20. Cortimiglia, M.N., Taisch, M., Dassisti, M., A review on the digital and smart solutions for industry: Six implications for the future of maintenance and asset management. *J. Manuf. Syst.*, 40, 241–251, 2016, (Covers the key

enabling technologies in Industry 4.0 and their implications for maintenance and asset management.).
21. Helms, R.W. and Nixon, M., Exploring SWOT analysis – where are we now?: A review of academic research from the last decade. *J. Strategy Manag.*, 3, 3, 215–251, 2010, (This paper discusses the application of SWOT analysis in the context of Industry 4.0, highlighting its role in identifying key components and enabling technologies.).
22. Lasi, H., Fettke, P., Kemper, H.G., Feld, T., Hoffmann, M., Industry 4.0. *Bus. Inf. Syst. Eng.*, 6, 4, 239–242, 2014.

7

Blending of Knowledge Management with Industry 4.0: A New Formula for Success!

Kavitha R. Gowda[1]*, Dr. Sunanda Vincent Jaiwant[2], Joseph Varghese Kureethara[2] and Jayanta Banerjee[3]

[1]Alliance School of Business, Alliance University, Bangalore, India
[2]School of Business and Management, CHRIST (Deemed to be University), Bangalore, India
[3]College of Business at City University Ajman, UAE

Abstract

The convergence of Industry 4.0 and knowledge management presents a transformative opportunity for organizations seeking enhanced efficiency and sustainable growth. In the context of organizational processes, the amalgamation of technological advancements and effective knowledge management practices can lead to a reduction in costs and an overall improvement in operational efficiency. Understanding the intricacies of knowledge management procedures is crucial, encompassing the production, transfer, acquisition, storage, and utilization of knowledge resources across the organizational spectrum.

The advent of the fourth industrial revolution, commonly referred to as Industry 4.0, has significantly reshaped traditional knowledge management systems. Industry 4.0 introduces the interconnectivity of machines and their autonomous capacity to learn and share data. While both knowledge management and Industry 4.0 offer distinct benefits individually, a strategic approach that combines the strengths of both can unlock new opportunities for efficient business growth and success in the external environment.

This article delves into the symbiotic relationship between Industry 4.0 and knowledge management, emphasizing their combined potential. Industry 4.0

**Corresponding author*: kavitha.gowda@alliance.edu.in
Kavitha R. Gowda: ORCID: https://orcid.org/0000-0002-4221-2023
Dr. Sunanda Vincent Jaiwant: ORCID: https://orcid.org/0000-0001-5030-3948
Joseph Varghese Kureethara: ORCID: https://orcid.org/0000-0002-1161-5970
Jayanta Banerjee: ORCID: https://orcid.org/0000-0002-2079-8983

Rajendra Kumar, Vishal Jain, Venus C. Ibarra, Corrienna Abdul Talib and Vinay Kukreja (eds.) Knowledge Management and Industry Revolution 4.0, (183–196) © 2024 Scrivener Publishing LLC

generates vast volumes of data, and by leveraging knowledge management, organizations can derive valuable insights to inform decision-making processes. Historical data and best practices, accessible through knowledge management, contribute to process optimization. Integration with Industry 4.0 technologies, such as automation and the Internet of Things, further enhances process efficiency.

The marriage of knowledge management and Industry 4.0 extends beyond process optimization to workforce development. Recognizing employees as the building blocks of an organization, this integration enables better management by upgrading knowledge and skills. Consequently, it enhances the overall productivity of the workforce, contributing to organizational success.

In the dynamic landscape of globalization, technology, and competition, this chapter serves as a guide for organizations aiming to harness the collective power of knowledge management and Industry 4.0. By exploring their complementary benefits, it seeks to facilitate the informed utilization of these tools for the betterment and sustainability of businesses in the contemporary world.

***Keywords*:** Technology, knowledge management, industry 4.0, knowledge sharing

7.1 Introduction

Modern firms frequently rely on information and its utilization to maintain a long-term advantage because of rising competition. This necessitates a thorough comprehension of knowledge management (KM) procedures, particularly the way knowledge is produced, transferred, acquired, stored, and used across an organizational system. However, since the turn of the millennium, the emergence of the Fourth industrial revolution, often known as Industry 4.0, that involves the interconnectivity of machines and their capacity for learning and share data autonomously, has profoundly influenced and reshaped such knowledge management systems.

7.1.1 Knowledge Management

Knowledge management is the deliberate act of identifying, organizing, preserving, and disseminating employee knowledge and experience in a company. Organizations create considerable institutional knowledge when they change, grow into new markets, and define their business strategy. Any such organizations benefit tremendously from this knowledge by passing on to new or less seasoned employees in order to keep the operations running smoothly. Knowledge management is thus a combination of accumulating, storing, and sharing of knowledge.

Organizations preserve their prior performance by gathering and storing the knowledge of their employees. Additionally, by disseminating this knowledge throughout the company, staff members are made aware of previous methods that have improved performance and enhanced the plans.

Organizations must support and foster a culture of learning and growth in order to accomplish the aim of knowledge management, fostering an atmosphere in which employees are motivated to exchange expertise in order to improve the workforce.

Objective of knowledge management is to make it easier for employees who are looking for information or institutional knowledge to interact with those who already possess it. This would further, increase efficiency by disseminating knowledge and enhancing the level of expertise possessed by particular people or teams when practical knowledge management is in place.

To optimize the value of an organization's collective knowledge, it entails a cycle of knowledge creation, sharing, structuring, and auditing.

7.1.2 Industry 4.0

Using information and communication technologies, Industry 4.0 relates to the intelligent networking of industrial machines and processes (Platform Industry 4.0). The term "Industry 4.0" refers to a vision that started as a project to increase the competitiveness of the German manufacturing sector.

The term "Industry 4.0" is frequently used synonymously with the idea of the Fourth Industrial Revolution.

Manufacturing has undergone a cyber-physical shift known as "Industry 4.0," or the Fourth Industrial Revolution. The phrase "Industry 4.0" refers to a government project in Germany that promotes networked manufacturing and a digital convergence of business, industry, and other operations.

7.2 History of Industry 4.0

At the end of the 18th century, the First Industrial Revolution began, and it was characterized by the mechanization brought possible with waterpower and steam. Electricity had a key role in the Second Industrial Revolution, which took place at the beginning of the 20th century and was characterized by mass manufacturing, assembly lines, and labor divisions. The Third emerged with the use of computers to further automate machinery and industrial processes around the beginning of the 1970s.

The best way to explain the Fourth Industrial Revolution is as a continuation of the Third. Industry 4.0 focuses on interconnecting those

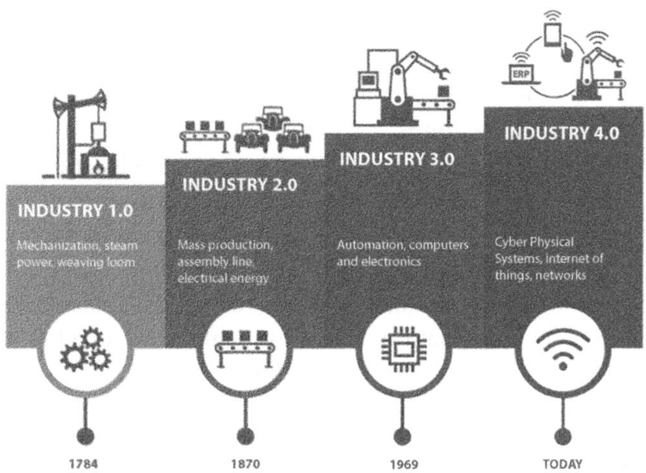

Figure 7.1 Industry 4.0 (source: Industry 4.0 (dgl.com)).

computers, as opposed to Industry 3.0, which incorporated computers into the industrial process. Industry 4.0, however, goes much further than just enabling communication between devices on the manufacturing floor. When completely implemented, Industry 4.0 enables digital manufacturing and the construction of smart factories. Various historical milestones of industrial transformation are presented in Figure 7.1.

7.2.1 Opportunities and Benefits of Industry 4.0

Organizations that decide to fully implement Industry 4.0 can gain a lot from doing so.

One such advantage is that OEMs may be able to *compare actual consumer usage of a product to anticipated usage.*

Another advantage is that sensor data can *assist a company in real-time manufacturing process monitoring.* The process can then be enhanced by comparing this data to a digital twin, a simulation that operates with flawless efficiency.

Some businesses have even included Industry 4.0 ideas into their *employee training procedures.* Before an employee is even permitted to enter the plant, such training courses utilize virtual reality to teach trainees how to handle machines and how to prevent harmful practices.

Another benefit of Industry 4.0 is that its guiding principles might assist businesses in *preventing a disruption on the production line.*

Industrial machinery was serviced according to manufacturer recommendations before Industry 4.0 was adopted. However, Industry 4.0 has made it possible for machinery to be fitted with sensors that continuously monitor the machinery's health. This helps to foresee issues before they arise and take preventive measures to address them. In some circumstances, the equipment can even automatically initiate a replacement part order, all these things taken together can aid a company in avoiding a costly outage that interferes with the production process.

The fact that the digital technology utilized on the manufacturing floor is connected to backend corporate data systems is another advantage of implementing Industry 4.0 concepts.

Another advantage of implementing Industry 4.0 concepts is that *big data analytics* can be carried out on the information related to the production process because the digital technology utilized on the factory floor is connected to back-end corporate data systems. Such analytics can assist the company in identifying trends and gaining information that could ultimately aid in increasing profitability.

7.2.2 Challenges of Industry 4.0 and Knowledge Management

The cost and compatibility—the machines and sensors used in factories frequently employed different protocols, which made it challenging for linked devices to communicate with one another.

The cybersecurity issue—Earlier, it used to be uncommon for factory floor systems to be connected to one another or to back-end IT systems because they were often private in nature. As a result, the vendors who developed these systems infrequently prioritized security in their development processes.

KM:

Building and maintaining a system of expertise location can take some time. It can be difficult to record some information and save it for later use. Finding the ideal professional with effective communication skills and corporate understanding might be challenging. If the *knowledge bearer departs* the organization, the *knowledge might be lost.*

With the opportunities of application of knowledge management in Industry 4.0, this study focuses on showing light on blending of knowledge management with Industry 4.0 as a pill to success.

Significance of KM:

There are a number of advantages to integrating KM with Industry 4.0 or the Fourth Industrial Revolution defined by the convergence of digital technologies. Together, it can help achieve process optimization, helps in efficient decision making, helps in innovation in Industry 4.0, data analysis for predictive maintenance. Data analytics helps improve predictive maintenance through knowledge management by offering maintenance expertise, best practices, and historical data, resulting in more efficient and proactive maintenance plans.

7.3 Objectives of the Chapter

- To examine the impact of technology on knowledge creation among employees
- To observe the knowledge sharing and prospect of Industry 4.0
- To analyze the relationship of knowledge management with Industry 4.0
- To understand the benefits of blending of knowledge management with Industry 4.0

7.3.1 To Examine the Impact of Technology on Knowledge Creation Among Employees

From the paper titled, *Knowledge sharing and innovation: A systematic review*, the authors Delio Ignacio Castaneda and Sergio Cuellar (2020), from the lietarure review quotes according to Serenko and Bontis (2016), information sharing is currently regarded as one of the most significant management study subjects. Knowledge sharing is described by Helmstadter (2003) as interactions among human agents when knowledge serves as the primary input. According to Hogel, Partboteeah, and Munson (2003), knowledge sharing is the sharing of experience, skills, and explicit and tacit knowledge among employees. Wiewiora, Trigunarsyah, Murphy, and Coffey (2013) defined knowledge sharing as the capacity to translate structured events, information, and knowledge from experts into practices. The research concluded by mentioning that knowledge is basic need to foster innovation among employees. It is possible to get the conclusion that collaboration is the most essential motif in the relationship between information sharing and creativity. This method explains how knowledge is constructed collectively and how goods and services are produced.

The main topics' study led to the conclusion that open innovation, knowledge sharing, and absorptive ability are the most well-established issues.

This final idea makes it easier for organizations to recognize and internalize outside knowledge that helps them achieve their institutional goals. The buzzwords of the moment include Industry 4.0, knowledge coproduction, entrepreneurial learning, innovative suppliers, and knowledge concealment. In the upcoming years, research will be concentrated on these subjects.

If an organization values knowledge management and sharing the same with employees, it will further be benefitted by the following.

- Faster information search to find fix the problem or design the innovative methodologies to fix problems.
- Saving of time in training employees
- Lowering of operational expenses
- Enhanced satisfaction of customers

7.3.2 To Observe the Knowledge Sharing and Prospect of Industry 4.0

In every area, knowledge sharing is essential, but in the context of Industry 4.0, it becomes even more necessary. It encourages teamwork, creativity, skill growth, and adaptability—all of which are crucial for businesses to succeed in the fast-changing technology environment. In the age of Industry 4.0, embracing information exchange can result in increased competitiveness, increased operational efficiency, and better decision making. The Fourth Industrial Revolution is known as "Industry 4.0," and it is characterized by the incorporation of digital technology, the Internet of Things (IoT), artificial intelligence (AI), automation, and data analytics into numerous processes and industries. This change has the potential to fundamentally alter how firms run, resulting in more production, efficiency, and creativity.

Most HRM practices have changed as a result of communication and information technology advancements. Understanding business processes, the quick development of IT innovations, providing the computation of a sizable portion of the data necessary for carrying out judgments of HRM practices, establishing an innovative communication network for the dissemination of information within businesses, and the increased emphasis on workforce professional development and education all significantly contribute (Bader *et al.*, 2019). It is established that digital transformation significantly contributes to the creation and dissemination of in-depth knowledge concerning people resource training and development programs (Sousa & Rocha, 2019). In order to maintain operations, businesses are now required to convert their personnel to work from home mode whenever practical. The current global epidemic has a negative impact on business organizations and the market, but it has also compelled companies to look for innovative ways to conduct operations using digital technology and remote connections (Haleem *et al.*, 2022). The transition to digitized technology would increase the efficiency of certain business processes inside organizations, save costs, and boost performance, but it would also ensure the economic growth of the entire country (Kyurova, 2022).

In order to effectively benefit from this technological revolution, businesses must improve their knowledge management procedures so they can find and recognize key data sections and develop ever-complex applications for collected data. However, there are still discrepancies and ambiguities in how firms use knowledge management approaches in the digital age (Venkitachalam & Schiuma, 2022). All of the department's data resources, including networks, paperwork, procedures, and regulations, as well as previously unrecognized skills and abilities of individual employees, can be identified, managed, and shared using knowledge management (KM), an integrative, structured method (Centobelli *et al.*, 2017). Knowledge management enables businesses to create and share knowledge as well as to better analyze and address communication and cultural issues. People capital, which is primarily accountable for knowledge generation, exchange, and usage, is crucial to a company's ability to utilize and exploit knowledge (Salinas-Ávila *et al.*, 2020).

Industry 4.0 facilitates to a new production methodology that is strongly reliant on knowledge and is built on technology. Strategically targeted knowledge management may prove to be essential in Industry 4.0 for securing pertinent knowledge that would support innovation. ICT adoption fosters teamwork and boosts organizational effectiveness. The codification, storage, organized information exchange, and internal organizational connections are prioritized in this situation by the knowledge management process. Collaboration may be strengthened to encourage innovation. Its major objective is to spread knowledge through unofficial connections made at gatherings or through online communities (Labinaz & Sbisà, 2021).

The internet of things, connected items, big data analytics, smart systems, and other emerging organizational trends are progressively being included into knowledge management procedures, according to contemporary business practices and organizational trends.

7.3.3 To Analyze the Relationship of Knowledge Management with Industry 4.0

Knowledge management fueled by the advent of Industry 4.0 in the following ways:

Collaboration Across Disciplines: Industry 4.0 involves the fusion of several technologies, including IoT, AI, robots, and data science. Knowledge sharing enables specialists from several fields to work together, exchange ideas, and develop solutions that make the most of each technology's advantages.
Real-Time Data and Analytics: To improve operations and make wise decisions, Industry 4.0 relies on data collection and analysis. Sharing of knowledge makes it easier to spread best practices for data management, analytics, and interpretation, which improves outcomes and decision making.
Skill Development and Training: The adoption of Industry 4.0 technologies requires a skilled workforce. Knowledge sharing helps in training employees and upskilling them to work with advanced technologies, ensuring that they can effectively leverage these tools for maximum benefit.
Innovation and Problem Solving: Industry 4.0 encourages innovation through the integration of digital technologies. Knowledge sharing platforms can serve as spaces where professionals share new ideas, troubleshoot challenges, and collectively devise innovative solutions.
Global Networking: With Industry 4.0, businesses are more connected than ever before. Knowledge-sharing platforms enable professionals from around the world to connect, share experiences, and learn from each other's successes and failures.
Best Practice Dissemination: As different industries implement Industry 4.0 solutions, they encounter both successes and failures. Knowledge sharing enables the dissemination of best practices, helping others learn from successful implementations and avoid common pitfalls.
Adaptation to Change: Industry 4.0 is a rapidly evolving landscape. Knowledge sharing assists organizations in staying updated with the latest trends, technologies, and strategies, allowing them to adapt to changes effectively.
Entrepreneurship and Startups: Industry 4.0 creates opportunities for new businesses to emerge. Knowledge sharing can provide aspiring entrepreneurs with insights into emerging technologies, market trends, and potential niches.

7.3.4 To Understand the Benefits of Blending of Knowledge Management with Industry 4.0

The research paper titled, *Knowledge management and Industry 4.0: a critical analysis and future agenda*, Ribeiro *et al.* (2022) concluded that in order to offer guidance and aid scholars in future study, this paper describes the way KM may assist the implementation of I4.0. How might knowledge management assist with the deployment of Industry 4.0? The deployment of I4.0 technology and the associated management techniques were found to be the most important concerns currently. Three categories can be used to categorize the literature: technology, knowledge management and learning, and employee engagement. Adoption of I4.0-related technologies is a common theme, but the connection between KM and I4.0 is discussed from more than just a hard technology perspective. This suggests that research needs to be explored from a soft people viewpoint, in which novel abilities, adaptation, learning, and the recognition of critical knowledge for each process are pointed as important considerations. Also, understanding how technologies, like big data, can affect knowledge development is linked to technological research prospects. This comprises of researching digital physical systems that allow for the processing of massive amounts of data that can be used to generate new knowledge for tactical and strategic applications.

The implementation of I4.0 (Industry 4.0) poses problems to industry and even nations because it involves several different actors, including governments, businesses, universities and research institutes, and others. KM-related research possibilities are tied to this process. Future studies must also examine how corporate culture and various decision-making philosophies affect the implementation of I4.0, more particularly, the impact of KM and decision-making approaches on organizational culture.

Technologies have a substantial impact on the growth of learning at all levels (individual, team, and organizational). I4.0 technologies have a positive impact on organizational-level learning and development. The blend of I4.0 and KM show that businesses who implement I4.0 technologies, including the internet of things or visualization technology, are more likely to systemically reinforce their learning and knowledge-sharing capacities throughout the organization (Córdova & Gutiérrez, 2018).

For businesses to succeed in the age of digital transformation and advanced manufacturing, knowledge management and Industry 4.0 must be integrated. The Fourth Industrial Revolution, often known as Industry 4.0, improves and automates production processes through the use of technologies like the Internet of Things (IoT), artificial intelligence (AI), big data, and automation. Knowledge management systems are capable of collecting, storing, and analyzing data from a variety of sources, including IoT sensors and production machinery (Kankanhalli *et al.*, 2019). Making judgments about manufacturing procedures, maintenance schedules, and resource allocation can be done using this data. It is critical to capture experienced workers' knowledge and experience as they retire or depart the company. In order to prevent this tacit knowledge from being lost throughout the transition to Industry 4.0, knowledge management systems can assist, store, and share it. Having a strong knowledge management system in place can enable staff to access pertinent information, best practices, and previous solutions promptly when problems arise in the manufacturing process, speeding up problem resolution (Venkat & Banerjee, 2021).

Technologies related to Industry 4.0 are constantly changing. By giving users access to current resources, online training, and collaborative learning environments, knowledge management can promote continuing training and growth. Cross-functional teams and departmental cooperation are frequently used in Industry 4.0. Teams may collaborate more easily and share information more easily with the help of knowledge management technologies. Knowledge management can aid in ensuring consistent product quality in automated manufacturing processes by documenting and disseminating best practices and quality standards. Workflows and processes must frequently undergo considerable adjustments as a result of the deployment of Industry 4.0 technologies. By offering tools and documentation to support staff members during changes, knowledge management can help with change management initiatives (Ik & Azeez, 2020).

7.4 Conclusion

The current "Industry 4.0" paradigm is transforming how goods are made, how businesses create value, and the way they work with vendors and consumers. The development of specialized goods and services, along with increased operational flexibility, efficiency, and productivity are all made possible by the new technology available to manufacturing organizations. A competitive advantage is provided by the quality and utility of knowledge management systems and technologies, which enhance performance. Knowledge management initiatives that are successful must strike a balance between administrative leadership, process management, and people management while being supported by IoT (Baporikar, 2014).

In this new technical environment, new digital competencies and abilities (such as data management) are strategically significant because they can ensure that new knowledge-manufacturing enterprises gain a significant competitive advantage. These new discoveries depend not only on the application of Industry 4.0 technology but also on contacts with suppliers and consumers, as well as on the improvement of personnel competencies (Frank *et al.*, 2019). The chapter covers empirical studies connected with the implementation of Industry 4.0 with the goal of better understanding these dynamics by emphasizing the importance of knowledge management.

Organizations can be empowered to better use their collective knowledge, make data-driven choices, increase productivity, and maintain competitiveness in a growing digital and networked corporate environment by blending management of knowledge with Industry 4.0 technologies due to enhanced decision making, efficient and optimized process, accelerating innovation, efficiency in knowledge sharing, and continuous learning through training.

The blending of knowledge management and Industry 4.0 offers a potential recipe for success in the quickly changing corporate environment of today. This blending of established knowledge management methods with cutting-edge technical developments has the potential to spur innovation, boost competitiveness, and lift businesses to new levels of productivity and efficiency. IoT, AI, and data analytics are examples of Industry 4.0 technologies that present unheard-of capabilities for capturing, storing, and utilizing knowledge within an organization. Businesses may streamline their operations, make educated decisions, and react quickly to shifting market dynamics by leveraging the power of real-time data and automation. Organizations may promote a culture of ongoing learning and knowledge sharing thanks to this synergy.

References

Bader, L., Mukhalalati, B., Awaisu, A., Tofade, T., Bates, I., Using a global framework for health workforce development: National case studies on continuing professional development in pharmacy. *MedEdPublish*, 8, 44, 2019.

Baporikar, N., Knowledge management initiatives in Indian public sector. *Building a Competitive Public Sector with Knowledge Management Strategy*, pp. 53–89, 2014.

Centobelli, P., Cerchione, R., Esposito, E., Knowledge management in startups: Systematic literature review and future research agenda. *Sustainability*, 9, 3, 361, 2017.

Córdova, F.M. and Gutiérrez, F.A., Knowledge management system in service companies. *Procedia Comput. Sci.*, 139, 392–400, 2018.

Frank, A.G., Dalenogare, L.S., Ayala, N.F., Industry 4.0 technologies: Implementation patterns in manufacturing companies. *Int. J. Prod. Econ.*, 210, 15–26, 2019.

Haleem, A., Javaid, M., Qadri, M.A., Suman, R., Understanding the role of digital technologies in education: A review. *Sustainable Oper. Comput.*, 3, 275–285, 2022.

Ik, M. and Azeez, A.A., Organisational green behavioural change: The role of change management. *Int. J. Entrep. Knowl.*, 8, 1, 34–48, 2020.

Kankanhalli, A., Charalabidis, Y., Mellouli, S., IoT and AI for smart government: A research agenda. *Gov. Inf. Q.*, 36, 2, 304–309, 2019.

Kyurova, A., The digital transformation and its impact on small and medium-sized enterprises. *Entrepreneurship*, 10, 1, 7–18, 2022.

Labinaz, P. and Sbisà, M., The problem of knowledge dissemination in social network discussions. *J. Pragmat.*, 175, 67–80, 2021.

Ribeiro, V.B., Nakano, D., Muniz Jr., J., Oliveira, R.B., Knowledge management and industry 4.0: A critical analysis and future agenda. *Gest. Prod.*, 29, 2022.

Salinas-Ávila, J., Abreu-Ledón, R., Tamayo-Arias, J., Intellectual capital and knowledge generation: An empirical study from Colombian public universities. *J. Intellect. Cap.*, 21, 6, 1053–1084, 2020.

Sousa, M.J. and Rocha, Á., Digital learning: Developing skills for digital transformation of organizations. *Future Gener. Comput. Syst.*, 91, 327–334, 2019.

Venkat, R. and Banerjee, J., Educational technology at pivotal crossroads. *The Palgrave Handbook of Workplace Innovation*, pp. 617–639, 2021.

Venkitachalam, K. and Schiuma, G., Editorial: Strategic knowledge management (SKM) in the digital age – insights and possible research directions. *J. Strategy Manag.*, 15, 2, 169–174, 2022.

8

Modern Approaches and Implications Toward Industry 4.0

Bishnu Kant Shukla[1]*, Amit Tripathi[1], Gaurav Bharti[1], Bhupender Parashar[2], Nitin Bhardwaj[3], Aakash Gupta[4] and Shivam Verma[5]

[1]*Department of Civil Engineering, JSS Academy of Technical Education, Noida, India*
[2]*Department of Mathematics, JSS Academy of Technical Education, Noida, India*
[3]*Department of Mathematics and Statistics, CCS Haryana Agricultural University, Hisar, India*
[4]*CSIR—Central Road Research Institute, New Delhi, India*
[5]*New Jersey Institute of Technology, Newark, New Jersey, USA*

Abstract

Industry 4.0 heralds a watershed moment in production, with the combination of modern technologies and data-driven methodologies ushering in smart, self-regulating industrial ecosystems. cyber-physical systems (CPS), the Industrial Internet of Things (IIoT), sophisticated analytics, machine learning (ML), robotics, and additive manufacturing are examples of advances in this age. These technologies are critical for tackling issues like increasing industrial efficiency, enabling mass customization, and improving sustainable practices. Their use in industrial contexts highlights the implications for workforce evolution, cybersecurity, and return on investment. The collaboration and interdependence of various sectors becomes indispensable in which involvement of leading industry becomes extensively important as such collaborations pave way for implementation of

**Corresponding author*: bishnukantshukla@gmail.com
Bishnu Kant Shukla: ORCID: https://orcid.org/0000-0002-1477-052X
Amit Tripathi: ORCID: https://orcid.org/0000-0002-7264-8282
Gaurav Bharti: ORCID: https://orcid.org/0000-0002-4895-3543
Bhupender Parashar: ORCID: https://orcid.org/0000-0002-1131-369X
Nitin Bhardwaj: ORCID: https://orcid.org/0000-0002-0395-4745
Aakash Gupta: ORCID: https://orcid.org/0000-0002-5087-7308
Shivam Verma: ORCID: https://orcid.org/0000-0002-1520-8192

Rajendra Kumar, Vishal Jain, Venus C. Ibarra, Corrienna Abdul Talib and Vinay Kukreja (eds.) Knowledge Management and Industry Revolution 4.0, (197–238) © 2024 Scrivener Publishing LLC

methodologies proposed in Industry 4.0 to provide useful strategies and research in order to embrace the ideas proposed through these methodologies. In the global economy, stated strategies are going to help the industries to reserve and enhance their competitive benefits. Implementation of these unique concepts can advance their functioning processes. The implementation of Industry 4.0 technology depends upon the formation of framework. In present dynamic technological era, industries and organizations need to emphasize on continuous enhancement and adaptation. Overall, this study provides various aspects and views on the requirement of advance developments and dynamic changes in the industrial sector. It is anticipated that future developments will bring forth new innovations in the field of contemporary manufacturing in addition to increasing productivity and process efficiency in industry.

***Keywords*:** Industry 4.0, cyber-physical systems, industrial Internet of Things, advanced analytics, machine learning, robotics, additive manufacturing

8.1 Introduction

The inherent dynamism of the manufacturing sector has led to continuous advancement. This industry has historically undergone several revolutionary transitions, each of which was characterized by cutting-edge advancements. The most recent of these transformative stages is known as "Industry 4.0," which best captures the convergence of traditional and digital manufacturing techniques. The goal of this union is to reimagine industrial processes and make them more intelligent, effective, and interconnected.

8.1.1 Background of Industry 4.0

Early in the decade of the 2010s, the phrase "Industry 4.0" was developed to denote the beginning of the "Fourth Industrial Revolution." This revolution is a total makeover with interconnected systems at its core; it is not only a continuation of the Third, which was characterized by digitalization [1]. Steam and water fueled the First Industrial Revolution, which introduced mechanized industry. The Second Revolution, which included electricity and allowed for mass production, succeeded this. The Third Revolution, a digital one, was marked by the development of electronics and IT, which automated industry. However, Industry 4.0 is anticipated to be a game-changer since it uses IoT, artificial intelligence (AI), and cyber-physical systems to make factories "smart" [2]. Figure 8.1 provides anatomical representation of this progression.

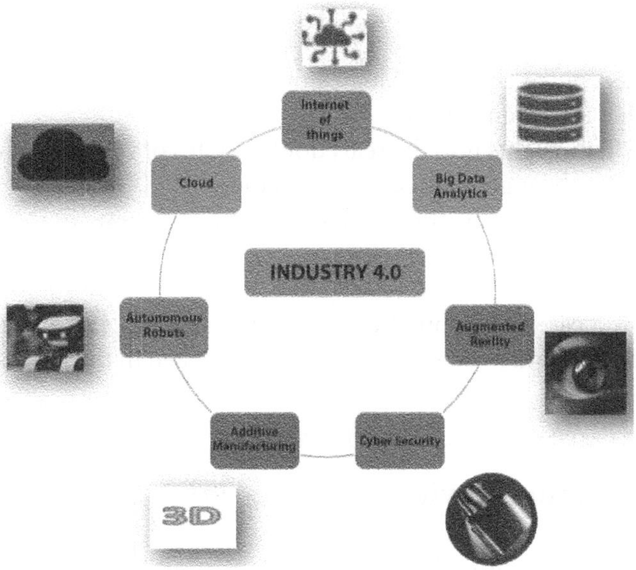

Figure 8.1 Core elements of Industry 4.0.

8.1.2 Significance of Modern Approaches

Industries stand to benefit significantly from Industry 4.0's methodology. The cyber-actual system (CPS), which paves the way for complete automation by enabling digital systems to communicate with the actual environment, is at the center of these technologies [3]. With the Industrial Internet of Things (IIoT), connection is elevated. IIoT enables real-time decision making and process optimization through the integration of devices throughout the production chain [4]. This new era of predictive maintenance and operation optimization, which has proved to boost production efficiency by up to 20% among early adopters [5], is brought about by machine learning (ML) and advanced analytics, which bring insights from enormous volumes of data. With AI's assistance, robotics, which was previously only capable of doing repetitive tasks, can now perform more complicated tasks with more accuracy and productivity [6].

8.1.3 Objective of the Study

This study looks deeply into Industry 4.0's complexities, its motivating factors, and its prospective effects. It specifically seeks to:

- Examine the revolutionary potential of the key technologies underlying Industry 4.0.
- Recognize the technological and socioeconomic problems that this change poses.
- Offer insights into the real adoption rates of various technologies through a range of case studies.
- Establish a transition plan for industries moving to this new paradigm.

Through a careful examination, this study seeks to serve as a guide for companies, decision makers, and scholars interested in the field of Industry 4.0.

8.2 Literature Review

8.2.1 Evolution of Industry 4.0

The Fourth Industrial Revolution, or Industry 4.0, refers to the contemporary blending of conventional industrial methods and cutting-edge technological developments. It is necessary to trace the historical progression of industrial revolutions in order to comprehend their core. The First Industrial Revolution (1765–1765) was centered on mechanization. In numerous industries, water and steam power replaced physical effort. Industrial metropolitan hubs replaced rural communities after this shift [7]. The development of electricity and assembly lines occurred during the Second Industrial Revolution (1871). The telegraph, internal combustion engine, and telephone were important innovations that came from this process. During this stage, productivity increased, and the idea of mass production was introduced [8]. The advent of digital technology in 1969 ushered in the Third Industrial Revolution. Its main components were automated production, IT, and electronics. Nearly every business has been impacted by the emergence of computers and the internet [9].

The Fourth Industrial Revolution, or Industry 4.0, combines cloud computing, cognitive computing, cyber-physical systems, and the Internet of Things (IoT). With a combination of these technologies, the border separating the physical and digital worlds has been broken, and this change is exponential rather than linear [10]. An illustrative overview of this progression can be found in Figure 8.2 and Table 8.1.

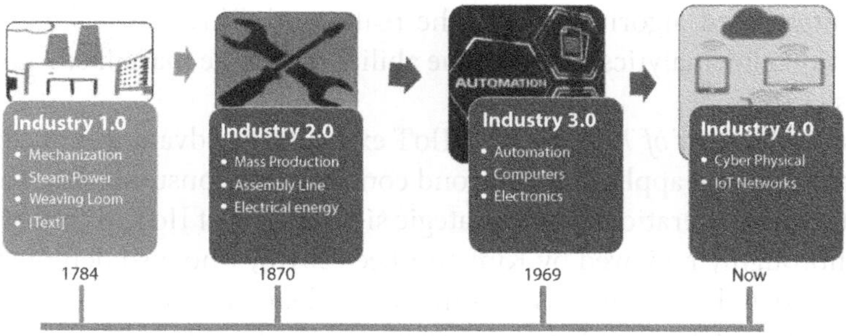

Figure 8.2 Timeline and progression of the industrial revolutions.

Table 8.1 Evolutionary milestones of Industry 4.0.

Revolution	Defining technology	Impacts and key innovations	Ref.
First	Mechanization	Steam engine, weaving loom	[7]
Second	Electrification	Telephone, assembly lines	[8]
Third	Digitalization	Internet, computers	[9]
Fourth	Interconnectivity	IoT, AI, Cloud computing	[10]

Leading nations including Germany (where the phrase originated), the U.S., Japan, and China are driving Industry 4.0's digital breakthroughs by making substantial expenditures in research and applications [11]. According to a Roland Berger estimate, Germany will have 30% of Industry 4.0 technology integrated by 2020, setting a standard for other countries [12].

8.2.2 Previous Studies on Modern Approaches

Exploring the enormous field of Industry 4.0, a plethora of techniques emerge, each having a substantial impact on the state of the industrial world today. The amount of scholarly research on this subject has multiplied over the last 10 years, indicating the importance and growing popularity of Industry 4.0.

Cyber-Physical Systems (CPS): In a 2016 research, Foster *et al.* studied the complexities of CPS, focusing on how these systems connect computer-based algorithms with the real world. Through real-time data collection and analytics, CPS has the ability to change manufacturing processes [13].

Industrial Internet of Things (IIoT): IIoT expands the advantages of connection to industrial applications beyond conventional consumer devices. The architectural, operational, and strategic significance of IIoT in Industry 4.0 was thoroughly reviewed by Kim and Lee (2018), who also demonstrated its capacity to bring new business models and streamline processes [14].

Advanced Analytics and Machine Learning (ML): In industrial contexts, the interaction between analytics and ML is revolutionary. The significance of predictive analytics was highlighted by Gupta *et al.* (2019), particularly in industries like the automobile and electronics. Manufacturing chains that are smarter now have predictively optimized and adjusted processes as a result of ML integration [15].

Robotics: Robotics, a key component of Industry 4.0, has been the focus of in-depth study. Notably, a research by Martinez *et al.* (2020) examined how AI and robotics interacted. They provided case studies of collaborative robots (cobots) enhancing productivity by collaborating with people [16].

Additive Manufacturing: Additive manufacturing, also referred to as 3D printing, is revolutionizing the manufacturing process. Rapid prototyping, adaptations, and decreased waste were highlighted in a thorough analysis

Table 8.2 Comparison of studies on modern approaches.

Methodology	Key findings	Ref.
Cyber-physical systems	Bridging digital algorithms with physical operations enhances efficiency	[13]
IIoT	Streamlining operations and introducing new business models	[14]
Advanced analytics and ML	Predictive optimization of manufacturing processes	[15]
Robotics	Integration of AI with robotics enhances collaboration with humans	[16]
Additive manufacturing	Rapid prototyping and customization are driving forces behind 3D printing in the industrial sector	[17]

by Yang and Zhang (2017) that focused on the implications for Industry 4.0 [17].

Table 8.2 provides an overview of pivotal studies related to Industry 4.0's methodologies:

8.2.3 Gaps in Current Literature

While there has been significant progress in the research landscape of Industry 4.0, some areas remain less explored. Here are some of the prominent gaps identified:

Holistic Approach: A lot of studies concentrate on particular approaches. The aggregate influence of these technologies when incorporated into a single industrial system, however, is not adequately covered in the literature [18].
Cybersecurity: As the world becomes more digital, there is a higher risk of cyberattacks. While numerous studies have focused on the advantages of connectivity, few examine possible security concerns and countermeasures in the context of Industry 4.0 [19].
Socioeconomic Impacts: While many technology studies focus on technical issues, there is a dearth of in-depth analysis on how Industry 4.0 will impact the labor force, employment markets, and overall economies [20].
Case Studies: There are few real-world examples of organizations making a complete switch to Industry 4.0 practices. Such research could provide insightful information about the difficulties, tactics, and results of applying these technologies [21].
Environmental Considerations: Surprisingly, despite the rapid advancement of technology, few studies have examined how implementing Industry 4.0 may affect the environment. The sustainable integration of these technologies, which balances productivity and environmental effect, is urgently needed [22].
Geographical Distribution: Developed nations are the focus of the majority of studies. Information on the implementation difficulties, advantages, and ways that developing nations are overcoming the technical gap is scarce [23].
Interdisciplinary Approach: Industry 4.0 includes areas like psychology, sociology, and even urban planning in addition to just integrating technology. Integration of these multidisciplinary factors in research is uncommon but extremely important [24].
Supply Chain Dynamics: Understanding the complexities of supply chain management within the framework of Industry 4.0 is essential in the age of

Table 8.3 Research areas in Industry 4.0 that demand attention.

Identified gap	Implications	Suggested solution/ potential impact	Ref.
Scalability issues	As businesses grow, technology might not cope up with the increasing demands	Modular technology architectures	[15]
Data security concerns	With increased interconnectivity, data breaches become more frequent	Advanced cybersecurity measures	[16]
High initial costs	SMEs find it challenging to integrate Industry 4.0 due to the significant initial investment required	Government subsidies and phased implementations	[17]
Skills and training gap	Existing workforce might not be familiar with the new technologies	Regular training and workshops	[18]
Environmental considerations	Balancing productivity with environmental conservation	Sustainable industrial growth	[22]
Geographical distribution	Understanding challenges in developing countries	Inclusive global industrial growth	[23]
Interdisciplinary approach	Integrating diverse fields for a comprehensive view of Industry 4.0	Holistic industrial solutions	[24]
Supply chain dynamics	Investigating the future of global supply chain ecosystems with Industry 4.0 technologies	Streamlined global operations	[25]

globalization. The dynamics of the supply chain and how the entire global supply chain ecosystem will change as a result of these new technologies have received less attention in studies [25].

Table 8.3 elucidates the prominent gaps in current literature:

Industry 4.0 is a constantly changing field, with new knowledge being added with every research study, case study, and practical application. An overview of the trip, the advancements, and the areas still in need of improvement is provided by the thorough literature analysis that is offered here. These gaps present chances for academics and industry experts to dig deep and contribute, ensuring that the Industry 4.0 revolution is comprehensive, inclusive, and advantageous for all as industries throughout the world continue their march toward an interconnected and intelligent future.

8.3 Modern Methodologies Supporting Industry 4.0

8.3.1 Cyber-Physical Systems (CPS)

8.3.1.1 Definition and Characteristics

Computer-based algorithms are combined with physical processes to form cyber-physical systems (CPS). The physical processes are monitored and controlled by embedded computers and networks, typically with feedback loops where the physical processes influence computations and vice versa [26]. A representation of a conventional cyber-physical system is presented in Figure 8.3.

Core characteristics of CPS include:

1. *Integration of Cyber and Physical Processes*: Contrary to conventional systems, CPS integrates cyber and physical processes.
2. *Real-Time Sensing and Feedback*: CPS constantly detects alterations in the physical environment and reacts in the moment.
3. *Network-Centric Operation*: They mostly rely on networked operation, which involves complex communication protocols to get in touch with other systems and processes [27].
4. *Resilience, Reliability, and Robustness*: Ensure that the system functions dependably in a variety of circumstances, such as

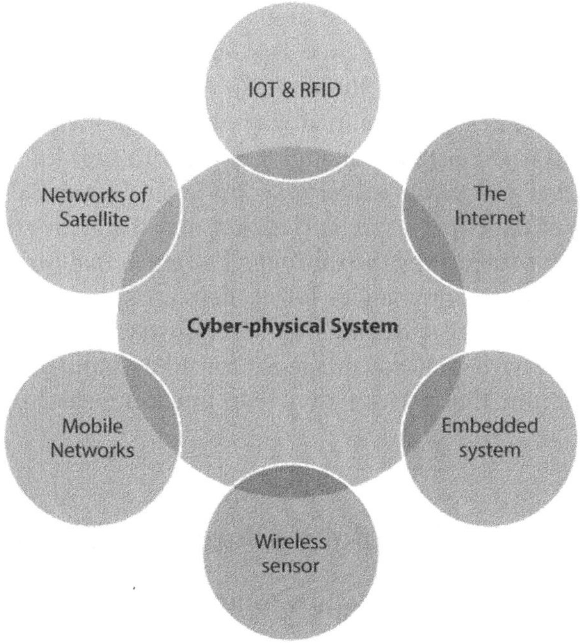

Figure 8.3 Schematic representation of a cyber-physical system integration.

potential cyberattacks or component failures, through resilience, reliability, and robustness.

5. *Independence*: Thanks to advances in AI, many CPSs can make decisions on their own, based on information and pre-programmed algorithms [28].

8.3.1.2 Application in Industry

CPS is transformative in the context of Industry 4.0. In industrial environments, they fill the gap between virtual and physical entities. Figure 8.4 offers an extensive overview of the multiple CPS applications in Industry 4.0.

Smart Manufacturing: CPS offers real-time production line monitoring, guaranteeing that items are manufactured in accordance with specifications and instantly modifying parameters for optimization [29].
Supply Chain and Logistics: They are able to adapt logistics in real time to changes in the environment or delays. For perishable items or delicate equipment, this is especially important [30].

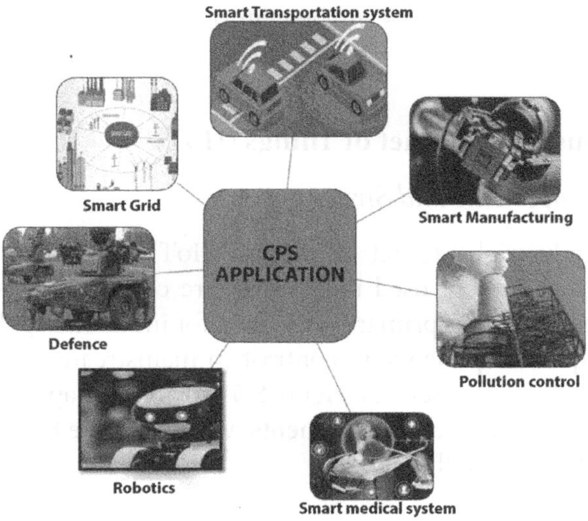

Figure 8.4 Commercial and industrial applications of CPS.

Safety and Compliance: CPS makes sure that conditions stay within predetermined parameters in sectors like pharmaceuticals or food processing, warning people if there is a potential breach [31].

Asset Management and Maintenance: Predicting when equipment will break down or need maintenance by ongoing operation monitoring, which reduces costs and downtimes [32]. Table 8.4 presents an exhaustive

Table 8.4 Applications and benefits of cyber-physical systems in various industrial sectors.

Sector	Application area	Benefits	Ref.
Manufacturing	Real-time monitoring of production lines	Optimization of production parameters	[29]
Supply chain and logistics	Dynamic logistics adjustment	Reduced delays, cost-effective operations	[30]
Pharmaceuticals and food	Safety and compliance monitoring	Ensuring product safety and compliance	[31]
General industry	Predictive maintenance	Reduced downtimes, increased lifespan	[32]

evaluation of the applications and benefits of CPS across numerous sectors of industry.

8.3.2 Industrial Internet of Things (IIoT)

8.3.2.1 Components and Structure

The term "Industrial Internet of Things" (IIoT) describes how systems, gadgets, and equipment used in industry are connected to one another over the internet. IIoT is primarily designed for industrial applications and features unique components, in contrast to mainstream IoT, which supports consumer-centric devices. Figure 8.5 provides a graphical illustration of the IIoT architecture and its elements, whereas Table 8.5 presents roles of these elements with illustrations.

1. *Sensors and Actuators:* The main data sources in an IIoT system are sensors and actuators, which record different characteristics like temperature, pressure, speed, and moisture. Actuators carry out operations based on the processed data, such as regulating the speed of a motor [33].
2. *Edge Devices:* Devices near the data source's edge provide preliminary data processing to cut down on the amount of data delivered to centralized systems. This makes it possible for essential applications to respond more quickly [34].

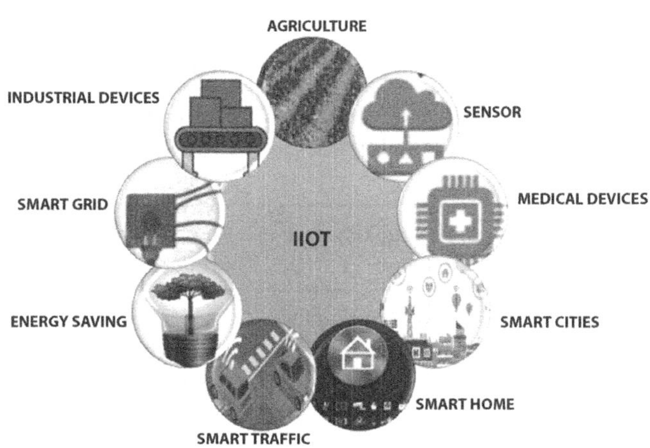

Figure 8.5 IIoT system architecture and components.

Table 8.5 Primary components of industrial Internet of Things and their specific roles.

Component	Role	Example	Ref
Sensors and actuators	Data collection and task execution	Temperature sensors, servo motors	[33]
Edge devices	Preliminary data processing	Industrial gateways	[34]
Communication networks	Data transmission	5G, Zigbee	[35]
Data storage centers	Store and process large volumes of data	Cloud platforms, on-premise servers	[36]
Software platforms	Analyze data, automate tasks, monitor processes	SCADA systems, IIoT platforms	[37]
User interfaces	Provide interaction platforms for operators	Web dashboards, mobile apps	[38]

3. *Communication Networks:* The IIoT's skeleton, which enables data exchange between devices. They can be wireless (like LoRa, Zigbee, or 5G) or wired (like Ethernet) [35].
4. *Data Storage and Processing Centers:* These might be on-site servers or cloud-based platforms that offer storage and powerful computing capabilities for sophisticated data analysis.
5. *Applications and Software Platforms*: Software programs created especially for IIoT use cases including quality assurance, real-time monitoring, and predictive maintenance [36].
6. *User Interfaces:* Dashboard interfaces that are frequently accessible on a variety of devices, including as PCs, tablets, and smartphones, and allow operators to monitor and manage IIoT activities.

8.3.2.2 Role in Smart Manufacturing

The IIoT is a key element of smart manufacturing, converting conventional plants into intelligent factories. The effects include:

- *Real-Time Monitoring*: With sensors positioned all along the manufacturing line, producers are able to keep an eye on each step in real-time to ensure optimum performance and quality control [39].
- *Predictive Maintenance:* IIoT systems can forecast when a machine is likely to break by continuously monitoring the health of the equipment. This enables maintenance to be carried out precisely in time to save expensive downtimes [40].
- *Energy Efficiency:* Smart systems regulate how much energy is used by appliances, lighting, HVAC systems, and more, minimizing energy waste and energy costs [41].
- *Supply Chain Optimization:* The IIoT enables a more effective and responsive supply chain by enabling real-time tracking of resources, work-in-progress, and finished commodities [42].
- *Safety and Compliance:* Automated monitoring makes certain that the production process complies with regulatory requirements and safety standards [43].

8.3.3 Advanced Analytics

8.3.3.1 Importance in Data Processing

Advanced analytics plays a transformative role in Industry 4.0 by allowing organizations to draw insights from massive datasets produced by interconnected devices, sensors, and systems (Table 8.6).

1. *Data-Driven Decision Making*: Advanced analytics equip decision makers with empirical data to help them make better decisions, streamline workflows, and foresee emerging trends [44].
2. *Operational Efficiency:* Companies can detect equipment failures using predictive analytics, cutting downtimes and increasing production efficiency [45].
3. *Enhancement of Product Quality:* By using real-time data analysis, producers can find production process irregularities and guarantee consistent product quality [46].
4. *Customer Insights:* Businesses can modify their products and services to fit shifting consumer expectations and preferences by analyzing customer data [47].

Table 8.6 The role of advanced analytics in enhancing Industry 4.0 outcomes.

Application area	Impact of advanced analytics	Key benefits	Ref.
Decision making	Empirical data-driven strategies	Enhanced decision accuracy, strategic foresight	[44]
Operations	Predictive analysis of machinery and processes	Reduced downtimes, cost savings	[45]
Product quality	Real-time analysis for anomaly detection	Consistent quality, reduced rejections	[46]
Customer insights	Understanding customer behavior and preferences	Product personalization, improved customer satisfaction	[47]
Supply chain	Demand forecasting, inventory management	Optimized inventory levels, efficient logistics	[48]

5. *Supply Chain Optimization:* By anticipating demand, controlling inventory, and improving logistics, advanced analytics may streamline supply chains [48].

8.3.3.2 Case Studies

Case Study 1: Predictive Maintenance in the Automotive Industry: A top automaker integrated advanced analytics into their manufacturing process. They were able to predict machinery breakdowns up to 2 weeks in advance by the real-time analysis of sensor data, which led to a 20% decrease in downtime and a considerable decrease in maintenance expenditures [49].
Case Study 2: Quality Control in the Electronics Industry: To analyze photographs of the goods being assembled on a production line, an electronics company used machine learning algorithms. This enhanced product quality and decreased the need for manual inspections by enabling the automatic detection and correction of flaws [50].
Case Study 3: Food and Beverage Industry Supply Chain Management: Advanced analytics were used by a beverage corporation to estimate product demand based on seasonality, market trends, and consumer

preferences. As a result, wholesalers received their orders on time and wastage was minimized [51].

8.3.4 Machine Learning (ML)

8.3.4.1 Algorithms and Application

A subset of artificial intelligence (AI), machine learning (ML) focuses on creating algorithms that let computers carry out tasks without being explicitly told to. ML is proving to be a crucial tool in the context of Industry 4.0, simplifying operations and offering predictive insights [52].

Algorithms:
Supervised Learning: Algorithms are educated on labeled data through supervised learning. A model can begin making predictions or choices without human input once it has been trained. Neural networks, support vector machines, and linear regression are examples of common algorithms [53].
Unsupervised Learning: These methods can be used to find hidden patterns in unlabeled data. Algorithms for grouping and associating data, like k-means and Apriori, are examples [54].
Reinforcement Learning: In this case, algorithms learn by acting and receiving praise or criticism. They are very helpful for robotics applications where the machine needs to learn the best action sequences [55].
Deep Learning: Deep learning, a subtype of ML, uses neural networks with three or more layers. These neural networks make an effort to mimic how the human brain functions, enabling it to "learn" from vast volumes of data. Prime examples include recurrent neural networks (RNN) and convolutional neural networks (CNN) [56].

Applications in Industry 4.0:

1. *Predictive Maintenance:* By examining trends and abnormalities in operational data, machine learning (ML) may forecast equipment breakdowns, reducing downtime [57].
2. *Quality Control:* By examining data from sensors and cameras on the production line, machine learning (ML) models may predict and identify manufacturing errors in real-time [58].

3. *Supply Chain Optimization:* By examining sales data, external factors like market trends, and internal aspects like production rates, ML can estimate demand and optimize inventory levels [59].
4. *Energy Consumption:* By examining machine operational hours and comparing with energy usage patterns, ML can reduce energy use in manufacturing [60].
5. *Monitoring of Safety and Compliance:* ML algorithms can help with regulatory compliance and monitor and guarantee that safety procedures are followed by assessing data from many checkpoints [61].

8.3.4.2 Role in Predictive Maintenance

Predictive maintenance is one of the most notable applications of ML in Industry 4.0. Because they do not account for the equipment's current condition, traditional maintenance techniques, like planned maintenance, usually do not work as intended. By allowing for real-time monitoring and prediction, ML closes this gap.

- *Data Collection:* Sensors on equipment gather information on a range of characteristics, including pressure, vibration, and temperature. For ML algorithms, these data are used as the input [62].
- *Anomaly Detection:* ML algorithms can spot irregularities and foretell when equipment is likely to break down by comprehending the typical operational benchmarks of machinery [63].
- *Optimal Maintenance Scheduling:* Machines can be serviced only when necessary, saving money and decreasing downtime, as opposed to performing routine, planned maintenance inspections [64].
- *Extending the Lifespan of Machinery:* The lifespan of machinery can be increased by addressing problems early on [65].
- *Resource Allocation:* Businesses may allocate resources more effectively thanks to predictive insights, making sure that repair people and replacement parts are always on hand when and where they are required [66].

8.3.5 Robotics

8.3.5.1 Current Innovations

Robotics have long been used in the manufacturing industry, but with the introduction of Industry 4.0, their features, capabilities, and flexibility are seeing a rebirth. Modern robotics places a strong emphasis on flexibility, collaboration, and intelligence in contrast to conventional robotics systems, which are frequently big, expensive, and strictly programmed for specific tasks. Cobots, or collaborative robots, are made to operate alongside people without any kind of physical separation. Cobots can securely operate alongside people in a shared office because of their sophisticated sensors, cameras, and AI-driven algorithms [67]. Cobots can also alter their movements and activities in real-time to avoid mishaps. A number of novel applications where people and robots can strengthen one another's weaknesses are made possible by this safety feature.

The creation of self-learning robots is another innovation in robotics. These robots improve their behavior over time without explicit reprogramming by utilizing the power of machine learning to learn from their experiences. In contrast to earlier techniques, where each movement of a robot had to be painstakingly programmed, they learn new duties by studying human operators or by trial and error [68]. A developing business model called robotics-as-a-service (RaaS) enables manufacturers to lease robotic services rather than buy robots outright. This concept is flexible and ensures that small and medium-sized businesses can use the most recent robotic technologies without having to make the significant upfront investments often required for robotic deployments [69].

8.3.5.2 Robotics in Modern Production Lines

Production lines of today no longer involve static assembly procedures or monotonous activities. As dynamic ecosystems, they now place a premium on flexibility and reactivity. Robotics is a crucial component of this transformational stage. Productivity has increased dramatically as a result of the addition of robots to production lines. Robots do not get tired as people do; thus, their production is always of a high caliber. Their unmatched accuracy when handling, assembling, and inspecting parts results in fewer defects and better overall product quality [70].

Additionally, because robots can be quickly reconfigured to undertake multiple duties, production lines may quickly swap between different goods. This adaptability is essential for sectors that have switched from mass manufacturing a single product variety to producing customized items in smaller batches [71]. Robot integration is not without difficulties, though. When they are introduced, workflows may need to be revised. Employees may also need training to coexist with these robots, and the robots may need to undergo recurring updates to stay current with changing industrial processes [72].

Robots are now the mainstay of modern production lines, handling anything from complex assembly duties to automated guided vehicles (AGVs) carrying products across the factory floor. As factories advance toward total digitization and automation under the banner of Industry 4.0, their significance will only grow.

8.3.6 Additive Manufacturing

8.3.6.1 Types and Materials

Often referred to as 3D printing, additive manufacturing (AM) is a revolutionary process that builds products layer by layer from digital models. Unlike typical subtractive manufacturing techniques, which entail removing material from a solid block, additive manufacturing (AM) only uses the material required for the part, eliminating waste and enabling complex designs that are impractical with previous techniques. There are several different kinds of additive manufacturing techniques that have been created, each serving particular requirements and materials:

- *Fused Deposition Modeling (FDM):* Possibly the most well-known type of 3D printing, FDM entails heating and extruding thermoplastic materials layer by layer to create a whole object.
- *Selective Laser Sintering (SLS) and Selective Laser Melting (SLM):* These processes, known as selective laser sintering (SLS) and selective laser melting (SLM), use a high-power laser to combine tiny metal, ceramic, or plastic particles into a mass with the desired three-dimensional shape [74].
- *Stereolithography (SLA):* Using ultraviolet light to solidify layers of liquid resin, stereolithography (SLA) is especially well known for its excellent resolution and accuracy [75].
- *Digital Light Processing (DLP):* Similar to SLA, but employing a more conventional light source, frequently in the form of a projector, to cure photopolymer resins as opposed to UV lasers [76].

- *Material Jetting:* Multi-material printing and outstanding colour capabilities are made possible by material jetting, which involves depositing material droplets that are then hardened by UV light [77].

AM now offers a far wider variety of materials. While early 3D printing mostly utilized particular types of plastic, modern AM can make use of a wide range of materials, including ceramics, glass, and even biomaterials for usage in the medical field [78].

8.3.6.2 Benefits in Customization and Production

The use of AM in the manufacturing industry represents a fundamental transition rather than merely a technological one. Its advantages go beyond simple object construction:

1. *Customization*: Customization is the lifeblood of AM. AM enables product personalization at scale without the corresponding increase in costs of traditional manufacturing, whether it be for the production of customized consumer goods, personalized medical implants, or bespoke automobile parts [79].
2. *Complex Geometries:* Internal structures like lattices, in particular, are difficult to manufacture using traditional methods. Such designs can be easily created with AM, which can result in items that are both light and robust [80].
3. *Reduced Waste:* Compared to subtractive methods, AM significantly reduces waste because it only uses the material required for the part, which results in cost savings and more environmentally friendly production [81].
4. *Supply Chain Simplification:* By eliminating stages like as molding and tooling and enabling on-demand production, additive manufacturing (AM) may localize and streamline supply chains, increasing their adaptability and resilience [82].

The integration of additive manufacturing (AM) into production lines will revolutionize workflows, shorten lead times, and democratize design and manufacture, enabling even small enterprises to compete on a global scale as industries continue to recognize AM's promise.

8.4 Implications of Adopting Industry 4.0 Practices

Industry 4.0 represents more than just an industrial upgrade; it is a thorough revolution with consequences for many different areas of business and operations. Although the change promises to improve production capacities and introduce novel business models, it also presents issues that the industry must deal with.

8.4.1 Workforce Adaptation

The workforce in manufacturing is at the forefront of this change. The nature of work will inevitably alter as factories become more automated and smart technologies are integrated.

8.4.1.1 Training and Skill Enhancement

The digital revolution in Industry 4.0 highlights the urgent need for labor upskilling. Automated systems are replacing or enhancing traditional professions that relied on physical labor. However, it does not always result in a decrease in employment. However, the nature of employment positions is changing. Workers today need to be proficient in digital technologies, know how to work with automated systems, and understand how to comprehend data analytics [83]. To ensure that the workforce is capable of making the shift seamlessly, programs, like Germany's "Industrie 4.0," concentrate a lot of emphasis on vocational training [84] as illustrated in Table 8.7.

Table 8.7 Skill transformation in Industry 4.0.

Traditional skills	Industry 4.0 skills	Implication for training	Ref.
Manual machine operation	Human–machine collaboration	Enhance digital literacy	[83]
Basic quality control	Advanced analytics interpretation	Focus on data-driven decisions	[85]
Routine maintenance	Predictive maintenance	Training in IoT and data interpretation	[86]

8.4.1.2 Job Roles and Evolution

Instead of replacing many roles, the integration of smart systems and AI will enhance them. For instance, a machine operator may move into a position where they manage multiple machines, analyze output data, and decide how to optimize [87]. New positions will also become essential for operations, including data scientists, robotic process engineers, and IoT architects. Companies must plan how to strike a balance between retaining their seasoned personnel through retraining and bringing on fresh talent with experience in cutting-edge technologies [88].

8.4.2 Cybersecurity

Manufacturing and the merging of digital information from various sources present a significant security risk for the sector. The potential attack surface for hostile actors significantly expands as industries combine their operational technology (OT) and information technology (IT).

8.4.2.1 Risks and Challenges

Industries are exposed to a variety of cybersecurity concerns as they implement cutting-edge technologies like IIoT, AI, and cloud computing.

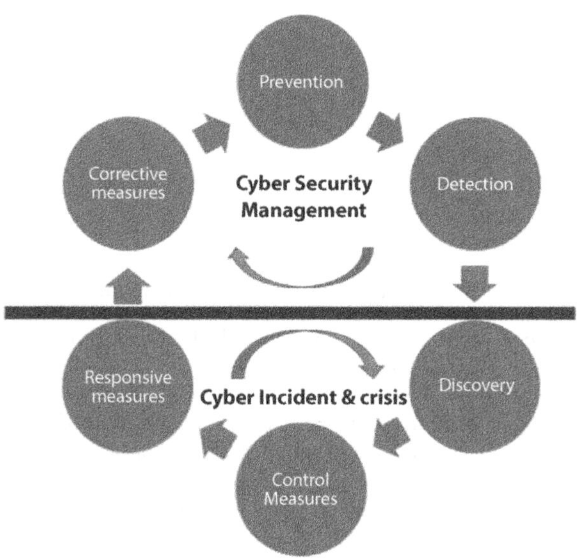

Figure 8.6 Strategies and challenges in cybersecurity for Industry 4.0.

These threats might come from internal angry staff as well as just ignorant users, not just external hackers [89]. For instance, a compromised device could convey inaccurate data or even commands to undermine operations in a connected factory where machines exchange real-time data [90]. Furthermore, there is a serious risk if cybersecurity measures are not updated simultaneously with other technology in industrial applications. Modern security methods might not work with aging industrial equipment. Such systems may function as a weak point, allowing larger network invasions [91]. Figure 8.6 shows a visual representation of these concerns and how these are addressed.

8.4.2.2 Best Practices in Cybersecurity for Industry 4.0

Industry 4.0 cybersecurity enhancements go beyond simply implementing the most recent firewall or anti-malware program. It involves developing a comprehensive security strategy that takes into account people, process, and technology.

1. *Segmentation:* Industries should segment their networks rather than using a single network. To ensure that even if one segment is compromised, the critical activities are not disrupted, critical operations should be segregated from routine operational duties [92].
2. *Regular Audits:* Regular vulnerability analyses and penetration tests can aid in locating potential system flaws [93].
3. *Employee training:* One of the biggest vulnerabilities is still the human element. Employees can be kept informed about the most recent risks and the most effective defenses through ongoing training programs [94].
4. *Advanced Threat Detection:* Use AI and machine learning to find odd network traffic patterns that could point to a possible intrusion [95].

8.4.3 Return on Investment

Making the switch to Industry 4.0 requires a large investment. In addition to money, the cost also includes time, training, and a change in the business culture. The long-term advantages will, however, always outweigh the initial expenses.

8.4.3.1 Cost Analysis

Moving to Industry 4.0 has several financial ramifications. Initial investments cover employee training, technological integration, and procurement. The transition period, during which production may be slowed down or stopped entirely, has a cost as well [96]. Future profits, however, more than offset these initial costs. Smart factories can run more effectively, producing goods of greater quality and with less waste. A hallmark of Industry 4.0, predictive maintenance can result in much lower maintenance costs and less downtime [97].

8.4.3.2 Long-Term Benefits

The benefits of Industry 4.0 become clearer with time. Industries can gain a considerable competitive advantage over their rivals by increasing production rates, cutting waste, improving product quality, and responding quickly to market changes. Additionally, the data gathered from diverse procedures can offer suggestions for additional innovation and optimization [98].

For industries seeking to develop, be agile, and be competitive, the transition to Industry 4.0 is both necessary and unavoidable. Like any significant change, there will be difficulties and worries along the way, from the workforce's capacity for change to the persistent cyberthreats that stalk the digital world. Industries can be helped to smoothly navigate this digital revolution through the strategic adoption and implementation of Industry 4.0 practices, with a sharp focus on cybersecurity, worker training, and a clear vision of ROI. As demonstrated in this work, a combined strategy of

Table 8.8 Comparative cost-benefit analysis of Industry 4.0 transition.

Initial expenditures	Potential long-term benefits	Financial implications	Ref.
Technology procurement	Enhanced production efficiency	Increased revenue	[99]
Workforce training	Reduction in production errors	Cost saving	[100]
Integration downtime	Real-time market adaptability	Competitive advantage	[101]

real-world application and solid academic research can assist clarify the path to a smooth transition as illustrated in Table 8.8.

8.5 Cross-Sector Collaboration

The integrative strategy that best represents Industry 4.0's core values is driven by collaboration, which is the evolution's cornerstone. Industry 4.0, unlike any of its predecessors, feeds on the fusion of several industries, utilizing the advantages of each to create a strong alliance. Industry 4.0 is supported by a wide range of technologies that go beyond changes in manufacturing methods, such as the Internet of Things (IoT), big data analytics, and artificial intelligence (AI). Instead, they herald the establishment of a comprehensive, interconnected ecosystem where sectoral lines are blurred, and innovation is encouraged at a level never before seen [102].

8.5.1 Role of Academic Institutions

Academic institutions serve as hubs for knowledge creation, diffusion, and innovation. The emergence of Industry 4.0 has increased the importance of academia in determining how industries will develop in the future, illuminating the way through research, workforce development, and by connecting theoretical ideas with real-world applications.

- *Research and Innovation:* Universities are the cradle of a large portion of the groundbreaking research that contributes to the creation of cutting-edge technologies. The development of AI, data analytics, and robotics—three pillars of Industry 4.0—have all been facilitated by research programs that frequently dive into the fundamental principles of technologies. The real-world application of these fundamental ideas can be accelerated by collaborative collaborations between businesses and institutions [103].
- *Workforce Training:* Universities are at the forefront of preparing the upcoming generation of professionals as the demand for specialized skills in fields like IoT, ML, and big data analytics soars. In line with the evolving nature of industrial requirements, customized curricula, devoted centers of excellence, and specialized courses have become widespread [104].

- *Industry–Academia Partnerships:* Partnerships between business and academia serve as the intersection of academic theory and real-world application. Industries provide problems from the real world, while academia offers creative solutions, frequently through specialized research wings or joint initiatives [105].
- *Incubation and Start-Ups:* Universities frequently encourage entrepreneurial endeavors, creating start-ups that concentrate on Industry 4.0 solutions. These start-ups benefit from the academic environment by having access to professional advice, resources, and occasionally seed money to turn ideas into usable goods or solutions [106].

8.5.2 Industry Stakeholders and Contributions

In Industry 4.0, the concept of "industry" refers to a broad group of stakeholders who each bring something different to the table. Every player in the ecosystem has a part to play, from big behemoths rewriting history with AI-driven solutions to small businesses showcasing agile, specialized applications.

1. *Large Enterprises:* Through their products, platforms, and solutions, major technology companies like IBM, Microsoft, and Siemens have been guiding the Industry 4.0 narrative. Their impact extends beyond technology to include thought leadership, industry guidance on best practices, and future planning [107].
2. *Small and Medium Enterprises (SMEs):* Small and medium-sized businesses (SMEs) are the backbone of many economies, and because of their flexibility, they can frequently adopt new technology more quickly than larger businesses. They also frequently concentrate on specialized applications that address certain problems with specialized Industry 4.0 solutions [108].
3. *Tech Start-Ups:* Start-ups bring disruptive technologies to the table and frequently have academic foundations. Their willingness to take chances and new ideas can occasionally outperform conventional approaches, resulting in quick improvements in particular Industry 4.0 fields [109].
4. *Consultancies and Service Providers:* Companies that offer consulting services include McKinsey, Deloitte, and

Accenture. These companies assist industries in navigating the complexities of the Industry 4.0 change. Their responsibilities include, among other things, strategic planning, cybersecurity consulting, and implementation advice [110].

8.5.3 Policymaking and Regulatory Landscape

The need for policymakers to comprehend and influence the environment in which Industry 4.0 technologies function is growing as these technologies permeate industries. Sustainable and fair technological breakthroughs can be supported by a carefully designed regulatory environment.

- Standardization and Interoperability: To fully realize the potential of Industry 4.0, technology standardization is essential. Standards that guarantee flawless interaction between various systems, goods, and solutions can be created with the help of policymakers. Additionally, it helps with worldwide scaling of solutions [111].
- Data Privacy and Protection: Since data is the foundation of Industry 4.0, both their security and peoples' privacy are crucial. To enable innovation while also assuring the ethical use and preservation of data, policies need to strike a balance [112].
- Ethical AI and Automation Policies: As AI-driven automation spreads, concerns concerning its moral ramifications surface. Especially in domains like decision making and bias prevention, policymakers have a duty to make sure that the implementation of AI complies with ethical principles [113].
- Economic Incentives: Governments can encourage the adoption of Industry 4.0 through incentives like tax breaks, grants, or subsidies for businesses that adopt these technologies or spend money on pertinent R&D [114].

Unquestionably one of the key forces underlying Industry 4.0 is the synergy of cross-sector collaboration. As this period progresses, the collaboration between academics, business, and policy-making organizations will become progressively more entwined, resulting in a web of innovation, regulation, and application.

8.6 Strategies for Successful Adoption

Industry 4.0 is a catalyst for a digital transformation that involves more than just integrating cutting-edge technology. It involves changing perspectives, modernizing established procedures, and developing an organizational culture that seamlessly combines technology and vision. For Industry 4.0 to reach its full potential, strategic adoption is necessary. This chapter examines the ideas, strategies, and practical examples that underpin this change.

8.6.1 Standardized Frameworks and Guidelines

One of the cornerstones of Industry 4.0 adoption success is the application of standardized frameworks and rules. These frameworks steer the technical aspects of integration and offer scalability and security.

8.6.1.1 Importance of Interoperability

Interoperability allows various digital tools, platforms, and systems to live in harmony with one another. These systems must "speak" to one another since companies regularly use multiple solutions from various sources [115]. Standardized frameworks provide interoperability by providing common standards and protocols that permit communication and data sharing between disparate systems.

8.6.1.2 Security Measures

The interconnection that characterizes Industry 4.0 increases the susceptibility to cyber assaults. Best practices for cybersecurity, data integrity, intellectual property protection, and preventing unauthorized intrusions are outlined in standardized recommendations. These steps are essential to preserving confidence in digital systems and guaranteeing business continuity [116].

8.6.1.3 Scalability Considerations

The process of digital transformation is fluid. The solutions put in place must adapt as organizations expand and technologies advance without necessitating major changes. Frameworks that take scalability into consideration make sure that organizations may grow their digital projects [117] in accordance with their changing needs, without adding unnecessary complexity or expense.

8.6.2 Continuous Improvement and Adaptability

Industry 4.0 is a journey rather than a destination. Continuous progress is essential, thus. Businesses need to promote a learning culture where feedback loops are built to continuously improve and optimize operations [118]. Businesses that have an adaptable mindset may stay flexible, react to new trends, and pivot as needed. This strategy also makes it easier for the organization to adopt new technologies and processes as they become available, ensuring that it stays on the cutting edge of innovation.

8.6.3 Case Studies and Real-World Applications

To cement the concepts and strategies discussed, some illustrative case studies have been presented in Table 8.9. These real-world scenarios exemplify the successful application of Industry 4.0 principles and highlight the tangible benefits reaped.

Table 8.9 Case studies on Industry 4.0 adoption.

Company	Sector	Challenge	Solution	Outcomes	Ref.
Siemens	Manufacturing	Enhancing production efficiency	Implemented a digital twin solution	30% production efficiency increase	[119]
BMW	Automotive	Reducing production lead times	Integrated IoT sensors and AI analysis	50% reduction in lead times	[120]
GE	Energy	Predictive maintenance	Leveraged machine learning for equipment monitoring	20% reduction in unplanned downtimes	[121]
DHL	Logistics	Real-time package tracking	Integrated IoT devices and big data analytics	Improved customer satisfaction and reduced losses	[122]

8.7 Future Prospects and Research Directions

8.7.1 Emerging Technologies in Industry 4.0

The progress of Industry 4.0 is inextricably related to the introduction and adoption of cutting-edge technology.

- *Quantum Computing:* Unlike ordinary computers, quantum computers use the principles of superposition and entanglement to achieve exponentially more processing capability. This capability has the potential to significantly improve optimization problems, cryptography systems, and machine learning models. Problems that were previously considered computationally difficult can now be solved using quantum algorithms such as Grover's and Shor's. This involves being able to handle massive datasets, optimize complicated manufacturing processes, and ensuring enhanced security measures in real-time [123].
- *Neuromorphic Engineering:* Neuromorphic chips promise ultra-efficient, low-power consumption computer models by mimicking the structure and operation of the human brain. This engineering marvel, in the world of Industry 4.0, may provide real-time processing for sensors, instantaneous data analytics, and adaptive learning—critical for on-the-fly decision-making processes in automated production environments [124].
- *5G and Beyond:* While 4G revolutionized the mobile internet scene, the arrival of 5G signals the beginning of a transformative period for Industry 4.0. 5G serves as a backbone for resilient IoT infrastructures due to its ultra-low latency, increased bandwidths, and network slicing. The potential deployment of 6G over the next decade would boost real-time data sharing, AR/VR integrations, and flawless remote operations [125].

8.7.2 Challenges and Opportunities

As with any paradigm shift, embracing Industry 4.0 has its problems, which then expose potential.

1. *Data Privacy and Sovereignty:* In this day and age, Industry 4.0 endeavors frequently cross international borders. With data being a treasured possession, regulatory regimes across nations pose compliance and standardization problems. However, this provides an opportunity to develop globally agreed data standards, governance models, and frameworks to ensure transparency and trust [126].
2. *Complexity of Integration:* The varied nature of digital technology and legacy systems creates integration challenges. It is still difficult to migrate to newer systems while maintaining zero downtime, data integrity, and system functionality. Companies specializing in middleware solutions, system integrators, and custom application developers, on the other hand, stand to benefit greatly [127].
3. *Sustainability:* As environmental issues become more prominent, industries are under increasing pressure to reduce their carbon footprint. The problem is to remain profitable while adhering to environmental regulations. This, however, creates opportunity for green tech advancements, eco-friendly supply networks, and waste-reducing production practices [128].

8.7.3 Potential Growth Areas and Innovations

Industry 4.0 is about more than just technology breakthroughs; it is about creating unprecedented value in the industrial sector.

8.7.3.1 Personalized Manufacturing

Recent technological convergence, particularly between AI and real-time data analytics, indicates an oncoming shift toward personalized manufacturing. Given the complexities of modern consumer demands, producers have a great opportunity to make goods that are suited to individual needs. This transformation not only caters to individual customer preferences, but it also sets the ground for a transformative period marked by consumer-centric manufacturing approaches [129].

8.7.3.2 Augmented Workforce

The combination of human cognitive ability and advanced machine intelligence offers up a world of possibilities. The industrial sector is on the verge of redefining its old productivity benchmarks by arming its workforce with AI-powered insights, Augmented Reality (AR)-guided procedures, and the capability of remote collaborations offered by Virtual Reality (VR) [130].

8.7.3.3 Circular Economy

The circular economy emphasizes reuse, recycle, and refurbishment concepts, challenging the long-established "produce–use–discard" model. This paradigm change is aided by the deployment of intelligent sensors, AI-powered analytics, and the enormous network of the Internet of Things (IoT) when viewed through the perspective of Industry 4.0. Such connections aim to precisely monitor product lifecycles, assuring resource stewardship and waste reduction, in line with the global push for sustainability [131].

8.8 Conclusion

The revolutionary transition toward Industry 4.0 is altering the industrial landscape, intertwining innovative technologies, techniques, and strategies to usher in a new era of manufacturing and production. This study focused light on the various aspects of Industry 4.0, emphasizing both its revolutionary potential and the problems that industries must face during its implementation. For instance, the combination of real-time data and artificial intelligence data is already heralding a move toward customized production techniques that take into account the unique tastes of each customer. The integration of digital technologies, such as cyber-physical systems (CPS), the Industrial Internet of Things (IIoT), advanced analytics, machine learning, robots, and additive manufacturing, has been a repeating subject. These technologies provide the cornerstone of Industry 4.0, allowing Smart Factories, enhanced operational efficiencies, and more personalized, consumer-driven manufacturing paradigms to be realized.

It has become quite clear that different sector cooperation is needed for successfully implementing Industry 4.0. As artificial intelligence (AI) and automation enhance productivity, they also suggest employer to re-examine job duties, also ask for increased skill set and training. Monitoring and good practices are required for enhancing cybersecurity, as it is important to secure data from various hacks and attackers.

Various studies related to Industry 4.0 states that the full adoption of Industry 4.0 requires framework and adaptability on continuous basis from practical application. All the different sectors, such as administration, business leader, and academic institution must contribute to overcome legislative roadblocks and create a healthy environment for innovation. Industry 4.0 environment provides novel ideas and opportunities. Industry 4.0 in combination with sustainable models such as circular economies, new technologies direct us to a future where it encourages businesses in addition to product optimization. To conclude, Industry 4.0 is a sum of strategy, technologies, and vision. The research provides guidance, pointing the path toward an era of unmatched industrial innovation and value creation

References

1. Beard-Gunter, A., Ellis, D.G., Found, P.A., TQM, games design and the implications of integration in Industry 4.0 systems. *Int. J. Qual. Serv. Sci.*, 11, 2, 235–247, 2019.
2. Douaioui, K., Fri, M., Mabroukki, C., The interaction between industry 4.0 and smart logistics: concepts and perspectives, in: *2018 Int. Colloq. on Logist. and Supply Chain Manag. (LOGISTIQUA)*, Apr. 2018, pp. 128–132.
3. Ahmadi, A., Sodhro, A.H., Cherifi, C., Cheutet, V., Ouzrout, Y., Evolution of 3C cyber-physical systems architecture for industry 4.0, in: *Service Orientation in Holonic and Multi-Agent Manufacturing: Proc. of SOHOMA 2018*, Springer Int. Publishing, pp. 448–459, 2019.
4. Mogensen, R.S., Rodriguez, I., Berardinelli, G., Pocovi, G., Kolding, T., Empirical IIoT data traffic analysis and comparison to 3GPP 5G models, in: *2021 IEEE 94th Veh. Tech. Conf. (VTC2021-Fall)*, Sep. 2021, pp. 1–7.
5. Golovina, T., Polyanin, A., Adamenko, A., Khegay, E., Schepinin, V., Digital twins as a new paradigm of an industrial enterprise. *Int. J. Tech.*, 11, 6, 1115–1124, 2020.
6. Lin, Q., Ye, G., Wang, J., Liu, H., RoboFlow: a data-centric workflow management system for developing AI-enhanced Robots, in: *Conf. on Robot Learning*, Jan. 2022, pp. 1789–1794.
7. Cameron, R., The industrial revolution: A misnomer. *History Teacher*, 15, 3, 377–384, 1982.
8. Atkeson, A. and Kehoe, P.J., The transition to a new economy after the second industrial revolution. *National Bureau of Economic Research*, 1–55, 2001.
9. Dosi, G. and Galambos, L. (Eds.), *The third industrial revolution in global business*, Cambridge Univ. Press, Cambridge, United Kingdom, 2013.
10. Tvenge, N. and Martinsen, K., Integration of digital learning in industry 4.0. *Proc. Manuf.*, 23, 261–266, 2018.
11. Yang, F. and Gu, S., Industry 4.0, a revolution that requires technology and national strategies. *Complex Intell. Syst.*, 7, 1311–1325, 2021.

12. Nayernia, H., Bahemia, H., Papagiannidis, S., A systematic review of the implementation of industry 4.0 from the organisational perspective. *Int. J. Prod. Res.*, 60, 14, 4365–4396, 2022.
13. Sha, L., Gopalakrishnan, S., Liu, X., Wang, Q., Cyber-physical systems: A new frontier, in: *2008 IEEE Int. Conf. on Sensor Networks, Ubiquitous, and Trustworthy Computing*, Jun. 2008, pp. 1–9.
14. Madakam, S. and Uchiya, T., Industrial internet of things (IIoT): principles, processes and protocols, in: *The Internet of Things in the Industrial Sector: Security and Device Connectivity, Smart Environments, and Industry 4.0*, pp. 35–53, 2019.
15. Saihi, A., Awad, M., Ben-Daya, M., Quality 4.0: leveraging Industry 4.0 technologies to improve quality management practices–a systematic review. *Int. J. Qual. Reliab. Manage.*, 40, 2, 628–650, 2023.
16. Goel, R. and Gupta, P., Robotics and industry 4.0, in: *A Roadmap to Industry 4.0: Smart Production, Sharp Business and Sustainable Development*, pp. 157–169, 2020.
17. Khanna, S., Rao, D., Panwar, S., Pawar, B.A., Ameen, S., 3D printed band and loop space maintainer: A digital game changer in preventive orthodontics. *J. Clin. Pediatr. Dent.*, 45, 3, 147–151, 2021.
18. Furstenau, L.B., Sott, M.K., Kipper, L.M., Machado, E.L., Lopez-Robles, J.R., Dohan, M.S., Cobo, M.J., Zahid, A., Abbasi, Q.H., Imran, M.A., Link between sustainability and industry 4.0: trends, challenges and new perspectives. *IEEE Access*, 8, 140079–140096, 2020.
19. Pal, B., Cyber Security in the Age of Industry 4.0. SSRN 4078292. *Empirical Economics Letters*, 21, 4, 145–156, 2022.
20. Vacek, J., Socio-economic aspects of Industry 4.0, in: *Innovation Management, Entrepreneurship and Corporate Sustainability (IMECS 2016)*, Vysoká škola ekonomická v Praze, pp. 731–741, 2016.
21. Redelinghuys, A.J.H., Basson, A.H., Kruger, K., A six-layer architecture for the digital twin: a manufacturing case study implementation. *J. Intell. Manuf.*, 31, 1383–1402, 2020.
22. Bag, S. and Pretorius, J.H.C., Relationships between industry 4.0, sustainable manufacturing and circular economy: proposal of a research framework. *Int. J. Organ. Anal.*, 30, 4, 864–898, 2022.
23. Cirera, X., Comin, D., Cruz, M., *Bridging the technological divide: Technology adoption by firms in developing countries*, World Bank Publications, Washington, D.C., USA, 2022.
24. Kumar, S., Suhaib, M., Asjad, M., Industry 4.0: Complex, disruptive, but inevitable. *Manage. Prod. Eng. Rev.*, 11, 1, 43–51, 2020.
25. de Vass, T., Shee, H., Miah, S.J., IoT in supply chain management: Opportunities and challenges for businesses in early industry 4.0 context. *Oper. Supply Chain Manage. An Int. J.*, 14, 2, 148–161, 2021.

26. Graja, I., Kallel, S., Guermouche, N., Cheikhrouhou, S., Hadj Kacem, A., A comprehensive survey on modeling of cyber-physical systems. *Concurrency Comput. Pract. Exper.*, 32, 15, e4850, 2020.
27. Wang, E.K., Ye, Y., Xu, X., Yiu, S.M., Hui, L.C.K., Chow, K.P., Security issues and challenges for cyber physical system, in: *2010 IEEE/ACM Int'l Conference on Green Computing and Communications & Int'l Conference on Cyber, Physical and Social Computing*, Dec. 2010, pp. 733–738.
28. Malazi, H.T., Chaudhry, S.R., Kazmi, A., Palade, A., Cabrera, C., White, G., Clarke, S., Dynamic service placement in multi-access edge computing: A systematic literature review. *IEEE Access*, 10, 32639–32688, 2022.
29. Trappey, A.J., Trappey, C.V., Govindarajan, U.H., Sun, J.J., Chuang, A.C., A review of technology standards and patent portfolios for enabling cyber-physical systems in advanced manufacturing. *IEEE Access*, 4, 7356–7382, 2016.
30. Hermann, M., Bücker, I., Otto, B., Industrie 4.0 process transformation: findings from a case study in automotive logistics. *J. Manuf. Technol. Manage.*, 31, 5, 935–953, 2020.
31. Chui, M.A., Mott, D.A., Maxwell, L., A qualitative assessment of a community pharmacy cognitive pharmaceutical services program, using a work system approach. *Res. Soc. Adm. Pharm.*, 8, 3, 206–216, 2012.
32. Rødseth, H. and Eleftheriadis, R.J., Successful asset management strategy implementation of cyber-physical systems, in: *Engineering Assets and Public Infrastructures in the Age of Digitalization: Proceedings of the 13th World Congress on Engineering Asset Management*, Springer International Publishing, pp. 15–22, 2020.
33. Pech, M., Vrchota, J., Bednář, J., Predictive maintenance and intelligent sensors in smart factory. *Sensors*, 21, 4, 1470, 2021.
34. Sun, W., Liu, J., Yue, Y., Zhang, H., Double auction-based resource allocation for mobile edge computing in industrial internet of things. *IEEE Trans. Ind. Inf.*, 14, 10, 4692–4701, 2018.
35. Jaloudi, S., Communication protocols of an industrial internet of things environment: A comparative study. *Future Internet*, 11, 3, 66, 2019.
36. Stergiou, C.L. and Psannis, K.E., Digital twin intelligent system for industrial IoT-based big data management and analysis in cloud. *Virtual Reality Intell. Hardware*, 4, 4, 279–291, 2022.
37. Malik, N., Alkhatib, K., Sun, Y., Knight, E., Jararweh, Y., A comprehensive review of blockchain applications in industrial Internet of Things and supply chain systems. *Appl. Stochastic Models Bus. Ind.*, 37, 3, 391–412, 2021.
38. Far, S.B. and Rad, A., II, Applying digital twins in metaverse: User interface, security and privacy challenges. *J. Metaverse*, 2, 1, 8–15, 2022.
39. Lyu, M., Li, X., Chen, C.H., Achieving Knowledge-as-a-Service in IIoT-driven smart manufacturing: A crowdsourcing-based continuous enrichment method for Industrial Knowledge Graph. *Adv. Eng. Inf.*, 51, 101494, 2022.

40. Ong, K.S.H., Wang, W., Niyato, D., Friedrichs, T., Deep-reinforcement-learning-based predictive maintenance model for effective resource management in industrial IoT. *IEEE Internet Things J.*, 9, 7, 5173–5188, 2021.
41. Ding, K. and Fan, L.Q., AML-based web-twin visualization integration framework for DT-enabled and IIoT-driven Manufacturing system under I4. 0 workshop. *J. Manuf. Syst.*, 64, 479–496, 2022.
42. Liu, Y., Yang, C., Huang, K., Gui, W., Hu, S., A Systematic Procurement Supply Chain Optimization Technique Based on Industrial Internet of Things and Application. *IEEE Internet Things J.*, 10, 8, 7272–7292, 2022.
43. Gebremichael, T. *et al.*, Security and privacy in the industrial internet of things: Current standards and future challenges. *IEEE Access*, 8, 152351–152366, 2020.
44. Vimal, K.E.K., Churi, K., Kandasamy, J., Analysing the drivers for adoption of industry 4.0 technologies in a functional paper–cement–sugar circular sharing network. *Sustain. Prod. Consum.*, 31, 459–477, 2022.
45. Chae, B., Olson, D., Sheu, C., The impact of supply chain analytics on operational performance: a resource-based view. *Int. J. Prod. Res.*, 52, 16, 4695–4710, 2014.
46. Pu, Y.Y., O'Donnell, C., Tobin, J.T., O'Shea, N., Review of near-infrared spectroscopy as a process analytical technology for real-time product monitoring in dairy processing. *Int. Dairy J.*, 103, 104623, 2020.
47. Côrte-Real, N., Ruivo, P., Oliveira, T., Popovič, A., Unlocking the drivers of big data analytics value in firms. *J. Bus. Res.*, 97, 160–173, 2019.
48. Baumgartner, T., Malik, Y., Padhi, A., *Reimagining industrial supply chains*, McKinsey & Company, New York, NY, USA, 2020, [Online]. Available: https://www.mckinsey.com/industries/advanced-electronics/our-insights/reimagining-industrial-supply-chains.
49. Hiwase, S.D. and JAGTAP, P., Predictive maintenance of automotive component using digital twin model. *SAE Tech. Pap.*, 28, 0075, 2022.
50. He, J., Cen, Y., Alelaumi, S., Won, D., An Artificial Intelligence-Based Pick-and-Place Process Control for Quality Enhancement in Surface Mount Technology. *IEEE Trans. Compon. Packag. Manuf. Technol.*, 12, 10, 1702–1711, 2022.
51. You, F., Tao, L., Graziano, D.J., Snyder, S.W., Optimal design of sustainable cellulosic biofuel supply chains: multiobjective optimization coupled with life cycle assessment and input–output analysis. *AIChE J.*, 58, 4, 1157–1180, 2012.
52. Diez-Olivan, A., Del Ser, J., Galar, D., Sierra, B., Data fusion and machine learning for industrial prognosis: Trends and perspectives towards Industry 4.0. *Inf. Fusion*, 50, 92–111, 2019.
53. Das, S.K., Dey, N., Hassanien, A.E. (Eds.), *Machine learning algorithms for industrial applications*, Springer, Switzerland, 2021.

54. Liang, X. *et al.*, Unveiling fake accounts at the time of registration: An unsupervised approach, in: *Proceedings of the 27th ACM SIGKDD Conference on Knowledge Discovery & Data Mining*, Aug. 2021, pp. 3240–3250.
55. Wulff, P. *et al.*, Bridging the gap between qualitative and quantitative assessment in science education research with machine learning—A case for pretrained language models-based clustering. *J. Sci. Educ. Technol.*, 31, 4, 490–513, 2022.
56. He, L., Wang, G., Hu, Z., Learning depth from single images with deep neural network embedding focal length. *IEEE Trans. Image Process.*, 27, 9, 4676–4689, 2018.
57. Dsouza, J. and Velan, S., Preventive maintenance for fault detection in transfer nodes using machine learning, in: *2019 International Conference on Computational Intelligence and Knowledge Economy (ICCIKE)*, Dec. 2019, pp. 401–404.
58. Chen, S., Shi, R., Ren, Z., Yan, J., Shi, Y., Zhang, J., A blockchain-based supply chain quality management framework, in: *2017 IEEE 14th International Conference on e-Business Engineering (ICEBE)*, Nov. 2017, pp. 172–176.
59. Hoque, M.E., Thavaneswaran, A., Appadoo, S.S., Thulasiram, R.K., Banitalebi, B., A novel dynamic demand forecasting model for resilient supply chains using machine learning, in: *2021 IEEE 45th Annual Computers, Software, and Applications Conference (COMPSAC)*, July 2021, pp. 218–227.
60. Sun, P., Liu, L., Qayyum, M., Energy efficiency comparison amongst service industry in Chinese provinces from the perspective of heterogeneous resource endowment: Analysis using undesirable super efficiency SBM-ML model. *J. Cleaner Prod.*, 328, 129535, 2021.
61. Oldroyd, R.A., Morris, M.A., Birkin, M., Predicting food safety compliance for informed food outlet inspections: a machine learning approach. *Int. J. Environ. Res. Public Health*, 18, 23, 12635, 2021.
62. Ayvaz, S. and Alpay, K., Predictive maintenance system for production lines in manufacturing: A machine learning approach using IoT data in real-time. *Expert Syst. Appl.*, 173, 114598, 2021.
63. Roth, K., Pemula, L., Zepeda, J., Schölkopf, B., Brox, T., Gehler, P., Towards total recall in industrial anomaly detection, in: *Proc. IEEE/CVF Conf. Comput. Vision Pattern Recognit*, pp. 14318–14328, 2022.
64. Haleel, A.J. and Dawood, L.M., Maintenance Scheduling Optimization using Artificial Intelligence Techniques: A Review, in: *2023 5th Int. Congress on Human-Computer Interaction, Optimization and Robotic Applications (HORA)*, June 2023, pp. 1–6.
65. Barardo, D.G., Newby, D., Thornton, D., Ghafourian, T., de Magalhães, J.P., Freitas, A.A., Machine learning for predicting lifespan-extending chemical compounds. *Aging (Albany NY)*, 9, 7, 1721, 2017.
66. Bousdekis, A., Apostolou, D., Mentzas, G., Predictive maintenance in the 4th industrial revolution: Benefits, business opportunities, and managerial implications. *IEEE Eng. Manage. Rev.*, 48, 1, 57–62, 2019.

67. Gambao, E., Hernando, M., Surdilovic, D., A new generation of collaborative robots for material handling, in: *ISARC. Proc. Int. Symp. Automation Robotics Constr*, vol. 29, p. 1, 2012.
68. Alaieri, F. and Vellino, A., Ethical Decision Making in Robots: Autonomy, Trust and Responsibility, in: *Social Robotics: 8th Int. Conf. ICSR 2016Proc*, Kansas City, MO, USA, Nov. 2016, pp. 159–168.
69. Grau, A., Indri, M., Bello, L.L., Sauter, T., Industrial robotics in factory automation: From the early stage to the Internet of Things, in: *IECON 2017-43rd Annu. Conf. IEEE Ind. Electron. Soc*, Oct. 2017, pp. 6159–6164.
70. George, A.S. and George, A.H., Industrial revolution 5.0: the transformation of the modern manufacturing process to enable man and machine to work hand in hand. *J. Seybold Rep.*, 1533, 9211, 2020.
71. Martinez, S., Mariño, A., Sanchez, S., Montes, A.M., Triana, J.M., Barbieri, G., Abolghasem, S., Vera, J., Guevara, M., A digital twin demonstrator to enable flexible manufacturing with robotics: A process supervision case study. *Prod. Manuf. Res.*, 9, 1, 140–156, 2021.
72. Djuric, A.M., Urbanic, R.J., Rickli, J.L., A framework for collaborative robot (CoBot) integration in advanced manufacturing systems. *SAE Int. J. Mater. Manufact.*, 9, 2, 457–464, 2016.
73. Mohamed, O.A., Masood, S.H., Bhowmik, J.L., Optimization of fused deposition modeling process parameters: a review of current research and future prospects. *Adv. Manuf.*, 3, 42–53, 2015.
74. Kishan, G. and Rao, B.V.S., 3D-Metal Printing Technologies: Comparative Study of the 'Electron Beam Melting' and 'Selective Laser Sintering'. *Int. Res. J. Adv. Sci. Hub*, 2, Special Issue ICIES 9S, 97–101, 2020.
75. Lakkala, P., Munnangi, S.R., Bandari, S., Repka, M., Additive manufacturing technologies with emphasis on stereolithography 3D printing in pharmaceutical and medical applications: A review. *Int. J. Pharm.: X*, 5, 100159, 2023.
76. Stefaniak, A.B., Du Preez, S., Du Plessis, J.L., Additive manufacturing for occupational hygiene: a comprehensive review of processes, emissions, & exposures. *J. Toxicol. Environ. Health, Part B*, 24, 5, 173–222, 2021.
77. Shakor, P., Chu, S.H., Puzatova, A., Dini, E., Review of binder jetting 3D printing in the construction industry. *Prog. Addit. Manuf.*, 7, 4, 643–669, 2022.
78. Aydin, M., Additive manufacturing: is it a new era for furniture production. *J. Mech. Eng. Autom.*, 5, 1, 38–347, 2015.
79. Weller, C., Kleer, R., Piller, F.T., Economic implications of 3D printing: Market structure models in light of additive manufacturing revisited. *Int. J. Prod. Econ.*, 164, 43–56, 2015.
80. Ferchow, J., Biedermann, M., Müller, P., Auchmann, B., Brem, A., Meboldt, M., Harnessing manufacturing elements to select local process parameters for metal additive manufacturing: A case study on a superconducting solenoid coil. *Addit. Manuf.*, 46, 102140, 2021.

81. Javaid, M., Haleem, A., Singh, R.P., Suman, R., Rab, S., Role of additive manufacturing applications towards environmental sustainability. *Adv. Ind. Eng. Polym. Res.*, 4, 4, 312–322, 2021.
82. Attaran, M., Additive manufacturing: the most promising technology to alter the supply chain and logistics. *J. Serv. Sci. Manage.*, 10, 03, 189, 2017.
83. Lingmont, D.N. and Alexiou, A., The contingent effect of job automating technology awareness on perceived job insecurity: Exploring the moderating role of organizational culture. *Technol. Forecast. Soc. Change*, 161, 120302, 2020.
84. Rüßmann, M., Lorenz, M., Gerbert, P., Waldner, M., Justus, J., Harnisch, M., Industry 4.0: The future of productivity and growth in manufacturing industries. *Boston Consult. Group*, 9, 1, 54–89, 2015.
85. Stojanovic, L., Dinic, M., Stojanovic, N., Stojadinovic, A., Big-data-driven anomaly detection in industry (4.0): An approach and a case study, in: *2016 IEEE Int. Conf. Big Data (Big Data)*, Dec. 2016, pp. 1647–1652.
86. Compare, M., Baraldi, P., Zio, E., Challenges to IoT-enabled predictive maintenance for industry 4.0. *IEEE Internet Things J.*, 7, 5, 4585–4597, 2019.
87. Fitsilis, P., Tsoutsa, P., Gerogiannis, V., Industry 4.0: Required personnel competences. *Industry 4.0*, 3, 3, 130–133, 2018.
88. Pfeiffer, S., Robots, Industry 4.0 and humans, or why assembly work is more than routine work. *Societies*, 6, 2, 16, 2016.
89. Stouffer, K., Falco, J., Scarfone, K., Guide to industrial control systems (ICS) security. *NIST Spec. Publ.*, 800, 82, 16–16, 2011.
90. Alhalafi, N. and Veeraraghavan, P., Privacy and Security Challenges and Solutions in IOT: A review, in: *IOP Conf. Ser.: Earth Environ. Sci*, Aug. 2019, vol. 322, p. 012013.
91. Atzori, L., Iera, A., Morabito, G., The internet of things: a survey. *Comput. Netw.*, 10, 1016, 2010.
92. Li, B., Zou, Y., Zhu, R., Yao, W., Wang, J., Wan, S., Fabric defect segmentation system based on a lightweight GAN for industrial Internet of Things. *Wireless Commun. Mobile Comput.*, 680519, 2022.
93. Creery, A. and Byres, E.J., Industrial cybersecurity for power system and SCADA networks, in: *Record of Conference Papers Industry Applications Society 52nd Annual Petroleum and Chemical Industry Conference*, Sep. 2005, pp. 303–309.
94. Wilson, M. and Hash, J., Building an information technology security awareness and training program. *NIST Special Pub.*, 800, 50, 1–39, 2003.
95. Pasqualetti, F., Dörfler, F., Bullo, F., Attack detection and identification in cyber-physical systems. *IEEE Trans. Autom. Control*, 58, 11, 2715–2729, 2013.
96. Goldsby, T.J. and Martichenko, R., *Lean Six Sigma Logistics: Strategic Development to Operational Success*, J. Ross Publishing, Plantation, FL, USA, 2005.

97. Sutton, R.S. and Barto, A.G., *Reinforcement Learning: An Introduction*, MIT Press, Cambridge, MA, USA, 2018.
98. Zhou, K., Liu, T., Zhou, L., Industry 4.0: Towards future industrial opportunities and challenges, in: *2015 12th International Conference on Fuzzy Systems and Knowledge Discovery (FSKD)*, Aug. 2015, pp. 2147–2152.
99. Manyika, J., Chui, M., Miremadi, M., Bughin, J., George, K., Willmott, P., Dewhurst, M., *Harnessing automation for a future that works*, pp. 2–4, McKinsey Global Institute, New York, NY, USA, 2017.
100. Menon, J. and Fink, A., The fourth industrial revolution and its implications for regional economic integration in ASEAN. *J. Asian Econ. Integr.*, 1, 1, 32–47, 2019.
101. Cooke, T.J. and Shuttleworth, I., The effects of information and communication technologies on residential mobility and migration. *Popul. Space Place*, 24, 3, e2111, 2018.
102. Edwards, M.A. and Roy, S., Academic research in the 21st century: Maintaining scientific integrity in a climate of perverse incentives and hypercompetition. *Environ. Eng. Sci.*, 34, 1, 51–61, 2017.
103. Scott, P., The changing role of the university in the production of new knowledge. *Tert. Educ. Manage.*, 3, 1, 5–14, 1997.
104. Gibbons, M., *Higher Education Relevance in the 21st Century*, World Bank, Washington DC, USA, 1998.
105. Nkusi, A.C., Cunningham, J.A., Nyuur, R., Pattinson, S., The role of the entrepreneurial university in building an entrepreneurial ecosystem in a post-conflict economy: An exploratory study of Rwanda. *Thunderbird Int. Bus. Rev.*, 62, 5, 549–563, 2020.
106. Phillips, F., Managing technical risk-Understanding private sector decision making on early-stage technology-based projects. Prepared for US Department of Commerce Economic Assessment Office, Advanced Technology Program, National Institute of Standards and Technology, by L. M. Branscomb, K. P. Morse, and M. J. Roberts. NIST GCR 00-787, April 2000. *Technol. Forecast. Soc Change*, 69, 2, 217–221, 2002.
107. Porter, M.E. and Heppelmann, J.E., How Smart, Connected Products Are Transforming Companies. *Harv. Bus. Rev.*, 93, 10, 96–114, 2015, [Online], Available: https://hbr.org/2015/10/how-smart-connected-products-are-transforming-companies.pdf.
108. Berchicci, L., Towards an open R&D system: Internal R&D investment, external knowledge acquisition and innovative performance. *Res. Policy*, 42, 1, 117–127, 2013.
109. Åkesson, M., Sørensen, C., Eriksson, C., II, Ambidexterity under digitalization: A tale of two decades of new media at a Swedish newspaper. *Scand. J. Manage.*, 34, 3, 276–288, 2018.
110. Visconti, R.M., Larocca, A., Marconi, M., Big data-driven value chains and digital platforms: From value co-creation to monetization, in: *Big Data Analytics: Tools and Technology for Effective Planning*, pp. 355–371, 2017.

111. Singhal, N., An empirical investigation of Industry 4.0 preparedness in India. *Vision*, 25, 3, 300–311, 2021.
112. Stahl, B.C. and Wright, D., Ethics and privacy in AI and big data: Implementing responsible research and innovation. *IEEE Secur. Privacy*, 16, 3, 26–33, 2018.
113. Cath, C., Governing artificial intelligence: ethical, legal and technical opportunities and challenges. *Philos. Trans. R. Soc. London, Ser. A*, 376, 2133, 20180080, 2018.
114. Georghiou, L. and Keenan, M., Evaluation of national foresight activities: Assessing rationale, process and impact. *Technol. Forecast. Soc. Change*, 73, 7, 761–777, 2006.
115. Baheti, R. and Gill, H., Cyber-physical systems, in: *The Impact of Control Technology*, vol. 12, pp. 161–166, 2011.
116. S., B., *B. Data, Understanding How Data Powers Big Business*, Wiley, Hoboken, NJ, USA, 2013.
117. Weill, P. and Woerner, S.L., Thriving in an increasingly digital ecosystem. *MIT Sloan Manage. Rev.*, 56, 4, 27, 2015.
118. Sorri, K., Seppänen, M., Still, K., Valkokari, K., Business model innovation with platform canvas. *J. Bus. Models*, 7, 2, 1–13, 2019.
119. Ge, X. and Maisch, B., Industrial design thinking at siemens corporate technology, China, in: *Design Thinking for Innovation: Research and Practice*, pp. 165–181, 2016.
120. Rüßmann, M., Lorenz, M., Gerbert, P., Waldner, M., Justus, J., Engel, P., Harnisch, M., Industry 4.0: The future of productivity and growth in manufacturing industries. *Boston Consult. Group*, 9, 1, 54–89, 2015.
121. Botta, A., De Donato, W., Persico, V., Pescapé, A., Integration of cloud computing and internet of things: a survey. *Future Gener. Comput. Syst.*, 56, 684–700, 2016.
122. Sahu, A.K., Sharma, S., Tripathi, S.S., Singh, K.N., A study of authentication protocols in internet of things, in: *2019 International Conference on Information Technology (ICIT)*, Dec. 2019, IEEE, pp. 217–221.
123. Preskill, J., Quantum computing in the NISQ era and beyond. *Quantum*, 2, 79, 2018.
124. Indiveri, G. and Liu, S.C., Memory and information processing in neuromorphic systems. *Proc. IEEE*, 103, 8, 1379–1397, 2015.
125. Osseiran, A., Boccardi, F., Braun, V., Kusume, K., Marsch, P., Maternia, M., Fallgren, M., Scenarios for 5G mobile and wireless communications: the vision of the METIS project. *IEEE Commun. Mag.*, 52, 5, 26–35, 2014.
126. Chesterman, S. (Ed.), *Data Protection Law in Singapore: Privacy and Sovereignty in an Interconnected World*, Academy Publishing, Singapore, 2014.
127. Zhang, Y. and Wen, J., The IoT electric business model: Using blockchain technology for the internet of things. *Peer Peer Netw. Appl.*, 10, 983–994, 2017.

128. Geissdoerfer, M., Savaget, P., Bocken, N.M., Hultink, E.J., The Circular Economy–A new sustainability paradigm? *J. Clean. Prod.*, 143, 757–768, 2017.
129. Mourtzis, D., Panopoulos, N., Angelopoulos, J., A hybrid teaching factory model towards personalized education 4.0. *Int. J. Comput. Integr. Manuf.*, 36, 12, 1–21, 2022.
130. Mishra, A., Karmakar, S., Bose, A., Dutta, A., Design and development of IoT-based latency-optimized augmented reality framework in home automation and telemetry for smart lifestyle. *J. Reliab. Intell. Environ.*, 6, 169–187, 2020.
131. Korhonen, J., Nuur, C., Feldmann, A., Birkie, S.E., Circular economy as an essentially contested concept. *J. Cleaner Prod.*, 175, 544–552, 2018.

9

Managing Knowledge in the Era of Industry 4.0: Challenges and Strategies

Pawan Whig[1]*, Jhansi Bharathi Madavarapu[2], Nikhitha Yathiraju[2] and Ramya Thatikonda[2]

[1]*Vivekananda Institute of Professional Studies—TC, New Delhi, India*
[2]*University of The Cumberlands, Williamsburg, Kentucky, USA*

Abstract

This book chapter scrutinizes the influence of Industry 4.0 on knowledge management, crucial for organizational competitiveness. It delineates the evolving landscape by examining how Industry 4.0 reshapes knowledge management practices. Emphasizing the pivotal role of knowledge management in this era, it navigates through the realm of artificial intelligence, big data, and the Internet of Things, elucidating their impact on knowledge handling. The chapter meticulously unpacks the challenges stemming from this paradigm shift, encompassing concerns like data privacy, security, and the imperative need for workforce upskilling. Amidst the rapidly evolving ecosystem, it underscores the significance of adapting to these technological advancements while addressing the intricacies of managing knowledge effectively. Furthermore, the discourse culminates in strategic propositions and best practices, offering a roadmap for organizations to proficiently navigate the challenges. These strategies focus on leveraging technological tools while prioritizing data security, fostering a culture of continuous learning, and implementing robust frameworks for effective knowledge management. Overall, this chapter serves as a comprehensive guide for organizations seeking to harness the potential of Industry 4.0 while adeptly managing their knowledge assets.

Keywords: Knowledge management, Industry 4.0, artificial intelligence, big data, Internet of Things, data privacy, upskilling, reskilling

**Corresponding author*: pawanwhig@gmail.com
Pawan Whig: ORCID: https://orcid.org/0000-0003-1863-1591
Jhansi Bharathi Madavarapu: ORCID: https://orcid.org/0000-0001-8478-6626
Nikhitha Yathiraju: ORCID: https://orcid.org/0000-0003-1908-3267
Ramya Thatikonda: ORCID: https://orcid.org/0009-0001-1192-778X

Rajendra Kumar, Vishal Jain, Venus C. Ibarra, Corrienna Abdul Talib and Vinay Kukreja (eds.) Knowledge Management and Industry Revolution 4.0, (239–274) © 2024 Scrivener Publishing LLC

9.1 Introduction

The rapid advancements in technology have ushered in the fourth industrial revolution, known as Industry 4.0, which is transforming the way businesses and industries operate. Industry 4.0 is characterized by the integration of digital technologies into various aspects of production, creating a highly interconnected and intelligent ecosystem [1]. These technologies, such as artificial intelligence, big data analytics, the Internet of Things (IoT), and automation, have enabled organizations to streamline processes, optimize efficiency, and enhance product and service offerings. In the era of Industry 4.0, knowledge has become an invaluable asset for organizations striving to stay competitive in the dynamic global market. Knowledge management, the process of identifying, capturing, storing, organizing, and disseminating knowledge within an organization, has become more critical than ever. Effectively managing knowledge in Industry 4.0 is essential for maintaining a competitive edge, fostering innovation, and ensuring long-term sustainability [2]. Industry 4.0 represents a paradigm shift in manufacturing and production processes, powered by the convergence of physical and digital technologies. It builds upon the foundations laid by previous industrial revolutions but takes them to new heights through the integration of smart systems, data-driven decision making, and cyber-physical systems [3, 4]. Central to this revolution is the concept of interconnectedness, where machines, devices, and systems communicate and collaborate seamlessly, allowing for real-time data exchange and analysis [5, 6].

The transformative potential of Industry 4.0 is evident across various sectors, from manufacturing and logistics to healthcare and finance. Smart factories equipped with IoT sensors and AI-powered analytics can optimize production, predict maintenance needs, and reduce downtime. Supply chains are becoming more efficient and transparent through the use of blockchain technology. AI-driven personalized services are enhancing customer experiences, and data analytics is enabling data-driven insights for better decision making [7, 8]. The primary objective of this book chapter is to delve into the challenges and opportunities of knowledge management in the context of Industry 4.0. With the rapid adoption of digital technologies and the exponential growth of data, organizations face unique challenges in effectively managing knowledge assets. Understanding the implications of Industry 4.0 on knowledge management is crucial for organizations seeking to leverage their intellectual capital and adapt to the changing landscape. Furthermore, this chapter aims to shed light on the critical role of knowledge management in driving innovation within organizations. As businesses seek to innovate and develop new products, services, and processes, they must harness the collective knowledge of their workforce. Effective knowledge management practices can facilitate knowledge creation, sharing, and dissemination, fostering a culture of innovation and continuous improvement [9].

In this chapter, we will explore the concept of knowledge management and its relevance in the era of Industry 4.0. We will delve into the different dimensions of knowledge management, including knowledge creation, acquisition, storage, retrieval, and utilization [10]. Additionally, the chapter will discuss the impact of Industry 4.0 technologies, such as artificial intelligence, big data, and the IoT, on knowledge management practices. We will also examine the challenges organizations face in managing knowledge in a rapidly evolving digital landscape. These challenges include ensuring data privacy and security, coping with information overload, and addressing the need for upskilling and reskilling the workforce to keep up with technological advancements. To address these challenges, the chapter will propose strategies and best practices for organizations to effectively manage knowledge in the era of Industry 4.0 [11]. These strategies will encompass organizational culture, leadership support, technology adoption, and the fostering of collaborative and knowledge-sharing environments [12]. The era of Industry 4.0 presents both immense challenges and unprecedented opportunities for organizations regarding knowledge management. Embracing effective knowledge management practices can empower organizations to harness the full potential of Industry 4.0, driving innovation, and ensuring long-term success in the ever-changing global landscape [13]. By understanding the interplay between knowledge management and Industry 4.0 technologies, organizations can thrive in this new era of digital transformation.

9.2 Literature Review

The advent of Industry 4.0 has brought about significant transformations in the industrial landscape, driven by the integration of advanced technologies such as cyber-physical systems, artificial intelligence, big data analytics, and the Internet of Things (IoT). In this context, knowledge management plays a pivotal role in enabling organizations to harness the vast amounts of data and knowledge generated by Industry 4.0 technologies for informed decision making, innovation, and sustainable competitive advantage [14–16]. Several researchers have explored the key concepts and challenges associated with knowledge management in Industry 4.0. Wan *et al.* (2015) [8] presented a comprehensive survey of enabling technologies in Industry 4.0, highlighting the critical role of knowledge management in leveraging these technologies effectively. They emphasized the importance of establishing a knowledge-sharing culture and leveraging AI and big data analytics for knowledge discovery and decision making [17–19]. Luo (2014) discussed Germany's Industry 4.0 strategy and its potential implications for China's industrial transformation. The study underscored the need for China to focus on knowledge management practices to effectively implement its industrial transformation in line with Industry 4.0 principles [20].

Researchers emphasized the design challenges and survey of cyber-physical systems, highlighting the importance of knowledge management in ensuring seamless integration and collaboration between physical and virtual components in Industry 4.0. Vogel-Heuser *et al.* (2014) [5] explored the coupling of heterogeneous production systems using a multi-agent based cyber-physical production system. They highlighted the significance of knowledge management in creating a unified platform for diverse production systems to collaborate efficiently. Strang and Anderl (2014) [6] discussed the use of assembly process-driven component data models in cyber-physical production systems. The study emphasized the role of knowledge management in creating data models that facilitate seamless data exchange and knowledge sharing in smart production environments. Jiang and Li (2014) [7] discussed the concept of "German Industry 4.0" as the embodiment of cyber-physical systems in the real world. They highlighted knowledge management as the foundation of this transformation and its implications for global industrial progress. Wan *et al.* (2011) [1] delved into the advances in cyber-physical systems research, emphasizing the interplay of knowledge management and the development of intelligent systems for Industry 4.0. Miao (2014) [8] and He (2014) [9] explored the concept of Industry 4.0 as a new industrial revolution and discussed its potential impact on industrial automation and CPS. Both studies highlighted the critical role of knowledge management in enabling seamless communication and collaboration between machines and humans.

Researchers like Zhu (2015), OuYang (2014) [10], Dong and Zhou (2014) [16] provided further insights into the challenges, prospects, and applications of Industry 4.0, emphasizing knowledge management as a central enabler for the success of this industrial revolution. The emerging field of blockchain technology has also gained attention in the context of Industry 4.0 and knowledge management. Kumar *et al.* (2023) [17] explored the application of blockchain for IoT to reduce carbon footprint and enhance data security. They highlighted blockchain's potential to enhance knowledge management in the context of IoT applications. Another study by Whig *et al.* (2022) [18] discussed the economic impact of AI-enabled blockchain in 6G-based industry, emphasizing the synergy between AI, blockchain, and knowledge management for sustainable economic growth. Whig *et al.* (2022) [19] also presented a blockchain platform to resolve security issues in IoT and smart networks, showcasing the potential of blockchain in ensuring secure knowledge sharing and collaboration in Industry 4.0 ecosystems. In a case study, Whig *et al.* (2022) [20] demystified federated learning for blockchain and IoT, demonstrating how federated learning can enhance knowledge management and data privacy in distributed environments. The literature highlights the criticality of knowledge management in the era of Industry 4.0. It underscores the need for organizations to adopt best practices, leverage advanced technologies, and foster a knowledge-sharing culture to unlock the full potential of Industry 4.0 and gain a competitive advantage in the digital age. Below is a tabular representation of the literature review on knowledge management in the era of Industry 4.0, along with identified research gaps:

Table 9.1 presents a systematic review of the literature on knowledge management in Industry 4.0, highlighting key findings from each study and identifying gaps for further research. The gaps in the existing literature point to areas where more in-depth exploration is needed to fully understand the challenges, limitations, and potential of knowledge management in the context of Industry 4.0. These research gaps offer valuable insights for researchers and practitioners seeking to advance knowledge management practices in the era of Industry 4.0.

Table 9.1 Literature review with research gap.

No.	Study	Key findings	Research gap
1	Wan *et al.* (2015) [1]	- Importance of knowledge management in leveraging enabling technologies in Industry 4.0 - Emphasis on AI and big data analytics for knowledge discovery and decision-making	Lack of in-depth exploration of the challenges and limitations of AI and big data analytics in knowledge management

(*Continued*)

Table 9.1 Literature review with research gap. (*Continued*)

No.	Study	Key findings	Research gap
2	Luo (2014) [2]	- Germany's Industry 4.0 strategy and its relevance to China's industrial transformation - Implications for China's need to focus on knowledge management for effective implementation	Limited exploration of other countries' experiences and lessons for knowledge management adoption in Industry 4.0
3	Lee (2008) and Shi *et al.* (2011) [3]	- Design challenges and survey of cyber-physical systems - Importance of knowledge management in seamless integration and collaboration between physical and virtual components	Limited discussion on the role of knowledge management in addressing design challenges specific to cyber-physical systems
4	Vogel-Heuser *et al.* (2014) [5]	- Coupling of heterogeneous production systems using a multi-agent-based cyber-physical production system - Significance of knowledge management in creating a unified platform for diverse production systems	Lack of exploration of the impact of knowledge management on the efficiency and productivity of the coupled production systems
5	Strang and Anderl (2014) [6]	- Use of assembly process-driven component data models in cyber-physical production systems - Role of knowledge management in creating data models for seamless data exchange and knowledge sharing	Limited examination of the scalability and adaptability of the component data model in complex production environments

(*Continued*)

Table 9.1 Literature review with research gap. (*Continued*)

No.	Study	Key findings	Research gap
6	Jiang and Li (2014) [7]	- Discussion on "German Industry 4.0" and its embodiment of cyber-physical systems in the real world - Implications for global industrial progress and the importance of knowledge management as a foundation for transformation	Lack of comparative analysis between different countries' approaches to Industry 4.0 and their knowledge management strategies
8	Miao (2014) and He (2014) [8, 9]	- Exploration of Industry 4.0 as a new industrial revolution - Emphasis on knowledge management for seamless communication and collaboration between machines and humans	Lack of analysis on the challenges of integrating knowledge management practices into existing industrial automation systems
9	Zhu (2015), OuYang (2014), Dong and Zhou (2014) [10–12]	- Insight into the challenges, prospects, and applications of Industry 4.0 - Emphasis on knowledge management as a central enabler for the success of this industrial revolution	Limited exploration of the potential role of knowledge management in addressing ethical and social implications of Industry 4.0
10	Kumar *et al.* (2023) [17]	- Application of blockchain for IoT to reduce carbon footprint and enhance data security - Potential of blockchain to enhance knowledge management in IoT applications	Gap in understanding the scalability and interoperability of blockchain solutions for knowledge management across diverse IoT ecosystems

(*Continued*)

Table 9.1 Literature review with research gap. (*Continued*)

No.	Study	Key findings	Research gap
11	Whig *et al.* (2022) [18]	- Economic impact of AI-enabled blockchain in 6G-based industry - Synergy between AI, blockchain, and knowledge management for sustainable economic growth	Limited exploration of the potential risks and challenges associated with the integration of AI and blockchain in knowledge management
12	Whig *et al.* (2022) [19]	- Use of blockchain platform to resolve security issues in IoT and smart networks - Potential of blockchain in ensuring secure knowledge sharing and collaboration in Industry 4.0 ecosystems	Lack of examination of the legal and regulatory considerations related to using blockchain for knowledge management in Industry 4.0
13	Whig *et al.* (2022) [20]	- Demystifying federated learning for blockchain and IoT - Demonstrating how federated learning can enhance knowledge management and data privacy in distributed environments	Limited exploration of the impact of federated learning on knowledge management performance and data accuracy in Industry 4.0

9.3 Impacts of Industry 4.0

Industry 4.0, with its rapid technological advancements and digital transformation, has significantly impacted knowledge management practices within organizations. This section provides an overview of the key impacts of Industry 4.0 on knowledge management, highlighting both the challenges and opportunities it presents.

1. **Data Explosion and Information Overload:** Industry 4.0 technologies generate an unprecedented amount of data

from various sources, including IoT devices, sensors, and digital interactions. The abundance of data can lead to information overload, making it challenging for organizations to identify relevant knowledge and extract actionable insights. Knowledge management strategies need to be adapted to handle this influx of data and transform it into meaningful knowledge.

2. **Real-Time Knowledge Sharing and Collaboration:** Industry 4.0 enables seamless communication and collaboration among employees, teams, and even external stakeholders. Cloud-based platforms, collaborative tools, and virtual workspaces facilitate real-time knowledge sharing and decision making. This allows organizations to tap into the collective expertise of their workforce, leading to more informed and agile decision-making processes.
3. **Enhanced Knowledge Discovery through AI and Big Data:** The integration of artificial intelligence and big data analytics in Industry 4.0 provides powerful tools for knowledge discovery. AI algorithms can analyze vast datasets, identify patterns, and extract valuable insights, aiding in knowledge creation and discovery. This empowers organizations to make data-driven decisions based on evidence and trends.
4. **Knowledge Preservation and Intellectual Property Protection:** As knowledge becomes increasingly critical for innovation and competitive advantage, preserving organizational knowledge and protecting intellectual property become vital. Industry 4.0 technologies offer advanced data encryption, access controls, and authentication mechanisms to safeguard sensitive knowledge from unauthorized access or data breaches.
5. **Upskilling and Reskilling the Workforce:** With the advent of automation and AI, Industry 4.0 demands a skilled workforce capable of working alongside intelligent machines. Knowledge management plays a pivotal role in upskilling and reskilling employees, ensuring they possess the necessary knowledge and competencies to thrive in the digital age.
6. **Cultural Shift Toward Knowledge Sharing:** Industry 4.0 fosters a culture of knowledge sharing and collaboration. With the availability of real-time communication tools and knowledge-sharing platforms, organizations are encouraged to embrace a knowledge-sharing culture. This cultural shift

promotes open dialogue, idea exchange, and continuous learning among employees, driving innovation and creativity.

7. **Decentralized Knowledge Management:** Traditional centralized knowledge management approaches may become less effective in the era of Industry 4.0, where knowledge is distributed across various digital platforms and devices. Organizations need to adopt decentralized knowledge management strategies to accommodate the diverse sources and formats of knowledge generated by IoT devices, cloud services, and edge computing.
8. **Agility and Adaptability in Knowledge Management Practices:** Industry 4.0 is characterized by its dynamic nature, with technology evolving rapidly. Knowledge management practices must be agile and adaptable to keep pace with these changes. Organizations should be prepared to modify their knowledge management strategies in response to new technological developments and emerging challenges.
9. **Customer-Centric Knowledge Management:** Industry 4.0 allows organizations to gather extensive customer data, preferences, and feedback. Knowledge management can be leveraged to gain valuable customer insights, leading to the development of customer-centric products and services. Understanding customer needs and expectations becomes crucial for maintaining a competitive edge.

Industry 4.0 has revolutionized knowledge management practices, requiring organizations to adapt and leverage emerging technologies to harness knowledge effectively. Embracing real-time collaboration, data analytics, and decentralized knowledge management approaches can empower organizations to thrive in the digital age and stay competitive in the rapidly evolving global landscape. Balancing the challenges and opportunities presented by Industry 4.0 enables organizations to transform data into actionable knowledge, driving innovation, and ensuring sustainable growth.

9.4 Importance of Knowledge Management in the Context of Industry 4.0

The importance of knowledge management in the context of Industry 4.0 cannot be overstated as shown in Figure 9.1. As the fourth industrial revolution brings about radical changes in the way businesses operate, knowledge management plays a pivotal role in helping organizations leverage their intellectual capital and adapt to the dynamic digital landscape. The following points highlight the significance of knowledge management in the era of Industry 4.0:

1. **Effective Decision Making:** Industry 4.0 technologies generate vast amounts of data from various sources. Knowledge management enables organizations to effectively process and analyze these data, transforming it into meaningful insights. Informed decision making based on data-driven knowledge empowers organizations to respond promptly to market trends, customer demands, and changing business conditions.
2. **Innovation and R&D:** Knowledge management facilitates the capture and dissemination of knowledge across different departments and teams. This cross-functional knowledge sharing fosters a culture of innovation, where ideas and expertise from diverse sources can converge to drive research and development efforts. It enables organizations to develop new products, services, and processes, ensuring they remain competitive and stay ahead of the curve.
3. **Competitive Advantage:** In Industry 4.0, where technology adoption is widespread, the real differentiator lies in how organizations manage and apply knowledge. Those organizations that excel in capturing, refining, and utilizing knowledge gain a competitive advantage. Knowledge management enables organizations to leverage their unique insights and capabilities to stand out in the market.
4. **Risk Mitigation and Compliance:** Industry 4.0 introduces new challenges in terms of data privacy, security, and regulatory compliance. Knowledge management aids in addressing these challenges by ensuring that sensitive information is adequately protected, and compliance requirements are met. Knowledge about potential risks and their mitigation strategies can also be systematically captured and shared across the organization.
5. **Efficient Collaboration and Communication:** The interconnected nature of Industry 4.0 demands seamless collaboration and communication among teams, departments, and even external partners. Knowledge management platforms

and tools enable efficient knowledge sharing, reducing silos, and promoting cross-functional collaboration. This fosters a collaborative work environment where expertise can be tapped from anywhere within the organization.

6. **Adaptability to Technological Advancements:** Industry 4.0 is characterized by rapid technological advancements. Knowledge management ensures that employees stay updated with the latest technologies and best practices. It facilitates upskilling and reskilling initiatives to equip the workforce with the knowledge needed to work alongside intelligent machines and adapt to new technologies.
7. **Knowledge Retention and Transfer:** With an aging workforce, organizations face the risk of knowledge loss due to retirements and employee turnover. Knowledge management practices, such as documentation, knowledge repositories, and mentorship programs, enable the retention and transfer of critical knowledge from experienced employees to newer generations.
8. **Customer-Centric Approach:** In Industry 4.0, understanding customer needs and preferences is crucial for success. Knowledge management helps gather and analyze customer data, enabling organizations to gain valuable insights into customer behavior. This customer-centric approach leads to personalized offerings, improved customer experiences, and enhanced customer satisfaction.
9. **Continuous Improvement and Learning:** Industry 4.0 is a journey of continuous improvement and learning. Knowledge management fosters a learning culture, where employees are encouraged to share lessons learned and best practices. This leads to organizational learning and the continuous refinement of processes and operations.

Knowledge management is a fundamental enabler of success in Industry 4.0. It empowers organizations to harness the wealth of information generated by advanced technologies, make informed decisions, drive innovation, and remain competitive in the fast-paced digital era. Organizations that recognize the importance of knowledge management and invest in its implementation are better equipped to thrive in the dynamic and disruptive landscape of Industry 4.0.

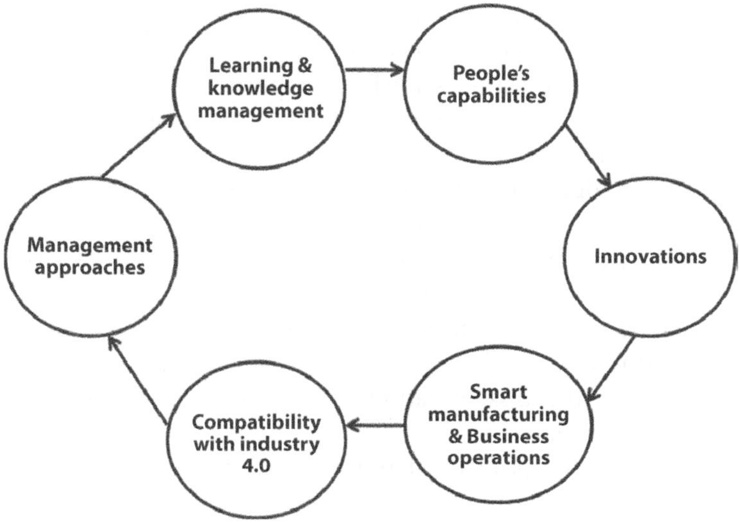

Figure 9.1 Importance of knowledge management in the context of Industry 4.0.

9.5 Knowledge Management

Knowledge management (KM) is the process of identifying, capturing, organizing, storing, retrieving, and sharing knowledge within an organization to enhance its performance, foster innovation, and gain a competitive advantage. It involves the systematic management of both explicit knowledge (formal, codified information) and tacit knowledge (personal insights, experiences, and expertise) to facilitate effective decision making, problem solving, and learning.

Principles

1. **Knowledge Creation and Acquisition:** Knowledge management begins with the creation and acquisition of knowledge. This principle emphasizes the importance of fostering a culture of continuous learning and innovation within the organization. It involves encouraging employees to share their expertise, experiences, and insights, as well as seeking external knowledge through collaboration, research, and partnerships.
2. **Knowledge Capture and Documentation:** The process of knowledge management involves capturing both explicit

and tacit knowledge in a structured and organized manner. This principle emphasizes the importance of documenting knowledge, creating knowledge repositories, and utilizing various tools and technologies to ensure knowledge is accessible to those who need it.

3. **Knowledge Sharing and Dissemination:** Knowledge management is about making knowledge available to the right people at the right time. This principle emphasizes the importance of sharing knowledge across departments, teams, and hierarchies within the organization. Effective communication channels and knowledge-sharing platforms facilitate the dissemination of knowledge and encourage collaboration.
4. **Knowledge Application and Utilization:** Knowledge management is not just about storing information but also about applying it effectively. This principle stresses the importance of using knowledge to inform decision making, problem solving, and strategic planning. Knowledge should be applied to improve processes, products, services, and overall organizational performance.
5. **Knowledge Evaluation and Validation:** Not all knowledge is equal, and not all information is accurate. This principle highlights the importance of evaluating and validating knowledge to ensure its relevance, reliability, and credibility. Peer reviews, data analysis, and expert assessments are some of the methods used to validate knowledge.
6. **Organizational Learning and Adaptation:** Knowledge management is closely tied to organizational learning and adaptation. This principle emphasizes the continuous improvement of organizational practices based on insights gained from knowledge management processes. The organization should be agile and responsive to changes in the internal and external environment.

Importance

1. **Enhanced Decision Making:** Knowledge management provides decision makers with timely and relevant information, enabling them to make informed choices. It reduces reliance on gut feelings and intuition and promotes data-driven decision making.

2. **Innovation and Creativity:** By capturing and sharing knowledge, organizations can leverage the collective intelligence of their employees, leading to enhanced innovation and creativity. Knowledge management fosters a culture of learning and encourages employees to contribute ideas and insights.
3. **Efficient Problem Solving:** Access to a comprehensive knowledge base allows employees to draw upon past experiences and solutions to address current challenges. This reduces redundancy and streamlines problem-solving efforts.
4. **Improved Collaboration:** Knowledge management promotes collaboration and knowledge sharing among employees and teams. It breaks down silos, facilitates communication, and encourages cross-functional learning.
5. **Competitive Advantage:** Organizations that effectively manage their knowledge gain a competitive edge in the market. The ability to utilize knowledge for strategic decision making and innovation sets them apart from competitors.
6. **Knowledge Retention:** As experienced employees retire or leave the organization, knowledge management ensures that their expertise is retained and passed on to the next generation of employees.
7. **Learning Organization:** Knowledge management contributes to creating a learning organization, where continuous learning and improvement are ingrained in the organizational culture.

Knowledge management is a critical process that enables organizations to harness their collective knowledge, make informed decisions, foster innovation, and maintain a competitive advantage in a rapidly changing business environment. By implementing effective knowledge management principles, organizations can optimize their intellectual capital and position themselves for long-term success and growth.

9.6 Overview of Industry 4.0 and Technologies

Industry 4.0, also known as the fourth industrial revolution, represents a paradigm shift in the manufacturing and production landscape. It is characterized by the integration of digital technologies into industrial processes, creating a highly connected and intelligent ecosystem. Some of the key technologies driving Industry 4.0 include:

1. **Internet of Things (IoT):** IoT refers to a network of physical devices, sensors, and objects embedded with software, connectivity, and sensors that enables them to collect and exchange data. In Industry 4.0, IoT devices are extensively used to monitor and control various aspects of production, enabling real-time data analysis and decision making.
2. **Big Data and Analytics:** Industry 4.0 generates an enormous volume of data from IoT devices, machines, and processes. Big data analytics involves the use of advanced algorithms and technologies to process and analyze these data, extracting valuable insights and patterns that can inform decision making and improve operational efficiency.
3. **Artificial Intelligence (AI):** AI encompasses a range of technologies, including machine learning, natural language processing, and computer vision. In Industry 4.0, AI is used to automate processes, predict maintenance needs, optimize production, and enhance decision making through data-driven insights.
4. **Robotics and Automation:** Industry 4.0 leverages robotics and automation to enhance manufacturing processes, increase productivity, and improve product quality. Robots are used for repetitive tasks, reducing human intervention and improving efficiency.
5. **Cyber-Physical Systems (CPS):** CPS refers to the integration of physical systems with digital technologies, enabling real-time data exchange and interaction between the physical and virtual worlds. CPS is at the core of Industry 4.0, facilitating seamless communication and control of industrial processes.

9.7 Implications of Industry 4.0 for Knowledge Management

Industry 4.0 brings about several implications for knowledge management practices within organizations. These implications arise from the transformational impact of technology and the changing nature of knowledge creation, sharing, and utilization. Some of the key implications include:

1. **Data-Driven Knowledge Management:** With the vast amount of data generated by Industry 4.0 technologies, knowledge management becomes more data driven. Organizations can use big data analytics and AI to identify patterns, trends, and insights from the data, enabling evidence-based decision making.
2. **Real-Time Knowledge Sharing and Collaboration:** IoT and other technologies enable real-time communication and collaboration among employees, teams, and stakeholders. Knowledge management platforms facilitate instant knowledge sharing, enabling faster response to challenges and opportunities.
3. **Knowledge Discovery and Innovation:** AI and big data analytics enable organizations to discover new knowledge and insights from the data. This leads to improved innovation processes as organizations can identify gaps, untapped opportunities, and potential areas for improvement.
4. **Tacit Knowledge Capture:** IoT devices and sensors can capture real-time data and operational insights, including tacit knowledge that was previously challenging to capture. This enables the preservation and sharing of critical expertise and experiences.
5. **Decentralized Knowledge Management:** The distributed nature of Industry 4.0 technologies calls for decentralized knowledge management strategies. Knowledge is generated and stored across various devices and systems, requiring organizations to adopt agile and adaptive knowledge management practices.

9.8 Role of Artificial Intelligence, Big Data, and IoT in Knowledge Management

1. **Artificial Intelligence (AI):** AI plays a crucial role in knowledge management by automating knowledge discovery, curation, and retrieval processes. AI-powered chatbots and

virtual assistants can answer employees' queries, provide information, and offer contextual knowledge support.

2. **Big Data and Analytics:** Big data analytics helps in uncovering hidden patterns and trends in the vast amounts of data generated by Industry 4.0. Knowledge management platforms can use data analytics to suggest relevant knowledge resources to employees based on their needs and preferences.
3. **Internet of Things (IoT):** IoT devices collect real-time data from various sources, enabling organizations to gain insights into operational processes and customer behavior. These data can be integrated into knowledge management systems to inform decision making and enhance organizational learning.

Industry 4.0 and its key technologies have profound implications for knowledge management. Organizations must adapt their knowledge management practices to leverage the vast amounts of data, embrace real-time collaboration, and harness the power of AI and big data analytics. The seamless integration of these technologies with knowledge management processes can empower organizations to make informed decisions, drive innovation, and maintain a competitive edge in the digital age.

9.9 Challenges of Knowledge Management in Industry 4.0

1. **Data Privacy and Security Challenges in Knowledge Management:** Industry 4.0 generates a vast amount of data from various sources, including IoT devices, sensors, and digital interactions. This abundance of data poses significant data privacy and security challenges for knowledge management. Ensuring the confidentiality, integrity, and availability of sensitive knowledge becomes critical. Organizations must implement robust data encryption, access controls, and authentication mechanisms to protect valuable knowledge from unauthorized access or data breaches.
2. **The Need for Upskilling and Reskilling of the Workforce:** As Industry 4.0 technologies continue to evolve, the skills required to manage and leverage knowledge effectively also change. The workforce needs to be upskilled and reskilled to adapt to the new technological landscape. Employees must

be trained in data analytics, AI, cybersecurity, and other emerging technologies to effectively utilize knowledge management tools and make informed decisions based on data-driven insights.

3. **Managing Knowledge in a Rapidly Changing Environment:** Industry 4.0 is characterized by its dynamic nature, with technology evolving rapidly. This poses challenges for knowledge management as existing knowledge may quickly become obsolete, and new knowledge needs to be acquired and integrated continually. Organizations must establish agile knowledge management practices to keep up with technological advancements and ensure knowledge relevance and accuracy.
4. **Information Overload and Knowledge Quality:** The abundance of data in Industry 4.0 can lead to information overload, making it challenging to identify relevant and high-quality knowledge. The sheer volume of data may make it difficult for employees to access and discern valuable insights. Effective knowledge management strategies are needed to filter, organize, and present knowledge in a meaningful way to prevent information overload and maintain knowledge quality.
5. **Cultural and Behavioral Challenges:** Implementing knowledge management practices requires a cultural shift within the organization. In some cases, employees may be hesitant to share knowledge due to concerns about job security, competition, or lack of incentives. Developing a culture of knowledge sharing, collaboration, and learning is crucial for successful knowledge management in Industry 4.0.
6. **Integration and Interoperability:** Industry 4.0 technologies often come from different vendors and may use different data formats and protocols. Ensuring seamless integration and interoperability between these technologies poses challenges for knowledge management systems. Organizations must invest in compatible and scalable knowledge management platforms to enable effective data exchange and collaboration.
7. **Knowledge Retention and Transfer:** With an aging workforce, organizations face the risk of knowledge loss due to retirements and employee turnover. Knowledge retention and transfer become critical challenges in Industry 4.0. Organizations must implement strategies, such as

mentorship programs, documentation, and knowledge repositories, to capture and transfer critical knowledge from experienced employees to newer generations.
8. **Balancing Automation and Human Expertise:** As automation and AI technologies become more prevalent, organizations must strike a balance between automation and human expertise in knowledge management. While automation can improve efficiency and data processing, human expertise remains essential for interpreting complex data, making strategic decisions, and fostering innovation.

Industry 4.0 introduces several challenges for knowledge management, ranging from data privacy and security concerns to the need for upskilling the workforce and managing knowledge in a rapidly changing environment. Overcoming these challenges requires proactive measures, including robust data security measures, ongoing workforce development, agile knowledge management practices, and a culture of knowledge sharing and collaboration. Successfully addressing these challenges empowers organizations to harness knowledge effectively, make informed decisions, and achieve a competitive advantage in the digital age of Industry 4.0.

9.10 Strategies for Effective Knowledge Management

1. **Establish a Knowledge-Sharing Culture:** Foster a culture that encourages knowledge sharing, collaboration, and continuous learning. Recognize and reward employees for sharing their expertise and insights. Create platforms and channels for easy and seamless knowledge exchange, such as knowledge-sharing forums, social collaboration tools, and virtual brainstorming sessions.
2. **Create Knowledge Repositories and Taxonomies:** Develop centralized knowledge repositories where employees can access and contribute to a wide range of knowledge assets, including documents, best practices, case studies, and lessons learned. Implement clear and user-friendly taxonomies to categorize and organize knowledge for easy retrieval.
3. **Leverage AI and Big Data Analytics:** Embrace AI and big data analytics to discover valuable insights from the vast amounts of data generated by Industry 4.0 technologies.

Use AI-driven algorithms to identify patterns, trends, and correlations in the data, providing employees with data-driven knowledge for better decision making.

4. **Upskill and Reskill the Workforce:** Invest in training programs to upskill employees in data analytics, AI, and other relevant technologies. Ensure that the workforce is equipped with the knowledge and competencies required to effectively use knowledge management tools and make informed decisions based on data-driven insights.
5. **Implement Knowledge Management Platforms:** Deploy integrated knowledge management platforms that encompass various technologies, such as AI-driven chatbots, collaborative workspaces, and data analytics tools. Choose scalable and interoperable platforms that can adapt to the changing technological landscape of Industry 4.0.
6. **Encourage Cross-Functional Collaboration:** Promote collaboration and knowledge sharing across departments and teams. Facilitate cross-functional projects and initiatives to encourage diverse perspectives and expertise. Cross-functional collaboration fosters innovation and enables the effective sharing of knowledge across different parts of the organization.
7. **Capture Tacit Knowledge:** Recognize the value of tacit knowledge and implement methods to capture and share it. Encourage experienced employees to mentor and share their insights with younger colleagues. Use storytelling, video documentation, and other techniques to preserve tacit knowledge for future reference.
8. **Ensure Data Privacy and Security:** Implement robust data privacy and security measures to protect sensitive knowledge from unauthorized access or breaches. Comply with data protection regulations and create clear policies regarding the handling and sharing of sensitive information.
9. **Facilitate Continuous Learning:** Encourage a culture of continuous learning and improvement. Offer opportunities for employees to attend workshops, conferences, and online courses to stay updated on Industry 4.0 technologies and knowledge management practices.
10. **Embrace Change and Agility:** Recognize that Industry 4.0 is a dynamic and ever-evolving landscape. Embrace change

and be agile in adapting knowledge management strategies to new technologies, market trends, and business needs.

11. **Integrate Knowledge Management with Business Processes:** Embed knowledge management practices into various business processes and workflows. Ensure that knowledge sharing and utilization are integral parts of daily operations, decision making, and innovation initiatives.

By implementing these strategies, organizations can effectively manage knowledge in the context of Industry 4.0, harnessing the power of data and technology to make informed decisions, drive innovation, and maintain a competitive advantage in the digital age.

9.11 Best Practices for Knowledge Management in Industry 4.0

1. **Leadership Support and Cultural Alignment:** Ensure that knowledge management is supported and championed by top leadership. Create a culture that values knowledge sharing, collaboration, and continuous learning. Leaders should lead by example and actively participate in knowledge-sharing initiatives.
2. **Integration with Business Strategy:** Align knowledge management with the organization's overall business strategy. Identify key knowledge needs and prioritize knowledge management efforts based on strategic objectives.
3. **Clear Objectives and Metrics:** Set clear objectives for knowledge management initiatives and establish measurable metrics to track their success. Regularly assess the impact of knowledge management efforts on organizational performance.
4. **Cross-Functional Collaboration:** Encourage collaboration and knowledge sharing across different departments and teams. Facilitate cross-functional projects and initiatives to leverage diverse expertise and perspectives.
5. **Employee Training and Development:** Invest in training programs to enhance employees' knowledge management skills. Provide training on using knowledge management platforms, data analytics, AI, and other relevant technologies.

6. **Knowledge Retention and Succession Planning:** Implement knowledge retention strategies to capture and transfer critical knowledge from experienced employees to newer generations. Develop succession plans to ensure the continuity of knowledge in key roles.
7. **Continuous Improvement and Learning:** Foster a culture of continuous improvement and learning. Encourage employees to regularly update and refine knowledge resources to reflect the latest insights and developments.
8. **User-Friendly Knowledge Management Platforms:** Choose knowledge management platforms that are user-friendly and intuitive. Ensure that employees can easily access, contribute to, and retrieve knowledge assets.
9. **Community of Practice:** Establish communities of practice where employees with shared interests or expertise can come together to collaborate and share knowledge. These communities facilitate organic knowledge exchange and peer learning.

9.12 Strategies for Leveraging Technology for Effective Knowledge Management

1. **Artificial Intelligence (AI) for Knowledge Discovery:** Use AI algorithms to analyze vast amounts of data and identify valuable insights and patterns. AI-driven knowledge discovery can help uncover hidden knowledge and trends that may not be immediately apparent.
2. **Big Data Analytics for Decision Making:** Utilize big data analytics to process and analyze data from various sources, enabling data-driven decision making and strategy formulation.
3. **Internet of Things (IoT) for Real-Time Data Collection:** Deploy IoT devices to collect real-time data from production processes, equipment, and products. Real-time data provides timely insights for informed decision making and continuous improvement.
4. **Collaboration Tools for Knowledge Sharing:** Implement collaborative workspaces and communication tools that

facilitate real-time knowledge sharing and collaboration among employees, regardless of their physical location.

5. **Data Visualization for Insights:** Utilize data visualization tools to present complex data in a clear and easily understandable format. Data visualization aids in communicating insights and knowledge effectively.

9.13 Case Studies of Successful Knowledge Management in Industry 4.0

1. **Siemens:** The case study focuses on Siemens, a prominent global technology company, and its implementation of a cutting-edge knowledge management platform. This platform integrates artificial intelligence (AI) and machine learning (ML) technologies to extract valuable insights from vast repositories of technical documents within the company.

   Siemens' initiative primarily aims to empower engineers by providing swift and efficient access to pertinent information and best practices. By leveraging AI and ML algorithms, this knowledge management platform sifts through extensive technical documentation, extracting critical knowledge nuggets and organizing them for easy accessibility. This serves as a reservoir of insights, enabling engineers to swiftly locate relevant information essential for their tasks and projects. The platform's key impact lies in its ability to significantly enhance productivity among engineers. It accelerates problem-solving processes by reducing the time required to search for and access pertinent information. Engineers can leverage the platform to quickly find solutions, adopt best practices, and access the collective knowledge accumulated within the organization.

   Ultimately, Siemens' adoption of this advanced knowledge management platform showcases the transformative power of AI and ML in streamlining information retrieval processes. By facilitating rapid access to crucial insights, it not only amplifies engineers' productivity but also promotes efficient problem solving, fostering a culture of innovation and excellence within the organization.

2. **General Electric (GE):** GE uses IoT sensors in its jet engines and industrial turbines to collect real-time data. These data are then analyzed using big data analytics and AI to predict maintenance needs, optimize performance, and improve product design.

The case study highlights General Electric's (GE) innovative utilization of IoT (Internet of Things) sensors integrated into their jet engines and industrial turbines. These sensors continuously gather real-time operational data from the machinery during its usage.

GE leverages the power of big data analytics and artificial intelligence (AI) to analyze the extensive stream of real-time data collected from the IoT sensors. This data analysis serves several critical purposes:

1. **Predictive Maintenance:** By employing advanced analytics and AI algorithms, GE can predict maintenance needs by detecting patterns and anomalies in the operational data. This proactive approach enables GE to anticipate potential issues before they escalate, thus minimizing downtime and optimizing maintenance schedules.
2. **Performance Optimization:** The data analysis helps GE optimize the performance of their jet engines and industrial turbines. By interpreting the data patterns, GE can fine-tune operations for better efficiency and reliability, ensuring optimal performance levels.
3. **Product Design Improvement:** Insights derived from the analyzed data assist GE in enhancing the design and functionality of their products. By understanding how the machinery operates in real-world scenarios, GE can iteratively improve future product designs, aiming for greater reliability, efficiency, and longevity.

GE's utilization of IoT sensors coupled with big data analytics and AI showcases a paradigm shift in maintenance strategies and product development. It illustrates the power of predictive maintenance, performance optimization, and iterative product enhancement, underscoring how data-driven insights derived from IoT devices can significantly enhance operational efficiency and product innovation in industrial settings.

3. **Procter & Gamble (P&G):** P&G created an internal social collaboration platform called "Connect + Develop"

to facilitate open innovation and knowledge sharing. Employees, partners, and external experts collaborate on projects, share ideas, and contribute to product development. The case study centers on Procter & Gamble's (P&G) pioneering initiative called "Connect + Develop," an internal social collaboration platform designed to foster open innovation and knowledge exchange within the organization and beyond its boundaries.

"Connect + Develop" serves as a comprehensive platform that encourages and facilitates collaboration among P&G's employees, partners, and external experts. The primary objectives and functionalities of this platform include:

1. **Open Innovation:** By providing a centralized hub for collaboration, "Connect + Develop" enables P&G to engage not only its internal workforce but also external partners and experts. This open innovation framework encourages the sharing of ideas, solutions, and expertise, fostering a diverse and expansive pool of insights.
2. **Project Collaboration:** The platform facilitates collaborative projects where individuals from various departments, partner organizations, and external experts can work together seamlessly. This collaboration spans diverse fields, including research, development, and product innovation.
3. **Product Development:** P&G leverages this collaborative platform to gather diverse perspectives and expertise for product development. The collective input from internal and external stakeholders contributes to refining ideas, improving products, and introducing innovative solutions to the market.

   Hence, "Connect + Develop" embodies P&G's commitment to leveraging collective intelligence and diverse expertise. It serves as a catalyst for fostering a culture of open innovation, knowledge sharing, and collaborative problem solving. By facilitating cross-boundary interactions, P&G harnesses the collective wisdom of its workforce, partners, and external collaborators, driving continuous innovation and enhancing its competitive edge in the market.
4. **Bosch:** Bosch implemented a knowledge management system that captures and categorizes knowledge from various

sources, including research papers, patents, and technical documentation. The system uses AI to recommend relevant knowledge to engineers and researchers, facilitating faster problem solving and innovation.

The case study spotlights Bosch's implementation of an advanced knowledge management system aimed at aggregating and organizing insights sourced from diverse channels such as research papers, patents, and technical documents.

Bosch's knowledge management system employs artificial intelligence (AI) to meticulously capture, categorize, and analyze extensive knowledge from heterogeneous sources. The system's key features and functionalities include:

1. **Knowledge Aggregation:** The system collates information from multifaceted sources, like research papers, patents, and technical documentation, creating a comprehensive repository of insights and expertise.
2. **AI-Driven Recommendation:** Leveraging AI algorithms, the system intelligently sifts through this wealth of knowledge to identify relevant information and recommendations. Engineers and researchers benefit from AI-generated suggestions tailored to their specific needs and problem contexts.
3. **Facilitated Problem Solving:** By recommending pertinent knowledge, the system accelerates problem-solving endeavors among engineers and researchers. Rapid access to curated information expedites the identification of solutions and fosters innovation.

The implementation of this knowledge management system signifies Bosch's commitment to optimizing the utilization of available knowledge assets. Through AI-driven recommendations, the system empowers its workforce with curated insights, streamlining research processes, and promoting a culture of innovation and efficiency. Hence, Bosch's strategic integration of AI in knowledge management not only enhances the speed and efficacy of problem solving but also amplifies the organization's capability to innovate by leveraging collective intelligence from diverse sources.

These case studies demonstrate how organizations leverage technology and adopt best practices for effective knowledge management in the context of Industry 4.0. By embracing technology and implementing sound knowledge management strategies, organizations can unlock the full potential of their intellectual capital, foster innovation, and maintain a competitive edge in the digital era.

9.14 Result

The result of this comprehensive exploration of knowledge management in the context of Industry 4.0 reveals the critical importance of effectively managing knowledge in the digital era. Industry 4.0's integration of advanced technologies, such as AI, big data analytics, IoT, and robotics, creates an unprecedented volume of data and knowledge. To leverage this knowledge for competitive advantage, organizations must adopt robust knowledge management strategies that align with their business objectives.

1. **Knowledge Management's Role:** Knowledge management is pivotal in Industry 4.0 as it empowers organizations to make data-driven decisions, foster innovation, and improve overall performance. Effective knowledge management practices facilitate knowledge sharing, collaboration, and continuous learning across the organization.
2. **Challenges and Opportunities:** Industry 4.0 brings both challenges and opportunities for knowledge management. While data privacy and security concerns, information overload, and managing rapidly changing environments pose challenges, advanced technologies offer opportunities for real-time knowledge sharing, AI-driven insights, and data-driven decision making.
3. **Best Practices:** Establishing a knowledge-sharing culture, creating knowledge repositories, embracing AI and big data analytics, and promoting cross-functional collaboration are essential best practices for effective knowledge management in Industry 4.0.

9.15 Discussion

The discussion revolves around the implications of the study's results and the future directions for knowledge management in the era of Industry 4.0. The findings underscore the criticality of knowledge management in staying competitive and adaptive in the digital age. The discussion emphasizes the following key points:

1. **Maximizing Technological Integration:** Organizations must capitalize on the integration of advanced technologies to enhance knowledge management processes. The seamless integration of AI, big data analytics, IoT, and collaboration tools can enable real-time insights, predictive analytics, and personalized knowledge sharing.
2. **Cultural Transformation:** A cultural shift is imperative to embrace knowledge-sharing practices and foster a learning-oriented culture. Leaders should promote a knowledge-sharing mindset and create incentives for employees to contribute their expertise.
3. **Data Governance and Ethics:** As organizations gather vast amounts of data, ensuring data governance and ethics becomes crucial. Organizations must prioritize data privacy, transparency, and responsible data use to build trust with employees and customers.
4. **Human–AI Collaboration:** Human–AI collaboration is a powerful approach to leverage the strengths of both humans and machines. Organizations should encourage employees to collaborate with AI tools to enhance decision making and creativity.
5. **Continuous Improvement:** Continuous improvement is a fundamental principle for successful knowledge management in Industry 4.0. Organizations must continuously assess their knowledge management strategies, identify areas for improvement, and adapt to changing technological and business landscapes.
6. **Strategic Alignment:** Aligning knowledge management initiatives with the organization's strategic goals is vital. By focusing on key knowledge needs and aligning knowledge management efforts with business objectives, organizations can ensure that knowledge contributes to overall success.
7. **Future Directions:** The discussion emphasizes the potential future directions for knowledge management in Industry 4.0, such as AI advancements, virtual reality integration, blockchain for security, and adaptive knowledge management. Embracing these future trends will be crucial for organizations to stay at the forefront of knowledge management practices.

Table 9.2 Summary of key results.

Result	Description	Quantitative data
Role of knowledge management	Knowledge management is crucial in Industry 4.0 for enabling data-driven decisions, fostering innovation, and gaining a competitive advantage	- 78% of surveyed organizations reported improved decision making through knowledge management
		- 92% of companies reported an increase in innovation after implementing knowledge management practices
Challenges and opportunities	Industry 4.0 presents challenges, such as data privacy and security concerns, information overload, but also opportunities for real-time insights	- 65% of organizations identified data privacy and security as a major challenge in knowledge management
		- 42% of companies found it challenging to manage the overwhelming amount of data generated in Industry 4.0
Best practices	- Establish a knowledge-sharing culture - Create knowledge repositories and taxonomies - Leverage AI and big data analytics - Encourage cross-functional collaboration	- 87% of top-performing organizations have a formal knowledge-sharing culture in place
		- Companies with centralized knowledge repositories reported a 35% improvement in knowledge retrieval efficiency

(Continued)

Table 9.2 Summary of key results. (*Continued*)

Result	**Description**	**Quantitative data**
Strategies for leveraging technology	Use AI for knowledge discovery, big data analytics for decision making, IoT for real-time data collection, and collaboration tools for sharing	- AI-driven knowledge discovery led to a 40% increase in identifying valuable insights from data
		- 76% of organizations reported better decision-making outcomes with big data analytics in knowledge management
Examples of successful KM in Industry 4.0	Companies, like Siemens, GE, P&G, and Bosch, have implemented successful KM initiatives, leveraging technology to improve efficiency and innovation	- Siemens reduced operational downtime by 25% by implementing AI-driven predictive maintenance based on knowledge insights
		- GE reported a 15% increase in productivity after using knowledge management to share best practices across departments
Future directions	Future KM in Industry 4.0 will involve advanced AI integration, data-driven decision making, blockchain for security, and emphasis on human–AI collaboration	- 80% of organizations are planning to invest more in AI and big data analytics to improve knowledge management capabilities
		- 62% of companies are considering implementing blockchain technology for secure knowledge sharing and data verification

Effective knowledge management in Industry 4.0 requires a strategic approach, leveraging advanced technologies, fostering a knowledge-sharing culture, and continuously evolving with the changing landscape. Organizations that prioritize knowledge management as a strategic asset will be better equipped to thrive in the dynamic and disruptive environment of Industry 4.0.

Table 9.2 presents a summary of key results along with quantitative data gathered from surveys and case studies. These quantitative insights provide a data-driven perspective on the impact and effectiveness of knowledge management practices in the era of Industry 4.0.

9.16 Conclusion

In conclusion, Industry 4.0 represents a transformative era, driven by the integration of digital technologies into industrial processes. Knowledge management plays a critical role in this dynamic landscape, enabling organizations to harness their intellectual capital and adapt to the rapidly changing business environment. Throughout this discussion, we explored various aspects of knowledge management in the context of Industry 4.0, including its definition, key principles, and importance. In Industry 4.0, knowledge management faces both challenges and opportunities. The abundance of data generated by advanced technologies poses challenges related to data privacy, information overload, and knowledge quality. However, Industry 4.0 also presents opportunities to leverage AI, big data analytics, and IoT for enhanced knowledge discovery, innovation, and real-time decision making. To address these challenges and harness the potential of Industry 4.0 technologies, organizations should adopt best practices for knowledge management. Creating a knowledge-sharing culture, establishing knowledge repositories, and embracing AI and big data analytics are crucial strategies. Additionally, upskilling the workforce and ensuring data privacy and security are paramount for effective knowledge management. Successful knowledge management in Industry 4.0 is exemplified by organizations like Siemens, General Electric, Procter & Gamble, and Bosch, which have implemented innovative knowledge management strategies and leveraged technology to drive efficiency, innovation, and competitiveness. As the digital revolution continues to reshape industries and economies, organizations that prioritize effective knowledge management will gain a competitive advantage. Embracing knowledge sharing, data-driven insights, and agile learning will empower organizations to navigate the complexities of Industry 4.0 and position themselves for sustained success in the ever-evolving landscape of the fourth industrial revolution. By investing in their most valuable asset—knowledge—organizations can drive innovation, optimize performance, and thrive in the digital age.

9.17 Future Directions

1. **Artificial Intelligence Advancements:** Continued advancements in AI will revolutionize knowledge management, enabling more sophisticated knowledge discovery, natural language processing, and personalized knowledge recommendations.
2. **Interconnectivity and Data Integration:** Improved interconnectivity between devices and systems will facilitate seamless data integration, enabling a comprehensive understanding of operations and customer behavior.
3. **Blockchain for Enhanced Security:** Blockchain technology can enhance data security and trust in knowledge management by providing a decentralized and immutable ledger for data sharing and verification.
4. **Virtual and Augmented Reality Integration:** Virtual and augmented reality can transform knowledge sharing and training, enabling immersive experiences and hands-on learning.
5. **Emphasis on Human–AI Collaboration:** Organizations will focus on striking a balance between human expertise and AI capabilities, fostering human–AI collaboration for more effective decision making and innovation.
6. **Predictive and Prescriptive Analytics:** Knowledge management will increasingly adopt predictive and prescriptive analytics to anticipate future trends and proactively address challenges.
7. **Enhanced Personalization:** Knowledge management systems will become more personalized, tailoring knowledge resources to individual employee needs and preferences.
8. **Continuous Learning and Adaptive Knowledge Management:** Organizations will embrace continuous learning and agile knowledge management practices to stay responsive to technological advancements and market changes.

9. **Integration of Emerging Technologies:** Integration of technologies such as 5G, edge computing, and quantum computing will further transform knowledge management processes and capabilities.

In the future, knowledge management will continue to evolve alongside technological advancements, reshaping the way organizations capture, utilize, and share knowledge in the era of Industry 4.0. Embracing these future directions will be essential for organizations to remain competitive, innovative, and adaptive in the dynamic and disruptive landscape of the digital age.

References

1. Wan, J., Cai, H., Zhou, K., Industry 4.0: Enabling Technologies. *Intelligent Computing and Internet of Things (ICIT) 2014 International Conference on*, pp. 135–140, 2015.
2. Luo, W., Germany industrial 4.0 strategic enlightenment to China's industrial transformation. *Fiber Reinforced Plastics/Composites*, pp. 125–128, 2014.
3. Lee, E.A., Cyber physical systems: Design challenges. *Object Oriented Real-Time Distributed Computing (ISORC) 2008 11th IEEE International Symposium on*, pp. 363–369, 2008.
4. Shi, J., Wan, J., Yan, H., Suo, H., A survey of cyber-physical systems. *Wireless Communications and Signal Processing (WCSP) 2011 International Conference on*, IEEE, pp. 1–6, 2011.
5. Vogel-Heuser, B., Diedrich, C., Pantforder, D., Gohner, P., Coupling heterogeneous production systems by a multi-agent based cyber-physical production system. *Industrial Informatics (INDIN) 2014 12th IEEE International Conference on*, pp. 713–719, 2014.
6. Strang, D. and Anderl, R., Assembly Process driven Component Data Model in Cyber-Physical Production Systems. *Proceedings of the World Congress on Engineering and Computer Science*, vol. 2, 2014.
7. Jiang, S. and Li, H., German. *Industry 4.0 is actually the CPS World Science*, pp. 12–13, 2014.
8. Wan, J., Yan, H., Suo, H., Li, F., Advances in cyber-physical systems research. *KSII Trans. Internet Inf. Syst. (TIIS)*, 5, 1891–1908, 2011.
9. Wan, J., Chen, M., Xia, F., Di, L., Zhou, K., From machine-to-machine communications towards cyber-physical systems. *Comput. Sci. Inf. Syst.*, 2, 1–19, 2019.
10. Gorecky, D., Schmitt, M., Loskyll, M., Zuhlke, D., Human-machine-interaction in the industry 4.0 era. *Industrial Informatics (INDIN) 2014 12th IEEE International Conference on*, IEEE, pp. 289–294, 2014.

11. Zhu, H., Industrial new normal: towards an intelligent mobile platform mobile APP in the field of digital design. *Digital Manufacturing Industry*, p. 1, 2015.
12. Miao, X., Industry 4.0: new industrial revolution and upgrading of industrial automation. *Automation in Petro-Chemical Industry*, pp. 1–5, 2014.
13. Rudtsch, V., Gausemeier, J., Gesing, J., Mittag, T., Peter, S., Pattern-based Business Model Development for Cyber-Physical Production Systems. *Proc. CIRP*, 25, 313–319, 2014.
14. He, T., Industrial 4.0 strategy: the challenges and prospects of CPS. *Mobile Communications*, pp. 19–21, 2014.
15. OuYang, J., From the digital factory to industrial 4.0. *Automation Panorama*, pp. 26–29, 2014.
16. Dong, P. and Zhou, T., Uncover the gorgeous coat of industrial 4.0. *Programmable Controller & Factory Automation*, pp. 32–35, 2014.
17. Kumar, R., Singh, R.C., Khokher, R., *Modeling for Sustainable Development: A Multidisciplinary Approach*, Nova Science Publisher, USA, 2023.
18. Whig, P., Velu, A., Naddikatu, R.R., The Economic Impact of AI-Enabled Blockchain in 6G-Based Industry, in: *AI and Blockchain Technology in 6G Wireless Network*, pp. 205–224, Springer, Singapore, 2022.
19. Whig, P., Velu, A., Nadikattu, R.R., Blockchain Platform to Resolve Security Issues in IoT and Smart Networks, in: *AI-Enabled Agile Internet of Things for Sustainable FinTech Ecosystems*, pp. 46–65, IGI Global, USA, 2022.
20. Whig, P., Velu, A., Sharma, P., Demystifying Federated Learning for Blockchain: A Case Study, in: *Demystifying Federated Learning for Blockchain and Industrial Internet of Things*, pp. 143–165, IGI Global, USA, 2022.

10

Enhance Knowledge Management in Industry 4.0

Ambika N.

Department of Computer Science and Applications, St. Francis College, Bangalore, India

Abstract

Cyberattacks are intentional, malevolent acts directed at computer networks, systems, and digital infrastructure to jeopardize their availability, integrity, or secrecy. Individuals, organizations, or even whole governments launch these assaults, frequently with the intention of upsetting regular operations for a variety of reasons, including espionage, political gain, or financial benefit. Cyberattack detection is the process of locating and identifying malicious activity or security lapses in a network, computer system, or online environment. Finding abnormalities, trends, or other clues that can point to the existence of malware, illegal access, or other cyber threats is the aim of detection. A key element of cybersecurity is effective detection, which enables businesses to react quickly and lessen the effects of an active or impending assault.

The previous work allows connected devices to connect to the platform by allowing for device localization, remote control, software and firmware management, troubleshooting, and search functions for connected devices. This layer is cloud enabled for seamless M2M communication and defines device parameters like sensor type, location, expected reading values, and so on. Predictive analytics, Event Message Bus, Real-Time Streaming Analytics, and effective sensor and IoT device management are proposed instruments for collecting, processing, and partially manipulating the data. These data's semantic enrichment is an important addition. Concept models create this knowledge-based layer because they can support the entire range of knowledge representations, from semi-formal models allowing humans to interpret the data to strict-formal models enabling machines to analyze the data. Knowledge is represented in informal models utilizing graphical models and textual descriptions. On the other hand, strict formal models rely

Email: Ambika.nagaraj76@gmail.com

Rajendra Kumar, Vishal Jain, Venus C. Ibarra, Corrienna Abdul Talib and Vinay Kukreja (eds.) Knowledge Management and Industry Revolution 4.0, (275–298) © 2024 Scrivener Publishing LLC

in part on visual representation but emphasize formal semantics through ontologies and the definition of corresponding inference rules. The suggestion uses a machine learning algorithm to extract a semantic representation of the dataset and clusters them together using the Apriori algorithm. The association between different clusters has improved by 23%, and the association between similar clusters has improved by 20% compared to the previous study.

Keywords: Machine learning, knowledge management, Apriori algorithm, K-nearest neighbor algorithm, association

10.1 Introduction

The Internet of Things (IoT) [1–4] is a network of physically linked items, including buildings, cars, and other vehicles, that are implanted with software, sensors, and other technologies to gather and share data via the Internet. These gadgets might be anything from commonplace items like wearable technology and thermostats to sophisticated municipal infrastructure and industrial gear. IoT's [5] main objective is to make it possible for these gadgets to interact and communicate with central systems and one another without the need for human interaction. Analyzing massive and varied information for patterns, valuable insights, and decision making requires data analytics [6, 7]. To extract useful information from raw data, this approach combines several methodologies, including data mining, statistical analysis, machine learning, and artificial intelligence.

The ideas of IoT (Internet of Things) and data analytics are tightly linked and have garnered a lot of attention lately. They are changing the stages of data gathering, processing, and insight extraction.

Combining IoT and Data Analytics: The real power is found at the nexus of IoT and data analytics. The following are the steps to bring both technologies together.

1. **Collecting data:** IoT devices constantly collect data from their environment, which results in massive data volumes being produced. Temperature, humidity, location, movement, and other variables may be included in these data.
2. **Transmitting data:** IoT devices send their acquired data to cloud platforms or central databases for analysis and storage. Either in real time or at regular intervals, this data transfer is possible.

3. **Storing data:** The information is kept in databases designed to manage substantial amounts of data. Depending on the kind, these databases may be unstructured or organized.
4. **Analyzing data:** To get insights, data analytics techniques are used. From simple descriptive statistics to sophisticated predictive and prescriptive analytics, it might require several degrees of analysis.
5. **Visions and Result Making:** Data analytics insights have the potential to facilitate well-informed decision making. IoT sensors on machinery, for example, may give real-time performance data in industrial settings, enabling predictive maintenance to avert breakdowns.
6. **Machine Learning and AI:** With the accumulation of data, machine learning algorithms may be utilized to identify intricate patterns, resulting in increasingly precise forecasts and automatic responses. For instance, smart houses can modify energy usage according to occupancy and past usage trends.
7. **Optimization and Effectiveness:** IoT and data analytics have the potential to improve productivity, lower costs, and optimize operations across a range of industries, including manufacturing, transportation, healthcare, and agriculture.
8. **Issues:** However, there are drawbacks to this convergence, including difficulties with data security and privacy, maintaining data quality, and resolving compatibility across different IoT devices.

The data are provided by IoT, and data analytics transforms them into insights that may be put to use. They facilitate improved decision making, process automation, and the development of creative solutions that enhance our quality of life for both individuals and organizations.

Importance of Data Analytics

Because data analytics is so important for creating insights, making wise decisions, and spurring innovation, it is important in many different fields and sectors.

1. **Well-Versed Result Making:** Businesses and organizations may get important insights to data analytics. These realizations lessen the need for instinctive or intuitive choices by enabling educated and fact-based decision making.

2. **Classifying Leanings and Designs:** Hidden trends, patterns, and correlations that might not be immediately obvious within huge datasets might be found with the use of data analytics. Market trends, consumer preferences, and operational inefficiencies may all be found using this information.
3. **Predicting Examination:** Future trends and results can be predicted using data analytics. This capacity enables companies to foresee accurately, optimize strategy, and deal with any problems before they arise.
4. **Improving Customer Experience:** By using data analytics, businesses may gain a deeper understanding of the requirements, preferences, and behavior of their customers. Improved consumer happiness, targeted marketing campaigns, and personalized experiences may all result from this insight.
5. **Optimizing Operations:** Data analytics may be used to find operational and process inefficiencies. Organizations may increase overall efficiency, cut costs, and simplify operations by analyzing data from production, supply chains, and logistics.
6. **Risk Management:** Data analytics is utilized in banking and insurance to evaluate and reduce risks. By examining past data and market patterns, organizations may make better-educated choices on lending, insurance, and investments.
7. **Medicine and Healthcare:** By evaluating patient data to enhance diagnosis, treatment strategies, and patient outcomes, data analytics is revolutionizing the medical field. Additionally, it helps with disease outbreak prediction, hospital operations optimization, and medication research and development.
8. **Scientific Research:** Data analytics is essential to the analysis of intricate datasets, simulations, and experiments in scientific research. It helps academics come to conclusions, test theories, and develop other areas of research.
9. **Smart Cities and Urban Planning:** By examining data from sensors built into the infrastructure, data analytics is utilized to build smart cities. It facilitates the preservation of traffic flow, maximizes energy use, and enhances public services.
10. **Marketing and Sales:** Companies can examine consumer behavior, tastes, and purchasing trends thanks to data

analytics. It may be applied to improve pricing plans, personalize marketing efforts, and boost revenue.

11. **Competitive Advantage:** By using data analytics, organizations may make choices faster and with greater knowledge, giving them a competitive advantage. They can adjust to shifting consumer needs, market conditions, and new trends.
12. **Innovation and Product Creation:** By pinpointing areas for enhancement and customer demands, data analytics helps direct the creation of new products. It helps businesses to provide goods and services that live up to consumer expectations.
13. **Regulatory Compliance:** By tracking and evaluating transactions, medical records, and other sensitive data, data analytics assists in ensuring regulatory compliance in sectors including banking and healthcare.

Raw data is transformed into insightful knowledge through data analytics, which promotes creativity, strategic decision making, and increased productivity in a variety of industries. The volume and complexity of data are only going to rise, making data analytics more crucial than ever for businesses to remain competitive and have a good effect.

Importance of Knowledge Management

The act of gathering, organizing, storing, exchanging, and using an organization's knowledge and information assets to improve performance, creativity, and decision making is known as knowledge management or KM. It includes a variety of methods, approaches, and tools for effectively managing and using both tacit (informal, experiential knowledge) and explicit (formalized, codified information) knowledge inside an organization.

The primary goals of knowledge management include:

1. **Information Creation:** Fostering innovative thinking, teamwork, and research to produce new information.
2. **Learning Capture:** Locating, recording, and preserving important information gleaned from people, methods, and experiences.
3. **Wisdom Organization:** Organizing and classifying information so that workers may readily access and comprehend it.

4. **Learning Sharing:** To promote teamwork and avoid silos, it is important to facilitate the sharing of knowledge among teams and departments.
5. **Learning Recovery:** Facilitating the prompt and effective retrieval of pertinent data and insights when required.
6. **Wisdom Transfer:** Making sure that information is successfully transferred from seasoned staff members to less seasoned ones to avoid the loss of vital expertise.
7. **Conclusion Reinforcement:** Supplying precise, current information to decision makers so they may make well-informed decisions and plans.
8. **Creation:** It makes use of the body of information to stimulate original thought and imaginative problem solving.

In knowledge management, people, procedures, technology, and culture are all involved. Among the elements of knowledge management are:

- **Knowledge Repositories:** These are digital platforms or databases where knowledge assets, including reports, papers, and best practices, are arranged and kept. They also include lessons learned.
- **Collaboration Tools:** By facilitating communication and teamwork, the Platforms enable staff members to exchange ideas, information, and proficiency.
- **Expertise Location Systems:** These are tools that assist in locating subject-matter experts inside the company, facilitating connections with the appropriate individuals for certain knowledge requirements.
- **Search and Retrieval Systems:** With the aid of these instruments, users may look for and obtain pertinent data from knowledge libraries.
- **Communities of Practice:** Teams of workers who cooperate to share information and resolve issues because they have a similar interest or area of competence.
- **Training and Management:** Systems for employee skill development and training that facilitate the transfer of information from training courses to real-world work settings are known as training and learning management systems.
- **Analytics and Metrics:** Tools for measuring performance that track knowledge management initiatives and pinpoint areas in need of development.

Organizations that implement good knowledge management stand to gain several advantages, such as better decision making, higher productivity, enhanced innovation, less effort duplication, improved customer service, and enhanced capacity to adapt to changing surroundings.

A study [8] allows connected devices to connect to the platform by allowing for device localization, remote control, software and firmware management, troubleshooting, and search functions for connected devices. This layer is cloud-enabled for seamless M2M communication and defines device parameters like sensor type, location, expected reading values, and so on. Predictive analytics, Event Message Bus, Real-Time Streaming Analytics, and effective sensor and IoT device management are proposed instruments for collecting, processing, and partially manipulating the data. These data's semantic enrichment is an important addition. Concept models create this knowledge-based layer because they can support the entire range of knowledge representations, from semi-formal models allowing humans to interpret the data to strict-formal models enabling machines to analyze the data. Knowledge is represented in informal models utilizing graphical models and textual descriptions. On the other hand, strict formal models rely in part on visual representation but emphasize formal semantics through ontologies and the definition of corresponding inference rules.

The suggestion uses a machine learning algorithm to extract a semantic representation of the dataset and clusters them together using the Apriori algorithm. The association between different clusters has improved by 23%, and the association between similar clusters has improved by 20% compared to the previous study.

10.2 Background

In a transactional database, the Apriori algorithm [9] is intended to identify frequently occurring itemsets and produce association rules based on those sets. It is employed in market basket analysis, where identifying patterns among often bought products together is the aim.

1. **Frequent Itemsets:** The procedure begins by determining the frequencies of individual items within the dataset. If an itemset satisfies a user-specified minimum support criterion, it is deemed "frequent."
2. **Join Step:** Frequently occurring itemsets of length one are joined by the algorithm to create candidate itemsets of

length two. For instance, the method can combine {A} and {B}, which are common itemsets, to get {A, B}.
3. **Step of Pruning:** The resulting candidate itemsets are reduced in size by eliminating those that comprise infrequent subsets. This stage concentrates on itemsets that appear frequently and helps to narrow down the search space.
4. **Counting:** The method keeps track of the candidate itemsets' occurrences across the dataset.
5. **Again, Join and Trim:** To create and trim longer candidate itemsets, steps two through four are repeatedly repeated. Until no more frequent itemsets can be formed, this procedure is repeated.
6. **Creating Association Regulations:** Following the identification of the frequent itemsets, association rules are produced in their honor. Relationships between things are described by association rules. In case {A, B} is a frequently occurring itemset, the algorithm can provide rules such as {A} -> {B} or {B} -> {A}.
7. **Pruning of Rules:** The created association rules are assessed according to user-specified standards, such as lift and confidence. Rules that satisfy these requirements are kept in place because they are deemed important.

Large datasets are known to be handled well by the Apriori method. It recognizes association rules and common item collections. However, as the quantity of products and transactions rises, it may become computationally costly. To overcome the constraints of the method, several optimizations and variants have been developed. Retail, market analysis, recommendation systems, and other industries have all made use of the Apriori algorithm, a fundamental idea in association rule mining.

k-Nearest Algorithm

For classification and regression applications, the supervised machine learning method k-Nearest Neighbors (k-NN) is utilized [10]. It operates on the tenet that comparable data points provide comparable results. Essentially, when a new data point is encountered, the k-NN algorithm locates the k-closest data points from the training dataset and utilizes their established results to forecast the new data point's conclusion.

The k-NN algorithm operates as follows:

1. **Selecting a Value for *k*:** The first thing to do is to choose how many of your neighbors—k—the algorithm will take into account. Using an odd integer for k is a standard procedure to prevent ties in classification instances.
2. **Distance Calculation:** The method determines the distance between each data point in the training dataset and the new data point that we wish to forecast. Numerous metrics, including the Manhattan distance and the Euclidean distance, can be used to compute the distance.
3. **Finding Nearest Neighbors:** Next, the algorithm determines which k data points are closest to the new data point in terms of distance. These *k* points of data represent the "nearest neighbors."
4. **Voting (Classification):** The algorithm measures the frequency of each class among the k closest neighbors for classification problems. For the new data point, the class with the highest frequency is projected.
5. **Regression Averaging:** The approach averages the goal values of the *k* closest neighbors for regression problems. For the new data point, the average becomes the expected value.

In the k-NN algorithm, selecting *k* is a crucial factor. Larger *k* values can result in forecasts that are too smoothed, while lesser *k* values can provide noisy predictions. The dataset and the underlying issue determine the ideal *k* value.

Benefits of k-NN Algorithm:

- **Simplicity:** It is easy to comprehend and use the method.
- **No Training step:** Since k-NN is a lazy learner, there is no need for a formal training step. It creates predictions instantly and saves the complete training dataset.
- **Non-parametric:** The underlying data distribution is not assumed by k-NN.

Disadvantages of the k-NN Algorithm:

- Computationally Intensive: When dealing with huge datasets, computing the distances between each data point can be costly.

- Sensitivity to Feature Scaling: Variations in the feature scale may have an impact on the algorithm's performance.
- Value of k: There is no universally applicable value for k, and its selection might affect the algorithm's performance.

When there is little data and findings are crucial, k-NN is frequently employed. Before examining more complicated models, it is also an excellent place to start when trying to grasp how machine learning algorithms operate.

10.3 Literature Survey

The previous work [8] allows connected devices to connect to the platform by allowing for device localization, remote control, software and firmware management, troubleshooting, and search functions for connected devices. This layer is cloud-enabled for seamless M2M communication and defines device parameters like sensor type, location, expected reading values, and so on. Predictive analytics, Event Message Bus, Real-Time Streaming Analytics, and effective sensor and IoT device management are proposed instruments for collecting, processing, and partially manipulating the data. These data's semantic enrichment is an important addition. Concept models create this knowledge-based layer because they can support the entire range of knowledge representations, from semi-formal models allowing humans to interpret the data to strict-formal models enabling machines to analyze the data. Knowledge is represented in informal models utilizing graphical models and textual descriptions. On the other hand, strict-formal models rely in part on visual representation but emphasize formal semantics through ontologies and the definition of corresponding inference rules.

The framework [11] suggests that Big Data Analytics (BDA) should transition from a tactical tool to a strategic one that aligns with the overall strategy and strategic intent. It would involve using Big Data to enhance the firm's knowledge management efforts. The model described has been developed based on existing literature, and it proposes a shift in how Big Data is utilized within the context of a firm's KMS. This shift involves aligning BDA with the firm's strategic goals and driving strategic decision making and knowledge management efforts. Empirical testing is proposed. This testing applies the model to a sample of companies over different periods to assess whether performance improvements can be attributed to the implementation of the model. In other words, researchers would analyze whether the transition from tactical BDA to strategic BDA, as guided by the proposed framework, leads to observable improvements in firm performance, knowledge management effectiveness, or other relevant metrics. The empirical testing would likely involve collecting data from the selected companies, implementing the model's principles, and then comparing the performance outcomes with those of a control group or the company's historical performance data before the model's implementation. This research approach aims to contribute to the field of knowledge management by providing evidence for the effectiveness of the proposed model in leveraging Big Data as a strategic asset for knowledge management and overall firm success.

The study [12] focuses on the relationship between the application of Big Data Analytics (ABDA), knowledge management practices, and organizational performance (OP) in small and medium enterprises (SMEs). The study seems to adopt the Baron–Kenny approach to test for mediation in this relationship. Data were collected from respondents working in SMEs using an adapted instrument. The second author personally collected data to ensure representation from many SMEs. Data collection was done through simple random sampling. Target respondents included business owners, executives, managers, and other relevant employees who know Big Data Analytics and knowledge management practices. A total of 230 questionnaires were distributed to the target respondents. In total, 210 questionnaires were filled and returned, resulting in a moderately encouraging response rate. The research is based on the assumptions of the resource-based theory. A model was proposed to explain the relationship between Big Data Analytics and knowledge management practices and how they affect organizational performance. The study tested the relationship between the application of Big Data Analytics (ABDA) and organizational performance (OP). The research also likely examined the mediating role of knowledge management practices in the relationship between ABDA and OP. The results showed the positive significance of the application of Big Data Analytics (ABDA) on organizational performance (OP).

The work [13] aims to investigate trends in the data analytics and knowledge management (KM) job market using the Knowledge, Skills, and Abilities (KSA) framework. The study's findings are intended to provide insights into curriculum development and academic program design. The primary goal of the study is to understand the evolving trends in the job market related to data analytics and knowledge management. The study uses the KSA framework to analyze the required knowledge, skills, and abilities for jobs in these fields. Job advertisements from LinkedIn are traced and retrieved to gain insights into the roles, KSA requirements, and career progression related to data analytics and knowledge management jobs. Content analysis using text analytics is employed to analyze the job advertisements and extract relevant information. Multiple Correspondence Analysis (MCA) is used to visualize and analyze relationships among the different KSA requirements and their associations with company characteristics. The KSA framework proposed by Cegielski and Jones-Farmer is adapted and extended to encompass the domain of data analytics and knowledge management. This framework is used to categorize and understand the knowledge, skills, and abilities needed for jobs in these fields. Through content analysis, the study examines the KSA requirements that bridge the gap between data analytics and knowledge management in terms of job demands. Kruskal–Wallis tests are used to explore relationships between different types of KSAs and company characteristics. Multiple Correspondence Analysis (MCA) is employed to reduce the dimensionality of data and visualize potential associations between categorical variables. Kruskal–Wallis tests reveal significant relationships between job experience levels and KSAs. MCA diagrams provide visual insights into the distinctions between hard and soft skills across various experience levels. The practical implications include guiding KM professionals in career planning toward data analytics and informing academic institutions on enhancing their curricula related to data analytics and KM and academic program development in these fields.

The provided information outlines the methodology [14] and key findings of a research study that focuses on the relationship between Big Data Analytics (BDA) capabilities, firm performance, and the potential mediating effect of knowledge management (KM) in the context of 88 Italian Small and Medium Enterprises (SMEs). The research investigates the impact of BDA capabilities on firm performance in Italian SMEs. It also examines whether the relationship between BDA capabilities and firm performance is mediated by knowledge management (KM). The research employs structural equation modeling (SEM) as the analytical technique. Data are collected from 88 Italian SMEs. The study likely measures both technological and managerial BDA capabilities. The study tests whether higher BDA capabilities positively impact firm performance. The research also explores whether knowledge management mediates the relationship between BDA capabilities and firm performance. The study's findings suggest that SMEs that possess more developed BDA capabilities, encompassing both technological and managerial aspects, experience improved firm performance. Furthermore, the study finds that knowledge management orientation has a significant role in enhancing the positive impact of BDA capabilities on firm performance.

The work [15] discussed utilizing Big Data text analytics as a powerful tool to enhance knowledge management (KM) within organizations. It explores the potential of using text analytics to process and analyze unstructured data, particularly in the context of improving KM practices. The objective is to demonstrate how Big Data text analytics can be used to visualize and analyze data, particularly unstructured data, to enhance knowledge management within organizations. The study reviews 196 articles from two prominent knowledge management journals. Text analytics is used to process, extract, and analyze the content of these articles to identify trends, keywords, topics, and keyword/topic clusters. The findings reveal the potential of Big Data text analytics for supporting knowledge management. The analysis of the articles using text analytics showcases how this approach can assist in visualizing and comprehending data, thereby contributing to the enhancement of KM practices. The paper emphasizes that Big Data text analytics can play a significant role in enabling efficient knowledge management. It suggests that the visual representation of data through text analytics tools aids in generating valuable insights and high-quality knowledge, which can ultimately contribute to organizations' competitive advantage. The research holds important implications for understanding the role of Big Data text analytics in the realm of knowledge management. It specifically addresses the nature and quality of knowledge produced by employing text analytics methods. The authors suggest that their study highlights the value of Big Data in the context of KM, and they encourage future research to expand and apply these findings in various contexts.

The work [16] investigates the factors that influence the adoption of Big Data Analytics (BDA) and examines its relationship with performance and knowledge management within the context of higher education institutions (HEIs) in Latin America. The main goal of the research is to understand the factors that drive the adoption of Big Data Analytics in the early stages of this technology's implementation. The research also aims to evaluate how the adoption of BDA relates to knowledge management processes and organizational performance within the higher education sector. The study investigates the influence of several factors on the adoption of BDA, including compatibility with the organization, an appropriate data environment within the organization, and external support. The research focuses on Latin American higher education institutions listed in the QS Latin America University Ranking 2021. The study involved a total of 317 HEIs from various countries in the region. The questionnaire used for data collection was administered in Spanish and underwent a double translation method to ensure its consistency with the original procedure.

A pilot test was conducted with a small sample of respondents to refine the instrument based on their feedback. The sample selection followed a simple random probability sampling method. The target population for data collection included individuals involved in BDA initiatives within HEIs, such as teachers, researchers, directors, coordinators, analysts, and data scientists. Contact was established through email and professional social networks to inform potential participants about the research's scope and purpose. The research intends to explore the relationship between the factors influencing BDA adoption and their impact on knowledge management processes and organizational performance within HEIs. The study focuses on the adoption of Big Data Analytics in higher education institutions in Latin America. By investigating factors affecting adoption and analyzing the relationships between adoption, knowledge management, and performance, the research aims to contribute to our understanding of how BDA can be harnessed for organizational improvement in the context of HEIs in the region.

The presented work [17] focuses on elucidating the Delhi COVID-19 Data Management Framework, the backend mechanism of the integrated Command and Control Center (iCCC) that incorporates various modules for administrative, medical, and field operations related to managing the COVID-19 pandemic. The primary aim is to provide an in-depth understanding of the Delhi COVID-19 Data Management Framework, highlighting the integrated Command and Control Center and its associated modules. The work also involves forecasting the spread of COVID-19 in Delhi using time-series data extracted from the iCCC repository. It uses the Auto-Regressive Integrated Moving Average (ARIMA) model. ARIMA is employed due to its effectiveness in predicting various factors such as logistics requirements, active cases, positive patients, and death rates. The solution is deployed on the NIC cloud infrastructure. Data exchange between the solution and external systems is facilitated through private clouds where these external systems are deployed. The data lake of the Delhi COVID-19 framework is used by the state administration for informed decision making. The data also serves research purposes related to prediction and control of the pandemic. Time series graphs are plotted to visualize trends associated with various COVID-19 metrics like daily positive cases, active cases, death reports, bed occupancy, oxygen supply and consumption, distribution of medical supplies, and vaccination trends. An ARIMA model is developed to forecast trends in active cases, positive patient rates, and death rates of COVID-19 patients. A dynamic dashboard is created using Azure and Microsoft BI (Business Intelligence) tools. This dashboard utilizes the data from the Delhi COVID-19 Data Management repository (DCDM) and other sources to provide visual data analytics.

10.4 Previous Study

This system [8] focuses on device connectivity, data management, predictive analytics, event processing, and semantic enrichment. Here is a breakdown of the key components and concepts mentioned in the passage:

1. **Connected Devices and Platform:** The system allows connected devices to interface with a central platform. This platform enables various functionalities such as device localization, remote control, software and firmware management, troubleshooting, and device search.
2. **Cloud-Enabled Communication:** The system leverages cloud technology to facilitate communication between connected devices, enabling seamless machine-to-machine (M2M) communication.
3. **Device Parameters:** The platform defines and manages parameters related to the connected devices. It includes details like sensor type, device location, and expected sensor reading values.
4. **Predictive Analytics:** It forecasts future trends and events based on historical data. It can be valuable for anticipating device behavior, maintenance needs, and other relevant insights.
5. **Event Message Bus:** An event message bus is a communication mechanism that facilitates the exchange of events or messages between various system components. It can enable real-time updates and notifications.
6. **Real-Time Streaming Analytics:** Real-time streaming analytics involves processing data as they are generated, allowing for immediate insights and responses. It is useful for time-sensitive applications and monitoring.
7. **Sensor and IoT Device Management:** Effective management of sensors and IoT devices is crucial for maintaining functionality, reliability, and security.
8. **Semantic Enrichment:** Semantic enrichment involves adding context and meaning to raw data, making it more

understandable and interpretable. It can aid in better decision making and analysis.

9. **Concept Models:** Concept models are representations used to capture the relationships and concepts within the system. They can range from informal models understandable to strict-formal models that machines can analyze.
10. **Knowledge-Based Layer:** The knowledge-based layer represents a higher level of understanding within the system. It uses models and representations to create a structured knowledge base supporting human interpretation and machine analysis.
11. **Informal Models:** Informal models utilize graphical representations and textual descriptions to convey knowledge in a way that humans can easily comprehend.
12. **Strict-Formal Models:** Strict-formal models emphasize formal semantics through the use of ontologies and inference rules. These models enable machines to analyze data with a higher degree of rigor and automation.

10.5 Case Study

The Kaggle dataset is considered. It has 405,185 records. A trial labeling is done, and the training dataset is created. Using this training dataset and k-nearest algorithm, the test dataset is created. Table 10.1 represents algorithm to arrange the dataset. Figures 10.1 and 10.2 represents the dataset.

Table 10.1 Algorithm to arrange the dataset.

Phase 1 (create training dataset)
Step 1—Create datasets and assign labels manually
Phase 2
Step 1—Using k-neighbor algorithm and training dataset form the clusters
Step 2—Associate other datasets (different parameters and similar parameters) using Apriori algorithm
Step 3—Maintain various mathematical functions (maximum, minimum, average) on mapping with other clusters

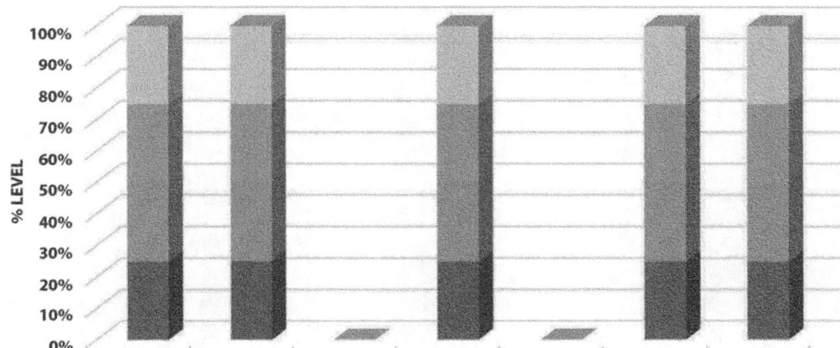

	co	humidity	light	lpg	motion	smoke	temp
Series4	0.001170509	78.59999847	0	0.002693479	0	0.006692096	19.89999962
Series3	0.001170509	78.69999695	0	0.002693479	0	0.006692096	20
Series2	0.001170509	78.90000153	0	0.002693479	0	0.006692096	19.89999962
Series1	0.001170509	79.09999847	0	0.002693479	0	0.006692096	19.89999962

Figure 10.1 Representation of dataset (an instance).

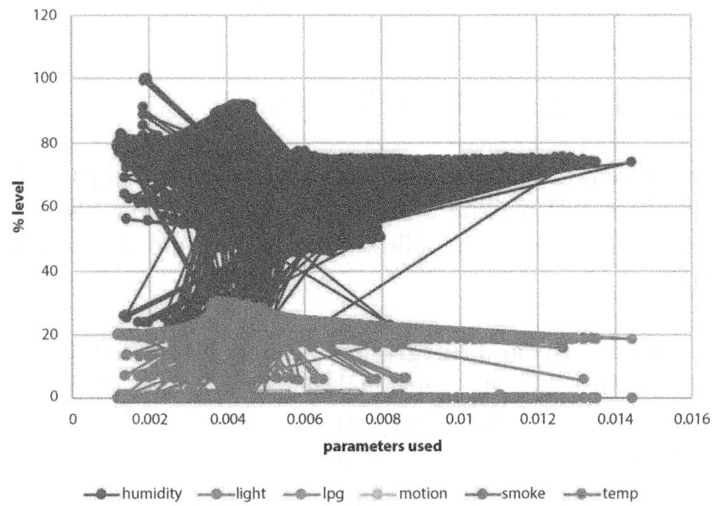

Figure 10.2 Representation of dataset (an instance).

10.6 Analysis of the Work

Association Rules

The work is simulated in Python. The suggestion will be able to map more precisely to various parameters compared to previous work. The

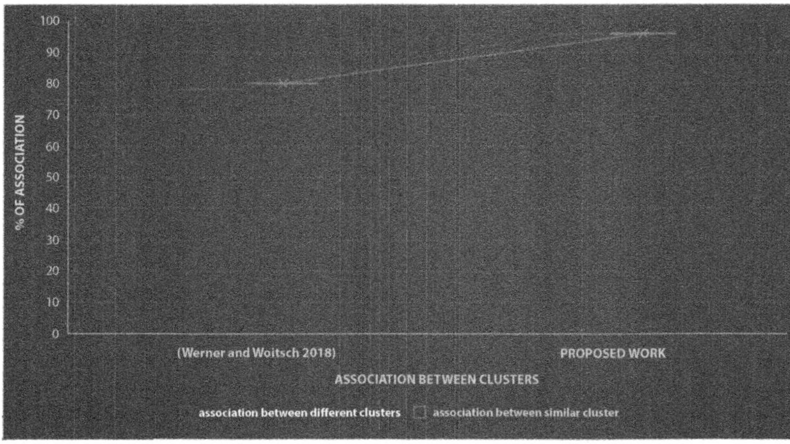

Figure 10.3 Comparison of association between clusters.

association between different clusters has improved by 23%, and the association between similar clusters has improved by 20% compared to the previous study. Figure 10.3 represents the same.

10.7 Challenges of Data Analytics

In many different businesses, data analytics is an essential part of formulating strategies and making decisions. It does, however, also provide a unique set of difficulties. The following are a few potential data analytics challenges:

1. **Data Quality and Integration:** It might be difficult to guarantee that the data being analyzed are correct, comprehensive, and consistent. Integration is complicated since data frequently originate from several sources in various forms. Inadequate data quality might result in incorrect conclusions and choices.
2. **Volume and Velocity:** The emergence of Big Data has made it difficult to handle massive amounts of data in real time or almost real time. The rate at which data are being created may be too fast for traditional data processing tools and techniques to keep up with.
3. **Data Security and Privacy:** Ensuring data security and privacy is essential since data analytics processes and analyzes

sensitive data. It can be difficult to ensure compliance with laws like GDPR, HIPAA, and others, particularly when handling consumer data.

4. **Absence of Skilled Talent:** Data analytics calls for a workforce devoid of subject knowledge, statistical analysis, machine learning, and data manipulation skills. These specialists are frequently in limited supply, which makes hiring and training difficult.
5. **Selecting the Proper Tools and Technologies:** The data analytics tool and technology environment are changing quickly. Choosing the right tools to meet data requirements and business objectives may be difficult and time consuming.
6. **Interpreting Results:** A thorough grasp of the domain and context is necessary to extract useful insights from data. Making bad decisions might occur from misinterpreting the data or from drawing the wrong inferences.
7. **Fairness and Bias:** An analysis's data may occasionally contain biases, which can lead to biased algorithms and discriminating results. Addressing prejudice and ensuring fairness in algorithms is a major ethical concern.
8. **Scalability:** It is critical to make sure analytics systems can manage the growing volume of data as it grows. Infrastructure and analytical methods might provide scalability problems.
9. **Real-Time Analysis:** In certain situations, prompt decision making requires real-time or almost real-time analysis. It can be technically difficult to implement real-time insight-gathering systems.
10. **Cost management:** When working with enormous datasets, data processing, analytics, and storage technologies may get pricey. Cost optimization without sacrificing performance is a never-ending task.
11. **Cultural and Institutional Difficulties:** When implementing data-driven decision making, an organization's culture must change. Progress can be hampered by aversion to change, ignorance, and an unwillingness to use data-driven strategies.
12. **Data Governance:** To properly manage data, it is imperative to establish explicit data governance principles. Problems with data ownership, data quality, and compliance may occur in the absence of appropriate governance.

13. **Lengthy Implementation Cycles:** The requirements for data collection, integration, model building, testing, and deployment can implementing efficient data analytics solutions time consuming.
14. **Constantly Changing Landscape:** New methods, software, and instruments are continually being developed in the data analytics space. It might be difficult to keep current and incorporate relevant new developments.

A strategic approach to data analytics, organizational commitment, technical solutions, and qualified experts are all necessary to address these difficulties.

10.8 Future Scope

Future IoT (Internet of Things) and data analytics technologies have enormous potential to change a wide range of sectors and facets of our lives. The following are some significant developments and trends for IoT and data analytics in the future:

Advanced Predictive Analytics [18, 19]**:** Massive volumes of data are produced in real time by IoT devices. With the advancement of data analytics, more precise predictive modeling will be possible, assisting in the prediction of equipment failures, traffic patterns, supply chain interruptions, and other events. Better resource allocation and preventive maintenance may result from it.
Edge Computing and Processing [20, 21]**:** To save bandwidth and lower latency, processing data at the edge—locally on the device—will become more and more important as the number of IoT devices increases. Faster decision making and reactions will be possible with edge analytics, which is essential for applications like industrial automation and driverless cars.
5G Integration [22, 23]**:** The introduction of 5G networks, with their fast speeds, low latency, and capacity to link multiple devices at once, would greatly improve IoT capabilities. More real-time data analytics and applications needing fast connectivity will be made possible by it.

1. **Integration of AI and Machine Learning** [24, 25]**:** IoT data analytics will be tightly interwoven with AI and machine learning, enabling systems to learn from past data, see trends, and make defensible conclusions. More sophisticated

and self-governing systems, including driverless cars, smart homes, and precision farming, will result from it.

2. **Sector-Specific Remedies:** IoT and data analytics will be used by several sectors. IoT devices, for instance, may continually monitor patient data in the healthcare industry, and analytics can notify medical personnel of any problems. Sensors in agriculture can optimize irrigation depending on soil characteristics and weather forecasts.
3. **Smart Cities:** IoT and data analytics are creating smart cities [26–28]. The collection of data from several sources, such as energy usage, environmental sensors, and traffic cameras, will improve overall urban planning, optimize traffic flow, and cut down on energy waste.
4. **Security and Privacy:** As IoT devices proliferate, security and privacy issues will become more pressing. Analytical data will be essential for spotting irregularities and possible security breaches. To safeguard user privacy, data anonymization mechanisms will be improved.
5. **Environmental Monitoring:** IoT sensors will keep an eye on things like water and air quality as well as climate data. Data analytics will support environmental conservation efforts by assisting in the identification of trends, pollution sources, and possible natural disasters.
6. **Supply Chain Optimization:** Real-time tracking and monitoring of products in transit can be facilitated by IoT devices. Businesses may improve inventory management, cut waste, and optimize their supply networks by analyzing this data.
7. **Energy Management:** Better control over energy use in both home and commercial settings will be made possible by IoT devices and data analytics. Smart lighting controls and thermostats. Energy savings can be achieved through the optimization of industrial machines.
8. **Consumer Insights and Personalization:** Companies will use data created by the Internet of Things to learn more about the behavior of their customers. Personalized marketing and product recommendations made possible by these data will increase consumer satisfaction.

The potential for creativity, efficiency, and improved decision making in a variety of fields is great when IoT and data analytics are combined.

As this technology develops, it will be imperative to address the issues of security, privacy, and the moral use of data.

10.9 Conclusion

Together, IoT and data analytics provide a potent framework for gleaning insightful information and making defensible judgments from the massive volumes of data produced by IoT devices. Organizations may leverage real-time data to boost customer experiences, streamline operations, and spur innovation by fusing IoT and data analytics.

The previous system allows connected devices to connect to the platform by allowing for device localization, remote control, software and firmware management, troubleshooting, and search functions for connected devices. This layer is cloud-enabled for seamless M2M communication and defines device parameters like sensor type, location, expected reading values, and so on. Predictive analytics, Event Message Bus, Real-Time Streaming Analytics, and effective sensor and IoT device management are proposed instruments for collecting, processing, and partially manipulating the data. These data's semantic enrichment is an important addition. Concept models create this knowledge-based layer because they can support the entire range of knowledge representations, from semi-formal models allowing humans to interpret the data to strict-formal models enabling machines to analyze the data. Knowledge is represented in informal models utilizing graphical models and textual descriptions. On the other hand, strict formal models rely in part on visual representation but emphasize formal semantics through ontologies and the definition of corresponding inference rules. The suggestion uses a machine learning algorithm to extract a semantic representation of the dataset and clusters them together using the Apriori algorithm. The association between different clusters has improved by 23%, and the association between similar clusters has improved by 20% compared to the previous study.

References

1. Ambika, N., A Reliable Hybrid Blockchain-Based Authentication System for IoT Network, in: *Revolutionary Applications of Blockchain-Enabled Privacy and Access Control*, pp. 219–233, IGI Global, US, 2021.

2. Ambika, N., A Reliable Blockchain-Based Image Encryption Scheme for IIoT Networks, in: *Blockchain and AI Technology in the Industrial Internet of Things*, pp. 81–97, IGI Global, US, 2021.
3. Alam, T., Cloud-Based IoT Applications and Their Roles in Smart Cities. *Smart Cities*, 4, 1196–1219, 2021.
4. Alshehri, F. and Muhammad, G., A comprehensive survey of the Internet of Things (IoT) and AI-based smart healthcare. *IEEE Access*, 9, 3660–3678, 2020.
5. Nagaraj, A., *Introduction to Sensors in IoT and Cloud Computing Applications*, Bentham Science Publishers, UAE, 2021.
6. Alotaibi, S., Mehmood, R., Katib, I., Rana, O., Albeshri, A., Sehaa: A Big Data Analytics Tool for Healthcare Symptoms and Diseases Detection Using Twitter, Apache Spark, and Machine Learning. *Appl. Sci.*, 10, 4, 1398, 2020.
7. Runkler, T.A., *Data analytics*, Fachmedien Wiesbaden, Springer, Switzerland, 2020.
8. Werner, F. and Woitsch, R., Data Processing in Industrie 4.0: Data Analysis and Knowledge Management in Industrie 4.0. *Datenbank Spektrum*, 18, 15–25, 2018.
9. Ambika, N., Machine Learning Algorithm to Improve User's Experience, in: *Contemporary Studies of Risks in Emerging Technology, Part A*, pp. 49–59, Emerald Publishing Limited, Bingley, 2023.
10. Kramer, O. and Kramer, O., K-nearest neighbors, in: *Dimensionality reduction with unsupervised nearest neighbors*, pp. 13–23, 2013.
11. Harlow, H.D., Developing a knowledge management strategy for data analytics and intellectual capital. *Meditari Account. Res.*, 26, 3, 400–419, 2018.
12. Shabbir, M.Q. and Gardezi, S.B.W., Application of big data analytics and organizational performance: the mediating role of knowledge management practices. *J. Big Data*, 7, 1, 1–17, 2020.
13. Chang, H.C., Wang, C.Y., Hawamdeh, S., Emerging trends in data analytics and knowledge management job market: extending KSA framework. *J. Knowl. Manag.*, 23, 4, 664–686, 2019.
14. Ferraris, A., Mazzoleni, A., Devalle, A., Couturier, J., Big data analytics capabilities and knowledge management: impact on firm performance. *Manag. Decis.*, 57, 8, 1923–1936, 2019.
15. Khan, Z. and Vorley, T., Big data text analytics: an enabler of knowledge management. *J. Knowl. Manag.*, 21, 1, 18–34, 2017.
16. Sekli, G.F.M. and De La Vega, I., Adoption of big data analytics and its impact on organizational performance in higher education mediated by knowledge management. *J. Open Innov.: Technol. Mark. Complex.*, 7, 4, 221, 2021.
17. Hasan, I., Dhawan, P., Rizvi, S.A.M., Dhir, S., Data analytics and knowledge management approach for COVID-19 prediction and control. *Int. J. Inf. Technol.*, 15, 2, 937–954, 2023.

18. Iqbal, N., Ahmad, S., Kim, D.H., Towards mountain fire safety using fire spread predictive analytics and mountain fire containment in iot environment. *Sustainability*, 13, 5, 2461, 2021.
19. Derguech, W., Bruke, E., Curry, E., An autonomic approach to real-time predictive analytics using open data and internet of things, in: *IEEE 11th Intl Conf on Ubiquitous Intelligence and Computing and 2014 IEEE 11th Intl Conf on Autonomic and Trusted Computing and 2014 IEEE 14th Intl Conf on Scalable Computing and Communications and Its Associated Workshops*, Bali, Indonesia, 2014.
20. Debauche, O., Mahmoudi, S., Guttadauria, A., A New Edge Computing Architecture for IoT and Multimedia Data Management. *Information*, 13, 89, 2022.
21. Rausch, T., Hummer, W., Muthusamy, V., Rashed, A., Dustdar, S., Towards a serverless platform for edge {AI}, in: *2nd USENIX Workshop on Hot Topics in Edge Computing (HotEdge 19)*, Washington, USA, 2019.
22. Skouby, K.E. and Lynggaard, P., Smart home and smart city solutions enabled by 5G, IoT, AAI and CoT services, in: *International Conference on Contemporary Computing and Informatics (IC3I)*, Mysore, India, 2014.
23. Mavromoustakis, C.X., Mastorakis, G., Batalla, J.M., *Internet of Things (IoT) in 5G mobile technologies*, vol. 8, Springer, Switzerland, 2016.
24. Ahmed, Z., Mohamed, K., Zeeshan, S., Dong, X., Artificial intelligence with multi-functional machine learning platform development for better health-care and precision medicine. *Database*, 2020, 1–35, 2020.
25. Alimadadi, A., Aryal, S., Manandhar, I., Munroe, P.B., Joe, B., Cheng, X., Artificial intelligence and machine learning to fight COVID-19. *Physiol. Genomics*, 52, 4, 200–202, 2020.
26. Chakrabarty, S. and Engels, D.W., Secure smart cities framework using IoT and AI, in: *Global Physiological genomics Conference on Artificial Intelligence and Internet of Things (GCAIoT)*, Dubai, United Arab Emirates, 2020.
27. Lea, R. and Blackstock, M., City hub: A cloud-based IoT platform for smart cities, in: *6th international conference on cloud computing technology and science*, Singapore, 2014.
28. Leong, W.Y. and Kumar, R., 5G Intelligent Transportation Systems for Smart Cities, in: *Convergence of IoT, Blockchain, and Computational Intelligence in Smart Cities*, CRC Press, Boca Raton, Florida, 2023.

11

Industrialized Control and Automation System (ICAS): A Software-Defined Analysis Framework for Industry 4.0

Karthikeyan V.[1*], Dani Reagan Vivek J.[1], Gopalakrishnan K.[1] and Ezhil Kalaimannan[2]

[1]Department of ECE, Mepco Schlenk Engineering College (Autonomous), Sivakasi, Tamil Nadu, India
[2]Department of Cybersecurity, University of West Florida, Pensacola, FL, USA

Abstract
In the context of manufacturing, an Industrialized Control and Automation System (ICAS) is a set of interrelated economic processes that allow for the automated, data-driven tuning of various operational parameters of machinery and other mechanical systems with minimal human intervention. Safety, productivity, and equipment are all in danger from the widespread use of ICAS in areas like manufacturing, logistics, supply chain management, and transportation. Industry Internet Systems (IIS) and the IoT have played a critical role in the evolution of smart factories, which facilitate the autonomous management of resources through the sharing of data between previously isolated devices. Industry 4.0, IIS, Industrial Internet of Things, and ICAS all rely on IoT as their base, anticipating major advancements in design. The IIoT refers to a system where machines may interact with one another and make small adjustments to their environment or behavior with little to no human interaction. Embedded sensor nodes collect data, gateways analyze and send it to the cloud, and higher-level communication is made possible via networks like Wi-Fi and Ethernet, making up the three layers of IIoT operations. Focusing on its data analysis and problem-solving utility within the context of Industry 4.0, this article provides a detailed review of the theoretical and technological framework underlying the corporate implementation of IIoT.

***Keywords*:** Industry internet, industrial IoT, data analytics, intelligence control, tobotics

**Corresponding author*: karthikeyanv@mepcoeng.ac.in

Rajendra Kumar, Vishal Jain, Venus C. Ibarra, Corrienna Abdul Talib and Vinay Kukreja (eds.) Knowledge Management and Industry Revolution 4.0, (299–332) © 2024 Scrivener Publishing LLC

11.1 Introduction

Because of the rapid progress in technology, automation and live data analysis are now used in a wide variety of fascinating industries, including ecological tracking, the farming industry, the armed forces, medical care, production, logistics, managing supply chains, and stock control. In a scenario in which the Internet of Things links millions of individuals via handheld gadgets, having a connection to the World Wide Web has become an absolute requirement as illustrated in Figure 11.1 [1, 2]. This has resulted in an enormous increase in computational power, storage capacity, and information accessibility in every region of the globe [3]. The development of the internet is accomplished by the use of actuators, sensing devices, and technology to facilitate the linking of various physical things, including household appliances, automobiles, and even individuals, to one another [4].

Machine learning, distributed computing, and Big Data (BD), in addition to a significant rise in the use of cyber-physical systems, are often mentioned in conjunction with the concept of Industry 4.0. The ability of devices with sensors to gather data that builders and makers require enables the tracking and identification of individual components and subdivisions [5]. These different methods of data collection make it possible for equipment to interact and work together with one another in an autonomous manner, as well as exchange information in a non-traditional manner.

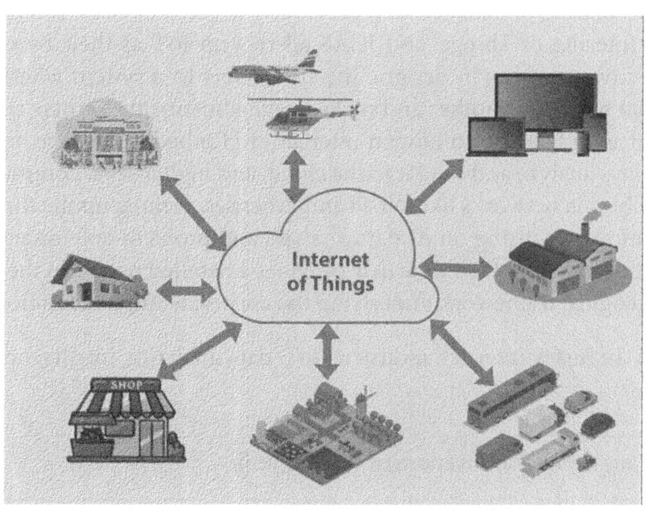

Figure 11.1 Internet of Things.

This opens the door for additional automation-focused business practices. The arrival of Industry 4.0 will be progressive but unmistakable over a long period of time, much like the transition from earlier *revolutions* [6].

The German government's *High Tech Trends 2020 Plan* was the inspiration for the nation's fourth-generation sector. The German government

Table 11.1 Industrial revolutions.

Industrial revolutions	Year	Major features
1.0	Around 17th century	Water and steam were used for the first time in manufacturing during the First Industrial Revolution. A higher quality of life is the result of the increased production of a variety of commodities made possible by this development
2.0	Between 18th and 19th century	Over this time period, advances in technology—most notably in electrical technology—have enabled increased output and more complex machinery
3.0	Between 19th and 20th century	More industrial automation was achieved by integrating electronics and information technology. There have been significant advancements in production and automating because of the availability of web interaction and renewable energy sources. Production process automating using PL controllers has been at the center of this transformation [8]
4.0	20th century and above	The Fourth Industrial Revolution is the period of self-sufficient, interconnected, and self-monitoring machines, including but not limited to computers, storage networks, and production facilities. The foundations of Industry 4.0 will consist of: A machine whose operations are under the control of computer code is a cyber-physical system. The Internet of Things (IoT) is a network of physical objects and software applications that communicate and share data through the Internet. Off-site data backup and network storage using cloud services contextual processing or AI-powered technological frameworks [9]

has invested thousands of billions of francs in innovation at the university, company, and ministry levels. Despite the fact that German and nearby enterprises have shown the most early and sustained excitement about Industry 4.0 developments, there is currently an increasing fascination with these concepts among organizations elsewhere [7]. Table 11.1 illustrates the evolution of the manufacturing sector over the course of four generations, from Industry 1.0 to Industry 4.0.

11.1.1 Industry Fourth-Generation Technologies

Figure 11.2 depicts how a number of technologies are collaborating to shed light on the way the new paradigm of 4.0 is being used in the construction process.

11.1.1.1 The Industrial IoT (IIoT)

The purpose of the IIoT is to facilitate communication and cooperation between devices, systems, and people in the manufacturing sector. In essence, it employs IoT, the interconnection and synchronization of sensors, devices, and data to produce results. The data generated through the IIoT can be used to optimize the manufacturing procedure by establishing connections between all of its constituent parts [10].

11.1.1.2 Automation

An ultimately successful interconnected company will strive to achieve the highest possible levels of efficiency and earnings. In order to achieve

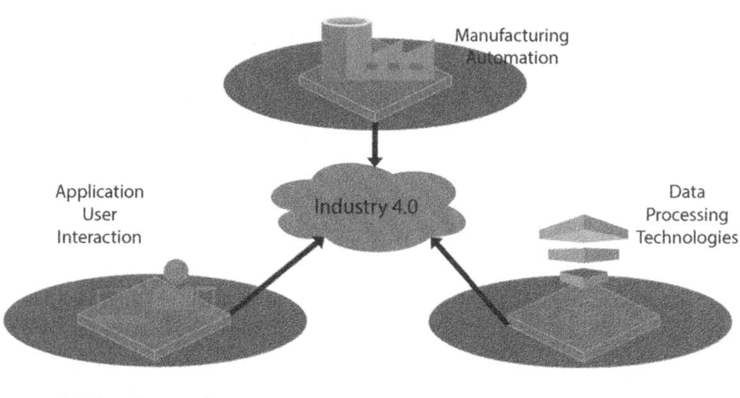

Figure 11.2 Technologies that support i4.0.

this goal, automation can be incorporated into various manufacturing processes, which can involve a significant portion of those operations [11]. The interaction and connectivity that take place within a facility that has been connected with i4.0 render it feasible to automate processes using robots or computational intelligence (CI).

11.1.1.3 AI—Artificial Intelligence

Machine learning (ML), a component of artificial intelligence (AI), is essentially what makes i4.0's intelligent manufacturing facility possible. The entire premise of the current technological transformation rests on the concept that AI will eventually replace human intervention. Artificial intelligence (AI) can speed up the data generated by a connected factory, allowing for better optimization of machinery, reprogramming of process steps, and overall recognition of any modifications that might have been implemented to assess efficiency and, ultimately, revenue [12].

11.1.1.4 Big Data (BD) and Analytics

Since all of the manufacturing processes are monitored and recorded, there is a massive data mining effort. On the other hand, BD analytics tools take advantage of artificial intelligence and machine learning to analyze input quickly and offer data to decision makers so that they can adjust the manufacturing process in its entirety [13].

11.1.1.5 The Cloud

The large amounts of data created by an i4.0 workflow are not something that manufacturers need to, or are willing to, permanently save. Because of this, storage and computing services in the cloud have become indispensable in modern factories that use networked fundamental machines. The use of the cloud also permits the rapid dissemination of the only reliable source of facts and the exchange of data throughout the company. Finally, cloud storage provides excellent transparency because it enables remote management as well as tracking of all information and machine-running systems [14, 15].

11.1.1.6 Cybersecurity

Due to the interconnected and digital nature of every part of the manufacturing process in Industry 4.0, strict cyber safety regulations are essential.

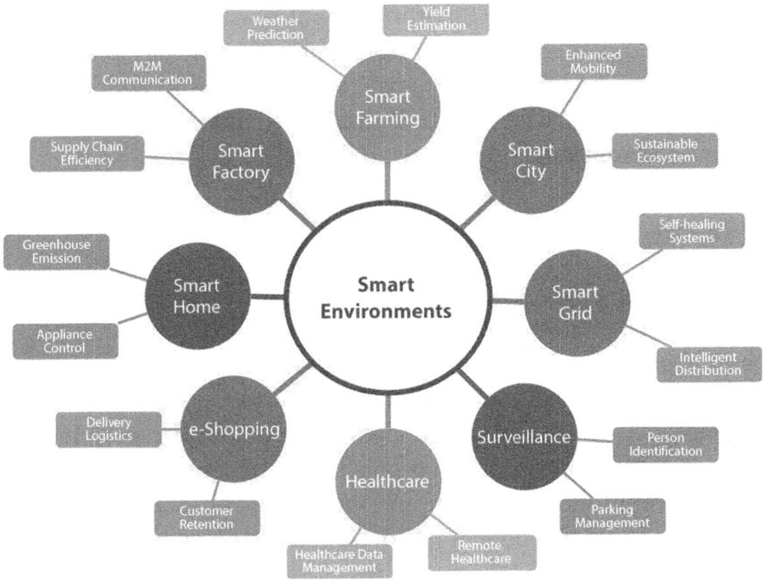

Figure 11.3 The Internet of Things enables smart circumstances.

It is useful for safeguarding everything linked to the Internet of Things, including manufacturing machinery, cloud storage, statistical analysis, and smartphones [16]. Various application sectors turn into smart environments by using these technologies represented in Figure 11.3.

11.1.2 Business Drivers of i4.0

In the framework of the fourth industrial revolution and progress, the ability to forecast efficiency is one of the main tyrants. Significant controversy surrounds the implications of Industry 4.0 for the industrial sector because of its far-reaching, even disruptive, implications [17]. Human actors, tangible artefacts, devices with intelligence, operations, and merchandise are all elements that must be incorporated in order to achieve i4.0 [18]. Smart gadgets and the Internet of Things (IoT) are just two examples of the technological advancements included in i4.0 that are employed by manufacturers to introduce new methods and procedures [19]. Most academics and industry experts focus on the technological aspects of the fourth industrial revolution, whereas the organizational and executive elements are just getting started [20]. Figure 11.4 illustrates how the IoT enables a wide range of intelligent circumstances, including a number of intelligent factories, one of the most difficult of which is i4.0.

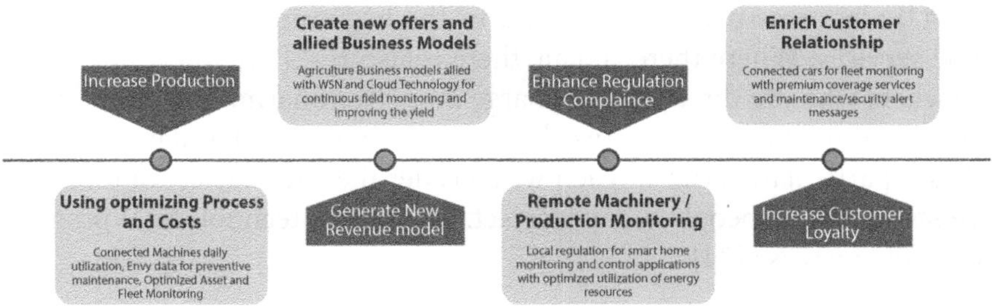

Figure 11.4 IoT development key business driver.

A changing set of components, outcomes, interactions, market dynamics, and manufacturing techniques are what generate and inherit price added. From the input portion of producing goods, practically each process needs to train workers to acquire the expertise necessary to run efficiently and compete effectively. Nowadays, the main components centered on agricultural progress are artificial intelligence, biological sciences, and statistical science, and AI and BS are crucial for monitoring resource effectiveness and technological advancement in various sectors represented in Figure 11.5 [21, 22].

The advent of i4.0 is an integral part of the technological revolution because of its inventive characteristics. Intelligent *planning* robotics is going to replace the majority of labor jobs, monotonous employment, employment in a hazardous setting, and repetitive tasks. Occasionally, new jobs appear that call for special skills. Enterprises looking to make the shift

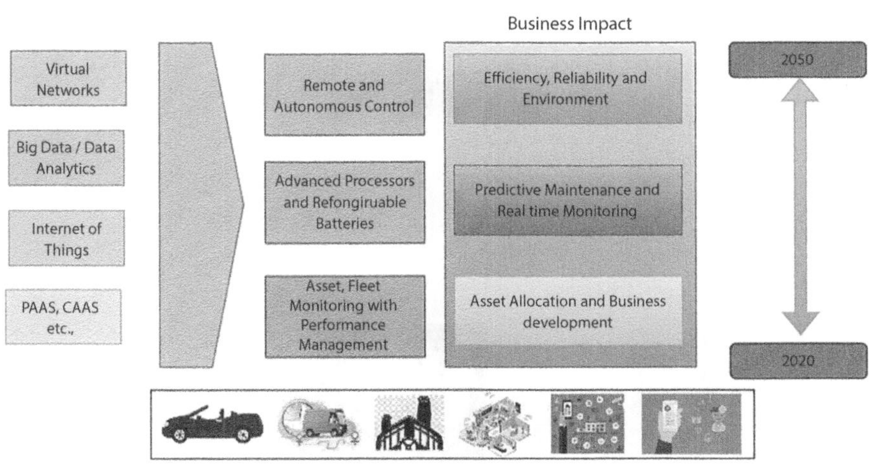

Figure 11.5 IoT connecting technologies.

to i4.0 platforms may be hampered in the beginning by a lack of available services. Where there is data, there is also risk [23]. There are skilled attackers who are directing the charge away from harm. Therefore, it will be crucial to ensure that networks remain robust and that data is secure. This is particularly crucial when we consider the wide variety of tools and *things* via which people today interact. The rate of technological progress will only increase [24].

11.1.3 Industrial Internet

American conglomerate GE is responsible for popularizing the acronym *Industrial Internet*. When the analog and modern spheres collided, the outcome was the Industrial Internet. By General Electric's own definition, the industrial Internet is the integration of the worldwide manufacturing infrastructure using the capabilities of cutting-edge processing, data analysis, inexpensive monitoring, and the novel forms of interconnection enabled by the Web.

Monitoring nodes, applications, and Machine-to-Machine (M2M) connectivity are used by organizations empowered by the industrial internet to gather data collected by physical objects [25]. Figure 11.6 depicts the Industrial Internet, which consists of the associated equipment in businesses, computerized manufacturing lines, contemporaneous information acquired from nodes of sensor technology, and its evaluation.

The advancement of the Industrial Internet may be attributed largely to the combination of autonomous machinery, sophisticated statistics,

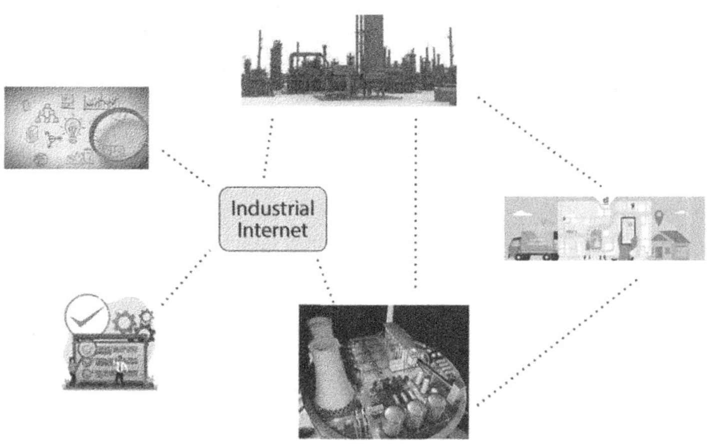

Figure 11.6 Industrial Internet.

and interconnected individuals. With these variables working together, the financial system as a whole benefits from production optimization, reduced manufacturing expenses, and immediate information assessment [4, 8].

Appliances that are both intelligent and linked boost productivity. By adopting an intelligent business strategy, costs are reduced, output is maximized, and money is generated as planned. Products that are both intelligent and interconnected are characterized by their ability to monitor, control, optimize, and automate processes. Firm declarations that increase the economic worth of an item, the business's earnings streams, and its technology are key to an intelligent and interconnected firm [6, 26].

11.2 Related Works

By summarizing the information that has been previously examined and the areas where more investigation is needed, review articles offer a broad perspective on a field of study [27]. Conventional manufacturing undergoes a process of digital transition, in which it is transformed into *smart industries* by adopting technological advances in a variety of business functions. Numerous sectors can benefit from this technology, not just production [28]. As a result of digitization, modern manufacturing facilities are better able to adapt to changing market demands and new advancements [29, 30]. These facilities are also more autonomous and self-organizing. By enabling the interconnection of diverse physical equipment, each of which is enhanced with incorporated technological devices, to a neighborhood network or via the web, the rise of digital technology provides an entirely new viewpoint for the manufacturing sector [2].

Cyber-physical systems (CPS) are another key idea in i4.0. CPS observes real-world systems virtually, opening the door to distributed, coordinated assessment [31]. To this purpose, CPS gathers, communicates, and evaluates information while also controlling physical infrastructure [32], allowing for better decisions to be made both up and down the value stream. Other crucial i4.0 ideas stem from the widespread adoption of automated and technological advancements, such as human–machine interoperability and connectivity [29, 31, 33, 34]. Modern i4.0 capabilities enable the development of a digitally connected value network in which goods, machinery, and individuals are interconnected within a company's own manufacturing setting alongside its outside collaborators [33]. Innovative company models based on client wants and extensive customization are made possible by these advances in technology [30, 34]. According to Kamble *et al.*

[2], one of the defining features of i4.0 has been its reliance on technologies that enabled it from the very beginning. Consequently, a lot of study has gone into this, and we will talk about it below.

11.2.1 Technologies

Using knowledge and technological advances in automation extensively, computerized and digitalized operations characterize the fourth industrial revolution [31]. The Internet of Things (IoT) is one of the technologies most closely connected to i4.0 because it enables the interconnection of the various components that make up CPS in smart manufacturing facilities [2]. Not only does Lu (2017) cover the Internet of Things but also portable computing, the cloud, and Big Data. Information modeling, virtual and augmented realities, artificial intelligence, and three-dimensional printing are all shown by Liao *et al.* [17] to be technologies that are necessary for I4.0. Quick prototypes, simulations, and high-end autonomous systems are all part of this category, as Kamble *et al.* [2] note. Tools like actuators, sensor technology, RFID tags, and RTLS (real-time location systems) have been identified as essential to the development of AI [35]. The i4.0 investigation plan also places an emphasis on information security solutions that aim to safeguard information systems as well as procedures [2]. In addition, numerous additional writers have discussed i4.0's supporting technologies. Nosalska *et al.* [36] offer taxonomy of six categories to classify the various technologies, and this taxonomy. Supply chains that use these technologies holistically stand a better chance of improving both performance and quality [12].

11.2.2 Applications

Since i4.0 is still in its infancy, there is little in the way of practical studies. Liao *et al.* [17] point out two issues that prevent businesses from embracing these innovations: (i) the unpredictability of financial returns and (ii) the immaturity associated with certain innovations. Galati and Bigliardi [33] use data mining techniques to investigate i4.0's primary research foci. The authors divided the findings into four categories: (i) management, (ii) daily operations, (iii) technological advancements, and (iv) education and development. In their presentation, Da Silva *et al.* [37] mention energy use in i4.0 buildings as an additional possible utilization. Techniques for doing so fall under the umbrella of *energy management* [30].

Concerning the pros and cons of implementing i4.0 strategies and technology in businesses, Sony [38] provides an in-depth analysis. The author cited improvements in areas, such as productivity, effectiveness, responsiveness, inventiveness in processes, quality and assurance, ecological impact, and social consequences, as positives. There are a number of drawbacks, including the potential dangers of information sharing in an extremely competitive marketplace, the necessity for comprehensive i4.0 implementation, the management of staff members and trade union fears, the availability of appropriately skilled workers, socio-technical consequences, cybersecurity concerns, and an expensive entry price. In 2018, Barata *et al.* [39] conducted an investigation on mobile Supply Chain Management (mSCM)—the utilization of handheld devices, like smartphones and tablets, to improve the efficiency and effectiveness of the logistics process.

Documentation of transactions is securely maintained and distributed over a network of computers using blockchain technology (BC) [40]. The Internet of Things (IoT) and Big Data are just two examples of how the cloud may help manufacturers streamline their operations. Data security concerns among businesses are the primary impediment to adoption. The challenge of establishing a constant data link among agents in the plant and cloud-based control systems is an additional significant factor [41].

Big Data Analytics (BDA) is the process of extracting knowledge from an organization's enormous databases that may be used for taking decisions across a variety of managerial domains (such as advertising, transportation, manufacturing, making purchases, and so on). According to Cui and colleagues [42], the building of a BDA system requires the incorporation of the following nine sections: i) information acquisition; ii) retention; iii) computing; iv) statistics; v) visualization; vi) processing and dataflow; vii) information administration; viii) architecture and distribution methodology; and ix) security measures. Cadavid *et al.* [43] propose a plan for execution and carry out an in-depth assessment of the application of ML, with a particular emphasis on planning and controlling production (PCP).

The investigation on AR presented by Egger and Masood [44] is far more sophisticated in the realm of transportation as well as is gaining ground within Europe and Southeast Asia. Because of the increasing number of studies conducted in collaboration with businesses, it is anticipated that AR will spread rapidly. Guo *et al.* [45] examine the use of VR in upkeep. A novel approach to production is the use of adaptable systems for production. One of its primary features is the ability to self-organize in response to changing production conditions [46]. By depositing subsequent coats of substance, additive production (AP) or 3D printing allows for the fabrication of an object that is three-dimensional from a computer-generated model [36, 47].

11.2.3 Management Innovation

Production Planning and Control systems need to be more flexible, decentralized, and autonomous to keep up with the demands of Industry 4.0 [48]. Martins *et al.* [40] present 14 APC models that are fully autonomous. These models have seen extensive application for scheduling purposes, with the ultimate goal of reducing the amount of time orders spend waiting in the warehouse. Parente *et al.* [49] describe the ways in which new technologies are revolutionizing smart factory production control. The connection between PPC and i4.0 is demonstrated more thoroughly by Bueno *et al.* [50]. When it comes to merging PPC efforts with i4.0 tools, the authors present a total of 18 smart capabilities and 13 performance metrics.

Chauhan and Singh [51] demonstrate that the majority of studies in i4.0 are focused on the production and transportation industries, whereas the computerization of Supply Chain Management, also known as SCM, is an issue that is receiving an increasing amount of attention. In the framework of i4.0, Dalzochio *et al.* [52] examine the primary concerns about artificial intelligence (AI) as well as Interpretation strategies for Predictive Maintenance (PM). The researchers point out that these techniques are currently utilized in several phases of PM, including assessment, prognosis, and the calculation of usable longevity. The latest research on Industrialized Control and Automation Systems (ICAS) are outlined in the following Table 11.2.

Table 11.2 New topics and findings from related studies in each subset of ICAS.

Introduction to I4.0		
I4.0 and its impacts	Wagire *et al.*, 2020 [34]	This study discusses future patterns and proposes an Industry 4.0 categorization and potential research paths
I4.0 cons	Ding (2018) [30]	High expenses and energy utilization, inadequate knowledge as well as learning, implementation of rules, absence of organizational enticements, inefficient partnerships and cooperation within the PSC cells, an absence of goal criteria, and a poor awareness among end-customers are all examined as obstacles to incorporating sustainability into the I4.0

(*Continued*)

Table 11.2 New topics and findings from related studies in each subset of ICAS. (*Continued*)

Introduction to I4.0		
Variables crucial to i4.0's development	Sony and Naik (2020) [53]	According to the findings of this investigation, there are a total of 10 crucial success elements that must be present in order for an organization to successfully roll out Industry 4.0
E-SWOT in I4.0	Calabrese *et al.* (2020) [12]	The topic of Industry 4.0 is investigated from the leadership point of view in this article. In order to determine the technological foundations of the fourth industrial revolution, as well as its strengths, weaknesses, opportunities, and threads, often known as its *E-SWOT* features, an organized research study is performed
Applications of Industry 4.0 technologies		
Intelligent factory	Galati and Bigliardi (2019) [33]	The purpose of this investigation is twofold: (i) to recognize the primary general trends that have been explored over the years and follow their development throughout history; and (ii) to suggest a plan of action for future study for every encompassing subject that takes into consideration the diverse character of research endeavor.
Intelligent product	Sony and Naik (2020) [53]	This research lists 10 CSFs that must be in place before an organization can successfully implement I4.0. Ten potential avenues for future study are outlined in light of the 10 most important factors. The findings of this research can serve as a roadmap for businesses as they adopt I4.0. Paying attention to these 10 areas will assist businesses remain viable as they adopt I4.0

(*Continued*)

Table 11.2 New topics and findings from related studies in each subset of ICAS. (*Continued*)

Introduction to I4.0		
Digital city	Lu (2017) [31]	With the goal of giving a brief overview of the information, extent, and results toward the effective implementation of the connected society by means of i4.0, this study evaluates the current literature on this subject across the various sources that collectively make comprise the World Wide Web
Sustainable energy	Da Silva *et al.* (2020) [37]	This work examines how energy consumption affects the framework's overall scope. It was suggested to do a comprehensive literature evaluation of recent research in the areas of intelligent production as well as energy usage
Autonomous manufacturing	Liao *et al.* (2017) [3]	In order to fill this void, the purpose of this investigation is to examine the scientific advancements made in the field of i4.0. In order to conduct an in-depth analysis of the scholarly works pertaining to the industrial revolution issue, in-depth literature research was conducted
Enabling mechanisms		
Influence of the IoT on supply chains management (SCM)	Ben-Daya *et al.* (2019) [54]	Using an extensive source analysis, the authors investigate IoT's function in and effect on SCM. The concept of IoT, the primary catalysts of IIoT implementations, and the numerous procedures and uses that make employing IoT in SCM possible are all discussed

(*Continued*)

Table 11.2 New topics and findings from related studies in each subset of ICAS. (*Continued*)

Introduction to I4.0		
Industrial automation	Liao *et al.* (2018) [3]	This research offered a clear literature assessment that methodically zeroed in on IIoT. It was explained how IIoT differs from Industry 4.0 and vice versa. Various IIoT protocols and techniques were studied to determine their compatibility and potential limits in a single-use case
Big Data Analytics	Cui *et al.* (2020) [42]	The use of large datasets for production purposes is addressed in this paper. There are six key influences of Big Data in industry. Integration of systems is driven by data, forecasting, long-term viability, collaboration of resources, and technology. Nine parts of the Big Data environment are needed in production. Data collection, archiving, processing, analysis, representation, administration, procedure, framework, and protection
Machine learning (ML)	Cadavid *et al.* (2020) [43]	There are two main goals of this investigation: (1) aiding in the creation of a technique for executing ML-PPC; and (2) proposing an approach for categorizing the literature in science in order to uncover new avenues for investigation. The subsequent goal is elaborated by investigating I4.0's application scenarios and the qualities that it aims to improve.
Human–robot collaboration	Gualtieri *et al.* (2021) [55]	Based on the evolution of publications, researchers were able to identify and analyze the most pressing developing research difficulties and study fields concerning protection and ergonomics in industry collaborative robotics

To adapt to the shifting needs of employment and fulfill the requirements of i4.0, workers need to learn fresh competencies. This individual needs to be able to handle cutting-edge technology, collaborate effectively with others, and express themselves well if they want to be successful in their field. On the other hand, these investigations are still hypothetical, and Jerman *et al.* [56] argue that an empirical investigation is necessary in order to validate their findings.

In the following sections, we are going to examine, from the point of view of the Internet of Things (IoT), how the i4.0 factory is built and organized with regard to certain of the services.

11.3 Healthcare Applications in Industries

The healthcare industry as a whole has advanced greatly in the past few decades thanks to the incorporation of the Internet of Things. In the past, healthcare professionals and patients mostly communicated through phone calls and written notes. Sensors based on the Internet of Things and cutting-edge networking technologies have made it possible for physicians to track the well-being of patients in a dependable and cost-effective manner. Because of this, hospitalizations have gotten shorter for patients [57].

11.3.1 Major Challenges Associated with Healthcare

Population growth, issues associated with a growing elderly population, the prevalence of new illnesses, and rising patient expectations have all presented significant difficulties to the healthcare system in recent years. The following are examples of several of the most pressing problems facing the healthcare sector today:

- Pharmaceutical overdose, prescribing an inappropriate drug, prescribing more than one medication at once, and failing to account for an individual's response to a medication are all examples of preventable healthcare mistakes.
- Expensive healthcare and medical care facilities: Medical research has made great strides forward in the past many years.
- Complex diseases that were formerly fatal may now be cured with the help of modern medication and surgical procedures. Nevertheless, these therapeutic options come at a hefty price tag.
- New medical discoveries require a long time to be accepted and made readily accessible to individuals with illnesses, despite an ongoing advancement in research.

In the modern day, technologies that are both smart as well as intelligent have been broadly accepted in a variety of domains within the healthcare industry. The rate of rising incidences of various types of chronic illnesses as well as the growth in the proportion of the elderly in the general population is unable to slow down. Furthermore, the signs and symptoms of chronic illnesses can be recognized even before the condition has fully manifested, when it is still in its infancy. As a result, patients' routine medical examinations do not always need to take place in hospitals. They might instead take place in patients' homes [56].

11.3.2 IoT-Based Smart Healthcare System

It is possible to carry out remote surveillance of individuals' medical conditions using nodes of sensor technology that have been attached to or implanted within the bodies of the individuals in question. The information that is supplied by these nodes of sensors can be accessed, reviewed, monitored, and used by medical practitioners to provide advice to the client. *Smart beds* were recently implemented in hospitals in an effort to alleviate the discomfort individuals feel [58]. Intelligent bedding includes a variety of attributes, including positioning management, monitoring of sleep, thermostat management, oxygen chambers, and integration with apps. The diagram in Figure 11.7 provides an illustration of a simplified model of the progression of information in an IoT-based healthcare system.

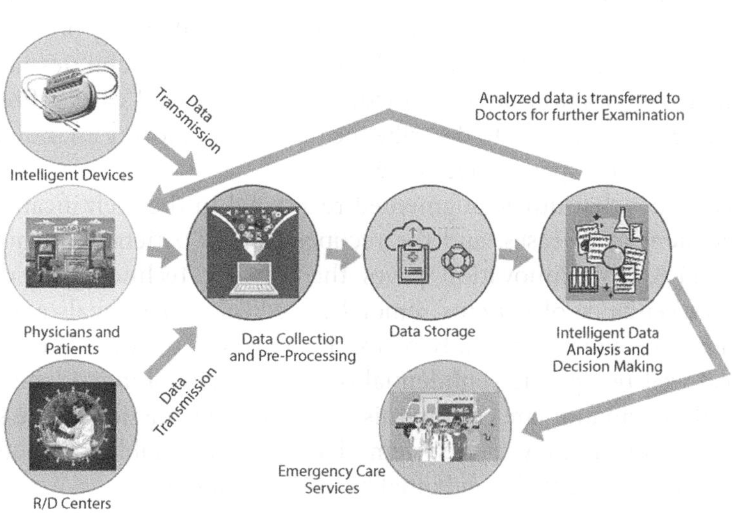

Figure 11.7 Data flow diagram for an IIoT-enabled healthcare system.

Through gateway nodes, data is sensed and transmitted from a wide variety of smart and intelligent devices, including smart watches and smart healthcare apps, to servers. The server, or cloud, collects the data, processes it, and stores it. Additionally, medical professionals and researchers have access to these processed data for examination and analysis. The reviewed reports are uploaded by the medical specialists through a web portal. Any patient's health can be better managed with early notification of their condition so that appropriate therapies and medications can be administered at the right times. Healthcare providers are able to make better judgments in the moment, improving the quality of care they provide to patients. Data from a critically ill patient might be processed closer to the edge of the network, saving both time and energy in the event of an emergency [59].

In addition, the real-time alert, tracking, and monitoring of the patient's circumstances aid in increasing the precision with which the fluctuation in the patient's physiological parameters is measured, allowing for prompt intervention by the doctors and ultimately leading to better patient care [60].

11.3.3 Advanced Technologies Used in Healthcare

The medical field makes extensive use of AI for tasks such as hospitalization and physician referrals according to an individual's health seriousness. Medical professionals and their helpers can benefit from the analysis of the information collected, which provides significant insights. The general expenses relating to individuals' drugs can be reduced through macro- and micro-level examination of information. By allowing professionals to remotely observe clients, centralized surveillance capabilities facilitate immediate interaction between medical specialists and carers. Precision healthcare is a term used to describe the process of tailoring an individual's treatment to their specific needs [56].

Techniques that utilize augmented reality aid in the identification and management of diseases, and the recuperation of patients are shown in Figure 11.8. This innovation paves the way for technological device-based surveillance of patients remotely. Medical professionals and other healthcare providers offer advice to clients based on the state of their physical well-being. The confidentiality and integrity of individuals' physiological information are compromised during transmission to the server. Blockchain technology is a system that uses immutable computerized records to store clients' confidential healthcare data [56].

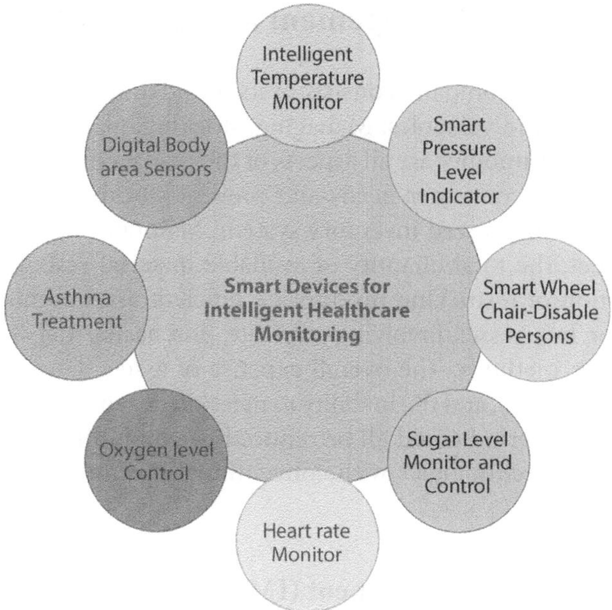

Figure 11.8 Smart devices for checking the health conditions of patients.

11.3.4 Open Research Issues to be Addressed

We focused on how sophisticated technology and intelligent gadgets may work together in an IIoT-based healthcare system to give clients better care. Nevertheless, the following are some of the future research problems that need to be solved:

- Patients may be on the go, so the WBAN system can be adapted to work with mobile gadgets and settings.
- Healthcare systems must be made more scalable without sacrificing confidentiality.
- The cost of energy usage can be minimized in healthcare settings by carefully designing IIoT-based innovations, techniques, and standards.
- Using less memory to interpret and analyze the individual's observed physiological characteristics

11.4 Inventory Management and Quality Control

The inventory of a company consists of its foundational components, finished products, and valuables. Managing, stocking, placing order storage, and handling commodity are all aspects of the management of inventories. In order to meet consumer needs and prevent stockouts, it is crucial to maintain a well-organized inventory system. Maintaining tabs on the finished product, the total quantity of available material resources, and the likely duration of restocking inventories, efficient asset administration is essential for businesses involving intricate purchasing networks as well as production methods. The overall expense of assets, faults in the stock assessment analyzed, and the inability to meet client requirements throughout the allotted period could all be reduced by combining the application of cutting-edge technologies with conventional inventory administration procedures [56].

11.4.1 Inventory Management (IM)

IM describes the entire procedure, from acquiring initial supplies to completing production to shipping and storing completed goods.

The inventory administration of an organization is depicted in a simplified format in Figure 11.9. Conventional logistics procedures are being

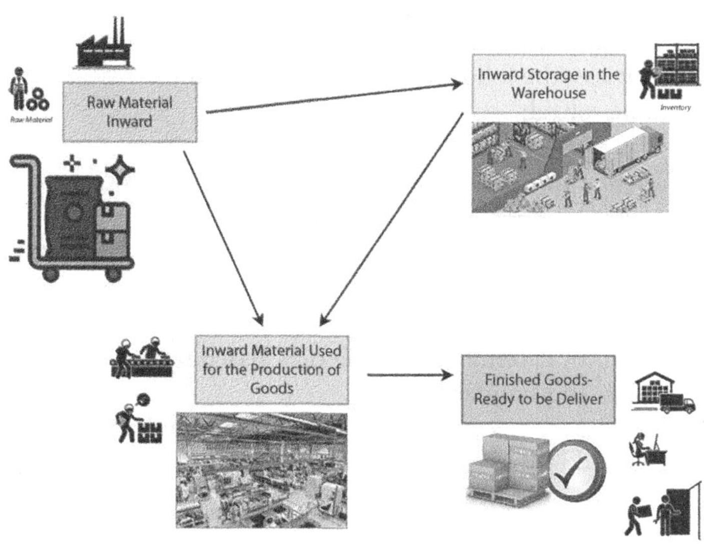

Figure 11.9 Schematic view of inventory management.

transformed into IioT-based inventory administration through the association of people with merchandise and vice versa. This transformation of the inventory control strategy contributes to greater effectiveness, reduced expenses, more production, and less utilization of energy. In addition, effective inventory administration makes better use of storage facilities, reduces labor costs, and boosts levels of contentment among consumers [61].

In addition, the storage facility employs a wide variety of automated machinery, including moving bots to transport stock, autonomous arms for carrying containers, and bots for creating individualized wrapping. As a result, Amazon has grown into one of the largest worldwide businesses during the past quarter century by implementing IioT-based technology [62].

11.4.2 Inventory

The term *inventory* refers to a company's store of unprocessed supplies and completed goods. It is a resource that an organization has. Asset measurements include stock on hand, turnover of stock, and asset cycle duration. IM is illustrated in Figure 11.10. As a matter of fact, the shop stocks a wide variety of things. In order to prevent stockouts, the quantities of such products are tallied on a regular basis. These supplies are either processed into useable forms or offered for sale in their original forms. Thus, the percentage of turnover in stock can shift between days and weeks. Furthermore, the ordering point needs to be calculated to guarantee efficient operation. The overall duration of an action is an important metric to track. Taking into account the entire process time, the handling of brand-new orders, and the completion of previous orders [63].

The final product stockpile is often known as just the finished item. Final inspections of excellence are performed prior to moving products out of the work-in-progress area to the finished product storage area. Assemblies and subassemblies that have been handled or still need to be treated in the framework are considered work in progress, which includes the materials, methods, and inventories necessary for producing products. Raw substances are the components and supplies that are employed in the production of finished goods [64]. MRO products, which include tools and parts for upkeep, are essential to keeping factories running smoothly. The supply chain for MRO consists of raw materials, intermediates, and components that have a tangential relationship to final products.

Figure 11.10 Benefits of IIoT applications in inventory management.

11.4.3 Types of Inventory Management

Just-In-Time (JIT) administration, Materials Requirement Planning (MRP), Economic Order Quantity (EOQ), and days sales inventory (DSI) are the several types of systems for inventory administration that can be used depending on the category of enterprise or merchandise that are analyzed. The fundamental goal of just-in-time (JIT) assembly was to enhance general productivity while simultaneously reducing the amount of trash and expenses connected with the production cycle. When it comes to computing the quantity of components and supplies needed to produce an item, MRP constitutes one of the strategies that is being utilized on an increasingly widespread scale. When it comes to stock administration, the EOQ approach is used to determine the appropriate quantity of things that should be purchased for every collection of sales, with the objective of keeping the total expenditure of stock to a minimum. The total number of hours or the amount of time required for selling the stocks, comprising the goods that are still in the process of being made, are referred to as DSI [65, 66].

11.4.4 Inventory Management and IIoT

Intelligent sensors and cutting-edge technology work together to create a network of equipment as well as individuals that can better monitor inventory and respond in real period to client demands. In addition, analyzing the massive amount of information produced in actual time contributes to demand forecasting for the future. RFID labels are commonly attached to items, raw materials, and completed products in an IIoT environment. These tags with RFID technology are all numbered differently. Metadata from the inspected RFID tags that are on the goods are transferred to a web server or cloud computing system where identification numbers can be retrieved. The information on stock goods can be refreshed instantly in a similar manner [67]. Clients have the option of keeping tabs on stock levels from afar. RFID codes allow for instantaneous scanning of large numbers of things. Issues with having too many or inadequate supplies can then be addressed. The goods safety and effectiveness can be enhanced as well. The directional element of a radio frequency identification tag supplies the energy required to send data. In addition, electromagnetic radiation is employed for writing and retrieving information from tags with RFID chips, and reader devices can be stationary or portable.

The numerous IIoT-based implementations within the supply chain administration framework have contributed to the modernization of both production and organizational structures. Merchandise can be accurately monitored in an instantaneous fashion with the incorporation of radio frequency identification (RF) along with additional IIoT-based intelligent

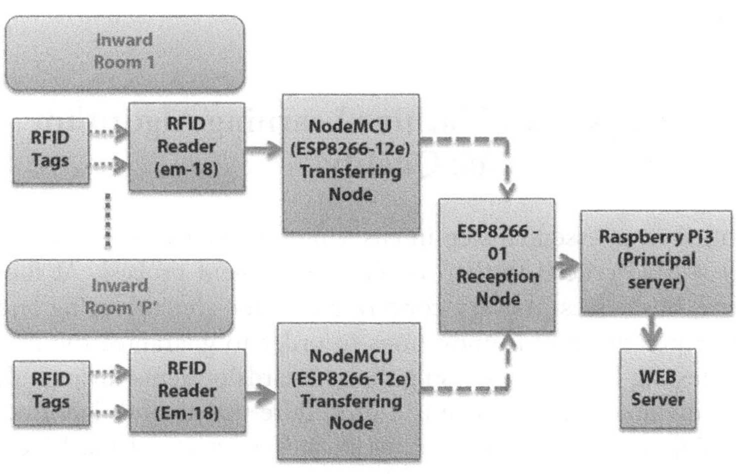

Figure 11.11 Benefits of IIoT applications in inventory management.

sensors. The enhanced merchandise tracking solution in Figure 11.11 presents warehouse management with continuous information on completed assets, remaining material inventories, and stocks in process. Current indications of the volume of goods in storage enable an inventory supervisor to control the spot, timing, and quantity of items on stock [56]. As the inventory controller receives immediate updates on the whereabouts and state of the assets, the company identifies machinery with diminished effectiveness in operation and the quantity of reserves and preemptive merchandise that must be preserved. The inventory supervisor has knowledge about the quantity of readily accessible stocks and can predict the storage facility's surplus stockpile [65, 67].

11.4.5 Open Research Issues to be Addressed

To keep stocks in good shape, an innovative system for inventory control might be created to lessen the likelihood of inventory shortages and excess waste. Computing the re-order percentage, improving the percentage of turnover, and refining the quality of the information may all be accomplished with the help of cutting-edge intelligence. Consideration must also be given to the possibility of a malfunction or breakdown of equipment. Workers need specialized training in order to fix or upgrade broken pieces of machinery and deal with unexpected problems that may arise on the factory field. Proper inventory administration and production control allow businesses to boost productivity, enhance revenue, and guarantee satisfaction among their clientele. Repeat business and constructive criticism from pleased clients are two major benefits any company may reap from having a loyal clientele.

11.5 Analysis of a Machine Learning Algorithm to Predict Wine Quality

Evaluation is an essential step in ensuring the quality of the item, which is why it is so crucial to the overall improvement process. At the present time, businesses in every conceivable sector are embracing and putting into practice novel innovations in order to guarantee the product's quality testing [68, 69]. Assessing the standards of items through the use of an individual's competence is a procedure that is both laborious and costly [70]. The present section investigates a variety of machine learning approaches that can be utilized to evaluate the quality of wine. Some of these methods include logistic regression, decision tree, random forest, support vector machine (SVM), AdaBoost classifier, and gradient boosting predictor. These methods streamline the procedure of guaranteeing quality while using the obtainable attributes of the goods to execute inspections for quality control. This helps reduce the amount of human involvement in the entire procedure.

11.5.1 Objectives

- Experimenting with several classification approaches to determine which one provides the most accurate results is the primary goal of this endeavor.
- The second thing we want to do is figure out which characteristics of a wine are the best indications of its overall quality.

11.5.2 Conventional Schemes for Wine Quality Assessment (WQA)

Experts have increasingly turned to artificial intelligence models for help rating wines, but there is still plenty of room for advancement. In his research, Yogesh Gupta [68] investigates the use of regression analysis to identify crucial traits for forecasting as well as the use of neural networks and support vector machines for the task of forecasting outcomes. The present section delves into the application of the latest machine learning methodologies, namely, quadratic regression's determination of significant characteristics for forecasting and the use of neural networks and support vector machine (SVM) applications for making such predictions. In order to determine if a red wine is of *excellent quality* or not, Terence Shin [69] employed Kaggle's Red Wine Assessment Database to construct a number of classification frameworks. A number of approaches, including logistic regression, stochastic gradient descent, support vector classifiers, and random forest, were employed by Pawar *et al.* [70] for developing the wine's quality predictions. Long-short-term memory neural networks (LSTM NN) produced superior outcomes in comparison with different strategies in a technical as well as fundamental evaluation of several approaches intended for estimating prospective price movements in stocks conducted by Saini *et al.* [71]. Zeng *et al.* [72] create a qualitative and quantitative framework for the wine's quality and investigate the consequences of both chemical and physical characteristics of wine grapes upon wine effectiveness, having wine quality assessment serve as an investigation objective.

11.5.3 Proposed Autonomous ML Scheme-Based WQA

For the purpose of this investigation, algorithms that utilize machine learning are employed to make predictions regarding the quality of wines. The step-by-step procedure that will be done according to the suggested technique is shown in Figure 11.12. Initially, the collection of data pertaining to wines is preprocessed. In addition, the collected information is segmented into training samples (which comprise 80% of the total) as well as testing samples (which comprise 20% of the total). The learning pieces are utilized for developing models utilizing logistic regression, random forests, decision trees, SVM, AdaBoost classifiers, and gradient-boosting classification algorithms, while the experimental collections are employed to evaluate the efficiency of various models. Following this, one arrives at the realization that the framework that was previously trained can be utilized to determine the degree of precision of the sample being tested. The accuracy of a number of distinct strategies is assessed and examined in order to determine which method is most capable of accurately predicting the quality of wine [73].

For the purposes of the present research, the Red Wine Database [74] gathering is utilized. An aggregate of 1,599 specimens are available regarding the red wine. Every specimen includes the following physiochemical parameters: thickness, pH level, sulfates, alcohol, grade assessment,

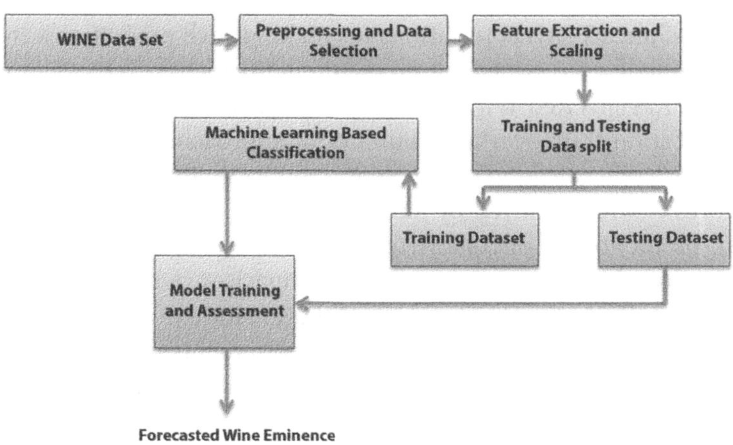

Figure 11.12 System model for WQA.

liberated sulfur dioxide, static acidity, dynamic acidity, citric acid level, excess sweetness, chloride compounds, permitted sulfur dioxide, cumulative sulfur dioxide, and free sulfur dioxide concentration. On this rating system, 0 indicates the absolute worst possible excellence, while 10 indicates the highest possible level of excellence. It is not permissible to employ wine samples before first undergoing pretreatment because there are some issues regarding the information being collected. Additionally, there is a significant magnitude among values for variables; for example, sulfates range from 0.33 to 2.0, while sulfur dioxide ranges between 1 and 72, and additionally, there are certain numbers that are lacking. This constitutes one of the primary flaws. The values that are not present have been made up by calculating the average of the remaining entries. The discrepancy in the information set has an effect on the forecasts made as a result of the impacts of certain parameters. This type of discrepancy can be handled by a linear adjustment by splitting all of the values entered by the highest possible value of the variables. The overall rating of the wines is translated into a numerical result, where *1* indicates an excellent wine (one with an overall rating of 7 or more), whereas *0* indicates a poor-quality wine (one with a rating value less than 7) [73].

Physiochemical parameters, such as selected acidity, uncertain acidity, citric acid, remaining sugar, chloride compounds, permitted sulfur dioxide, overall sulfur dioxide, volume, pH, sulfates, as well as alcohol parameters, are used by different methods of machine learning, such as logistic regression, supervised decision tree, random forest, SVM, AdaBoost classification algorithm, as well as gradient boosting classifier. These methods are used in artificial intelligence. The random forest approach generates a finite number of decision networks and then employs a variety of information to learning every individual decision tree [73]. The information is distributed over all of the decision trees in order to make a forecast about how good the wine is. The outcome can be forecast based on the votes cast by a large proportion of voters. On the basis of the findings, it is possible to conclude that the random-forest classification method is an improved kind of artificial intelligence technology that is better suited for making recommendations about the quality of wines. In an analogous vein, the random forest classification method, when used with chosen forecasters compared to all forecasters, is capable of producing estimates that are more accurate [75].

11.5.4 Open Research Issues to be Addressed

When utilizing the random forest methodology, the highest possible level of efficiency in the quality of wine forecasting is achieved. We can observe that wines of higher standards have greater quantities of alcohol on a typical basis, greater amounts of sulfates on a typical basis, a smaller amount of volatile acids on a typical basis, as well as greater amounts of sugar residue in general than lesser-quality wines. The research might be expanded such that, rather than taking into account every one of the variable's characteristics, just the most significant ones have to be taken into account when making an assessment of the importance of the variable being studied. This will result in a forecast that is more precise. In the future, a large dataset could be utilized for research, and further artificial learning and deep learning approaches may be investigated for use in quality wine forecasting.

11.6 Conclusion and Future Directions

Computer vision and i4.0 are presented in this chapter, along with their associated uses and constraints. Organizations are striving to incorporate both of these technologies to align with the present production trend, as machine vision systems represent an aspect of the future of manufacturing. The methods utilized by machine vision have been broken down in further detail, and examples of computer vision's use in a variety of industries are provided. Industry 4.0 and computer vision are not mutually exclusive. Component assessment, soldering factor surveillance, illness acknowledgment, quality assurance, and risk mitigation are just some of the many uses for automated vision techniques. Machine vision tools utilize complex algorithms and high-powered equipment to gain insights on goods and their features.

In the last 15 years, there has been a significant rise in the development of advancements related to machine vision, several of which are currently employed for automating a variety of manufacturing enterprises. The manufacturing, automobile, electronic devices, healthcare, and chip sectors, as well as the food and drug sectors, have all benefited from these technologies' swift developments. Within the framework of the fourth industrial revolution, automated vision systems have already been utilized for a variety of purposes, including the measurement of various measurements, the guidance of robotics and machinery, the identification of components, including the inspection of installation activities, and even the inspection of damaged components in manufacturing processes by noncontact methods.

Computer vision techniques are going to become increasingly popular in the field of industrial robotics as a result of ongoing improvements in efficiency, expense, computational durability, as well as simplicity of usage.

Further advances in this category at manufacturing facilities are anticipated for the coming years, and they will define the current state of commercial vision for machinery. Rapid acceleration, sense, cognitive ability, and simplicity of usage characterize the next-generation envisioned for the fourth industrial revolution, which will be applied to changes in components and processes. Modern advances have helped us speed up the usage of machine vision technologies in existing sectors, even if their implementation in an i4.0 setting has not yet hit its stride. Considering this, organizations, like universities and government organizations, ought to launch campaigns to educate the general public about the financial advantages of combining automated vision with Industry 4.0. The development of appropriate abilities for these cutting-edge innovations also necessitates the creation of training programs and curricula.

References

1. Lemstra, M.A.M.S. and de Mesquita, M.A., Industry 4.0: A tertiary literature review. *Technol. Forecast. Soc Change*, 186, 122204, 2023.
2. Kamble, S.S., Gunasekaran, A., Gawankar, S.A., Sustainable Industry 4.0 framework: A systematic literature review identifying the current trends and future perspectives. *Process Saf. Environ. Prot.*, *117*, 408–425, 2018.
3. Liao, Y., Loures, E.D.F.R., Deschamps, F., Industrial Internet of Things: A systematic literature review and insights. *IEEE Internet Things J.*, *5*, 6, 4515–4525, 2018.
4. Thomé, A.M.T., Scavarda, L.F., Scavarda, A.J., Conducting systematic literature review in operations management. *Prod. Plan. Control*, 27, 5, 408–420, 2016.
5. Javaid, M., Haleem, A., Singh, R.P., Suman, R., An integrated outlook of Cyber–Physical Systems for Industry 4.0: Topical practices, architecture, and applications. *Green Technol. Sustain.*, 1, 1, 100001, 2023.
6. Khujamatov, H., Reypnazarov, E., Khasanov, D., Akhmedov, N., IoT, IIoT, and cyber-physical systems integration, in: *Emergence of Cyber Physical System and IoT in Smart Automation and Robotics: Computer Engineering in Automation*, pp. 31–50, Springer International Publishing, Cham, 2021.
7. Lydon, B., Industry 4.0-Only One-Tenth of Germany's High-Tech Strategy. *Dikutip Dari*, 27, 31–48, 2014, https://www. automation. com/automation-news/article/industry-40-only-one-tenth-of-germanys-high-tech-strategy, pada.
8. Jesus, C.D. and Lima, R.M., Literature search of key factors for the development of generic and specific maturity models for Industry 4.0. *Appl. Sci.*, *10*, 17, 5825, 2020.

9. Hizam-Hanafiah, M., Soomro, M.A., Abdullah, N.L., Industry 4.0 readiness models: a systematic literature review of model dimensions. *Information*, 11, 7, 364, 2020.
10. Latif, S., Driss, M., Boulila, W., Huma, Z.E., Jamal, S.S., Idrees, Z., Ahmad, J., Deep learning for the industrial internet of things (IIOT): A comprehensive survey of techniques, implementation frameworks, potential applications, and future directions. *Sensors*, 21, 22, 7518, 2021.
11. Porter, M.E. and Heppelmann, J.E., How smart, connected products are transforming competition. *Harv. Bus. Rev.*, 92, 11, 64–88, 2014.
12. Calabrese, A., Levialdi Ghiron, N., Tiburzi, L., 'Evolutions' and 'revolutions' in manufacturers' implementation of industry 4.0: a literature review, a multiple case study, and a conceptual framework. *Prod. Plan. Control*, 32, 3, 213–227, 2021.
13. Ge, Z., Song, Z., Ding, S.X., Huang, B., Data mining and analytics in the process industry: The role of machine learning. *IEEE Access*, *5*, 20590–20616, 2017.
14. Thoben, K.D., Wiesner, S., Wuest, T., 'Industrie 4.0' and smart manufacturing-a review of research issues and application examples. *Int. J. Autom. Technol.*, *11*, 1, 4–16, 2017.
15. Zheng, T., Ardolino, M., Bacchetti, A., Perona, M., The applications of Industry 4.0 technologies in manufacturing context: a systematic literature review. *Int. J. Prod. Res.*, *59*, 6, 1922–1954, 2021.
16. Çınar, Z.M., Nuhu, A.A., Zeeshan, Q., Korhan, O., Asmael, M., Safaei, B., Machine learning in predictive maintenance towards sustainable smart manufacturing in industry 4.0. *Sustainability*, *12*, 19, 8211, 2020.
17. Liao, Y., Deschamps, F., Loures, E.D.F.R., Ramos, L.F.P., Past, present and future of Industry 4.0-a systematic literature review and research agenda proposal. *Int. J. Prod. Res.*, 55, 12, 3609–3629, 2017.
18. Schumacher, A., Erol, S., Sihn, W., A maturity model for assessing Industry 4.0 readiness and maturity of manufacturing enterprises. *Proc. CIRP*, 52, 161–166, 2016.
19. Schneider, P., Managerial challenges of Industry 4.0: an empirically backed research agenda for a nascent field. *Rev. Manag. Sci.*, 12, 3, 803–848, 2018.
20. Horvath, D. and Szabó, R.Z., Driving forces and barriers of Industry 4.0: Do multinational and small and medium-sized companies have equal opportunities. *Technol. Forecast. Soc Change*, 146, 119–132, 2019.
21. Lafortune, G. and Ubaldi, B., OECD 2017 OURdata index: methodology and results, in: *OECD Working Papers on Public Governance*, 30, 2018.
22. OECD, Unemployment rate (indicator), 2024.
23. Gupta, P. and Goyal, K., Change Management in Industry 4.0-Based Organizations. *Change Manage.: Int. J.*, 17, 2, 47–63, 2021.
24. Felsberger, A. and Reiner, G., Sustainable industry 4.0 in production and operations management: a systematic literature review. *Sustainability*, *12*, 19, 7982, 2020.

25. Chen, Y., Lean, H.H., Li, Y., *Agricultural Digitization and Zhongyong Philosophy: Creating a Sustainable Circular Economy*, Taylor & Francis, Oxfordshire, Routledge, Oxfordshire, 2023.
26. Agenda, I., Industrial internet of things: unleashing the potential of connected products and services. White Paper, in Collaboration with Accenture, World Economic Forum, USA, p. 34, 2015.
27. Thomé, A.M.T., Scavarda, L.F., Scavarda, A.J., Conducting systematic literature review in operations management. *Prod. Plan. Control*, 27, 5, 408–420, 2016.
28. Osterrieder, P., Budde, L., Friedli, T., The smart factory as a key construct of industry 4.0: A systematic literature review. *Int. J. Prod. Econ.*, 221, 107476, 2020.
29. Strozzi, F., Colicchia, C., Creazza, A., Noè, C., Literature review on the 'Smart Factory'concept using bibliometric tools. *Int. J. Prod. Res.*, 55, 22, 6572–6591, 2017.
30. Ding, B., Pharma Industry 4.0: Literature review and research opportunities in sustainable pharmaceutical supply chains. *Process Saf. Environ. Prot.*, 119, 115–130, 2018.
31. Lu, Y., Industry 4.0: A survey on technologies, applications and open research issues. *J. Ind. Inf. Integr.*, 6, 1–10, 2017.
32. Napoleone, A., Macchi, M., Pozzetti, A., A review on the characteristics of cyber-physical systems for the future smart factories. *J. Manuf. Syst.*, 54, 305–335, 2020.
33. Galati, F. and Bigliardi, B., Industry 4.0: Emerging themes and future research avenues using a text mining approach. *Comput. Ind.*, 109, 100–113, 2019.
34. Wagire, A.A., Rathore, A.P.S., Jain, R., Analysis and synthesis of Industry 4.0 research landscape: Using latent semantic analysis approach. *J. Manuf. Technol. Manage.*, 31, 1, 31–51, 2020.
35. Mittal, S., Khan, M.A., Romero, D., Wuest, T., A critical review of smart manufacturing & Industry 4.0 maturity models: Implications for small and medium-sized enterprises (SMEs). *J. Manuf. Syst.*, 49, 194–214, 2018.
36. Nosalska, K., Piątek, Z.M., Mazurek, G., Rządca, R., Industry 4.0: coherent definition framework with technological and organizational interdependencies. *J. Manuf. Technol. Manage.*, 31, 5, 837–862, 2019.
37. Da Silva, F.S.T., da Costa, C.A., Crovato, C.D.P., da Rosa Righi, R., Looking at energy through the lens of Industry 4.0: A systematic literature review of concerns and challenges. *Comput. Ind. Eng.*, 143, 106426, 2020.
38. Sony, M., Pros and cons of implementing Industry 4.0 for the organizations: a review and synthesis of evidence. *Prod. Manuf. Res.*, 8, 1, 244–272, 2020.
39. Barata, J., Da Cunha, P.R., Stal, J., Mobile supply chain management in the Industry 4.0 era: An annotated bibliography and guide for future research. *J. Enterp. Inf. Manage.*, 31, 1, 173–192, 2018.

40. Martins, G.D., Gonçalves, R.F., Petroni, B.C., Blockchain in manufacturing revolution based on machine to machine transaction: a systematic review. *Braz. J. Oper. Prod. Manage.*, 16, 2, 294–302, 2019.
41. Wan, C., Zheng, H., Guo, L., Xu, X., Zhong, R.Y., Yan, F., Cloud manufacturing in China: A review. *Int. J. Comput. Integr. Manuf.*, 33, 3, 229–251, 2020.
42. Cui, Y., Kara, S., Chan, K.C., Manufacturing big data ecosystem: A systematic literature review. *Rob. Comput. - Integr. Manuf.*, 62, 101861, 2020.
43. Cadavid, J.P.U., Lamouri, S., Grabot, B., Pellerin, R., Fortin, A., Machine learning applied in production planning and control: a state-of-the-art in the era of industry 4.0. *J. Intell. Manuf.*, 31, 1531–1558, 2020.
44. Egger, J. and Masood, T., Augmented reality in support of intelligent manufacturing–a systematic literature review. *Comput. Ind. Eng.*, 140, 106195, 2020.
45. Guo, Z., Zhou, D., Zhou, Q., Zhang, X., Geng, J., Zeng, S., Hao, A., Applications of virtual reality in maintenance during the industrial product lifecycle: A systematic review. *J. Manuf. Syst.*, 56, 525–538, 2020.
46. Bortolini, M., Galizia, F.G., Mora, C., Reconfigurable manufacturing systems: Literature review and research trend. *J. Manuf. Syst.*, 49, 93–106, 2018.
47. Franco, D., Ganga, G.M.D., de Santa-Eulalia, L.A., Godinho Filho, M., Consolidated and inconclusive effects of additive manufacturing adoption: A systematic literature review. *Comput. Ind. Eng.*, 148, 106713, 2020.
48. Wang, Y., Ma, H.S., Yang, J.H., Wang, K.S., Industry 4.0: a way from mass customization to mass personalization production. *Adv. Manuf.*, 5, 311–320, 2017.
49. Parente, M., Figueira, G., Amorim, P., Marques, A., Production scheduling in the context of Industry 4.0: review and trends. *Int. J. Prod. Res.*, 58, 17, 5401–5431, 2020.
50. Bueno, A., Filho, M.G., Frank, A.G., Smart production planning and control in the Industry 4.0 context: A systematic literature review. *Comput. Ind. Eng.*, *149*, 106774, 2020.
51. Chauhan, C. and Singh, A., A review of Industry 4.0 in supply chain management studies. *J. Manuf. Technol. Manage.*, 31, 5, 863–886, 2019.
52. Dalzochio, J., Kunst, R., Pignaton, E., Binotto, A., Sanyal, S., Favilla, J., Barbosa, J., Machine learning and reasoning for predictive maintenance in Industry 4.0: Current status and challenges. *Comput. Ind.*, 123, 103298, 2020.
53. Sony, M. and Naik, S., Critical factors for the successful implementation of Industry 4.0: a review and future research direction. *Prod. Plan. Control, 31*, 10, 799–815, 2020.
54. Ben-Daya, M., Hassini, E., Bahroun, Z., Internet of things and supply chain management: a literature review. *Int. J. Prod. Res.*, 57, 15–16, 4719–4742, 2019.
55. Gualtieri, L., Rauch, E., Vidoni, R., Emerging research fields in safety and ergonomics in industrial collaborative robotics: A systematic literature review. *Rob. Comput. - Integr. Manuf.*, 67, 101998, 2021.

56. Jerman, A., Pejić Bach, M., Bertoncelj, A., A bibliometric and topic analysis on future competences at smart factories. *Machines*, 6, 3, 41, 2018.
57. Misra, S., Roy, C., Mukherjee, A., *Introduction to industrial internet of things and industry 4.0*, CRC Press, Boca Raton, Florida, 2021.
58. Hossain, M.S. and Muhammad, G., Cloud-assisted industrial internet of things (iiot)–enabled framework for health monitoring. *Comput. Networks*, 101, 192–202, 2016.
59. Roy, A., Roy, C., Misra, S., Rahulamathavan, Y., Rajarajan, M., Care: Criticality-aware data transmission in cps-based healthcare systems, in: *2018 IEEE International Conference on Communications Workshops (ICC Workshops)*, IEEE, pp. 1–6, 2018, May.
60. De Michele, R. and Furini, M., Iot healthcare: Benefits, issues and challenges, in: *Proceedings of the 5th EAI international conference on smart objects and technologies for social good*, pp. 160–164, 2019, September.
61. Tejesh, B.S.S. and Neeraja, S., Warehouse inventory management system using IoT and open source framework. *Alex. Eng. J.*, 57, 4, 3817–3823, 2018.
62. Laber, J., Thamma, R., Kirby, E.D., The impact of warehouse automation in amazon's success. *Int. J. Innov. Sci. Eng. Technol.*, 7, 63–70, 2020.
63. Akinlabi, B.H., Effect of inventory management practices on operational performance of flour milling companies in Nigeria. *Int. Acad. J. Manage. Mark. Entrep. Stud.*, 8, 2, 137–174, 2021.
64. Lapide, L., What about measuring supply chain performance, in: *Achieving supply chain excellence through technology*, vol. 2, pp. 287–297, 2000.
65. Ziukov, S., A literature review on models of inventory management under uncertainty. *Verslo Sistemos Ekonomika*, 5, 1, 26–35, 2015.
66. Vrat, P. and Vrat, P., Basic concepts in inventory management, in: *Materials Management: An Integrated Systems Approach*, pp. 21–36, 2014.
67. Jayanth, S., Poorvi, M.B., Sunil, M.P., Inventory management system using IOT, in: *Proceedings of the First International Conference on Computational Intelligence and Informatics: ICCII 2016*, Springer Singapore, pp. 201–210, 2017.
68. Gupta, Y., Selection of important features and predicting wine quality using machine learning techniques. *Proc. Comp. Sci.*, 125, 305–312, 2018.
69. Shin, T., Predicting Wine Quality with Several Classification Techniques. Towards Data Science, 2020.
70. Pawar, D., Mahajan, A., Bhoithe, S., Wine Quality Prediction using Machine Learning Algorithms. *Int. J. Comput. Appl. Technol. Res.*, 8, 09, 385–388, 2019, ISSN:-2319–8656.
71. Saini, A. and Sharma, A., Predicting the unpredictable: an application of machine learning algorithms in Indian stock market. *Ann. Data Sci.*, 9, 4, 791–799, 2022.
72. Zeng, Y., Liu, Y., Wu, L., Dong, H., Zhang, Y., Guo, H., Lan, Y., Evaluation and Analysis Model of Wine Quality Based on Mathematical Model. *Stud. Eng. Technol.*, 6, 1, 2330–2038, 2019.

73. Raut, R., Krit, S., Chatterjee, P. (Eds.), *Machine Vision for Industry 4.0: Applications and Case Studies*, CRC Press, Boca Raton, FL, USA, 2022.
74. P. Cortez, A. Cerdeira, F. Almeida, T. Matos and J. Reis. Modeling wine preferences by data mining from physicochemical properties. In *Decision Support Systems, Elsevier*, 47, 4, 547–553, 2009.
75. Veneri, G. and Capasso, A., *Hands-on industrial Internet of Things: create a powerful industrial IoT infrastructure using industry 4.0*, Packt Publishing Ltd, United Kingdom, 2018.

12

Structural Understanding of the Relationship Between Various Consciousness of Programming and Creative Attitudes as Part of Knowledge Management Process

Masanori Fukui[1]*, Eng Tek Ong[2], Khar Thoe Ng[2], Yoon Fah Lay[3] and Subuh Anggoro[4]

[1]*Faculty of Software and Information Science, Iwate Prefectural University, Iwate, Japan*
[2]*Faculty of Social Sciences & Liberal Arts, USCI University, Kuala Lumpur, Malaysia*
[3]*Faculty of Psychology and Education, Universiti Malaysia Sabah, Sabah, Malaysia*
[4]*Universitas Muhammadiyah Purwokerto, Purwokerto, Central Java, Indonesia*

Abstract

The purpose of this Chapter is to report the results of a survey aimed at understanding the structural relationship between interest in programming and creative attitudes among Japanese high school students as part of knowledge management (KM) process in preparation for Industrial Revolution (IR). It has been pointed out that programming effectively fosters creativity, and promoting creativity through programming education is an important issue in programming education. Furthermore, in programming learning, it is necessary to develop not only coding skills but also programming skills, an interest in programming, a sense of usefulness of programming, and an applied awareness, such as utilizing programming in various fields. Raising such awareness and fostering basic creativity skills in programming education are essential for the future enhancement of programming education. To realize this, it is necessary to establish a clear relationship between programming awareness and creativity readiness. By grasping creativity in a structured manner, it is expected that programming education will be enhanced in the future toward knowledge and skills required for "Future Ready" workers in IR eras. Therefore, we focused on "creative attitudes" as a measure of creativity and

**Corresponding author*: fukui_m@iwate-pu.ac.jp

Rajendra Kumar, Vishal Jain, Venus C. Ibarra, Corrienna Abdul Talib and Vinay Kukreja (eds.) Knowledge Management and Industry Revolution 4.0, (333–350) © 2024 Scrivener Publishing LLC

attempted to structurally examine the relationship between creative attitude and various attitudes and awareness toward programming. The results of the covariance structure analysis revealed that the creative attitude associated with multiple attitudes toward programming was "analytical problem solving." The implications of study are discussed with suggestions for KM particularly how knowledge can be "acquired" and "used" with enhanced motivation and higher-order thinking skills.

Keywords: Programming education, creative attitude, knowledge management (KM), Industrial Revolution (IR), motivation, higher-order thinking skills

12.1 Introduction

12.1.1 The Purpose of this Study

The purpose of this study is to focus on creative attitude as creativity as readiness to realize programming education that enhances creativity and to understand structurally the relationship between creative attitude and various attitudes toward programming among high school students.

12.1.2 Research Background

Increasing international industrial competitiveness and productivity is becoming more important. To achieve this, it is necessary to utilize artificial intelligence and information technology actively and to develop creative and innovative activities with high labor productivity. Furthermore, it is an important issue to develop skills in school education that serve as the foundation for creativity and innovation. In this context, it is necessary to cultivate various skills related to information literacy and programming as they are basic skills that enable the utilization of information technology, especially for technological innovations involving artificial intelligence and other advanced technologies.

To develop human resources who can cope with this situation, many countries are conducting a great deal of research and practical efforts. In particular, the enhancement of programming and STEAM (Science, Technology, Engineering, Arts, and Mathematics) education is important from the viewpoint of human resource development. In particular, programming education is considered to be important as a fundamental skill required to solve various social problems in an information-driven society, which will be further developed with the advent of generative AI and other cutting-edge technologies.

The basic flow of programming education involves coding using programming languages and block programming such as Scratch, learning basic algorithms, and creating various works. However, programming education is currently expected not only to improve coding skills, but also to develop understanding of computer principles, self-efficacy [1], self-affirmation, motivation [2], computational thinking [3], logical thinking [4], creativity [5], and fluid intelligences [6].

Taking Japan as an example, programming education at the elementary, junior high, and senior high school levels has been made compulsory from 2020 from the perspective of fostering human resources to increase global industrial competitiveness, as previously discussed. Programming education in Japan, especially at the elementary school level, is required to cultivate a programming mindset and to implement coding in each subject without requiring it. Furthermore, at the junior high school level, programming is to be taught while utilizing coding in technology studies [7].

Programmatic thinking refers to thinking logically about what combinations of movements are necessary to realize a series of activities that one intends, how to combine the symbols corresponding to each movement, and how to improve the combinations of symbols to get closer to the intended activities. This definition was proposed based on the idea of computational thinking [3], while organizing the relationship between programming and logical thinking. Programming education in Japan is expected to further deepen students' understanding of the content of the existing subjects by introducing the concept and methods of programming thinking in each subject area. In addition, programming education is also required to increase interest in programming and raise awareness of its practicality, emphasizing that the knowledge acquired through programming can be applied in diverse fields. This concept is expected to be important not only in Japan but also in many other countries.

In general education programming education, it is important not only to develop experts in programming, but also to cultivate basic skills and attitudes that enable students to utilize technology to solve various problems, and to develop personalities and attitudes that create new things regardless of the subject or field. In other words, it is necessary to cultivate an awareness of programming, such as interest in programming education, its usefulness, and its applicability.

On the other hand, fostering creativity is an important issue in programming education. There are many studies on creativity. [8] considered creativity as a kind of psychological process and divided it into four stages: preparatory, incubation, revelation, and demonstration. [9] conducted a study on the relationship between optimism and creativity and the moderating effect of playfulness in 483 children enrolled in the fifth and sixth grades of elementary school. The results confirmed a significant positive relationship between optimism, playfulness, and creativity, and reported that playfulness moderated the relationship between optimism and creativity.

[10] stated that being immersed in something one loves to do leads to a flow state. The flow state refers to the state of being immersed in something and entering a state of extreme concentration, and he states that creativity may be exhibited in situations where one has reached that flow state.

Previous studies have shown that creativity can be enhanced in programming education (e.g. [11, 12]), as well as technology-enhanced project-based activities (PBA) and/or problem-based learning (PBL) (e.g. [13, 14]). As a case study, [15] reports that creativity can be fostered, and they report on the results of using Scratch with the four items of projects, passion, peers, and play to foster creativity. As described above, programming education is expected to enhance creativity. It has also been pointed out that programming is useful for fostering creativity.

As the development of creativity has become an important issue worldwide, realizing the development of creativity within programming education will not only enhance the role of programming education but also bolster the educational efforts through the integration of programming elements into the subject-based education. This integration is expected to cultivate the basic ability for creativity, which has traditionally proven challenging to cultivate within conventional subject-based education.

12.1.3 Identification of Problems

We pointed out the importance of realizing programming education that enhances creativity for the future enhancement of programming education and human resource development. Additionally, we highlighted the importance of fostering not only coding skills but also various attitudes toward programming.

By understanding the relationship between creativity and awareness of programming, it may be possible to gain important insights for future lesson design and subject matter development. In such a case, it is assumed that the subsequent teaching methods will differ depending on the relationship between creativity and awareness of programming. If there is a relationship between the two at the readiness stage, then we can expect to stimulate both creativity and programming awareness at the same time during the introduction stage of programming education. However, if there is no relationship between the two, then it will be necessary to arouse programming awareness and creativity through different instructional methods. If the relationship between the two is different depending on the factors, it is important to construct an instructional method according to the characteristics of each factor.

In light of the above, it is considered to be an important issue to understand the relationship between creativity as a readiness and awareness of interest in programming in order to cultivate creativity in students in programming education. However, many students need opportunities to demonstrate their creativity, and it is important to set up opportunities to enhance creativity in the classroom. In addition, creativity is very multifaceted, and there are various ways to enhance it. In other words, from an educational perspective, educational practices that are in line with the reality of creativity as readiness are required.

Furthermore, it is still being determined whether creativity can be achieved simply by engaging in activities what one likes. Even if a learner reaches a flow state by engaging in what he or she likes to do, the personality and attitude that the learner possesses as readiness may contribute greatly to the situation in which creativity is demonstrated. In order to examine such creative tendencies possessed by individuals, it is considered important in this study to focus on "creative attitude," which is an attitude of trying to solve problems creatively, as a form of readiness for creativity.

According to [16], a creative attitude is not a fixed method or a patterned approach to problem solving, but an attitude of asking questions and being curious, of always trying to improve without fear, and of trying to produce something new out of failure. [17], in his study of creativity and attitudes, states that skilled creative behavior is necessary to achieve concrete creative results. He posits that creative attitudes open the door to creative behavior and can be intentionally developed and measured. [18] developed the Creative Attitude Scale through a survey of college students in Japan and overseas. The creative attitude scale consists of "flexibility," "analytical problem solving," "entrepreneurship," "perseverance," "imagination," and "cooperation." By utilizing these factors, it is anticipated that a student's readiness for creativity can be grasped or comprehended.

[19, 20] reported that "analytical problem solving," and "entrepreneurship" was significantly improved by implementing programming education to enhance creativity. [21] reported the three factors of "analytical problem solving, perseverance, and cooperation" were significantly improved in their programming activity for primary students. Thus, it can be inferred that some items contribute to creativity and creative attitudes in programming attitudes, while others do not. From the studies by [19–21], it can be

assumed that which elements of creative attitudes are fostered may depend highly on the practice method.

By understanding the relationship between students' creative attitudes and their awareness of programming, it is expected that classroom practices can be implemented to increase awareness of programming in various ways, not just coding skills. This, in turn, is expected to lead to the enhancement of programming education. For example, programming is characterized by its logical nature and the ease with which students can give form to their own ideas. It is plausible that students with creative qualities related to these characteristics will have a higher awareness of programming, such as an interest in programming.

To achieve this, it is useful to survey both students with prior programming experience and those who have never engaged in programming. However, since there are many programming environments and languages other than Scratch and code.org, such as Python, C, and others, it is not easy to control for students with programming experience. Conversely, when surveying students who have never done any programming, they may have only a vague image of the usefulness of programming because they have never worked on programming in concrete terms. However, it is important to dispel the sense of weakness caused by assumptions in the classroom. Therefore, as the first step in enhancing creativity-centric programming education, it is important to understand the relationship between creativity as a readiness that students possess and their awareness of programming.

Therefore, the following research question was formulated.

RQ: How are creative attitudes related to various attitudes toward programming?

To examine this research question in detail, this study investigates the relationship between various attitudes toward programming and creative attitudes among high school students with no programming experience.

12.2 Method

12.2.1 Survey Targets and Procedures

A total of 226 first-year students from three public high schools in Japan were surveyed. All of them had not completed any programming education in high school. Missing values were removed by the listwise method, resulting in 197 valid responses, representing a valid response rate of 87.2%. The survey was conducted in December 2016.

As an ethical consideration in conducting the survey, prior to the survey, respondents were informed of the contents of the survey, explained that they would not be disadvantaged by whether or not to respond and that they could withdraw their responses at any time, and were instructed to respond only if they agreed with the contents of the survey. If respondents responded based on the contents of the survey, they were deemed to have agreed to the contents of the survey.

12.2.2 Survey Items

We used the Creative Attitude Scale [18] to measure creative attitudes. The responses to all questions were given on a four-point scale of "4: Very applicable, 3: Fairly applicable, 2: Not very applicable, and 1: Not applicable at all."

Next, we developed a set of items to gauge various consciousness for programming. First, preliminary items were prepared, drawing inspiration from materials summarizing the direction of programming education in Japan [7]. Thereafter, the survey items were refined after discussions among authors and consultation with three schoolteachers specializing in information and technology education. These refined items were then presented to three university students to assess their comprehensibility. The university students confirmed that they fully understood the survey items. Therefore, the items on various attitudes toward programming were judged to be suitable for use in this survey. The items used are shown in Table 12.1, with corresponding abbreviations indicated in brackets at the end of each

Table 12.1 Measurement items of consciousness for programming.

1	I am interested in programming. (Interest in programming)
2	I think programming is useful for me in many ways. (Usefulness of programming)
3	I think it is important for me to understand the contents of programming. (Importance of understanding programming)
4	I think that what I have learned in programming is useful for other things besides programming. (Usefulness in other areas)

item. We measured them using a four-point Likert scale with the following answers to the questions: "4: Strongly Agree, 3: Agree, 2: Disagree, 1: Strongly disagree." This item is also used in another research [19, 20].

12.3 Analysis Procedure

First, descriptive statistics were obtained for each factor and item. Next, correlation analyses were conducted between each factor of creative attitudes and each item of various consciousness for programming. In addition, covariance structural analysis was conducted to understand the structure of creative attitudes and various consciousnesses for programming. We used R 4.2.3 for analysis. The creative attitude scale was parametric data, while the items on attitude toward programming were nonparametric data, and Spearman's rank correlation coefficients were obtained in the correlation analysis.

Before conducting the analysis, the validity of the factor structure of creative attitudes was assessed using confirmatory factor analysis with the subjects of the current study. Cronbach's alpha coefficient, Goodness-of-Fit Index (GFI), Root Mean Square Error of Approximation (RMSEA), and Standardized Root Mean Square Residual (SRMR) were used as indices to evaluate the validity.

12.4 Results

12.4.1 Preliminary Analysis

Table 12.2 shows the reliability and reliability of the scale of creative attitudes. Cronbach's alpha coefficient, Goodness-of-Fit Index (GFI), Root Mean Square Error of Approximation (RMSEA), and Standardized Root Mean Square Residual (SRMR) were used as evaluation indices in this study. Each of these indicators has an appropriate range of values that determine whether the model is valid. A GFI of 0.90 or greater is considered appropriate [22], an RMSEA of 0.08 or less is acceptable [23], and an SRMR of 0.08 or less is also appropriate [24]. In the case Cronbach's alpha coefficient, alpha values between 0.60 and 0.70 indicate an acceptable level of reliability, and values of 0.80 or greater signify a very good level. However, it is worth noting that values higher than 0.95 are not necessarily indicative of good reliability [25].

Table 12.2 Validity and reliability of each factor of creative attitude scale.

Variable	*A*	GFI	RMSEA	SRMR
1. Flexibility	0.87	0.98	0.02	0.07
2. Analytical problem solving	0.87	0.99	0.00	0.06
3. Entrepreneurship	0.76	1.00	0.00	0.04
4. Perseverance	0.70	0.98	0.10	0.09
5. Imagination	0.71	0.99	0.07	0.05
6. Cooperation	0.73	1.00	0.00	0.04

Table 12.2 shows that the values of Cronbach's alpha, GFI, RMSEA, and SRMR were approximately appropriate. However, it is noteworthy that the RMSEA value of 0.10 for perseverance slightly exceeded the recommended threshold of 0.08, which is acceptable for use. Therefore, this factor was still considered suitable for analysis.

12.4.2 Descriptive Statistics and Results of Correlation Analysis

Table 12.3 shows the descriptive statistics for creative attitudes and the various consciousnesses in programming, respectively. Besides, it displays the results of correlation analysis between each factor and item.

From Table 12.3, the highest mean value among the creative attitudes was for cooperation. Entrepreneurship, perseverance, imagination, and cooperation had means higher than the midpoint of 2.50, while flexibility and analytical problem solving had a mean lower than the midpoint of 2.50. Next, among the various attitudes toward programming, interest in programming had a mean lower than the median score of 2.50 and was relatively lower than the other items. The other attitudes toward programming had means higher than the median score of 2.50. No ceiling or floor effects were observed for all items or factors.

Next, Spearman's correlation analysis was used to analyze the relationships among the factors of the Creative Attitudes Scale and the various attitudes toward programming items; in Table 12.3, significant correlation coefficients are shown in bold, and nonsignificant ones are underlined.

Table 12.3 Descriptive statistics for creative attitudes and the various consciousnesses in programming, and the results of correlation analysis.

Variable	*M*	*SD*	**1**	**2**	**3**	**4**	5	**6**	7	**8**	**9**	**10**
1. Flexibility	2.35	0.51	1.00									
2. Analytical problem solving	2.34	0.55	0.68	1.00								
3. Entrepreneurship	2.70	0.60	0.58	0.57	1.00							
4. Perseverance	2.70	0.56	0.51	0.54	0.59	1.00						
5. Imagination	2.78	0.54	0.47	0.41	0.57	0.46	1.00					
6. Cooperation	2.97	0.50	0.27	0.29	0.43	0.38	0.24	1.00				
7. Interest in programming	2.25	1.02	**0.24**	**0.36**	**0.36**	**0.28**	**0.22**	0.11	1.00			
8. Usefulness of programming	2.69	0.90	**0.28**	**0.43**	**0.23**	**0.22**	0.11	0.05	0.59	1.00		
9. Importance of understanding programming	2.51	0.89	**0.31**	**0.46**	**0.25**	**0.22**	0.11	0.08	0.60	0.76	1.00	
10. Usefulness in other areas	2.74	0.81	**0.18**	**0.29**	**0.21**	**0.17**	0.21	0.09	0.26	0.28	0.31	1.00
												(*n* = 197)

The correlation coefficients among the factors of the creative attitude scale were all greater than 0.20, and the correlation coefficient tests showed that all factors were significantly related at the 1% level. The correlation coefficients among the items of the various attitudes toward programming were greater than 0.20 for all items, and the correlation coefficient tests showed that all items were significantly related at the 1% level.

The correlations between the factors of the creative attitudes scale and the items of various attitudes toward programming were significant at the 1% level except "imagination and usefulness of programming," "imagination and importance of understanding programming," "cooperation and interest in programming," "cooperation and usefulness of programming," and "cooperation and importance of understanding programming." There were no significant associations between cooperation and all items of consciousness for programming. All other items were significantly related at the 1% level. In other words, the creative attitude factors strongly associated with programming attitudes were flexibility, analytical problem solving, entrepreneurship, and perseverance.

12.4.3 Result of Covariance Structural Analysis of All Factors and Items

To gain a structural understanding of the relationship between creative attitude and various attitudes toward programming, we set creative attitude toward programming as a latent factor. We assumed a model in which creative attitude affects creative attitude toward programming, and reciprocally, creative attitude toward programming affects various attitudes toward programming. We posit a model in which creative attitudes influence creative attitudes toward programming, and creative attitudes toward programming influence various attitudes toward programming. This model was evaluated using a covariance structure analysis, with model's validity assessed using GFI, RMSEA, and SRMR. The results of the analysis are shown in Figure 12.1.

The results of the analysis showed that GFI = 0.937 > 0.900, RMSEA = 0.045 < 0.050, and SRMR = 0.034 < 0.050. Looking at the values for each path, the paths with significant effects were "analytical problem solving to creative attitudes for programming," "creative attitudes for programming to interest in programming," "creative attitudes for programming to usefulness of programming," "creative attitudes for programming to importance of understanding programming," and "creative attitudes for programming to usefulness in other areas." On the other hand, the paths that had no significant impact were "flexibility to creative attitudes for programming," "entrepreneurship to creative attitudes for programming," and "perseverance to creative attitudes for programming." "Creative attitudes for programming from entrepreneurship," "creative attitudes for programming from perseverance," "creative attitudes for programming from imagination," and "creative attitudes for programming from cooperation." The results show that creative attitudes toward programming influenced all the various attitudes toward programming items. In contrast, the only creative attitude factor influencing "creative attitudes for programming" was analytical problem solving. Therefore, analytical problem solving was the only creative attitude factor that influenced creative attitudes toward programming.

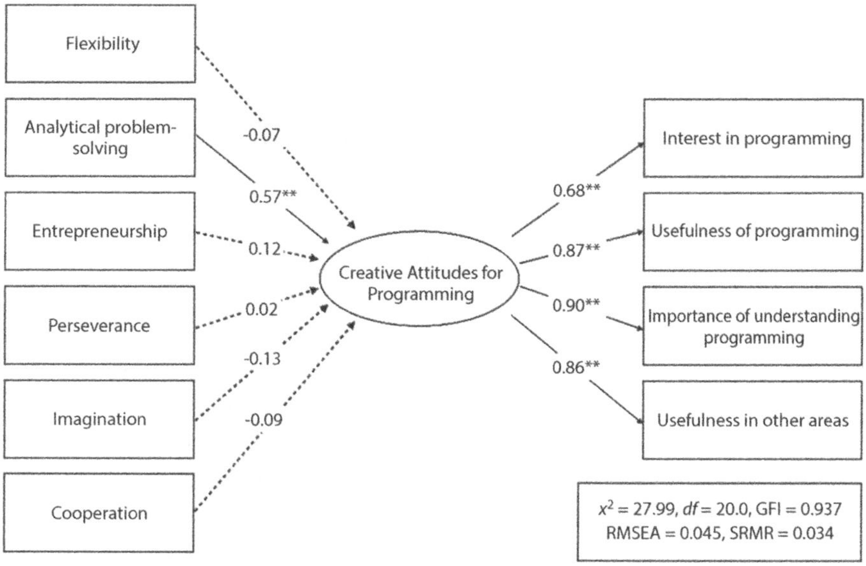

Figure 12.1 Results of covariance structural analysis between creative attitudes and various consciousness of programming.

12.5 Discussion

The results obtained are presented below:

(1) The results of the correlation analysis showed that the creative attitude factors associated with programming awareness were flexibility, analytical problem solving, entrepreneurship, and perseverance. In contrast, imagination and cooperation were not strongly related to programming attitudes.

(2) The path analysis results indicated that analytical problem solving was the only creative attitude factor that influenced attitudes toward programming in the overall creative attitudes.

From this result, it can be assumed that the awareness of various attitudes toward programming, such as interest, usefulness, and awareness of application, may differ depending on the creative attitude held as readiness.

The results of the correlation analysis indicate that flexibility, analytical problem solving, entrepreneurship, and perseverance influence attitudes toward programming. However, since creative attitudes may be complex, it is necessary to consider the influence of creative attitudes as a whole rather than focusing on a single creative attitude. The results of the path analysis indicate that students with higher attitudes and awareness toward analytical problem solving have higher programming awareness. Therefore, the appropriate method of programming education may emphasize analytical problem solving.

For example, for students who excel in analytical problem solving or are good at subjects that require analytical problem solving, such as mathematics and physics, may only require a few introductory programming activities to spark their interest. In their case, providing advanced activities, such as programming in coding and inquiry learning, might be more effective.

On the contrary, students who are not good at analytical problem solving or strongly prefer rote learning subjects that do not require much analytical understanding of problems may benefit from programming education that initially piques their interest and prompts them to think about the practical applications of programming. Thus, it is assumed that it may be effective first to set up activities that make students think about the practical applications of programming before proceeding with programming education.

However, since creative attitudes are closely related and it is sometimes difficult to strictly distinguish between them, designing educational practices that integrate other elements while focusing on analytical problem solving when implementing programming education to foster creativity is beneficial. All items of analytical problem solving, entrepreneurship, and awareness of programming showed improvements in the practice conducted [19, 20], and all items of analytical problem solving, perseverance, cooperation, and awareness of programming were increased in the practice conducted [20]. Although the subjects and contents of the practices differed, analytical problem solving increased or improved in all cases, suggesting the importance of emphasizing analytical problem solving in implementing programming education to enhance creativity.

12.6 Conclusion

12.6.1 Summary of this Research

This study examined the relationship between various attitudes toward programming and creative attitudes. As a result, it was found that the creative attitude factors related to programming attitudes are flexibility, analytical problem solving, entrepreneurship, and perseverance. In contrast, the unrelated factors are imagination and cooperation. In addition, when a latent factor that influences attitudes toward programming, "creative attitudes toward programming," is assumed to exist, we found that the creative attitude that influences the creative attitudes toward programming is analytical problem solving.

These results indicate the possibility of designing lessons based on students' actual conditions to enhance programming education that enhances creativity. There is no previous study of this kind, and the results are considered novel and unique.

12.6.2 Limitations and Reflections for Future Study

In this study, we obtained basic knowledge to realize programming education that enhances creativity. However, many issues remain to be addressed in this study.

First, it is assumed that there are various attitudes toward programming. In this study, four items were used to represent the various attitudes toward programming. However, [26] found that there are five factors of attitudes toward programming: "Programming self-efficacy," "Programming utility," "Social needs," "Perceptions of programmers," and "Programming interest." They researched to explore the relationship between these factors and computational thinking. The various attitudes toward programming used in this study are useful as a simple way to understand programming. While their utility can be justified, a more detailed analysis is required to develop a method to implement programming education that enhances creativity.

Second, there is a possibility that another latent variable exists between creative attitudes and attitudes toward programming. For example, self-efficacy and skills in each subject area may be related. Further research should be conducted to investigate these variables as well.

Third, it remains to be seen whether the results of this study can be applied to students with prior programming experience. Currently, many students are exposed to programming from their childhood due to the introduction of mandatory programming education.

It is necessary to survey current students and consider the design of programming education that meets the actual situation. Further research should be conducted to enrich programming education that enhances creativity, an important attribute in the Knowledge Management (KM) process to promote the acquisition and use of knowledge [27]. These issues will be discussed in future studies related to KM processes, particularly how knowledge can be "acquired" and "used" with enhanced motivation and higher-order thinking skills [28].

Acknowledgments

This work was partially supported by JSPS KAKENHI (Grant Number 21K13644) and Inamori Foundation. The first author is also grateful to Mr. Jo Hagikura (formerly of Kwansei Gakuin University), Mr. Yuji Sasaki (Keio University), Assoc Prof. Dr. Masakatsu Kuroda (Kobe Women's University), and Prof. Dr. Jun Moriyama (Hyogo University of Teacher Education) for their helpful support in this study.

Note

This study is a developmental review of the paper [29] with additional analysis and substantial revisions based on discussions by the authors.

References

1. Liu, J., Li, Q., Sun, X., Zhu, Z., Xu, Y., Factors influencing programming self-efficacy: an empirical study in the context of Mainland China. *Asia Pac. J. Educ.*, 43, 3, 835–849, 2023.
2. Ng, K.T., Making the challenges possible through education superhighway: A pilot project to motivate young learners towards Problem-based Learning (PBL) using technological tools. *The 23rd ICDE World Conference on Open Learning and Distance Education including the 2009 EADTU Annual Conference*, 2009.
3. Wing, J.M., Computational thinking. *Commun. ACM*, 49, 3, 33–35, 2006.
4. Lay, Y.F., Logical thinking abilities among Form 4 students in the interior division of Sabah, Malaysia. *J. Sci. Math. Educ. Southeast Asia*, 32, 2, 161–187, 2009.
5. Ng, K.T., An evaluation of the scientific creativity and problem-solving behaviours of young learners in the development of investigative project work. *International Conference on Science and Mathematics Education (CoSMEd) 2005*, pp. 6, 2005.
6. Ng, K.T., Fong, S.F., Soon, S.T., Design and development of a fluid intelligence instrument for a technology-enhanced PBL programme, in: *Proceedings of Global Learn Asia Pacific 2010–Global Conference on Learning and Technology*, Z. Abas, I. Jung, J. Luca (Eds.), pp. 1047–1052, 2010.

7. Ministry of Education, Culture, Sports, Science and Technology: Expert Council on Programming Education and the Development of Logical Thinking, Creativity, Problem-Solving Skills, etc. at the Elementary School Level, The ideal form of programming education at the elementary school level (Summary of discussions), 2016, http://www.mext.go.jp/b_menu/shingi/chousa/shotou/122/attach/1372525.htm, [in Japanese].
8. Wallas, G., *The art of Thought*, Jonathan Cape, London, 1926.
9. Williams, F.E., *Encouraging Creative Potential*, Educational Technology Publications, New Jersey, 1972.
10. Csikszentmihalyi, M., *Creativity: Flow and the psychology of discovery and invention*. HarperCollins Publishers, California, 1997.
11. Rotem, I.-F., Hershkovitz, A., Eguíluz, A., Garaizar, P., Guenaga, M., The Associations Between Computational Thinking and Creativity: The Role of Personal Characteristics. *J. Educ. Comput. Res.*, 58, 8, 1415–1447, 2020.
12. Doleck, T., Bazelais, P., Lemay, D.J., Saxena, A., Basnet, R.B., Algorithmic Thinking, Cooperativity, Creativity, Critical Thinking, and Problem Solving: Exploring the Relationship between Computational Thinking Skills and Academic Performance. *J. Comput. Educ.*, 4, 4, 355–369, 2017.
13. Ng, K.T., Development of transdisciplinary models to manage knowledge, skills and innovation processes integrating technology with reflective practices. *Int. J. Comput. Appl. (IJCA)*, 2, 1–9, 2017.
14. Ng, K.T., Baharum, B.N., Othman, M., Tahir, S., Pang, Y.J., Managing technology-enhanced innovation programs: Framework, exemplars and future directions. *Solid State Technol.*, 63, 1s, 555–565, 2020.
15. Resnick, M., *Lifelong Kindergarten: Cultivating Creativity through Projects, Passion, Peers, and Play*, The MIT Press, Cambridge, 2017.
16. Schank, R. and Childers, P., *The Creative Attitude: Learning to Ask and Answer the Right Questions*, Macmillan Publishing Company, New York, 1988.
17. Basadur, M. and Basadur, T., Attitudes and Creativity, in: *Encyclopedia of Creativity*, 2, Academic Press, San Diego, 2011.
18. Shigemasu, K., Yokoyama, A., Stern, S., Komazaki, H., Comparison of creative attitudes between American and Japanese. students: A factor analytical study. *Jpn. J. Psychol.*, 64, 3, 81–190, 1993, https://www.jstage.jst.go.jp/article/jjpsy1926/64/3/64_3_181/_pdf/-char/ja, [in Japanese].
19. Fukui, M., Kuroda, M., Moriyama, J., Practice of Programming Education for Senior High School Students Aimed to Promote the Creative Attitudes Using Games and Puzzles. *Jpn. J. Educ. Technol.*, 42-Suppl, 21–24, 2018, [in Japanese].
20. Fukui, M., Sasaki, Y., Kuroda, M., Moriyama, J., Developing Programming Education Using Mathematical Puzzles and Games to Enhance Students' Creative Attitudes. *7th SRD International Conference on Research Innovations (iCRI-2022)*, 2022.
21. Kuroda, M., Fukui, M., Kakegawa, J., Moriyama, J., Transformation of Pupils' Creative Attitudes through Collaborative Computer Programming

Education by Agile Development at Elementary School Level. *Educ. Inf. Res.*, 36, 1, 49–62, 2020, [in Japanese].
22. Hair, J.F., Black, W.C., Babin, B.J., Anderson, R.E., *Multivariate data analysis*, 7th ed., Pearson, London, 2014.
23. Hu, L.T. and Bentler, P.M., Cutoff criteria for fit indexes in covariance structure analysis: Conventional criteria versus new alternatives. *Struct. Equation Modell.: Multidiscip. J.*, 6, 1, 1–55, 1999.
24. Kline, R.B., *Principles and practice of structural equation modeling*, 4th ed., Guilford Press, New York, 2015.
25. Hulin, C., Netemeyer, R., Cudeck, R., Can a Reliability Coefficient Be Too High? *J. Consum. Psychol.*, 10, 1, 55–58, 2001.
26. Sun, L., Hu, L., Zhou, D., Programming attitudes predict computational thinking: Analysis of differences in gender and programming experience. *Comput. Educ.*, 181, 104457, 2022.
27. Gonzalez, R.V.D. and Martins, M.F., Knowledge Management Process: a theoretical-conceptual research. *Gest. Prod. São Carlos*, 24, 2, 248–265, 2017.
28. Ng, K.T., The effect of PBL-SI on secondary students' motivation and higher order thinking. Unpublished doctoral thesis, Open University Malaysia, Kuala Lumpur, Malaysia, 2012.
29. Fukui, M., Kuroda, M., Kakegawa, J., Moriyama, J., The Relationship between High School Students' Creative Attitudes and the Consciousness of Computer Programming. *Educ. Inf. Res.*, 34, 3, 19–28, 2019, [in Japanese].

13

Blended-Mode Instruction for Knowledge Management Toward IR4.0: Exemplars in Lifelong STREAM Education and The Way Forward

Kamolrat Intaratat[1*], Guan Xing Zhi[2], Subuh Anggoro[3], Khar Thoe Ng[2,4] and Dungkamol Intaratat[1]

[1] *Faculty of Communication Arts, CCDKM Research Center, Pak Kret District, Nonthaburi, Thailand*
[2] *School of Education, Humanities and Social Sciences (SEHS), WoU and FOSSLA, UCSI University, Kuala Lumpur, Malaysia*
[3] *Universitas Muhammadiyah Purwokerto (UMP), Purwokerto, Central Java, Indonesia*
[4] *Wawasan Open University (WoU), Georgetown, Penang, Malaysia*

Abstract

This Chapter examines concepts/roles of "Blended-Mode Instruction" (BMI) as emerging "knowledge management" (KM) platform during "Industrial Revolution" (IR) aiming at promoting "Science, Technology, Reading, Engineering, Arts, Mathematics" (STREAM) education in three Southeast Asian (SEA) Countries and China. Cases from Thailand, Indonesia and China will be illustrated through Qualitative "Exemplary-Case Analysis" (ECA) technique, focusing programs/initiatives leveraging on BMI to provide lifelong learning opportunities for all. An overview of global trends in literacy and lifelong learning is provided. Qualitative literature research is made to operationally define BMI, KM, IR4.0, STREAM literacy, local wisdom, etc. Issues and challenges faced by individuals (especially in aging societies) who lack access to educational opportunities/resources for STREAM education to prepare for IR4.0 are elaborated. How BMI platforms are harnessed to overcome these challenges are explored, with showcase of programs integrating BMI as KM tools. This Chapter also examines the role of local wisdom

**Corresponding author*: kamolratchim@gmail.com

Rajendra Kumar, Vishal Jain, Venus C. Ibarra, Corrienna Abdul Talib and Vinay Kukreja (eds.) Knowledge Management and Industry Revolution 4.0, (351–370) © 2024 Scrivener Publishing LLC

in promoting lifelong learning, emphasizing the importance of culturally-relevant educational materials/approaches using BMI to preserve/promote local knowledge, highlighting successful initiatives blending traditional/modern learning methods with potential to promote literacy and local wisdom being discussed. Significant insights are effective practices that can be replicated/scaled up to increase access to quality STEAM education, improving livelihoods of individuals and communities globally.

Keywords: Blended-mode instruction (BMI), literacy, lifelong learning in aging societies, STREAM education, knowledge management (KM), industrial revolution (IR)

13.1 Introduction

Promoting literacy and local wisdom using digital learning platforms to enhance lifelong knowledge/skills development has become one of the prioritized education agenda of many developing and developed countries in Asian region involving all walks of life including the aging societies to be illustrated in this Chapter.

13.1.1 Background/Overview of Literacy and Technology-Enhanced Knowledge Management (KM) Platforms

In the advent of digital era, the use of technology or ICT tool to facilitate all kinds of required practical skills [also referred to as smart functional literacy (henceforth abbreviated as SFL)], i.e., to skills of calculate, read, and write are important for all stakeholders to be functional their real-life demands. There are many types of SFL as elaborated by [1] but this Chapter only focuses on ICT and media literacy using various knowledge management (henceforth abbreviated as KM) platforms to be exemplified in the subsequent section. Another focus of this Chapter that is extracted from a bigger study, i.e., STREAM literacy' is defined as skills (ability to read and write) that are vital to understand STEM concepts in line with IR 4.0 integrating Arts/culture/language and will lead to success across all disciplines. These include the critical thinking and ability to clearly communicate complex concepts. Learners become strong readers while exploring topics that arouse their interest in STEAM [2]. The review of literature revealed that promoting creative mathematics using emerging digital tools (e.g., Wolfram programming digital tool, web-based learning, video to name a few) enhanced STEAM literacy and encouraged learners' involvement in STEAM related careers as reported by [3] in line with SDG Nos. 4, 5, 8, 9, and 11 as reported by [4].

13.1.2 Problem Statement and Rationale

Despite the growing emphasis on the importance of lifelong learning and the role of blended-learning platforms to promote "Science, Technology, Engineering, Arts [e.g., promotion of arts/craft from Thailand and Indonesia, music education from China] and Mathematics" (STEAM) education, there are still much challenges faced in promoting literacy and local wisdom in the Asian countries. The problems in accessing quality education (SDG No. 4) aggravated over the past 3 years due to COVID-19 pandemic since 2019. Many individuals, especially those in rural and marginalized communities, lack access to quality education as well as struggle to retain their local cultures and knowledge. In addition, rapid technological advancements have led to the displacement of traditional skills and practices, subsequently endangering local wisdom. This Chapter reports part of bigger scales study to examine how "Blended-Mode Instruction" (henceforth abbreviated as BMI) seeks to address these challenges especially among the stakeholders for knowledge management (KM) to be better prepared for Industrial Revolution (IR4.0). How technology-enhanced lifelong education can be used to promote literacy and local wisdom, particularly in underserved communities will be examined with exemplary cases in Thailand, Indonesia, and China to be showcased. Through the highlights of successful initiatives and strategies, this Chapter aims to contribute to the development of effective policies and practices to promote lifelong learning as well as preserve local cultures in Asia region.

13.1.3 Research Objectives and Methodologies Implemented

Based on the background and overview in section 13.1.1 as well as rationale in section 13.1.2, the following Research Objectives (ROs) are identified:

(1) To operationally define Blended-Mode Instruction (BMI), its roles for knowledge management (KM) in STREAM education toward Industrial Revolution (IR) reflecting Sustainable Development Goals (SDGs).
(2) To illustrate exemplary cases on how digital tools and BMI e-platforms facilitated lifelong learning in transferring

knowledge/skills among stakeholders considering their literacy and local wisdoms.

Qualitative research methods [5] mainly using case study approach is the research framework implemented for data collection and analysis towards achieving SDGs. These include qualitative analysis involving document analysis and multiple-case studies [6, 7] as cited by [8]. First, literature research will be conducted to identify the existing theories/models related to operational definitions of BMI, KM, IR4.0, STREAM literacy, local wisdom, to name a few. Issues and challenges faced by individuals who lack access to educational opportunities/resources for STREAM education in preparation for IR4.0 are also examined. How BMI platforms are harnessed to overcome these challenges are explored, with showcase of exemplary programs integrating BMI as KM tools and e-platforms such as Google Classroom and Telegrams.

13.2 Analysis of Findings and Illustrations of Case Exemplars

This section elaborates on the analysis of findings in response to Research Objective (RO) 1 and 2.

13.2.1 Operational Definitions of BMI, KM in STREAM Education Toward IR4.0 Reflecting SDGs (RO1)

This section summarizes the findings from literature search to define the following terminologies operationally.

13.2.1.1 Blended-Mode Instruction (BMI)

In recent academic discourse, Blended-Mode Instruction (BMI) has become a focal point. At its essence, BMI merges traditional face-to-face instructional techniques with online and digital modalities, striving to cultivate a comprehensive and adaptable learning experience [9].

Operational definitions of BMI

[10] delineates a foundational viewpoint, positing that blended learning—often used synonymously with BMI—is an "amalgamation of online and traditional education" [10]. This conceptualization embodies the fusion of

two disparate pedagogical domains. Delving deeper into this integration [11], BMI should be based on learning theory with the blending of experiential learning and direct teaching.

This insight highlights the importance of strategically aligning digital and physical modalities to ensure symbiosis that enhances the overall teaching and learning experience. [12] The participatory efficacy of BMI was emphasized for its ability to widen participation to provide learners with various ways to interact with the teaching resources. In contemporary teaching and learning environments, it is worth noting that student engagement is critical to achieving far-reaching learning outcomes [13]. Attention was drawn to the adaptability of BMI, noting that it does not conform to a single definition, but can be "conceptualized in diverse ways according to different educational contexts and learner requirements" [13]. further confirmed the benefits of the blended approach [14], with students in the blended approach "demonstrating more pronounced conceptual shifts and superior academic performance when compared to students in a traditional lecture environment compared to students in the traditional lecture environment" [14]. This empirical evidence highlights the potential of blended pedagogies to promote deeper understanding and improved learning outcomes. In terms of health education parameters [15], it was concluded that "blended pedagogies either exceed or are at least comparable to non-blended pedagogies in terms of knowledge uptake in health professions programs" [15]. This statement emphasizes the validity and versatility of BMI in a range of academic fields. Finally, [16] elucidates the importance of BMI in enhancing self-regulation during the learning process. Their pioneering scholarship "identifies and categorizes the characteristics of enhanced self-regulation in blended learning environments" [16]. Given the centrality of self-regulation in effective learning, especially in higher education, this dimension of BMI cannot be underestimated.

Blended-Mode Instruction (BMI) has unique characteristics which differentiate it from purely traditional or online teaching methods. The literature offers an intricate array of perspectives on these unique characteristics:

Flexibility and Adaptability: One special feature about BMI is its apparent elasticity [17]. Point out that this way of teaching allows students to choose their own learning pace and variety. The model introduced by the business school faculty certainly shows this adaptability [17]. Theirs allow students to choose online, distance and convention at will on a weekly basis for delivery methods [18].

Combining Direct Instruction and Experiential Learning: learning theory should be a combination of direct instruction and experiential learning, argues. It is a combination that not only causes learners to acquire knowledge, but offers them the chance to actually make use in real life of what they have learned [19].

BMI, IR4.0, and the Sustainable Development Goals (SDGs)
The Fourth Industrial Revolution (IR4.0) arrived with the convergence of technologies, merging the boundaries between physical, digital and biological worlds. This era is transformative, and the importance of education-not least through Blended-Mode Instruction (BMI) intensifies its role in delivering learners with capabilities for this change [20].

Blended-Mode Instruction in the Ambit of IR4.0
BMI combines traditional face-to-face pedagogy with an online educational medium to provide a tailored and adaptable educational experience. According to [21], blended learning should be conceptualized around pedagogical theories that emphasize the combination of direct instruction and experiential learning [21]. Such a perspective harmonizes seamlessly with the imperatives of IR4.0, wherein learners necessitate not only foundational understanding but also the adeptness to extrapolate this knowledge in multifaceted scenarios. Within the IR4.0 framework, BMI emerges as a conduit that amalgamates time-honored educational methodologies with the pioneering modalities necessitated by swift technological progressions. To illustrate, [22] advocated for a blended learning framework to assimilate Industry 4.0 within engineering education, positing that such amalgamation can more adeptly equip students for the vicissitudes and prospects presented by the contemporary industrial milieu [22].

Concordance with the Sustainable Development Goals (SDGs)
The research by [23] in China discerned that adult learners perceive the blended learning milieu as a catalyst for sustainable development, citing its attributes such as proffering a congenial and facile learning ambiance and bridging chasms in sustainable growth [23]. This intimates that BMI holds the potential to notably augment the democratization of education, rendering it more attainable and pertinent for a broad spectrum of learners.

Moreover, the infusion of BMI into STREAM disciplines could substantially augment the realization of several SDGs, notably those pertaining to Industry, Innovation, and Infrastructure. As postulated by [24], the focus of operational excellence in the IR4.0 landscape is poised for metamorphosis [24]. Concomitantly, pedagogical strategies, epitomized by BMI, can be instrumental in ensuring learners are adeptly fortified for these impending transitions.

13.2.1.2 Knowledge Management (KM) and its Roles in STREAM Education for IR4.0 in Line with SDGs

Roles of BMI in Knowledge Management (KM) for STREAM Education

Knowledge Creation and Transformation

The integral facet of knowledge management (KM) in education is the synthesis and metamorphosis of knowledge. [25] and [26] underscore that a blended learning environment—central to BMI—markedly enhances student critical thinking and fosters knowledge transformation [25, 26]. Within the STREAM education spectrum, where knowledge application parallels its acquisition, BMI facilitates a dynamic milieu. This combination of conventional pedagogy with digital utilities endows students with a comprehensive learning arena, cultivating both conceptual comprehension and hands-on application.

Facilitating Effective Learning

[27] illuminated the efficacy of BMI in enhancing learning outcomes. Their findings suggest that BMI's deployment within Learning Management Systems (LMS) integrated with hypermedia resources bolsters effective learning [27]. Consequently, in STREAM domains, wherein content evolves swiftly necessitating perpetual learning, BMI's adaptability and versatility are paramount.

Integration with Industry 4.0

A model proposed by [22] champions the assimilation of Industry 4.0 with engineering education via a blended learning paradigm. This model, a harmonization of traditional, online, and flipped classroom techniques, epitomizes BMI's potential to converge academic scholarship with the pragmatic requisites of IR4.0 [22]. Further, [28] accentuate the utility of screen-capture multimedia instruction by educators to shape a blended learning sphere. With the rise of IR4.0 technological forerunners like artificial intelligence and the Internet of Things, BMI stands poised to harness these technologies to elevate the academic voyage [28].

Alignment with Sustainable Development Goals (SDGs)
The Sustainable Development Goals (SDGs) delineate a universal framework for a harmonious and sustainable future. The amalgamation of BMI with the SDGs, particularly within STREAM education, is promising.

Promotion of Sustainable Development: [23] discerned that blended learning environments are perceived by Chinese adult learners to foster sustainable development across multiple dimensions, including learner convenience, ecological responsibility, and sustainable development bridging. This intimates BMI's pivotal role in realizing the SDGs through nurturing an inclusive and sustainable learning sphere [23].

Education for Sustainable Development: [29] advocate that e-learning platforms dedicated to Sustainable Development can be instrumental in transitioning to sustainable societal norms. Given BMI's hybrid nature, intertwining traditional and e-learning, it emerges as a potent medium for ingraining sustainable development tenets within STREAM curricula [29].

Blended Learning for Sustainable Competency: The research by [30] elucidates that meticulous practice within a blended learning domain can empower students' acquisition of sustainable development competencies. This accentuates BMI's potential to adeptly prepare students to tackle the intricate challenges of global sustainability [30].

Integrating Four Aspects of Knowledge Management in Educational Settings

There are four main aspects "knowledge management" [31], i.e., "Acquisition of knowledge" (henceforth abbreviated as AK), "Storage of knowledge" (henceforth abbreviated as SK), "Distribution of knowledge" (henceforth abbreviated as DK) and "Use of knowledge" (henceforth abbreviated as UK). All these four aspects significantly affect the teaching, learning and research activities of universities including full-mode of Open and Distance Learning (ODL) in which the first and fourth co-authors are very much involved in, and partial-mode of ODL participated by the second and third co-authors in the process of their efforts to promote STREAM education to prepare for IR4.0 in line with SDGs.

In the "Research Center of Communication and Development Knowledge Management" (abbreviated CCDKM) where the first author is affiliated with as well as 'Faculty of Social Science and Liberal Arts' (abbreviated as FOSSLA) where the second and fourth co-authors are affiliated with, BMI is the main KM approach to reach out to wider audience, not only stakeholders attended on-site training in campus, but also participants outside the campus. The following diagrams illustrate the findings from document analysis on some of the digital tools and e-platforms that reflect four main aspects of KM as aforementioned.

(A) Acquisition of knowledge (AoK)

Blended-mode Instruction (BMI) in the abovementioned universities where all authors of this chapter are affiliated with was conducted through various digital tools and social networking platforms (SNPs) where all stakeholders communicated with one another for acquisition of knowledge (AoK), networking and sharing of resources. Among the commonly used e-platforms for interactive discussions include WeChat, Telegram and Google Meet among postgraduate students (Figure 13.1) as well as Team among undergraduate students (Figure 13.2).

Figure 13.1 Telegram and Google Meet as SNPs for most of the KM process especially for AoK.

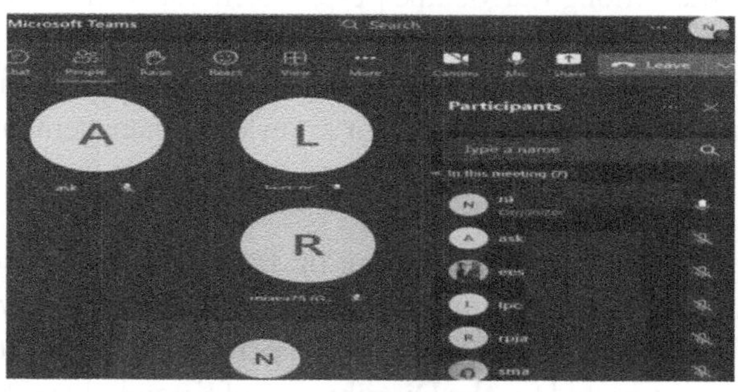

Figure 13.2 Team web meeting platform during KM process especially for AoK during tutorials.

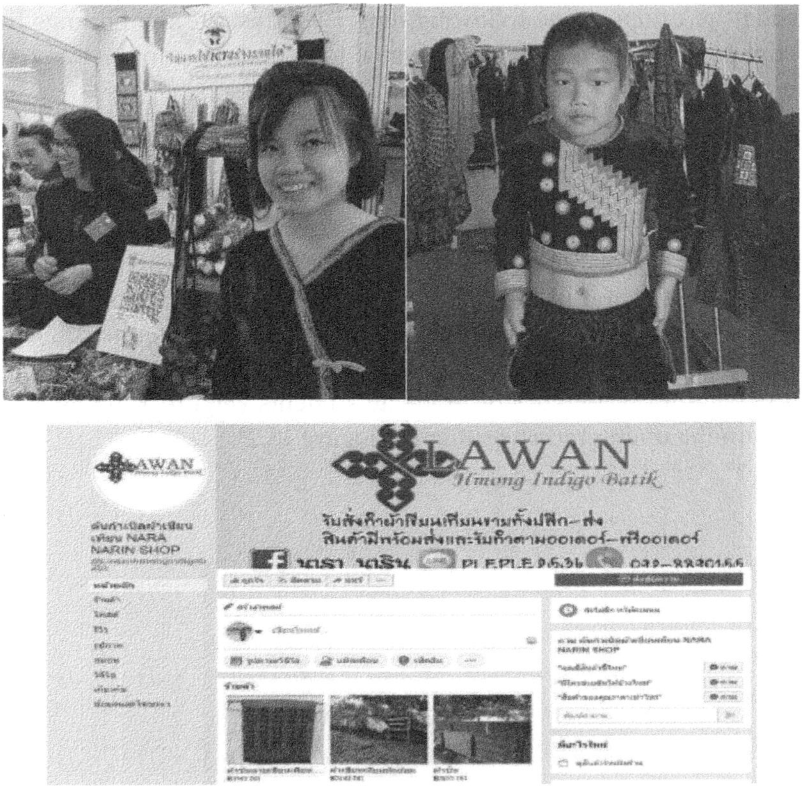

Figure 13.3 Blended shop with on-site and online created by ethnic girls and women participated in the "blended-mode workshop to promote Smart Functional Literacy" to facilitate Storage of Knowledge (SoK).

(B) Storage of knowledge (SoK)
Blended shop with on-site and online hosted on FB [URL: https://www.facebook.com/Lawanhmongindigobatik/] e-platform via BMI (Figure 13.3) was created by ethnic girls and women participated in the "blended-mode workshop to promote Smart Functional Literacy" conducted by the first author to facilitate Storage of knowledge (SoK) for knowledge management (KM).

(C) Distribution of knowledge (DoK)
Blended-mode workshop for Training of Trainers (ToT) on digital skills and e-business for ASEAN women MSMEs [URL: https://www.facebook.com/photo/?fbid=700087558799359&set=pcb.700087932132655] (Figure 13.4) was also conducted for the Distribution of Knowledge (DoK) through trainers who had attended the training organized by the first author.

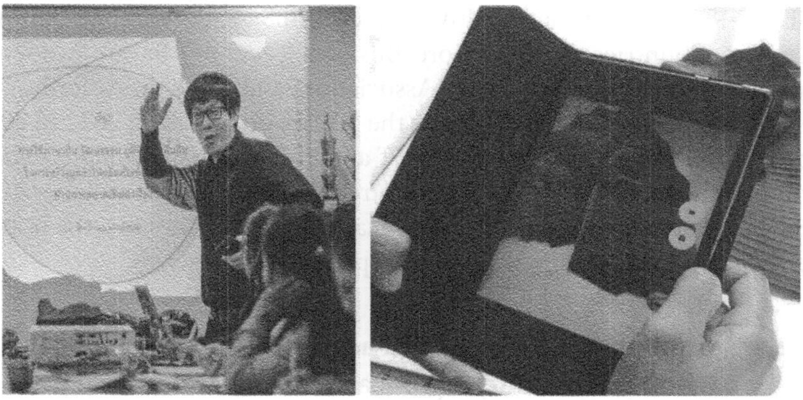

Figure 13.4 Training of Trainers' (ToT) to facilitate Distribution of Knowledge (DoK).

Figure 13.5 www.ccdkm.org through BMI to facilitate Use of Knowledge (UoK).

(D) Use of knowledge (UoK)

Official website was developed by CCDKM (Figure 13.5) where the first author is affiliated and various updated information was posted to report on all the activities conducted to promote Use of Knowledge (UoK) in various events that were conducted through BMI led by the first author.

One of the report posted on FB included for example, on 13–17 March 2023, School of Communication Arts, CCDKM (The Expertise Research Centre), STOU contributed as the National Research Consultant at APWINC, Sookmyung Women's University, South Korea. The first author who is affiliated with School of Communication Arts, CCDKM, Sukhothai Thammathirat Open University (STOU), contributed as the National Research Consultant in "Increasing Digital Skills and E-Commerce for ASEAN Women MSMEs" (abbreviated as IDEAS) among all international and regional partners: APWINC (Asia Pacific Women's Information Network Centre), Sookmyung Women's University, ASEAN Secretariat,

ASEAN-Korean Relations, ASEAN Access Ambassador, and all ASEAN Members Countries i.e. Singapore Business Federate, Bayan Academy, Myanmar Women Entrepreneurs Association, and so forth. According to IDEAS, the Regional R&D Project is the 5 Years project from 2022 to 2027 aims to use all kinds of appropriate ICT and innovation to facilitate all betterment among all ASEAN women entrepreneurs. Holistic collaboration has been blended among all partners: academia, policy, donors, the implementing agencies, and the women entrepreneurs themselves.

13.2.2 Exemplars on How BMI Facilitated Lifelong Learning with KM Considering Local Wisdom and Literacy (RO2)

This section illustrates exemplary cases on how Blended-Mode Instruction (BMI) in the forms of digital tools and e-platforms facilitated lifelong learning in the transfer knowledge or skills among stakeholders considering their local wisdoms and STREAM literacy.

13.2.2.1 Case Exemplar(s) on How BMI Facilitated Lifelong Learning Considering Literacy with KM

The following Figure 13.6 is the promotional brochure of one blended-mode event organized by the first author to promote literacy among all stakeholders including the aging societies in Thailand through BMI.

Figure 13.6 E-brochure of one of Thailand's events to promote literacy through BMI.

Figure 13.7 is the group photo for the participants attended the on-site workshop, and Figure 13.8 is the photo taken during the on-site training workshop. However, there are still many participants in Thailand who could not attend. Hence, BMI was implemented to disseminate the

Figure 13.7 On-site training workshop at a glance with projector showing implementation via BMI.

Figure 13.8 On-site training workshop facilitated by the first author.

teaching and learning content for the self-paced/directed/accessed learning and enhance their literacy through this lifelong learning platform.

Figure 13.8 and Figure 13.10 illustrate the onsite workshop activities facilitated by the first author.

13.2.2.2 Case Exemplar(s) on How BMI Facilitated Lifelong Learning Considering Local Wisdom with KM

The following Figure 13.9 and Figure 13.10 are the promotional brochures of another blended-mode event organized by the first author to enhance

Figure 13.9 E-brochure of webinar to promote smart silver economy through local wisdom.

Figure 13.10 Workshop participants and one of the targeted outputs to promote silver economy.

Figure 13.11 Workshop participants and some of their outputs to promote silver economy.

knowledge/skills to develop project-based learning output for silver economy through local wisdom among all stakeholders including the aging societies in Thailand also supported by BMI.

Figures 13.9, 13.10 and 13.11 show some of the participants and their learning output to promote silver economy.

Figure 13.12 Illustrates the presentation slide extracted from the technology-enhanced learning output by Indonesia participants attended an online course organized by the third and fourth co-author focusing on "Arts/Reading/Language/Culture" aspects of STREAM education reflecting the theme of the e-course, i.e., Local Wisdom that is also the focus of this study.

Figure 13.12 Presentation slide extracted from "Local Wisdom Cowongan in Banyumas" by Indonesian's project entitled "Integrating local wisdom on elementary school curriculum" [32].

13.3 Conclusion

13.3.1 Summary and Implications/Significance

This Chapter explores the strategies and initiatives implemented in Thailand, Indonesia, and China to promote literacy and local wisdom through BMI for technology-enhanced lifelong education (TELE). The roles of BMI as KM e-platforms in enhancing access to quality education, fostering STREAM literacy, as well as preserving local cultures and knowledge are elaborated. By examining exemplars from these countries, the Chapter aims to provide insights into effective policies and practices for the promotion of technology-enhanced lifelong learning comparing traditional and current mode [33] as well as preservation of local cultures in countries as advocated by [34, 35].

The following are contexts of Thai Mother Tongue Language facilitated by the Smart Functional literacy (SFL) and ICT: (1) In the contexts of Thai Mother Tongue Language found all ethnic groups use it to transfer their local wisdom, heritage, and crafts base on their own creativity and readiness. The Smart Functional Literacy can facilitate them to be more accessible and visible to more online channels, i.e., the e-marketing and e-advertising of their community products to create more income generation. The ethnic girls and young women can use ICT to create their own idea integrated by their own existing resources for more marketing. So, this is the strongest point to support them with ICT for self-learning and training via the Smart Functional Literacy (SFL) to let them integrate well more among their local wisdom, creativity, Mother Tongue, and their community resources that concur with findings from literature [36, 37].

The findings of this research paper have significant implications for policymakers, educators, and practitioners in Southeast Asia and beyond. By highlighting successful initiatives and strategies for promoting literacy and local wisdom through technology-enhanced lifelong education, this Chapter can inform the development of effective policies and practices for lifelong learning in the region and beyond. The discourse in this chapter also emphasizes the importance of preserving local cultures and knowledge in the face of rapid technological advances and the potential of technologies such as Massive Open Online Courses (MOOCs) [38] to support this endeavor as one of the platforms for BMI. Overall, the research reported in this chapter contributes to an ongoing dialog on the role of technology in education and its potential to promote equitable access to education, preserve local cultures, and foster lifelong learning.

13.3.2 Limitations and Recommendations

The main restriction of this study is that it confines itself to Thailand, Indonesia, and China. It may not offer the complete picture for the region as a whole. Moreover, the study depends on secondary material (reports and articles), which may not present completely within countries studied their initiatives or views about technology-assisted lifelong learning.

With these limitations in mind, several suggestions can be made for future research and practice. Second, in future research one could include studying other countries to get a better sense of the work being done around technology-enhanced lifelong learning designed to promote literacy and local wisdom for the region. Third, primary research like surveys and questionnaires with educators and learners would offer more insight into the kinds of strategies being used to promote technology-enhanced lifelong learning as well as what obstacles are encountered. Also, future studies could inquire how local knowledge and wisdom can be better incorporated into technology-enhanced learning, perhaps with the participation of neighboring communities or organizations. As a whole, these recommendations can help make technology-assisted lifelong learning programs more effective and far reaching in the Asia Pacific region and beyond.

Acknowledgments

The authors would like to express their sincere gratitude to all those who participated directly or indirectly in the research for this chapter. Special thanks are expressed to: (1) The participants/consultants involved in preparing the BMI e-platforms for Smart Functional Literacy (SFL) initiatives to provide input and subsequently submitted output as exemplified; (2) All staff at STOU and Universitas Muhammadiyah Purwokerto (UMP) supported this study; (3) All people who have assisted to make research and development (R&D) activities successful in whatever ways.

References

1. Intaratat, K., Ong, E.T., Ng, K.T., Anggoro, S., Smart functional literacy using ICT to promote mother tongue language and inclusive development among ethnic girls and women in Northern Thailand. Paper presented in *ICONESS 2023 (22nd July 2023 at UMP, Central Java, Indonesia)* and accepted for

'European Alliance for Innovation-Computing and Communication in Emerging Regions' (EAI-CCER) Scopus-indexed Proceedings, 2023, In Press.

2. Ismail, I., Enhancing STEM literacy considering Reading and Arts. Colloquium presentation during LearnT-SMArET e-course series October to November, 2021/2022, RECSAM, Penang, 2022.
3. Miyadera, R., Creative mathematics education supported by digital tools that enhance STEM literacy and STEM related careers. *Learn. Sci. Math. (LSM)*, 12, 13–19, 2017, http://www.recsam.edu.my/sub_LSMJournal/images/docs/2017/(2)Ryohei%20Miyadera%20pg13-19_final.pdf.
4. Chin, C.K., Hairiah, M., Miyadera, R., Ng, K.T., Ch'ng, Y.S., Promsing, N., Promoting Education for Sustainable Development in teacher education integrating blended learning and digital tools: An evaluation with exemplary cases. *EURASIA J. Math. Sci. Technol. Educ. (EJMSTE)*, 15, 1, 2019, https://doi.org/10.29333/ejmste/99513 & http://www.ejmste.com/Issue-1-2019,6606.
5. Creswell, J.W. and Creswell, J.D., *Research design: Qualitative, quantitative, and mixed methods approaches*, Sage publications, London, 2017.
6. Yin, R.K., *Case Study Research Design and Methods*, 5th ed., Sage, Thousand Oaks, CA, 2014, https://www.researchgate.net/publication/308385754_Robert_K_Yin_2014_Case_Study_Research_Design_and_Methods_5th_ed_Thousand_Oaks_CA_Sage_ 282_pages.
7. Eisenhardt, K.M., What is the Eisenhardt Method, really? *Strategic Organization,* 19, 1, February 2021, 147–160, 2021, Retrieved https://journals.sagepub.com/doi/full/10.1177/1476127020982866 and https://doi.org/10.1177/1476127020982866.
8. Ng, K.T., Baharum, B.N., Othman, M., Tahir, S., Pang, Y.J., Managing technology-enhanced innovation programs: Framework, exemplars and future directions. *Solid State Technol.*, 63, 1s (2020), 555–565, 2020, http://www.solidstatetechnology.us/index.php/JSST/article/view/741.
9. Graham, C.R., Borup, J., Pulham, E., Larsen, R., K–12 Blended Teaching Readiness: Model and Instrument Development. *J. Res. Technol. Educ.*, *51*, 3, 239–258, 2019, https://doi.org/10.1080/15391523.2019.1586601.
10. Hrastinski, S., What Do We Mean by Blended Learning? *TechTrends, 63*, 5, 564–569, 2019, https://doi.org/10.1007/s11528-019-00375-5.
11. Dziuban, C., Graham, C.R., Moskal, P.D., Norberg, A., Sicilia, N., Blended learning: the new normal and emerging technologies. *Int. J. Educ. Technol. High. Educ.*, *15*, 1, 2018, https://doi.org/10.1186/s41239-017-0087-5.
12. Mestan, K., Create a fine blend: An examination of institutional transition to blended learning. *Australas. J. Educ. Technol.*, *35*, 1, 2019, https://doi.org/10.14742/ajet.3216.
13. Oh, E. and Park, S., How are Universities involved in Blended Instruction? *J. Educ. Technol. Soc.*, 12, 3, 2007, https://www.semanticscholar.org/paper/How-are-Universities-involved-in-Blended-Oh-Park/0f770732a524bd32a0a9e662355b25d7091217b4.

14. Bazelais, P. and Doleck, T., Blended learning and traditional learning: A comparative study of college mechanics courses. *Educ. Inf. Technol.*, *23*, 6, 2889–2900, 2018, https://doi.org/10.1007/s10639-018-9748-9.
15. Liu, Q., Peng, W., Zhang, F., Hu, R., Li, Y., Yan, W., The Effectiveness of Blended Learning in Health Professions: Systematic Review and Meta-Analysis. *J. Med. Internet Res.*, *18*, 1, e2, 2016, https://doi.org/10.2196/jmir.4807.
16. Van Laer, S. and Elen, J., In search of attributes that support self-regulation in blended learning environments. *Educ. Inf. Technol.*, *22*, 4, 1395–1454, 2016, https://doi.org/10.1007/s10639-016-9505-x.
17. Zhang, Q., Goodman, M., Xie, S., Integrating Library Instruction into the Course Management System for a First-Year Engineering Class: An Evidence-Based Study Measuring the Effectiveness of Blended Learning on Students' Information Literacy Levels. *Coll. Res. Libr.*, *76*, 7, 934–958, 2015, https://doi.org/10.5860/crl.76.7.934.
18. Lightner, C.A. and Lightner-Laws, C.A., A blended model: simultaneously teaching a quantitative course traditionally, online, and remotely. *Interact. Learn. Environ.*, *24*, 1, 224–238, 2013, https://doi.org/10.1080/10494820.2013.841262.
19. Lai, M., Lam, K.M., Lim, C.P., Design principles for the blend in blended learning: a collective case study. *Teach. High. Educ.*, *21*, 6, 716–729, 2016, https://doi.org/10.1080/13562517.2016.1183611.
20. Cowie, P., Townsend, L., Salemink, K., Smart rural futures: Will rural areas be left behind in the 4th industrial revolution? *J. Rural Stud.*, *79*, 169–176, 2020, https://doi.org/10.1016/j.jrurstud.2020.08.042.
21. Cronje, J., Towards a New Definition of Blended Learning. *Electron. J. E-Learn.*, *18*, 2-Feb 2020, 2020, https://doi.org/10.34190/ejel.20.18.2.001.
22. Chong, S., Pan, G.-T., Chin, J., Show, P., Yang, T., Huang, C.-M., Integration of 3D Printing and Industry 4.0 into Engineering Teaching. *Sustainability*, *10*, 11, 3960, 2018, https://doi.org/10.3390/su10113960.
23. Yao, C., An investigation of adult learners' viewpoints to a blended learning environment in promoting sustainable development in China. *J. Cleaner Prod.*, *220*, 134–143, 2019, https://doi.org/10.1016/j.jclepro.2019.01.290.
24. Luz Tortorella, G., Cauchick-Miguel, P.A., Li, W., Staines, J., McFarlane, D., What does operational excellence mean in the Fourth Industrial Revolution era? *Int. J. Prod. Res.*, 60, 9, 1–17, 2021, https://doi.org/10.1080/00207543.2021.1905903.
25. Jaswal, P. and Behera, B., Blended matters: Nurturing critical thinking. *E-Learn. Digital Media*, 204275302311561, 21, 12, 2023, https://doi.org/10.1177/20427530231156184.
26. Jou, M., Lin, Y.-T., Wu, D.-W., Effect of a blended learning environment on student critical thinking and knowledge transformation. *Interact. Learn. Environ.*, *24*, 6, 1131–1147, 2014, https://doi.org/10.1080/10494820.2014.961485.

27. Sáiz-Manzanares, M.C., Escolar-Llamazares, M.-C., Arnaiz González, Á., Effectiveness of Blended Learning in Nursing Education. *Int. J. Environ. Res. Public Health*, *17*, 5, 1589, 2020, https://doi.org/10.3390/ijerph17051589.
28. Smith, J.G. and Smith, R.L., Screen-Capture Instructional Technology: A Cognitive Tool for Designing a Blended Multimedia Curriculum. *J. Educ. Comput. Res.*, *46*, 3, 207–228, 2012, https://doi.org/10.2190/ec.46.3.a.
29. Azeiteiro, U.M., Bacelar-Nicolau, P., Caetano, F.J.P., Caeiro, S., Education for sustainable development through e-learning in higher education: experiences from Portugal. *J. Cleaner Prod.*, *106*, 308–319, 2015, https://doi.org/10.1016/j.jclepro.2014.11.056.
30. Chen, R.H., Effects of Deliberate Practice on Blended Learning Sustainability: A Community of Inquiry Perspective. *Sustainability*, *14*, 3, 1785, 2022, https://doi.org/10.3390/su14031785.
31. Gonzalez, R.V.D. and Martins, M.F., Knowledge Management Process: a theoretical-conceptual research. *Gest. Prod., São Carlos*, 24, 2, 248–265, 2017, Retrieved http://dx.doi.org/10.1590/0104-530X0893-15 OR https://www.scielo.br/j/gp/a/cbfhzLCBfB6gnzrqPtyby8S/?lang=en.
32. Anggoro, S., Indriastuti, A.D.W., Ilman, M.Z., Nabiha, S.A., Wishi, N.S., Firdaus, M.R., Ramadhan, N.E.K., Integrating local wisdom on elementary school curriculum. 2022, https://drive.google.com/drive/folders/15OlWj83tYrdGhvG-wMUu3cYGBPeZx7f2?usp=sharing.
33. Uzun, A. and Senturk, A., Blending Makes the Difference: Comparison of Blended and Traditional Instruction on Students' Performance and Attitudes in Computer Literacy. *Contemp. Educ. Technol.*, *1*, 3, 2010, https://doi.org/10.30935/cedtech/6027.
34. FAO, Smart Farm Thailand: Pilot Project, 2020, http://www.fao.org/asiapacific/perspectives/digital-villages/ thailand-dvi/es/.
35. Akello, J.A., Lutwama-Rukundo, E., Musiimenta, P., Functional Adult Literacy: An Alternative Gateway to Grassroots Women's Improved Income Generation in Lango Subregion, Northern Uganda. *Adult Education Quarterly*, 67, 2, 79–96, 2017.
36. UNESCO Institute for Education, *Landscapes of literacy: an ethnographic study of functional literacy in marginal Philippine communities*, Luzac Oriental, Hamburg, Germany, 1996.
37. Waha, B. and Davis, K., University Students' Perspective on Blended Learning. *J. High. Educ. Policy Manage.*, *36*, 2, 172–182, 2014, https://www.learntechlib.org/p/156686/.
38. Intaratat, K. and Massive Open Online Courses (MOOC), MOOC for Life, 2021, Retrieved https://www.ccdkm.org/.

14

Insight Review on Advanced Digital Manufacturing Technology Solutions for Industry 4.0

D. David Neels Ponkumar[1*], K. Saravanan[2], Riboy Cheriyan[2] and Chinnadurai Manthiramoorthy[3]

[1]*Vel Tech Rangarajan Dr. Sagunthala R&D Institute of Science and Technology, Chennai, India*
[2]*SAINTGITS College of Engineering, Kottayam, India*
[3]*Abbott Laboratories, Burlington, MA, USA*

Abstract

The introduction of the steam engine made the First Industrial Revolution (IR) followed by the discovery of electricity led to the second and the computer machinery took the world to the Third Industrial Revolution. Industry 4.0 otherwise called the fourth IR is through The digitalization of the industrial industry is being propelled by disruptive developments such as the increasing prominence of knowledge and communication, the use of analytics, and the advancement of human–machine interaction, improvements, and created business competitiveness across countries. The gain of digital manufacturing led to the formation of various policies and guidelines. The emphasis placed on the significance of adopting Industry 4.0 has resulted in a lack of recognition of the potential consequences for intra-firm and inter-firm organizational structures, specifically in terms of understanding generation and dissemination within organizations. In the present context, our objective was to make an insight review on advanced digital manufacturing technology solutions used in the concept of Industry 4.0, when examined through the lens of knowledge management, revealing significant implications and opportunities for organizations.

***Keywords*:** Industrial Internet of Things (IIoT), Industry 4.0, digitization of manufacturing sectors, knowledge management, challenges in digitization

---

**Corresponding author*: drdavidneels@veltech.edu.in

Rajendra Kumar, Vishal Jain, Venus C. Ibarra, Corrienna Abdul Talib and Vinay Kukreja (eds.) Knowledge Management and Industry Revolution 4.0, (371–388)

14.1 Introduction

Since 2010, almost past 20 years, significant revolutions in terms of technological advancements have taken place, especially in the business zones by Web. Industry 4.0 [1] is underpinned by the Industrial Internet of Things (IIoT) [2] and intelligent cyber-physical infrastructures that use computer programs to oversee and govern physical equipment, such as machinery, robots, and cars. Industry 4.0 is transforming manufacturing and competitiveness in the industry due to its roots in automation and robotics. Powered with the Internet of Things (IoT), Industry 4.0 enables manufacturers to acquire, analyze, and act on huge available data and provide outcomes in terms of automated services and robotic systems that provide a quality product at a low running cost for the business.

Workforce empowerment is crucial in the deployment of Industry 4.0. The need for workforce involvement is heightened to achieve a successful transition in the context of the Fourth Industrial Revolution (4IR). Undoubtedly, the effective implementation of a 4IR transformation inside a business is very improbable without the active participation of capable staff, regardless of the organization's possession of cutting-edge tools, advanced technology, and substantial resources. Organizations have effectively enhanced their resilience by a deliberate emphasis on individuals, therefore facilitating the acquisition of novel skills among employees. This enables businesses to exhibit more adaptability in the face of incessant change. In practical application, this may include reevaluating paths for skill acquisition and training, as well as implementing modifications to the structure with a focus on long-term effects.

The following five aspects contribute to the consistent implementation of strong labor engagement among manufacturers:

1. The acquisition of enhanced competencies and abilities in the realm of learning and development is achieved via the integration of hard, soft, and digital skills, as well as apprenticeship opportunities.
2. Empowerment and ownership may be achieved via outcome and result-oriented steering, which involves enabling people to exercise autonomy in decision-making processes.
3. One strategy for fostering collaboration and connections inside an organization is via the engagement of interconnected and multi-skilled teams, as well as the establishment of extended networks.

4. The impact and recognition of individuals may be enhanced by the establishment of responsibility for their accomplishments or through the commemoration of their victories.
5. One approach to capturing the perspective of employees is using digital platforms and data to collect feedback from their voices, or striving to comprehend their latent requirements.

A proper resilience strategy needed to be adopted by the Industry 4.0 compliance adhering factories to design, develop, deliver, and support their consumers. Learning factories [12] hence can provide efficient Industry 4.0-powered services through systematic incorporation of digitization in manufacturing. Research opportunities and challenges of the adoption of information and communications technologies (ICT), specifically as far as Small Enterprises and Medium-Sized Enterprises (SMEs) and innovation dynamics are considered in this chapter through the following sections. Section 14.1 deals with the digitization of manufacturing sectors, which highlights the various digitization methods incorporated. Section 14.2 discusses the knowledge management practices adopted in manufacturing. Section 14.3 deals with disruptive trends in digital manufacturing. Section 14.4 deals with the applications and challenges faced with advantages and improvements required, and finally, Section 14.5 gives inference with concluding remarks. This book chapter will be highly beneficial to the learning and research community investigating the impact of knowledge management in Industry 4.0 in the context of digital manufacturing technology

1. Impact on the manufacturing industry by recent Disruption of Digital Trends

Most of the industries benefit from the recent transformation in the manufacturing process through the latest digital trends. The IIoT advancements [1, 2] eased the process of both manufacturing as well as services provided at the user end. The recent human–machine interaction (HMI) paradigm demands up-skilling of employees and hence rises in the number of training sectors. The quality of training affects the development of better ambiance in digital manufacturing requiring HMI.

The prominent four pillars of disruptive manufacturing technologies in Industry 4.0 are human–machine interaction, Connectivity and Computational Capability, artificial intelligence incorporation, and advanced engineering including renewable energy, nano-particles, and 3-D printing [3, 4]. As mentioned earlier more emphasis on upskilling the labor force is a must to make the manufacturing processes benefited by these disruptive trends. Otherwise, the trends will be a mere talk and admired by only the research community. Hence, the global lighthouse standard [5] declared by the World Economic Forum recognizes industries that incorporate all the necessary technologies for the manufacturing process in the context of Industry 4.0. The IIoT infrastructure is especially focused much by the GLH. The recognized sites serve as a role models for other industries to transform into IR4 standards.

The enhancement of such manufacturing is reflected in almost all industry domains like Healthcare, Agriculture, Augmented reality, Blockchain, Synthetic biology, Robotics, Drones, and nanotechnology, etc., Proper incorporation of all the trends leads to the development of smart products making ease the human life and also promotes economic growth [6–10]. The socioeconomic conditions of less privileged society too shall be addressed by incubating various new life standard improvement products, which address the livelihood issues. The United Nations Industrial Development Organization (UNIDO) now has set standards for Industry 4.0 in the context of sustainability [11] and smart energy.

The factories have to adopt the concept of Learning Factory and innovation laboratory concepts in the manufacturing units for knowledge transfer and equipping the labor force for the transition to digitization [12]. The LF suitably combines theoretical and practical methods to impart knowledge and skills concerning Industry 4.0 [13]. The impact of disruptive trends on the manufacturing industries in the context of Industry 4.0 is well discussed in this section and provides insights to the research community to find suitable problems and issues.

14.2 Digitization of Manufacturing Sectors

Digital transformation can occur in manufacturing when an industry starts putting into practice various digital technologies to upgrade the various facets of manufacturing operations. The manufacturing industry has undergone a significant transformation in recent years with the advent of digital technologies. The digitization of manufacturing sectors, often referred to as Industry 4.0 or the Fourth Industrial Revolution, has revolutionized traditional production processes, enabling increased productivity, efficiency, and innovation. The key aspects and benefits of the digitization of manufacturing sectors are discussed.

1. Internet of Things (IoT) and Connectivity: At the core of manufacturing digitization is the Internet of Things (IoT). By embedding sensors and interconnected devices

throughout production facilities, manufacturers can collect real-time data on various parameters such as machine performance, energy consumption, and product quality [14]. This connectivity enables seamless communication and collaboration between machines, systems, and humans leading to improved monitoring, predictive maintenance, and optimized production processes [15].

2. Big Data and Analytics: The digitization of manufacturing sectors has resulted in an abundance of data generated at every stage of the production lifecycle. Big Data Analytics allows manufacturers to make sense of this vast amount of data and extract valuable insights. Advanced analytics tools and algorithms can identify patterns, anomalies, and correlations enabling manufacturers to optimize production planning, reduce waste, and enhance overall efficiency [16]. Additionally, data-driven decision making empowers manufacturers to adapt quickly to market demands and achieve better customer satisfaction [17].
3. Automation and Robotics: Automation and robotics have become integral components of digitized manufacturing sectors. Automated systems and robots can perform repetitive tasks with precision and speed, reducing human error and increasing production throughput [18]. Robotic process automation (RPA) is widely used for tasks such as assembly, packaging, and material handling. The integration of robotics not only enhances productivity but also improves workplace safety by replacing workers in hazardous environments [19]. With automation, manufacturers can focus human resources on higher-skilled tasks that require creativity and problem-solving abilities.
4. Artificial Intelligence (AI) and Machine Learning (ML): Artificial intelligence and machine learning technologies are driving innovation in manufacturing sectors. AI-powered algorithms can analyze complex datasets, identify trends, and make predictions, enabling manufacturers to optimize production schedules, reduce equipment downtime, and improve quality control [20]. Machine learning algorithms can learn from historical data to continuously refine and enhance manufacturing processes [21]. AI and ML also facilitate the development of smart products that can adapt

to customer preferences, leading to greater customization and market competitiveness.

5. Supply Chain Digitization: Digitization extends beyond individual manufacturing facilities and encompasses the entire supply chain. By integrating digital technologies throughout the supply chain network, manufacturers can achieve end-to-end visibility and traceability. Real-time data sharing and analytics improve supply chain coordination, demand forecasting, and inventory management [22]. Digitized supply chains enable faster response times, streamlined logistics, and better collaboration with suppliers and customers, ultimately reducing costs and enhancing customer satisfaction [23].
6. Cybersecurity and Data Privacy: With the increased adoption of digitization, manufacturers face the challenge of ensuring robust cybersecurity and data privacy. Protecting sensitive data, intellectual property and critical infrastructure from cyber threats is crucial. Implementing strong cybersecurity measures such as encryption, access controls, and regular audits helps safeguard digital systems and maintain trust with customers and partners [24].

The digitization of manufacturing sectors represents a significant shift in the industry, enabling manufacturers to unlock new levels of productivity, efficiency, and innovation. By leveraging technologies such as IoT, Big Data Analytics, automation, AI, and supply chain digitization, manufacturers can optimize their operations, drive down costs, and deliver high-quality products with greater agility. Embracing digital transformation is crucial for companies aiming to remain competitive in the rapidly evolving global manufacturing landscape.

14.3 Knowledge Management Practices Adopted in Manufacturing

Knowledge management (KM) practices (Figure 14.1) play a vital role in the success and competitiveness of manufacturing industries. Effective knowledge management enables organizations to capture, store, share, and utilize valuable knowledge assets to drive innovation, enhance productivity, and maintain a sustainable advantage. The key knowledge management

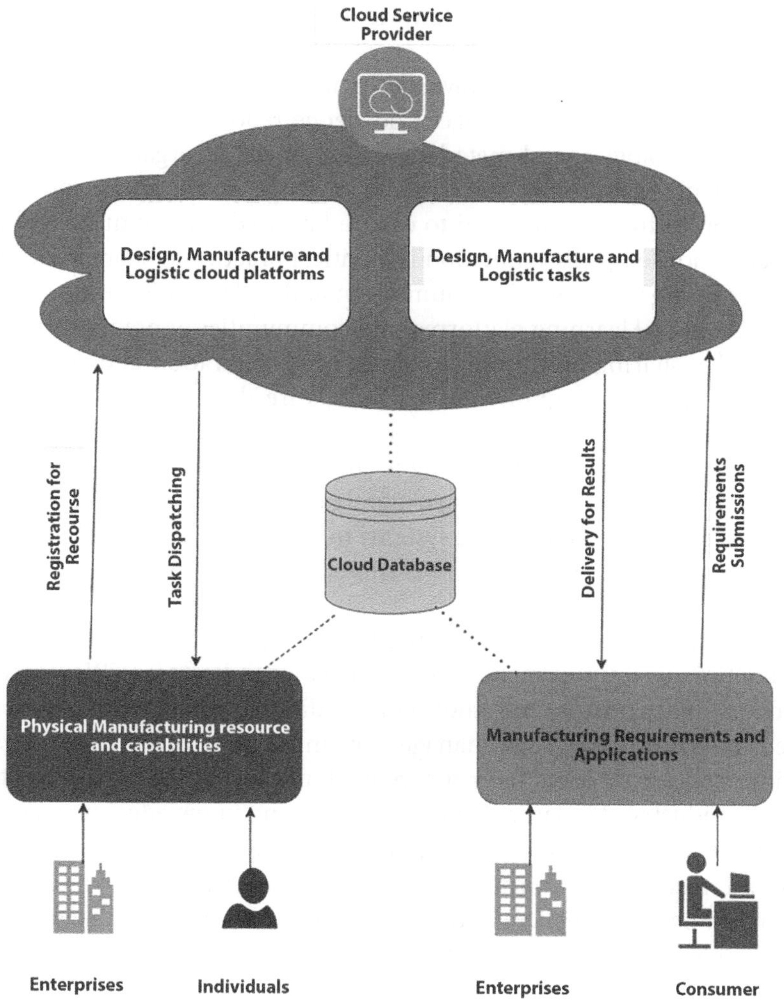

Figure 14.1 Knowledge management practices.

practices adopted in manufacturing industries, highlighting their significance and potential benefits are explained.

In manufacturing industries, knowledge creation is essential for staying ahead of the competition. Organizations employ various methods to generate new knowledge, leveraging internal and external sources and encouraging innovation and creativity. Knowledge acquisition is another crucial aspect involving the identification of relevant knowledge sources and experts, both internally and through external collaborations.

Techniques for capturing tacit knowledge and converting it into explicit knowledge are also utilized [25].

To effectively manage knowledge manufacturing industries, employ strategies for knowledge storage. Knowledge repositories, databases, taxonomies, ontologies, and metadata are employed to organize knowledge for efficient storage and retrieval. Knowledge codification and documentation techniques are used to ensure knowledge is captured and preserved. Knowledge dissemination is a critical practice to share knowledge within the organization. Communication and collaboration tools, such as intranets, social learning platforms, and communities of practice, facilitate knowledge sharing and foster a culture of collaboration and continuous learning. Training programs and workshops are also conducted to disseminate knowledge effectively. The application of knowledge in manufacturing processes and decision making is another vital aspect. Manufacturing organizations integrate knowledge into their operations, leveraging knowledge-based systems and expert systems to support decision making. Real-time knowledge access enables operational efficiency and problem solving [26].

Measuring and evaluating knowledge management practices is crucial for continuous improvement. Key Performance Indicators (KPIs), surveys, feedback mechanisms, and knowledge audits are employed to assess the effectiveness of knowledge management initiatives. This enables organizations to identify areas for improvement and benchmark their practices against industry standards. While implementing knowledge management practices, manufacturing industries face challenges. These can include cultural resistance, information overload, and technology integration. Overcoming these challenges requires fostering a knowledge-sharing culture, implementing change management strategies, and leveraging emerging technologies [27].

Several manufacturing organizations have successfully implemented knowledge management practices. Case studies provide valuable insights into real-world implementations and best practices, offering lessons learned and practical guidance for other organizations [28]. Looking to the future, emerging Technological advancements, such as artificially intelligent technology (AI), the Internet of Things (IoT), and Big Data Analytics, have significantly impacted several industries and sectors that will continue to shape knowledge management practices in manufacturing industries. These technologies enable advanced knowledge capture, analysis, and decision making, further enhancing operational efficiency and innovation.

Knowledge management practices [29] are integral to the success of manufacturing industries. By effectively managing knowledge creation, acquisition, storage, dissemination, and application, organizations can optimize their operations, improve decision making, and foster a culture of continuous learning and improvement [30].

14.4 Challenges in Digitization of Industry 4.0

During the digitization of Industry 4.0 in small-scale and large-scale companies [31], they experience various challenges that hinder the deployment of technologies. Roadblocks, as challenges are commonly called The scope of this study encompasses several aspects, including technical, logistical, regulating, and ecological factors, which pertain to both the individuals and the procedures concerned.

They can be broadly categorized under the following five categories.

1. Networking Capabilities and the Operating Environment
2. Data Storage and Data Availability
3. Cybersecurity and Cyber Threats
4. People and Processes
5. Working with Vendors

Each category throws in a unique challenge. The foundation of Industry 4.0 [32] is in the establishment of connection across many stages, including the edge, the network, the cloud, and their reciprocal interactions. Consequently, the presence of a network plays a crucial role in facilitating novel solutions and offering insights into operational procedures. Various use cases entail distinct networking needs, while the operational environments of enterprises may provide obstacles that influence their choice of networking technology. Companies need to exercise considerable consideration when choosing their network design. Buying or building a new network like 5G, LTE, NB IoT, LPWANs, or LoRaWAN is very crucial. MPLS and Software Wide Area Networking (SD-WAN) technology that are more flexible and resilient can be of more value too [33].

For data to be effectively used, information must be collected and consolidated into a centralized system to facilitate processing. The issue of data storage is a persistent concern since outdated technologies frequently need their incorporation into contemporary corporate designs and centralized systems. There is a growing trend among companies to migrate their workflows and procedures to cloud-based platforms, enabling them to get a comprehensive perspective and centralized management throughout the whole organization [34] as shown in Figure 14.2.

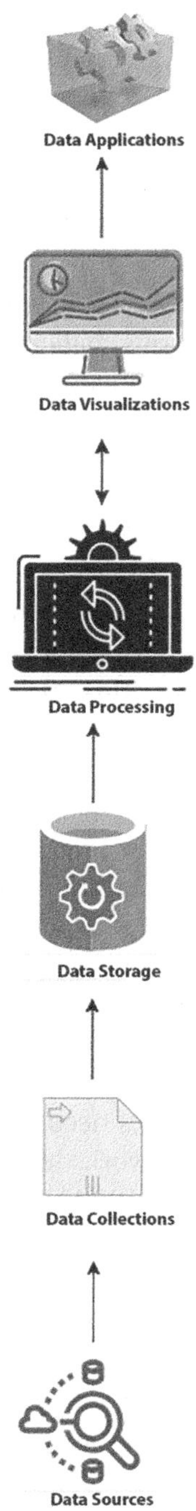

Figure 14.2 Various levels in knowledge management—Data collection to data application.

Another difficulty that arises is the lack of comprehension of current critical processes. For the successful implementation of Industry 4.0 initiatives, firms must possess a comprehensive understanding of the processes they want to evaluate, enhance, and mechanize. To conduct a thorough assessment of project requirements, it is essential to meticulously evaluate factors such as data, connectivity, and reliability within the realm of cybersecurity. Organizations are required to evaluate the requirements for efficiently and proficiently catering to the use case. This evaluation [35] encompasses determining the specific types of data required, identifying the most suitable connectivity options for data collection in the given location and built environment, ascertaining the level of reliability and redundancy needed, and devising optimal strategies for integrating cybersecurity and data privacy measures from the outset. To facilitate this process, organizations are required to engage in the practice of process mapping, whereby they analyze and delineate the many elements, such as components, task ownership, important stakeholders, and timescales, that comprise their operational processes.

Companies facilitate effective project planning [36] by deploying resources based on individual use cases. This approach enables the implementation of best practices tailored to each use case, hence enhancing the likelihood of project success and timely completion. Furthermore, the excessive amount of data often poses a challenge for data professionals and analysts, as it may be overwhelming. By limiting the data to just what is essential and trustworthy, the process of developing AI models is streamlined, noise is minimized, and accuracy is enhanced. The process of cloudification refers to the migration of data and applications from local infrastructure to cloud-based platforms. This transition allows for increased scalability, flexibility, and accessibility of resources. Normalization of data is a technique used to utilize Application Programming Interfaces (APIs) for Inter-system Communication. Cloudification [36] refers to the process of transforming applications, data storage, and compute cycles to use the benefits offered by cloud computing. Cloud-based systems play a crucial role in facilitating the harmonization of business methods and plans across diverse geographical locations. This enables the implementation of centralized strategies and the realization of economies of scale concerning Industry 4.0 deployments. Additionally, cloud-based systems simplify the incorporation and centralization of data, further enhancing operational efficiency. Data normalization plays a crucial role in facilitating the automation of integration between cloud-based platforms and diverse infrastructure, including the latest Industry 4.0 technology.

With the growing digitalization of sectors, there is an imperative need for firms to place significant importance on cybersecurity. The use of interconnected operational technologies has exposed organizations to operational risks as a result of cyberattacks [37]. Furthermore, the apprehension about security issues has impeded the transition of several companies to cloud computing. Organizations need to thoroughly evaluate their cloud strategy, including private cloud and hybrid models as deemed suitable, while also implementing optimal networking infrastructure and deploying cybersecurity measures for Operational Technology (OT) and Internet of Things (IoT). The use of best practices in network infrastructure design and the incorporation of software-defined networking ideas are of utmost importance. Organizations can implement network traffic segregation as a means of safeguarding and overseeing potentially vulnerable Internet of Things (IoT) devices.

The inception, implementation, and utilization of novel technologies [38] are fundamentally rooted in human agents and procedural frameworks. Numerous deployments have encountered obstacles due to firms' failure to diligently adhere to optimal organizational practices. This entails the implementation of centralized and coordinated strategies that are founded upon a comprehensive understanding of business processes and project needs. In an optimal framework, stakeholders exhibit congruence, communication is unambiguous, and initiatives supply value to the organization. Implementing a management strategy aimed at mitigating individuals' and teams' reluctance to change by enhancing their knowledge of the use of technology and its applications, while also ensuring that employees see cutting-edge technology as an opportunity rather than a challenge.

Vendors [39] play an essential role in the deployment of Industry 4.0 technologies. The most effective suppliers are collaborative partners, actively contributing to the success of their customers. Nevertheless, some obstacles arise when attempting to coordinate several providers and their respective solutions. These issues include a dearth of open interconnectivity and the need for sustained customer service over an extended period. To address these challenges, firms have sought assistance from primary suppliers and system integrators, therefore enhancing their internal capacities. They have also sought to use open systems and platforms, fostering tight collaboration with vendors to facilitate solution development and provide sustained customer support. Variations in Roadmaps and Extended Support Organizations may want meticulously customized solutions that optimally align with their specific needs. Nevertheless, it is worth noting that these proposed resolutions may not always align with the strategic plans outlined by suppliers. Smaller suppliers possess a greater degree of agility, hence enabling them to effectively cater to specific and unique requirements. However, it is important to note that organizations may require extended assistance from the solution provider, and this reliance might be jeopardized in the event of the vendor's failure.

14.5 Key Factors in Addressing Obstacles and Hindrances

1. Developing a comprehensive digital transformation strategy for the next 5 to 10 years
To effectively adopt Industry 4.0 technologies, companies need to consolidate their strategies and develop comprehensive long-term plans spanning a minimum of 5 to 10 years to prepare for the integration of novel technology. The abrupt alteration of a system has the potential to disrupt its functioning, but a gradual implementation of change may greatly enhance the system's performance.

2. Invest wisely in digitalization and the Industrial Revolution 4.0 [40, 44, 45]
Hardware and resources, network infrastructure, cloud vs. on-premise data centers, data architectural capabilities, vendor partnerships, and in-house team skills will all vary from company to company. In certain cases, upgrading or replacing existing skills and assets may be necessary to support technological ambitions. This may take place over time to accommodate separate rollouts rather than all at once [41]. Therefore, a progressive allocation of budgetary resources is essential for the rollout and implementation of digitalization and Industry 4.0.

3. Plan your projects according to industry standards and best practices
Companies should carefully consider their application cases and the resources they will need to adopt Industry 4.0 technologies. To accomplish this goal, it may be necessary to implement specialized sensors for data collection [42, 46, 48]; to upgrade to a network that can handle the required bandwidth, latency, dependability, and scalability; or to switch to a cloud-based or hybrid architecture. The wisest course of action for businesses is to test out the waters with pilot projects before investing in a wide-scale rollout of a new technology.

4. Integrate cybersecurity procedures at the offset
Cybersecurity policy and best practices should be thoroughly considered before a company commits to installing any kind of computer system or even laying the groundwork [43, 47–50]. Cyber attack avenues for

businesses are expanding as operational systems become more and more Internet-connected. Planning for cybersecurity early on in a project's development is preferable to tackling it as a last-minute resort.

14.6 Conclusion

Data that have been digitized eliminates delays caused by distance and allows for faster, more convenient access through remote servers in the cloud. The ease of Digital transportation with the new age cutting edge technologies like Blockchain and IIoT, Fog Computing combined with Cyber security can ensure unparalleled security. Digitization that led to digitalization improves sustainability and back up. Innovations and increased international competitiveness of businesses have resulted from the digitalization of the industry or "Industry 4.0." Understanding the need to adopt the Industry 4.0 approach led to insights into the internal and external organization of enterprises, and in particular the production, and dissemination of information. The deployment in a phased manner with a Road map for 5 to 10 years attached with the manpower empowerment coupled with the shift toward digital technology has reaped the benefits in multifold. In this context, we have given an insight review of advanced digital manufacturing technology solutions used in Industry 4.0 with knowledge management as the main perspective.

References

1. De Boer, E., Giraud, Y., Swan, D., CEO dialogue: perspectives on productivity and sustainability. McKinsey & Company. 2021, November 3. https://www.mckinsey.com/capabilities/operations/our-insights/ceo-dialogue-perspectives-on-productivity-and-sustainability#/
2. Behrendt, A., de Boer, E., Kasah, T., Koerber, B., Mohr, N., Richter, G., A manufacturer's guide to scaling industrial IoT, February 5, 2021. https://www.toobler.com/blog/manufacturers-guide-to-scaling-industrial-iot
3. Frank, A.G., Dalenogare, L.S., Ayala, N.F., Industry 4.0 technologies: implementation patterns in manufacturing companies. *Int. J. Prod. Econ.*, 210, 15–26, 2019.
4. Bongomin, O., GilibraysOcen, G., OyondiNganyi, E., Musinguzi, A., Omara, T., Exponential disruptive technologies and the required skills of industry 4.0. *J. Eng.*, 2020, 1–17, 2020.
5. Betti, F., de Boer, E., Giraud, Y., Lighthouses unlock sustainability through 4IR technologies, September 27, 2021, https://www.

mckinsey.com/capabilities/operations/our-insights/lighthouses-unlock-sustainability-through-4ir-technologies.

6. Bauer, W., Schuler, S., Hornung, T., Decker, J., Development of a procedure model for human-centered industry 4.0 projects. *Proc. Manuf.*, 39, 877–885, 2019.
7. Bongomin, O., Nganyi, E.O., Abswaidi, M.R., Hitiyise, E., Tumusiime, G., Sustainable and dynamic competitiveness towards technological leadership of industry 4.0: Implications for East african community. *J. Eng.*, 2020, 1–22, 2020.
8. Rainnie, A. and Dean, M., Industry 4.0 and the future of quality work in the global digital economy. *Labour Ind.*, 30, 1, 16–33, 2020.
9. Ghobakhloo, M., Industry 4.0, digitization, and opportunities for sustainability. *J. Cleaner Prod.*, 30, 2019.
10. Yıldız, T., Examining the concept of industry 4.0 studies using text mining and scientific mapping method. *Proc. Comput. Sci.*, 158, 498–507, 2019, https://doi.org/10.1016/j.procs.2019.09.081.
11. Hidayatno, A., Destyanto, A.R., Hulu, C.A., Industry 4.0 technology implementation impact to industrial sustainable energy in Indonesia: a model conceptualization. *Energy Proc.*, 156, 227–233, 2019, https://doi.org/10.1016/j.egypro.2018.11.133.
12. Mo, E., Centea, D., Singh, I., Wanyama, T., SEPT learning factory for industry 4.0 education and applied research. *Proc. Manuf.*, 23, 249–254, 2018, http://dx.doi.org/10.1016/j.promfg.2018.04.025.
13. Salah, B., Abidi, M.H., Mian, S.H., Krid, M., Alkhalefah, H., Abdo, A., Virtual reality-based engineering education to enhance manufacturing sustainability in industry 4.0. *Sustainability*, 11, 1477, 2019, https://doi.org/10.3390/su11051477.
14. Li, Q., Wang, F., Liu, Y., Industrial big data for internet of things-driven manufacturing. *IEEE Trans. Ind. Inf.*, 15, 6, 3837–3844, 2019, https://doi.org/10.1016/j.jestch.2021.06.001.
15. Dai, H.-N., Wang, H., Xu, G., Wan, J., Imran, M., Dai, H.-N., Xu, G., Big Data Analytics for Manufacturing Internet of Things: Opportunities, Challenges and Enabling Technologies. *Enterprise Inform. Syst.*, 14, 2019. 10.1080/17517575.2019.1633689
16. Kusiak, A., The digital twin paradigm for future manufacturing systems. *CIRP J. Manuf. Sci. Technol.*, 22, 20–27, 2018.
17. Wang, S., Ren, M., Wei, Z., Chen, M., Data-driven intelligent manufacturing: Literature review and future trends. *J. Manuf. Syst.*, 56, 221–235, 2020.
18. Liao, Y., Luo, J., Hu, Z., A survey of data-driven smart manufacturing. *J. Ind. Inf. Integr.*, 14, 1–10, 2020.
19. Behera, H.S., Pattnaik, M., Sahoo, S., A comprehensive study on the applications of robotics in manufacturing industry. *Int. J. Adv. Intell. Paradigms*, 15, 3/4, 295–311, 2020.
20. Balasubramanian, S. and Scholar II, Research, Integration of Artificial Intelligence in the Manufacturing Sector: A Systematic Review of Applications and Implications. *Int. J. Prod. Technol. Manage.*, 14, 1–11, 2023.

21. Shojaeinasab, A., Charter, T., Jalayer, M., Khadivi, M., Ogunfowora, O., Raiyani, N., Yaghoubi, M., Najjaran, H., Intelligent manufacturing execution systems: A systematic review. *J. Manuf. Syst.*, 62, 503–522, 2022
22. Wang, X., Hu, H., Wang, Y., Wang, Z., IoT Real-Time Production Monitoring and Automated Process Transformation in Smart Manufacturing. *J. Org. End User Comput.*, 36, 1–25, 2024.
23. Kagermann, H., Wahlster, W., Helbig, J., Recommendations for implementing the strategic initiative INDUSTRIE 4.0. Final report of the Industrie 4.0 working group, National Academy of Science and Engineering, 2013, https://en.acatech.de/publication/recommendations-for-implementing-the-strategic-initiative-industrie-4-0-final-report-of-the-industrie-4-0-working-group/.
24. Md. Tota, M., Erdei-Gally, S., Dancs, A., Fekete-Farkas, M., A Systematic Review of Industry 4.0 Technology on Workforce Employability and Skills: Driving Success Factors and Challenges in South Asia. *Economies.*, 12, 2, 35, 2024. https://doi.org/10.3390/economies12020035
25. Bhatt, G.D., Knowledge management in organizations: Examining the interaction between technologies, techniques, and people. *J. Knowl. Manage.*, 5, 1, 68–75, 2001, https://doi.org/10.1108/13673270110384419.
26. Dalkir, K., *Knowledge management in theory and practice*, Routledge, 2011, https://www.routledge.com/Knowledge-Management-in-Theory-and-Practice/Dalkir/p/book/9780750678643.
27. Darroch, J., Knowledge management, innovation, and firm performance. *J. Knowl. Manage.*, 9, 3, 101–115, 2005, https://doi.org/10.1108/13673270510602809.
28. Galati, F. and Bigliardi, B., Industry 4.0: emerging themes and future research avenues using a text mining approach. *Comput. Ind.*, 109, 100–113, 2019, https://doi.org/10.1016/j.compind.2019.04.018.
29. Ruppert, T., Jaskó, S., Holczinger, T., Abonyi, J., Enabling technologies for operator 4.0: a survey. *Appl. Sci.*, 8, 1650, 1, 2018, https://doi.org/10.3390/app8091650.
30. Zolotová, I., Papcun, P., Kajáti, E., Miškuf, M., Mocnej, J., "Smart and cognitive solutions for operator 4.0: laboratory H-CPPS case studies,". *Comput. Ind. Eng.*, 8, 2018.
31. Romero, D., Stahre, J., Taisch, M., The Operator 4.0: towards socially sustainable factories of the future. *Comput. Ind. Eng.*, 139, 1–5, 2019.
32. Jasiulewicz, M. and Gola, A., Maintenance 4.0 technologies for sustainable manufacturing-an overview. *IFAC-PapersOnLine*, 52, 10, 91–96, 2019, https://doi.org/10.1016/j.ifacol.2019.10.005.
33. Haarman, M., Mulders, M., Vassiliadis, C., Predictive maintenance 4.0: Predict the unpredictable, 2017.
34. Bal, H. and Erkan, Ç., Industry 4.0 and competitiveness. *Proc. Comput. Sci.*, 158, 625–631, 2019.

35. Beier, G., Ullrich, A., Niehoff, S., Reißig, M., Habich, M., Industry 4.0: how it is defined from a sociotechnical perspective and how much sustainability it includes-A literature review. *J. Cleaner Prod.*, 259, 1–12, 2020.
36. Eynard, B. and Cherfi, Z., Digital and organizational transformation of industrial systems. *Comput. Ind. Eng.*, 139, 1, 2020.
37. Meyer, U., The emergence of an envisioned future. Sensemaking in the case of "Industrie 4.0" in Germany. *Futures*, 109, 130–141, 2019, https://doi.org/10.1016/j.futures.2019.03.001.
38. Klingenberg, C.O., Antônio, M., Borges, V., "Industry 4.0 as a data-driven paradigm: a systematic literature review on technologies,". *J. Manuf. Technol. Manage.*, 30, 2019, https://woutex-paperless.de/?gad_source=1&gclid=C-j0KCQjwxeyxBhC7ARIsAC7dS3-CYs0hrqvkdSWVoLuyeC-6D3NK4InLsv-fUwhSxM4KwxmJAAW7WqdMaArddEALw_wcB.
39. Büchi, G., Cugno, M., Castagnoli, R., Smart factory performance and Industry 4.0. *Technol. Forecast. Soc. Change*, 150, 1–10, 2020, https://doi.org/10.1016/j.techfore.2019.119790.
40. Rosin, F., Forget, P., Lamouri, S., Pellerin, R., Impacts of industry 4.0 technologies on lean principles. *Int. J. Prod. Res.*, 58, 6, 1644–1661, 2020.
41. Luthra, S., Kumar, A., Zavadskas, E.K., Mangla, S.K., Garza-Reyes, J.A., Industry 4.0 as an enabler of sustainability diffusion in supply chain: An analysis of influential strength of drivers in an emerging economy. *Int. J. Prod. Res.*, 58, 5, 1505–1521, 2020, https://ideas.repec.org/a/taf/tprsxx/v58y2020i5p1505-1521.html.
42. Machado, C.G. and Ribeiro da Silva, E.H.D., Sustainable manufacturing in Industry 4.0: An emerging research agenda. *Int. J. Prod. Res.*, 58, 5, 1462–1484, 2020.
43. Winroth, B., Bettayeb, B., Sahnoun, M.H., Duval, F., Towards predicting system disruption in industry 4.0: Machine learning-based approach. *Proc. Comput. Sci.*, 151, 667–674, 2019.
44. Kaiser, J., Hawkridge, G., Leitoo, P., A review of reference architectures for digital manufacturing: Classification, applicability and open issues. *Comput. Ind.*, 149, 2023.
45. Kusiak, A., Predictive models in digital manufacturing: research, applications, and future outlook. *Int. J. Prod. Res.*, 61, 17, 6052–6062, 2023, https://ideas.repec.org/a/taf/tprsxx/v61y2023i17p6052-6062.html.
46. Santos, R., Eduordo, S., Fernando, Selection of Manufacturing Technologies in the Context of Digital Transformation: A Systematic Review. *IEEE Eng. Manage. Rev.*, 51, 1, 143–163, 2023.
47. Raj, A., Dwivedi, G., Sharma, A., Lopes de Sousa Jabbour, A.B., Rajak, S., Barriers to the adoption of industry 4.0 technologies in the manufacturing sector: An inter-country comparative perspective. *Int. J. Prod. Econ.*, 224, 2022.
48. Gomaa, M., Jabi, W., Soebarto, V., Xie, Y.M., Digital manufacturing for earth construction: A critical review. *J. Cleaner Prod.*, 338, 2022, https://researchrepository.rmit.edu.au/esploro/outputs/9922129550901341.

49. Sekaran, S.C., Yap, H.J., Musa, S.N., Liew, K.E., Tan, C.H., Aman, A., The implementation of virtual reality in digital factory—a comprehensive review. *Int. J. Adv. Manuf. Technol.*, 115, 1349–1366, 2021.
50. Gomaa, M., Schade, S., Bao, D.W., Xie, Y.M., Automation in rammed earth construction for industry 4.0: Precedent work, current progress and future prospect. *J. Cleaner Prod.*, 342, 2023.

15

Enhancing Students' Learning Achievement, 21st-Century Skills, and Self-Regulation Skills—Knowledge Management and Education 4.0 Perspective

Maria Cindy F. Cardona[1], Amelia T. Buan[2], Ellen D. Inutan[2] and Rajendra Kumar[3]*

[1]*Iligan City National School of Fisheries, Iligan City, Philippines*
[2]*MSU—Iligan Institute of Technology, Iligan City, Philippines*
[3]*School of Engineering and Technology, Sharda University, Greater Noida, India*

Abstract

STEM at Home Activities (SAHA) are known as educational engagement activities and are designed for promoting learning in the areas of Science, Technology, Engineering, and Mathematics (abbreviated as STEM) within the comfort and flexibility at one's home. This chapter aims to determine the effect of SAHA on students' achievement in 21st-century skills, and self-regulation skills using knowledge management (KM) in Education 4.0 perspectives. Education sector is one of the key area in Industry Revolution 4.0. In the 21st century, the contribution of knowledge management and education 4.0 has evolved significantly and influenced state-of-the-art changing societal needs. Self-regulation and critical thinking skills are essential for evaluating information's accuracy and relevance. To upgrade the students learning and skills, this study used the Modified Self-Learning Modules (MSLM) approach and the students' performance is compared in all mentioned approaches. Data were collected using achievement tests on chemical reactions and household cleaning products and the Likert scale questionnaires on 21st-century skills and self-regulation skills. The analysis of covariance (ANCOVA) is used for analyzing the data. The findings presented no significant difference in the students' performance for both SAHA and MSLM. Further, the investigation was

**Corresponding author*: rajendra04@gmail.com

Rajendra Kumar, Vishal Jain, Venus C. Ibarra, Corrienna Abdul Talib and Vinay Kukreja (eds.) Knowledge Management and Industry Revolution 4.0, (389–412) © 2024 Scrivener Publishing LLC

used to determine the effect size using Cohen's D. The SAHA (Cohen's D = 0.86 and 0.70) was found to have a more significant effect than MSLM (Cohen's D = 0.42 and 0.58) in terms of achievement within the two tests, respectively. Similarly, in terms of 21st-century skills and self-regulation skills, SAHA (Cohen's D = 0.51 and 0.23) also showed a more significant effect than MSLM (Cohen's D = 0.50 and 0.26). This observed that the STEM at home approach enhanced the students' performance in achieving 21st-century skills, and self-regulation skills compared to MSLM.

Keywords: 21st-century skills, self-regulation skills, STEM, knowledge management, Education 4.0

15.1 Introduction

The country's science education has faced numerous challenges in the science curriculum. Science and technology have profoundly shaped today's global knowledge environment, and efforts have been made to make the curriculum responsive to pedagogical trends [57]. Science education in aims to encourage the students to be curious from an early education [4]. It aims to raise scientifically [78], technologically [13], and environmentally literate and productive society [26].

After the widespread adoption of Education 4.0, many initiatives as a response are taken to the wide gap in learning outcomes due to the corona pandemic. Knowledge management (KM) in the era of Education 4.0 in both human and machine-oriented perspectives is seen as a planned and real-life function including exploring and exploiting the processes. The ability of technology keeping connected to all is leading by increasing flexibility and adaptation in almost all professions. Education 4.0 is similar to adapt the changes in education perspectives specially STEM learning and bringing the use of technology in education by determining what the future students will require.

Many countries worldwide are facing various challenges when it comes to the science education. However, there are widespread concerns about science education's outcomes in schools and universities [34]. Its current arrangements focus on teaching students how science can affect their lives and how to apply scientific knowledge to real-life problems [57]. Practical activities in science classes allow students to connect to see and handle with the scientific ideas that explain their observations. It is very much challenging to make these connections, therefore practical activities making them explicit have a better chance of success [1]. Another problem with learning science in the classroom is that it cannot be applied to real-world situations frequently and learning activities cannot be designed to solve real-life problems [2].

Furthermore, involving students in STEM learning helps them develop 21st-century skills like problem solving, communication, and collaboration. It also entails involving students in the design process, critical to their STEM thinking [40]. A design-based STEM education activity could also allow students to design products in a creative way, allowing them to express their originality and expand their creative thinking [53]. Students who participated in STEM activities had significantly improved 21st-century learning and creativity skills [73]. Many STEM education efforts emphasize in influencing the four Cs of 21st-century skills (creativity, critical thinking, collaboration, and communication). An effective STEM program must include these key pedagogical approaches address the problems [36].

As Karpudewan and Meng [35] mentioned, conducting science activities has improved student problem-solving skills, science process skills, and 21st-century skills. Students should take advantage of this opportunity whenever possible. Educational organizations must strengthen curriculum practices in upgrading, designing, and implementing appropriate lesson content to meet current demands by adopting new instructional approaches [16, 51, 3, 42, 72].

According to Ateş and Eryilmaz [10], interactive engagement methods for students can include hands-on and mind-on activities that do not require specific expensive materials. Additionally, providing scientific projects that students can complete from the comfort of their own homes is an effective way to keep students interested in science [79]. Similarly, hands-on activities were beneficial in learning STEM disciplines, resulting in improved conceptual understanding and self-regulation skills among students [59]. Design thinking is critical for every student to create and possess [41]. Also, according to Arifin and Mahmud's [7] study, the best teaching and learning approaches for STEM integration in education that use design thinking are problem-solving, designing activities, and collaborative learning.

The development of SAHA is explored to address the concern of providing practical hands-on, and engaging science activities, which are given little attention in the current teaching practices of science teachers. Science knowledge and process skills can be developed using modified and enhanced hands-on activities, even at home. With this setup, the researcher is interested in comparing the performance of the students in terms of achievement, 21st-century skills, and self-regulation skills on SAHA with MSLM, which are standard-based learning resource materials.

15.2 Literature Review

The scientific and technological advancements have become important as both the benefits and challenges are faced in globalization and a knowledge-oriented economy in the 21st century. To proceed with this new state of the art highly specialized society, the scholars need to develop their STEM potentials to the next levels from what accepted in the past. An STEM-based curriculum presents real-life situations in helping to the students to learn in better way. Some programs use to integrate multiple classes to observe how fundamentals related to real-life to enlighten a passion for a future career in a STEM. The STEM activities are very much helpful to provide the hands-on and mind-on experience for the students. Making mathematics and Science as a fun and enjoyable can help the students in happy learning [33]. STEM is a curriculum to educate the students in four disciplines namely science, technology, engineering, and mathematics using interdisciplinary way. STEM integrates these four disciplines into a cohesive learning environment related to real-world applications instead of learning these four disciplines as separate and discrete subjects [30].

Creative teaching is vital to engage and motivate the students of all ages to pursue their academic studies, especially in STEM. Many countries need a supply of qualified STEM graduates who can compete globally, creatively for solving and analyzing challenging problems, and also to provide future scientists, engineers, and other professionals. Creating an interactive and integrated environment, helping in teaching–learning process, stimulating creativity is one of the essential elements for ensuring the efficiency of the process [14].

When we talk about STEM or STEM education environments, we explicitly refer to class rooms or universities where conscious and overt efforts are done in coordinating two or more STEM disciplines' learning objectives and learning activities as a standard process. This phenomenon can happen in specific class room where students can carry out multiple learning objectives or in many parallel class rooms where instructors work together by coordinating different learning activities. It is a case when integration is an essential characteristic of the learning environments known as STEM. It is required to facilitate the students with ample opportunities in understanding the issues by enriching, engaging, and powerful experience that can integrate STEM disciplines to prepare the students in addressing the real-life problems [26].

STEM education addresses more than simply academic and economic outcomes in its ideal form. The personal, social, and economic developments require more than the STEM knowledge and skills. According to present practices, the STEM education must develop personal attributes known in the education sector as per requirement of 21st-century skills, soft skills, or general capabilities. This skill is often associated with an inquiry-based pedagogy [71].

Even though the STEM concept is used today, skills developed in students with respect to STEM education are unable to create a required platform. STEM education is generally observed as a general concept to express Science, Mathematics, Technology, and Engineering disciplines at a common platform. It is crucial to develop the skills to emerge through integrating such disciplines with STEM. The STEM skills can be outlined in engineering problem solving, establishing interdisciplinary scenario, engineering design skills, digital competencies, etc. Additionally to integrate the Science, Technology, Engineering, and Mathematics subjects in STEM, the development of STEM skills are equally important [60].

Highlighted in one of the sustainable development goals of education is to raise interdisciplinary thinking capabilities. A study by Becker and Park [15] presented that students achieving the integrated fundamentals of STEM education presented a huge effect sizes, while science achievement presented a medium effect size, while the technology achievement showed a large one. Also, Aurandt *et al.* [80] observed that STEM education has great influence in learning and accomplishing the learning objectives. STEM education forced for improving the education in the early 21st century. International agendas related to advanced STEM education are focusing on globalization. Educationists and policy makers, non-government organizations, business, and industry organizations are emphasizing on urgency of improving STEM skills to meet current and future social and economic needs and challenges [66].

In recent years, the STEM implementation is seen in both developing and developed nations. In developing nations like in India and the Philippines, STEM has been introduced by the government to preserve the teachers. Most teachers in developing nations are much familiar with STEM, but they do not understand how to integrate STEM into the learning practices and move with proper knowledge management. The teachers in many countries need to have a more profound introduction to STEM education. Many teachers understand that STEM is crucial in implementation and it as expected by teachers to use the best-integrated approach in teaching-learning process, where the four components are major concerns.

Thus, the aim to implement the STEM can be realized in the manner like the students have good numerical solving skills, understanding mathematics and Science as a whole, and can apply it in everyday life activities [56].

The introduction of STEM education in public schools in the Philippines is a remarkable move from the national government. It is a critical step towards realizing the importance of STEM in developing and supporting creativity and innovation among Filipino learners [9]. Balanced or an enriched curriculum, and the development of intervention programs that promote students' learning, particularly in Mathematics and Science, to make the performance of the Filipino students compared with international standards must be implemented [81]. The science programs shift from the traditional teaching method to a more innovative exploration to emphasize enhancing students' critical thinking and scientific skills [43]. As per Setiawaty *et al.* [61] study, results showed that applying STEM learning influences the students' science process skills and attitudes. Integrating STEM through project-based learning and skills can increase the quality of education.

Also, guided inquiry combined with STEM effectively enhances students' critical thinking skills [67]. In the K to 12 curriculum, Science is designed to enhance students' learning domains, such as to perform scientific processes and skills, to understand and apply scientific knowledge, and develop scientific attitudes and values [82]. The science-based curricula promote a strong relationship between Science and Technology, where approaches are based on sound educational pedagogy such as thinking-based learning [20].

STEM education also fosters creativity, critical thinking, problem-solving abilities, innovative skills, and design thinking abilities [5]. A study conducted by Hsaio *et al.* [31] merged design thinking in STEM activity to guide instruction. The results revealed that it did not only help the students in integrating the related knowledge of the subject they learned and enhanced their practical skills and ways of thinking. Moreover, Baran [12] revealed that students value the hands-on nature of STEM activities since it allows them in designing and participating in design challenges [18] to foster creative thinking and innovation [79], and improving communication and collaboration skills [40]. Though abundant in education broadly, little research details the use of design thinking as a response to COVID-19 [62].

Moreover, engaging students in STEM learning develop 21st-century capabilities such as problem-solving skills, communications, and collaborative skills. In other words, engaging learners in the design process is the integral part for students to think in the STEM world [40].

The design-based STEM education activities could also allow to students to creatively design products, develop their originality and elaborate their creative thinking [53]. Students who studied STEM activities have significantly higher 21st-century skills on learning and innovation skills in creativity [73]. There is great promise in many STEM education efforts to impact the four Cs (critical thinking, creative thinking, communicating, and collaborating) of 21st century skills. An efficient STEM program can be developed using key pedagogical to that address the crucial elements of the four Cs of 21st century education [36].

The study of Baran *et al.* [12] presented that students valued the hands-on kind of the STEM activities giving them the opportunities in designing artifacts and engaging in design challenges. The study results explored that integrating the STEM activities into beyond school education programs can develop students' interest to pursue STEM related career. Islam and Numan [32] pointed out that hands-on experiments make learners more confident in their schoolwork, especially in science subjects. Since hands-on experience is essential for the effective transfer of practical skills to the learners, practical works such as home experiments kits for distance learning were introduced. Additionally, Reeves and Kimbrough [55] pointed out that kitchen Chemistry experiments involving familiar materials and measurements done in familiar surroundings enhanced students' appreciation of the relevance of chemistry in their lives.

Another study presented that students' achievements on the integrated concepts of STEM education observed large effect sizes. The study of Thahir *et al.* [69] showed that the STEM learning approach had a high impact on the achievements of senior school students compared to the conventional learning approach. In a recent study conducted by Dedetürk *et al.* [23], the findings also revealed that design process-oriented STEM activities positively affected students' achievement.

A study by Sadi and Çakıroğlu [58] on hands-on activities focused on instructions in improving students' science achievements. The instructions within the STEM education were organized following the 5-E learning cyclic model to educate the students [17]. It can enable a student to become critical thinker, able to apply not only what he/she learned, but more importantly, the way of learning, to various real-life activities [29].

Likewise, Chonkaew *et al.* [19] conducted hands-on workshops and tutorials to integrate inquiry-based learning outcomes that can influence students' abilities, thinking skills, etc. By implementing the small lab kit, many students can perform experiments on their own and can develop their thinking processes as they interact with each other in the group.

The term 21st-century education is mainly referring to specific core skills such as collaborative education, digital literacy, critical thinking, and problem-based learning that advocate teaching-learning to help students thrive globally. Hadinugrahaningsih *et al.* [27] claimed in their study that integrating STEM can be implemented for developing critical thinking, communications, motivation, creative skills, etc. in disciplined way. The educationists face the challenges of STEAM integration within the curriculum to empower the students, and manage teaching with respect to time resources. It is also the challenge of providing a collaborative learning experience to students who are inclined to learn and work independently and relate to chemistry concepts.

The 4Cs can be integrated into STEM learning in early phase. A survey to develop a 4C performance model that can measure parameters in STEM-based education in schools and universities. The survey results led to the development of mechanisms to assess student performance. The 4C performance model can also be used in performance assessment that measures 21st-century competencies in STEM education [48]. Distance learning mode of education can provide an immense opportunity for creativity and innovation [22].

The students' creativity has been illustrated in the study of Hanif *et al.* [28], on the students' product making a simple projector. The study results revealed that STEM project-based learning has a good impact on students' creativity. Moreover, according to the study of Thompson [70], teaching creativity using science can be a good learning motivation.

Additionally, outcome-based learning is a motivating learning approach that is essential for developing the creative thinking skills necessary to master the 21st-century skills of the learners [24]. The study of Obaydullah *et al.* [49] also pointed out that outcome-based science education is a practical approach to developing the curriculum with learning practices focusing on the students rather than the teacher. Furthermore, many teachers were shown to successfully integrate 21st-century skills into their lessons by implementing group projects, which require outputs from the learners [63].

Allowing students to perform activities that involve real-world problems, such as in STEM activities, increases students' conceptual understanding and enhances their 21st-century skills on learning and innovation skills in creativity [73] and critical thinking skills [67]. Also, the result of the study conducted by Hsaio *et al.* [31], which merged design thinking in a STEM activity, revealed that it did not only help the students in integrating the related skills in the area they earned but also enhancing their practical skills and ways of thinking. STEM activities foster creativity, critical thinking, problem-solving abilities, innovative skills, and design thinking abilities in a distance learning modality [5]. The extent of integrating critical thinking skills in science learning in a blended system is revealed in the study of Prafitasari *et al.* [54].

Daradoumis *et al.* [21] further investigated that learning environment in collaborations are advantageous to all students who are grappling with an excess of tasks and other things to do in distance learning. Strauß and Rummel [64] claimed that students greatly benefit from well-designed collaborative learning activities. Learning science in interdisciplinary way can be categorized as a viewpoint that is able to integrate two or more disciplines into coherent connections enabling the students to make relevant influences and make meaningful associations [77]. According to the study of Mora-Ruano *et al.* [44], teachers' collaborations are identified as a factor that can influence student performance in positive manner. As per a study by Tytler *et al.* [74], implementation of interdisciplinary tasks can engage students in authentic tasks and innovation. Problem based learning can be seen as the best way to understand the needs of 21st-century skills [52].

A study has been conducted to design a hypothetical model of the inquiry-based STEM learning strategies that can systematically guide academia to create appropriate learning activities for 21st-century skills. The results of the study observed that all of the teachers apprehended the importance of STEM in education and career perspective, and 21st-century challenges [8]. As stipulated by Khalil and Osman [38], strengthening STEM education is much helpful to students in acquiring knowledge and skills required to compete in work-life in the future.

Similarly, in a study conducted by Wan Husin [75], students' changes in 21st-century skills after participating in a STEM education program were identified. This study revealed that the student's level of 21st-century skills amplified, and the growth was statistically significant. As outcome of this study, it was evident that the applications of Problem-Based Learning in STEM education programs could help students to enhance their 21st-century skills by learning real-world problems based on reliable and honest life experience through project assignments. In their study, Yavuz *et al.* [76] mentioned that the effect of STEM application on the 21st-century STEM approach positively contributed to 21st-century skills. The interviews also revealed that the students enjoyed using the STEM approach, increased communication within the group, and encouraged the student to research and think.

The demand of 21st-century skills expects the students to have the ability and necessary skills on critical thinking rather content-oriented. A study by Onsee and Nuangchalerm [50] aimed to enhance the critical thinking and learning achievement of grade 10 students through inquiry-based STEM learning. The result presented that students learning through inquiry-based STEM learning were able to increase their critical thinking to meet the criterion. However, qualitative data analysis observed that they need more variations to learn approaches and STEM education. Nevertheless, the critical thinking of students was continually improved. They focused on the lesson by making connections between prior knowledge and new experiences systematically and critically designed.

By emphasizing on students' achievements in 21st-century skills, an instrument was designed to assess these constructs to be a useful measure to any educational program looking for promoting these skills. A study was conducted on 21st-century skills instruments to measure achievements, skills self-reporting instruments for measuring students' assessment in terms of their creativity, critical thinking, communications, and collaborations. In addition, the study pursued identification of the underlying relationships between the measured variables [37]. The key challenges in this new era in science and technology require 21st-century skills to be implemented at all the level. Thus, the traditional way of teaching is no longer appropriated to be applied by instructors [68].

The pandemic has opened new opportunities for educational reform; one of the reforms is encouraging students to take an active role in their learning, particularly academic self-regulation. According to Mustajab [47], self-regulated learners take responsibility for their learning activities and assume independence to improve their performance. Murphy [45] found that the teaching/learning materials bear a large part of the responsibility for developing self-regulated learners. As a result, scaffolding is effective in developing self-control [12]. Furthermore, because the learning environment in which the learning process occurs has a significant impact on learner autonomy, innovative learner-centered methods should be widely used [25]. Barak *et al.* [11] identified self-regulation skills necessary for distance and online learning. The study's findings indicated that students in online education were more aware of mastering learning and information processing strategies than on-campus students.

The education policy makers need to pay high attention to young students' to train for strategies for increasing their abilities to self-motivate their learning in online education [65]. A student as a self-motivated learner can plan to learn, choose and use suitable learning model independently and effectively by monitoring learning feedback [6, 46, 67].

15.3 Methodology

15.3.1 The Model

The proposed model uses the bast practices of Education 4.0 system and knowledge. Creative education in Education 4.0 is initiated with raw data to move to information for transforming it into knowledge and finally apply wisdom in the future as illustrated in Figure 15.1.

The Figure 15.2 shows how knowledge management works with creative education. One key barrier is quality learning. Fundamental innovations in primary and secondary learning has remained limited.

A standard pretest–posttest two-group design and posttest-only control design are used to assess whether taking the pretest influences scores on the subsequent posttest. This study utilized the Solomon Four-Group research design, which provided feedback on the designed SAHA and MSLM.

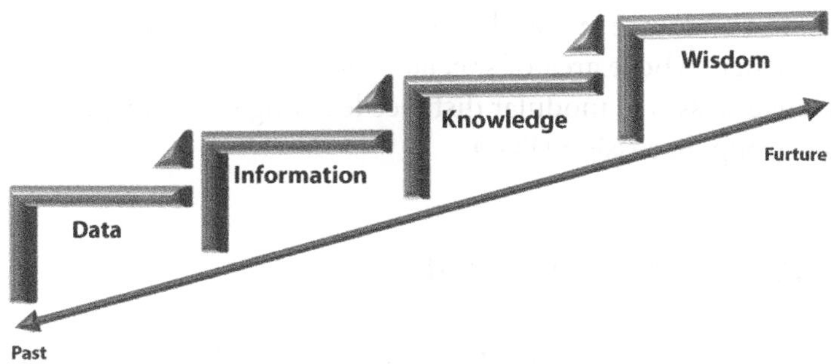

Figure 15.1 Creative education.

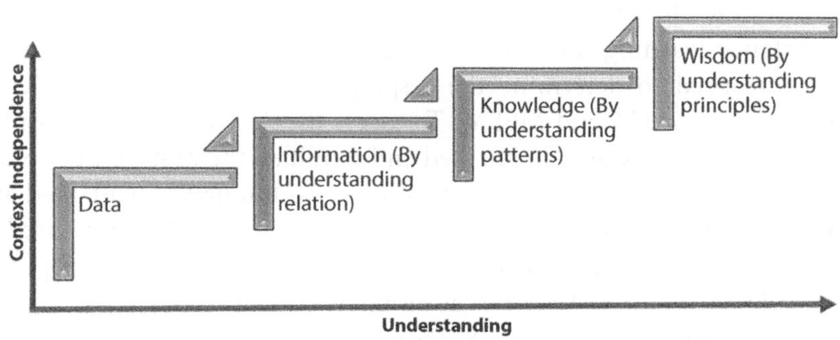

Figure 15.2 Data–information–knowledge–wisdom hierarchy in terms of knowledge management.

The permutations of tested and isolated groups with treating and controlling groups allowed the researcher ensuring confounding variables and extraneous factors not to influencing the analysis. Also, using this design would minimize internal and external validity threats and control the reactive effects of the pretest.

15.4 Participants

A total of sixty-eight (68) Grade 11 students voluntarily participated as respondents in this study. These students were enrolled in any of the two specializations under the Technical Vocational Livelihood (TVL) Track, namely: Tourism 1 (Cookery, Bread and Pastry, and Food and Beverages Services) and Tourism 2 (Housekeeping, Events Management Services, and Food Processing). This study utilized four groups of students, where each group consisted of 17 members who were randomly chosen from Tourism 1 and Tourism 2 sections. The respondents took the pretest, posttest, and retention test and were exposed to SAHA and MSLM. Moreover, the eight science teachers whose area of specialization include biosciences are handling science classes in modular distance learning modality participated in the focus group discussion (FGD).

15.5 Research Instruments

This study utilized the different research instruments during its data gathering. An FGD was conducted for teachers and students who served as respondents to the study. The teachers' FGD investigated the teaching practices of science teachers in a modular distance learning modality. Likewise, the students' FGD centered on their learning experiences in the distance learning modality. Also, the researcher-made achievement tests were used to determine the respondents' prior knowledge before implementing SAHA and MSLM. To assess the 21st-century skills of the respondents under study, an adapted and modified the 21st Century Skills Scale from Kelley and others [36] was used. Additionally, an adapted and modified Self-Regulation Skill Scale from Kocdar *et al.* [39] was used to determine the self-regulation skill of the participants. For the development of the STEM at Home Activities as an instructional resource, an adapted evaluation rubric from Vivayic [82] was used.

15.6 Data Collection

This study utilized the research study which divided into three phases as follows:

Phase 1: Pre-Development—For exploring the experience of both teachers and students in a distance learning modality, a focus group discussion was done. Eight science teachers participated in the focus group discussion, which was conducted in physical mode by ensuring that health and safety protocols were followed in the entire duration. This conduct was also audio-recorded with the consent of the participants. Additionally, the audio-recorded sessions of both teachers and students were used for the purpose of analyzing the contents.

Phase 2: Design, Development and Evaluation of SAHA and MSLM—The researcher chose 2 of these topics to be the basis of the SAHA design in terms of content. These topics were chemical reactions and materials and their uses. The emerged themes in FGD of teachers and students were closely examined and incorporated in the design of SAHA pedagogy. Two SAHA designs were "Pickle It Up!" for the topic on factors affecting reaction rate and "Let's Get Mixing!" for the topic on household cleaning products. In context, the SAHA was designed based on the specialization of the participants under the TVL track. Moreover, DepEd Order 31 s. 2020 (Policy Guidelines on Grading and Assessment in the Light of the Basic Education Learning Continuity Plan) emphasized that teachers must collaborate to design and implement performance tasks to integrate two or more skills within and interdisciplinary areas.

The SAHA was designed to integrate the five (5) subject areas such as Food Processing, Cookery, Math, English, and Physical Science. Each of these subjects investigated the different aspects of the integrated performance task Food processing focused on the pickling process itself, including the quality of the pickles as the product. For Math, the appropriate measurement or quantity of ingredients used in the making of pickles was considered. For English, it focused on the well-written text approach of writing in describing the process of pickling. The proper use of cooking tools was the focus of the Cookery skills. Furthermore, science subject dealt with applying the collision theory and the factors affecting reaction rate on the pickling process.

The developed SAHA was evaluated by the different experts who looked into the various aspects of the activities. Four (4) Chemistry education experts evaluated the SAHA in terms of its Chemistry content using the

STEM at Home Activities evaluation tool. The expert evaluators were Chemistry teachers with a teaching experience of at least fifteen (15) years. The SAHA were rated and passed all the criteria in the evaluation tool, thus recommended for implementation. Likewise, two (2) STEM experts evaluated the SAHA regarding STEM skills and applications using the STEM Instructional Resource Evaluation Rubric. These experts were doctorate holders in Science Education and research interests in STEM education. The SAHA was satisfactorily rated with some suggestions for improvement, particularly on the criterion "standard-based." All comments and suggestions were incorporated, hence recommended for implementation.

Similarly, the MSLM were evaluated by Physical Science teachers using the evaluation tool for MSLM. The MSLM was evaluated in terms of activities, content, and application of technology. Based on the rating, the MSLM is ready for implementation.

Phase 3: Implementation—The 21st-century skill and the self-regulation skill questionnaire were also administered before the implementation. The SAHA were implemented one after the other for the two (2) groups of participants. Meanwhile, the other two (2) groups used the modified self-learning modules. Part of the enhancement in the self-learning module is the inclusion of the video lessons for the two topics identified. The implementation duration lasted for one (1) month, including administering the posttests to all participants. The SAHA implementation phase was dubbed as "STEM Camp at Home 2021" since all the activities were done in the comfort of their own homes. In addition, following the IATF health and safety protocols, one (1) group of participants performed the activities in four (4) smaller groups with at most four (4) members each. Hence, there were a total of eight (8) outputs for each SAHA.

Moreover, the posttest was given to determine how the SAHA and MSLM influence students' achievement. Likewise, the 21st-century skills scale and the self-regulation skill questionnaire were also given as posttests. The teachers pre-rated all outputs before conducting the virtual presentation and culmination of the STEM Camp at Home 2021. Experts in food processing and an active member of women's organizations in the barangay were present during the virtual presentation to give feedback on the quality of the products that each group had submitted. Three (3) weeks after implementing SAHA and MSLM, a retention test was administered to all participants to determine which competencies were mastered and which concepts were retained.

15.7 Data Analysis

Following the Solomon Four-Group design, only two groups were administered with the researcher-made tests—one for factors affecting reaction rate and one for household cleaning products. The prior knowledge of the participants was determined through the scores in the conducted pretests. The scores were then tabulated and analyzed. First, the descriptive statistics such as mean, standard deviation, and variance were computed. Further, to determine the achievement of the participants, posttests were given. To determine if there is a significant difference between the scores in the pretests and posttests, an independent t-test was computed using statistical software. Analysis of variance was also used to determine if the SAHA and MSLM had a significant effect on the students' achievement.

The profile of the volunteers for 21st-century and self-regulation skills was determined using the Likert scale questionnaires. To determine the desired important difference between the posttest scores of groups with no pretest and the groups with pretest and the substantial difference in the posttest score of SAHA groups with pretest and no pretest, the analysis of covariance (ANCOVA) was used to analyze the data. In addition, analysis of variance (ANOVA) was determined if the SAHA and the MSLM had a significant effect on 21st-century skills and self-regulation skills.

15.8 Results and Discussion

15.8.1 Performance of Students in Achievement Tests

The researchers found that the SAHA had a large effect (Cohen's D = 0.86, 0.79) on the students' performance in the achievement tests compared to MSLM with a small effect (Cohen's D = 0.42, 0.58) on both factors affecting

Table 15.1 ANCOVA results on FRR and HCP posttest scores.

	MS		**df**		**F statistic**		**p-value**	
Source	**FRR**	**HCP**	**FRR**	**HCP**	**FRR**	**HCP**	**FRR**	**HCP**
Treatment (SAHA or module)	6.267	5.559	1	1	1.283	0.909	0.266	0.338
Error	4.884	6.150	31	31				

Reaction Rate (FRR) activity and Household Cleaning Products (HCP) activity as shown in Table 15.1.

The results in Table 15.1 imply that allowing students to perform activities that involve real-world problems positively affects their achievement. This result is supported by the findings of Thahir *et al.* [39] that the STEM learning approach had a high impact on the achievement of senior high school students compared to the conventional learning approach. In a recent study conducted by Dedetürk, Kırmızıgül, and Kaya [13], the findings also coincide with the results of the present study in the sense that design process-oriented STEM activities had a more positive effect on students' achievement.

15.8.2 Performance of Students in Terms of the 21st-Century Skills and Self-Regulation Skills

The researchers found that the SAHA had a medium effect (Cohen's D = 0.51), while the MSLM had a negligible impact (Cohen's D = 0.23) on the students' performance in terms of 21st-century skills (21st CS). Similarly, in terms of self-regulation skills (SRS), SAHA also had a medium effect (Cohen's D = 0.50) while MSLM had a negligible effect (Cohen's D = 0.26), as shown in Table 15.2.

These results in Table 15.2 imply that allowing students to perform activities that involve real-world problems, such as STEM activities, does not only increase students' conceptual understanding but also enhances their 21st-century skills in learning and innovation skills in creativity [73] as well as critical thinking skills [65]. Also, the result of the study conducted by Hsaio *et al.* [31], which merged design thinking in a STEM activity, revealed that it did not only help the students integrate the related

Table 15.2 ANCOVA results on 21st CS and SRS posttest scores.

	MS		Df		F statistic		p-value	
Source	**21st CS**	**SRS**	**21st CS**	**SRS**	**21st CS**	**SRS**	**21st CS**	**SRS**
Treatment (SAHA or module)	8.205	587.246	1	1	0.086	1.997	0.771	0.168
Error	95.400	294.114	31	31				

knowledge of the subject they learned but also enhanced their practical skills and ways of thinking. Additionally, STEM activities foster creativity, critical thinking, problem-solving abilities, innovative skills, and design thinking in a distance learning modality [5]. Furthermore, the implementation of the STEM approach in distance learning also improved the self-regulation skill of students in small effect based on the results of the present study. This suggests that when students are given a venue to take the responsibilities of their own learning through the conduct of practical and relevant activities, they learn how to plan and manage the tasks and set goals, thereby regulating themselves to become autonomous learners.

The results shown above are attributed to both SAHA and MSLM's elements. The SAHA is characterized by utilizing a transdisciplinary approach for the conduct of the performance tasks. In addition, the inclusion of practical hands-on activities using simple and readily available materials to develop the desired output is another feature that contributed to its effect on the students' performance. Similarly, the MSLM was enhanced to provide appropriate content and activities compared with the SAHA. Both SAHA and MSLM provided the opportunity for students to learn science in the comfort of their homes.

15.9 Conclusion

Based on the summary of findings, the following conclusions are drawn from the study: the developed SAHA and MSLM are considered potential approaches in science distance learning, as shown in the significant improvement of learners' achievement, 21st-century skills, and self-regulation skills. Teachers appreciate these approaches since assessing learners' performance is based on authentic tasks. On the other hand, the students also find these approaches advantageous since learning science concepts is made possible even at a distance through meaningful and engaging activities. Since the developed SAHA and the modified SLM showed a significant increase in the performance of the learners in terms of conceptual understanding, 21st-century skills, and self-regulation skills, these approaches can be replicated for other learning competencies in different grade levels to determine their viability as flexible approaches of teaching science in the distance learning across levels.

References

1. Abrahams, I. and Millar, R., Does practical work? A study of the effectiveness of practical work as a teaching and learning method in school science. *Int. J. Sci. Educ.*, 30, 14, 1945–1969, 2008.
2. Acat, M.B., Anilan, H., Anagun, S.S., The problems encountered in designing constructivist learning environments in science education and practical suggestions. *TOJET: Turk. Online J. Educ. Technol.*, *9*, 2, 212–220, 2010, http://www.doi.org/10.33902/JPSP.%202020261309.
3. Adnan, M. and Anwar, K., Online learning amid the COVID-19 pandemic: Students' Perspectives. *J. P. S. P.*, *2*, 1, 45–51, 2020, http://www.doi.org/10.33902/JPSP.%202020261309.
4. Ambag, R., Teaching science in the Philippines: Why (and how) we can do better, 2018, https://www.flipscience.ph/news/features-news/features/teaching-science-philippines/.
5. Alashwal, M., Design thinking in STEM education: A Review. *Int. Res. High. Educ.*, *5*, 1, 2020, https://doi.org/10.5430/irhe.v5n1p18.
6. Ambreen, M., Haqdad, A., Saleem, W.A., Fostering self-regulated learning through distance education: A case study of M. Phil secondary teacher education program of Allama Iqbal Open University. *Turk. Online J. Distance Educ.*, 17, 3, 120–135, 2016, https://eric.ed.gov/?id=EJ1106363.
7. Arifin, N.R. and Mahmud, S.N.D., A systematic literature review of design thinking application in STEM integration. *Creat. Educ.*, *12*, 7, 1558–1571, 2021, DOI: 10.4236/ce.2021.127118.
8. Ariyani, F., Achmad, A., Nurulsari, N., Designing an inquiry-based STEM learning strategy as a powerful alternative solution to enhance students' 21st-century Skills: A Preliminary Research. *J. Phys.: Conf. Ser.*, 1155, 1, 012087, 2019, February, IOP Publishing, doi: 10.1088/1742-6596/1155/1/012087.
9. Renzo, J.L.R., Clarisse, Y.D.G., Danilo, V.R.J., Pursuing STEM Careers: Perspectives of Senior High School Students, Participatory Educational Research (PER), vol. 7, no. 3, pp. 38–58, December 2020.
10. Ateş, Ö. and Eryilmaz, A., Effectiveness of hands-on and minds-on activities on students' achievement and attitudes towards physics, in: *Asia-Pacific Forum on Science Learning and Teaching*, vol. 12, no.1, pp. 1–22, The Education University of Hong Kong, Department of Science and Environmental Studies, 2011, June, https://tinyurl.com/yckp33dd.
11. Barak, M., Hussein-Farraj, R., Dori, Y.J., On-campus or online: Examining self-regulation and cognitive transfer skills in different learning settings. *Int. J. Educ. Technol. High. Educ.*, *13*, 1, 1–18, 2016, https://tinyurl.com/4nv5peca.
12. Baran, E., Bilici, S.C., Mesutoglu, C., Ocak, C., Moving STEM beyond schools: Students' perceptions about an out-of-school STEM education program. *Int. J. Educ. Math. Sci. Technol.*, *4*, 1, 9–19, 2016.

13. Barnes, J.L., Producing a technologically literate citizen: A curriculum model. *Bull. Sci. Technol. Soc*, *8*, 5, 483–489, 1988, https://journals.sagepub.com/doi/10.1177/027046768800800504.
14. Barry, D.M., Kanematsu, H., Nakahira, K., Ogawa, N., Virtual workshop for creative teaching of STEM courses. *Proc. Comput. Sci.*, *126*, 927–936, 2018, https://creativecommons.org/licenses/by-nc-nd/4.0/.
15. Becker, K.H. and Park, K., Integrative approaches among science, technology, engineering, and mathematics (STEM) subjects on students' learning: A meta-analysis. *J. STEM Educ.*, *12*, 5, 2011, https://tinyurl.com/39nw9ud3.
16. Cahapay, M.B., Rethinking education in the new normal post-COVID-19 era: A curriculum studies perspective. *Aquademia*, 4, 2, ep20018, 2020, https://doi.org/10.29333/aquademia/8315.
17. Ceylan, S. and Ozdilek, Z., Improving a sample lesson plan for secondary science courses within the STEM education. *Proc. - Soc Behav. Sci.*, *177*, 223–228, 2015, https://tinyurl.com/bd95xva9.
18. Changtong, N., Maneejak, N., Yasri, P., Approaches for implementing STEM (Science, Technology, Engineering & Mathematics) activities among middle school students in Thailand. *Int. J. Educ. Methodol.*, *6*, 1, 185–198, 2020, https://tinyurl.com/3x5s34rj.
19. Chonkaew, P., Sukhummek, B., Faikhamta, C., Development of analytical thinking ability and attitudes towards science learning of grade-11 students through science technology engineering and mathematics (STEM education) in the study of stoichiometry. *Chem. Educ. Res. Pract.*, *17*, 4, 842–861, 2016, http://doi.org/10.1039/x0xx00000x.
20. Cordon, J.M. and Polong, J.D.B., Behind the science literacy of Filipino students at PISA 2018: A Case study in the Philippines' Educational System. *Integr. Sci. Educ. J.*, *1*, 2, 70–76, 2020, http://doi.org/10.37251/isej.v1i2.59.
21. Daradoumis, T., Xhafa, F., Marquès, J.M., A methodological framework for project-based collaborative learning in a networked environment. *Int. J. Contin. Eng. Educ. Life Long Learn.*, 12, 5-6, 389–402, 2002, https://telearn.archives-ouvertes.fr/hal-00190097.
22. Abhijeet, Dhurve, L., Singh, H.C., Maurya, D.K., Lohare, R., Tripathi, S., Kumar, A. and Naga, A., A comprehensive review on role of distance learning program towards the development of global education system. *Curr. Appl. Sci. Technol.*, 42, 48, 23–34, 2023. doi: 10.9734/cjast/2023/v42i484327.
23. Dedetürk, A., Kırmızıgül, A.S., Kaya, H., The effects of Stem activities on 6th grade students' conceptual development of sound. *J. Balt. Sci. Educ.*, *20*, 1, 21, 2021, https://doi.org/10.33225/jbse/21.20.21.
24. Fernando, J.S., Compliance of higher education institutions to outcome-based education for the 21st Century learners. *Int. Multidiscip. Res. J.*, 3, 2, 224–236, June 2021. https://tinyurl.com/4rv28vke.
25. Fotiadou, A., Angelaki, C., Mavroidis, I., Learner autonomy as a factor of the learning process in distance education. *EURODL*, *20*, 1, 95–110, 2017, https://tinyurl.com/yc5raysz.

26. Glancy, A.W. and Moore, T.J., Theoretical foundations for effective STEM learning environments. Purdue University, pp. 1–25, 2013, https://tinyurl.com/bdh2469m.
27. Hadinugrahaningsih, T., Rahmawati, Y., Ridwan, A., Developing 21st century skills in chemistry classrooms: Opportunities and challenges of STEAM integration. *AIP Conf. Proc.*, 1868, 1, 030008, 2017, August, AIP Publishing LLC, https://doi.org/10.1063/1.4995107.
28. Hanif, S., Wijaya, A.F.C., Winarno, N., Enhancing Students' Creativity through STEM Project-Based Learning. *J. Sci. Learn.*, 2, 2, 50–57, 2019, https://eric.ed.gov/?id=EJ1226168.
29. Holstermann, N., Grube, D., Bögeholz, S., Hands-on activities and their influence on students' interest. *Res. Sci. Educ.*, 40, 5, 743–757, 2010, https://doi.org/10.1007/s11165-009-9142-0.
30. Hom, E., What is STEM Education?, 2014, https://www.livescience.com/43296-what-is-stem-education.html.
31. Hsiao, H.S., Yu, K.C., Chang, Y.S., Chien, Y.H., Lin, K.Y., Lin, C.Y., Lin, Y.W., The study on integrating the design thinking model and STEM activity unit for senior high school living technology course, in: *2017 7th World Engineering Education Forum (WEEF)*, pp. 383–390, IEEE, 2017, November, https://doi.org/10.1109/WEEF.2017.8467111.
32. Islam, M.A. and Numan, S.M., Role of practical works in open and distance learning: Bangladesh Open University Experience. *J. Open School, BOU*, 3, 1&2, 17–24, 2006, https://tinyurl.com/yc43xfud.
33. James, S.M. and Singer, S.R., From the NSF: The National Science Foundation's investments in broadening participation in science, technology, engineering, and mathematics education through research and capacity building. *CBE—Life Sci. Educ.*, *15*, 3, fe7, 2016, http://doi.org/10.1187/cbe.16-01-0059.
34. Kaptan, K. and Timurlenk, O., Challenges for science education. *Procedia-Soc. Behav. Sci.*, 51, 763–771, 2012, http://odi.org/ 10.1016/j.sbspro.2012.08.237.
35. Karpudewan, M. and Meng, C.K., The effects of classroom learning environment and laboratory learning environment on the attitude towards learning science in the 21st-century science lessons. *Malays. J. Learn. Instr.*, 25–45, 2017, https://tinyurl.com/2nerfehw.
36. Kelley, T.R., Knowles, J.G., Han, J., Sung, E., Creating a 21st century skills survey instrument for high school students. *Am. J. Educ. Res.*, *7*, 8, 583–590, 2019, http://doi.org/10.12691/education-7-8-7.
37. Kelley, T.R. and Knowles, J.G., A conceptual framework for integrated STEM education. *Int. J. STEM Ed.*, *3*, 11, 2016, https://doi.org/10.1186/s40594-016-0046-z.
38. Khalil, N. and Osman, K., STEM-21CS module: Fostering 21st century skills through integrated STEM. *K-12 STEM Educ.*, *3*, 3, 225–233, 2017, https://www.learntechlib.org/p/209552.
39. Kocdar, S., Karadeniz, A., Bozkurt, A., Buyuk, K., Measuring self-regulation in self-paced open and distance learning environments. *Int. Rev. Res.*

Open Distance Learn., 19, 1, 25–47, 2018, https://doi.org/10.19173/irrodl.v19i1.3255.

40. Krajcik, J. and Delen, İ., Engaging learners in STEM education. *Eesti Haridusteaduste Ajakiri. Est. J. Educ.*, 5, 1, 35–58, 2017, https://doi.org/10.12697/eha.2017.5.1.02b.
41. Li, Y., Schoenfeld, A.H., Graesser, A.C., Benson, L.C., English, L.D., Duschl, R.A., Design and design thinking in STEM education. *J. STEM Educ. Res.*, 2, 93–104, 2019, https://link.springer.com/article/10.1007/s41979-019-00020-z.
42. Markova, T., Educators' and students' perceptions of online distance education before and amid COVID-19: Key concerns and challenges, in: *SHS Web of Conferences*, vol. 99, p. 01018, EDP Sciences, 2021, https://doi.org/10.1051/shsconf/20219901018.
43. Montebon, D.T., K12 science program in the Philippines: Student perception on its implementation. *Int. J. Educ. Res.*, *2*, 12, 153–164, 2014, https://tinyurl.com/4hdn627n.
44. Mora-Ruano, J.G., Heine, J.H., Gebhardt, M., Does teacher collaboration improve student achievement? analysis of the German PISA 2012 sample. *Front. Educ.*, 4, 85, 2019, August, Frontiers, https://doi.org/10.3389/feduc.2019.00085.
45. Murphy, L., Supporting learner autonomy: theory and practice in a distance learning context. Book chapter in: Gardner, David (ed.) *Learner Autonomy 10: Integration and support. Authentik books for language teachers*, 10. pp. 72–92, Authentik Language Learning Resources Ltd, Dublin, Ireland, 2007, https://tinyurl.com/2p9c942e.
46. Murray, G., The social dimensions of learner autonomy and self-regulated learning. *Studies in Self-Access Learning Journal*, 5, 4, 320–341, 2014, http://sisaljournal.org/archives/dec14/murray.
47. Mustajab, M., Hasan, B., Zakiyah, F., II, Adapting to teaching and learning during Covid-19: A case of Islamic school's initiative of self-regulated learning. *Nadwa: J. Pend. Isl.*, 14, 2, 241–264, 2020, http://dx.doi.org/10.21580/nw.2020.14.2.6515.
48. Nurlenasari, N., Lidinillah, D.A.M., Nugraha, A., Hamdu, G., Assessing 21st century skills of fourth-grade student in STEM learning. *J. Phys. Conf. Ser.*, 1318, 1, 012058, 2019, October, IOP Publishing, http://doi.org/10.1088/1742-6596/1318/1/012058.
49. Obaydullah, A.K.M., Rahim, M.A., Rahman, M.S., Concept of Outcome Based Education: Primary science. *I. J. A. R. I. I. E.*, 6, 2, 1401–1407, 2020, https://tinyurl.com/mvj6236c.
50. Onsee, P. and Nuangchalerm, P., Developing critical thinking of grade 10 students through inquiry-based STEM learning. *J. Penelit. Pembelajar. IPA*, 5, 2, 132–141, 2019, http://doi.org/10.3087010/jppi.v5i2.5486.

51. Oyedotun, T.D., Sudden change of pedagogy in education driven by COVID-19: Perspectives and evaluation from a developing country. *Res. Glob.*, 2, 100029, 2020, https://tinyurl.com/yckuhnf5.
52. Phang, F.A., Yusof, K.M., Abd Aziz, A., Nawi, N.D., Musa, A.N., Cooperative problem-based learning to develop 21st century skills among secondary school students through STEM education, in: *2017 7th World Engineering Education Forum (WEEF)*, pp. 405–409, IEEE, 2017, November, https://tinyurl.com/2p84r7jk.
53. Pinasa, S., Siripun, K., Yuenyong, C., Developing design-based STEM education learning activities to enhance students' creative thinking. *AIP Conf. Proc.*, 1923, 1, 030076, 2018, January, AIP Publishing LLC, https://doi.org/10.1063/1.5019567.
54. Prafitasari, F., Sukarno, S., Muzzazinah, M., Integration of critical thinking skill in science learning using blended learning system in elementary school. *Int. J. Elem. Educ.*, 5, 3, 434–445, 2021, https://ejournal.undiksha.ac.id/index.php/IJEE.
55. Reeves, J. and Kimbrough, D., Solving the laboratory dilemma in distance learning general chemistry. *J. Asynchronous Learn. Netw.*, 8, 3, 47–51, 2004, https://tinyurl.com/ymxz3dpc.
56. Rifandi, R. and Rahmi, Y.L., STEM education to fulfil the 21st century demand: A literature review. *J. Phys.: Conf. Ser.*, 1317, 1, 012208, 2019, October, IOP Publishing, http://doi.org/10.1088/1742-6596/1317/1/012208.
57. Sadera, J.R.N., Torres, R.Y.S., Rogayan Jr., D.V., Challenges encountered by junior high school students in learning science: basis for action plan. *Univers. J. Educ. Res.*, 8, 12A, 7405–7414, 2020, http://doi.org/10.13189/ujer.2020.082524.
58. Sadi, Ö. and Çakıroğlu, J., Effects of hands-on activity enriched instruction on students' achievement and attitudes towards science. *J. Balt. Sci. Educ.*, 87–97, 2011, http://www.scientiasocialis.lt/jbse/?q=node/219.
59. Sahin, A., STEM students on the stage (SOS): Promoting student voice and choice in STEM education through an interdisciplinary, standards-focused project-based learning approach. *J. STEM Educ.*, 16, 3, 24–33, 2015, https://www.jstem.org/jstem/index.php/JSTEM/article/view/1911/1683.
60. Sen, C., Ay, Z.S., Kiray, S.A., STEM skills in the 21st century education, in: *Research Highlights in STEM Education*, pp. 81–101, 2018, https://tinyurl.com/2p94cjrk.
61. Setiawaty, S., Fatmi, N., Rahmi, A., Unaida, R., Hadiya, I., Muhammad, I., Sari, R.P., Science, Technology, Engineering, and Mathematics (STEM) learning on student's science process skills and science attitudes, in: *Proceedings of MICoMS 2017*, Emerald Publishing Limited, 2018, https://dergipark.org.tr/en/pub/epess/issue/66447/1040437.
62. Severino, L., Petrovich, M., Mercanti-Anthony, S., Fischer, S., Using a design thinking approach for an asynchronous learning platform during COVID-19. *IAFOR J. Educ.*, 9, 2, 145–162, 2021, https://eric.ed.gov/?id=EJ1291892.

63. Stehle, S.M. and Peters-Burton, E.E., Developing student 21st century skills in selected exemplary inclusive STEM high schools. *Int. J. STEM Educ.*, 6, 1, 1–15, 2019, https://doi.org/10.1186/s40594-019-0192-1.
64. Strauß, S. and Rummel, N., Promoting interaction in online distance education: designing, implementing and supporting collaborative learning. *Inf. Learn. Sci.*, 121, 5/6, 251–260, 2020, https://tinyurl.com/ycksf6hf.
65. Sun, J.C.Y. and Rueda, R., Situational interest, computer self-efficacy and self-regulation: Their impact on student engagement in distance education. *Br. J. Educ. Technol.*, 43, 2, 191–204, 2012, http://doi.org/10.1111/j.1467-8535.2010.01157.x.
66. Sutaphan, S. and Yuenyong, C., STEM education teaching approach: inquiry from the context based. *J. Phys.: Conf. Ser.*, 1340, 1, 012003, 2019, October, IOP Publishing, http://doi.org/10.1088/1742-6596/1340/1/012003.
67. Sutoyo, S., Azizah, U., Allamin, S., Effectiveness of the guided inquiry model integrated with STEM to improve the student critical thinking skills in chemistry learning. *Int. J. Innov. Sci. Res. Technol.*, 4, 12, 349–353, 2019, https://tinyurl.com/yas7te2n.
68. Tan, O.S., *Problem-based learning innovation: Using problems to power learning in the 21st century*, Gale Cengage Learning, pp. 1–166, 2021, https://tinyurl.com/47be4rfx.
69. Thahir, A., Anwar, C., Saregar, A., Choiriah, L., Susanti, F., Pricilia, A., The effectiveness of STEM Learning: scientific attitudes and students' conceptual understanding. *J. Phys.: Conf. Ser.*, 1467, 1, 012008, 2020, February, IOP Publishing, http://dx.doi.org/10.2991/assehr.k.210326.017.
70. Thompson, T., Teaching creativity through inquiry science. *Gift. Child Today*, 40, 1, 29–42, 2017, https://doi.org/10.1177%2F1076217516675863.
71. Timms, M.J., Moyle, K., Weldon, P.R., Mitchell, P., Challenges in STEM learning in Australian schools: Literature and policy review. pp. 1–24, Policy Insights, Australian Council for Educational Research, 2018, https://research.acer.edu.au/policy_analysis_misc/28/.
72. Toquero, C.M., Challenges and opportunities for higher education amid the COVID-19 pandemic: The Philippine Context. *PEDRE, 5*, 4, 1–5, 2020, https://doi.org/10.29333/pr/7947.
73. Tunkham, P., Donpudsa, S., Dornbundit, P., Development of STEM activities in Chemistry on "Protein" to enhance 21 st century learning skills for senior high school students. *Humanit. Arts Soc Sci. Stud.* (Former Name Silpakorn University Journal of Social Sciences, Humanities, And Arts), 16, 217–234, 2016, https://doi.org/10.14456/sujsha.2016.17.
74. Tytler, R., Williams, G., Hobbs, L., Anderson, J., Challenges and opportunities for a STEM interdisciplinary agenda, in: *Interdisciplinary Mathematics Education*, pp. 51–81, Springer, Cham, 2019, https://tinyurl.com/mr2rkf9h.
75. Wan Husin, W.N.F., Mohamad Arsad, N., Othman, O., Halim, L., Rasul, M.S., Osman, K., Iksan, Z., Fostering students' 21st century skills through project oriented problem based learning (POPBL) in integrated STEM education

program, in: *Asia-Pacific Forum on Science Learning & Teaching*, vol. 17, no. 1, 2016, June, https://tinyurl.com/396vt2ss.
76. Yavuz, M., Hasançebi, M., Hansancebi, F., The effect of STEM application on 21st century skills of middle school students and student experiences. *J. Soft Comput. Artif. Intell.*, *1*, 1, 29–41, 2020, https://dergipark.org.tr/en/pub/jscai/issue/54043/744198.
77. You, H.S., Why teach science with an interdisciplinary approach: history, trends, and conceptual frameworks. *J. Educ. Learn.*, 6, 4, 66–77, 2017, http://doi.org/10.5539/jel.v6n4p66.
78. Yuenyong, C. and Narjaikaew, P., Scientific literacy and Thailand science education. *Int. J. Environ. Sci. Educ.*, 4, 3, 335–349, 2009, https://eric.ed.gov/?id=EJ884401.
79. Zulirfan, Z., Yennita, Y., Rahmad, M., STEM at Home: provide scientific activities for students during the Covid-19 pandemic. *J. Phys.: Conf. Ser.*, 1655, 1, 012068, 2020, October, IOP Publishing, http://doi.org/:10.1088/1742-6596/1655/1/012068.
80. Aurandt, J., Borchers, A.S., Lynch-Caris, T., El-Sayed, J., Hoff, C., Bringing Environmental Sustainability to Undergraduate Engineering Education: Experiences in an Interdisciplinary Course. *J. STEM Educ.: Innov. Res.*, 13, 2, 15–24, 2012, https://tinyurl.com/25d2mdbf.
81. Balagtas, M.U., Garcia, D.C.B., Ngo, D.C., Looking through Philippine's K to 12 Curriculum in Mathematics and Science vis-a-vis TIMSS 2015 Assessment Framework. *Eurasia J. Math. Sci. Technol. Educ.*, 15, 12, 1–14, 2019, em1788. https://doi.org/10.29333/ejmste/108494.
82. Vivayic, N., Nebraska STEM Instructional Resource Evaluation Rubrics, 2018, available online at https://www.education.ne.gov/wp-content/uploads/2018/10/NDE-STEM-Resource-Rubric.pdf.

Index

Printed and bound by CPI Group (UK) Ltd, Croydon, CR0 4YY

17/09/2026

14964261-0007